Embracing the Stranger

Embracing *the* Stranger

Intermarriage and the Future of the
American Jewish Community

Ellen Jaffe McClain

BasicBooks
A Division of HarperCollins*Publishers*

Designed by Elliott Beard

Library of Congress Cataloging-in-Publication Data
McClain, Ellen Jaffe.
    Embracing the stranger : intermarriage and the future of the American Jewish community / by
Ellen Jaffe McClain.
        p.   cm.
    Includes bibliographical references and index.
    ISBN 0-465-01908-0
    I. Interfaith marriage—United States. 2. Judaism—United States. 3. Jews—United States—
Psychology. 4. Jews—United States—Identity. I. Title
HQI031.M43 1995
306.84'3—dc20   95–35291
                                                                                  CIP

95 96 97 98 ♦/HC 9 8 7 6 5 4 3 2 1

For SPENCER,
never really a stranger,
and in memory of
RALPH STEVENS and FRED SHULDINER,
two men who showed, every day, what it means
to be a good Jew and a *menschedik* human being.

Contents

Preface

It takes a certain amount of chutzpah for a junior high English teacher whose most visible role in Jewish institutional life is the vice-presidency of her synagogue to decide to write the next big book on intermarriage. That's why I'm constantly amazed by the number of people who have supported my work on this project during the past four years. My first thanks go to the scores of rabbis, academics, Jewish communal workers and educators, psychotherapists, and other professionals with insight into the various facets of the intermarriage debate who took the time to share their knowledge and experience with me. Because they took me seriously, I began to take myself and this book seriously.

Thanks also to the hundred-plus people who told me about their lives, relationships, and, in some cases, spiritual journeys. Their candor and eloquence color the pages of this book and give faces to people who are all too often treated as statistics or, worse, as enemies to American Jewry.

My parents, Mort and Lois Jaffe, laid the foundation for my Jewish identity, and the rabbi of our temple during my adolescence, Robert D. Schreibman, taught me how to begin building on that foundation. The passion for Judaism he communicated to me informs every paragraph of this book.

I am grateful to my editor at Basic Books, Steve Fraser, for supporting me and my work not only by accepting the project for publication but for his infinite patience with a writer who thought no one would believe her unless she backed up every statement three different ways, quoting five different experts. I must also thank historian Elaine Tyler May, who put me in touch with Steve after my proposal had been sent back by sixteen other editors. She insists her intervention had little to do with placing my book, but if nothing else—we met through her reader's query—she reinforced my confidence in the positive power of fate.

Special thanks go to my agent, Barbara Markowitz, who kept the faith through those sixteen rejections and always promoted my vision with enthusiasm and vigor. My career as a writer would not be possible without her.

Finally, I thank my husband, Spencer Gill. He supported me in every way during what turned out to be a very lonely process. Academics and Jewish professionals writing this kind of book can consult each other about their work, but I had only Spencer to use as sounding board and spare brain. If he got sick of listening to me think out loud, he never let on, and he was always there to give me feedback and keep me going when my faith in my own vision faltered. Writing this book changed both our lives, and I am grateful that Spencer has chosen to link his life with mine.

Embracing the Stranger

Introduction

Have you ever experienced that moment when you realized that some situation or condition you thought was peculiar to you actually was shared by others? That sudden knowledge, as refreshing as a sea breeze on a hot day, as deliciously relaxing as a warm bath, that you're not alone, it isn't just you, you're not crazy?

That moment came to me in a UCLA lecture hall, late on a brisk afternoon in January 1990, at a session of *Tikkun* magazine's first Los Angeles Conference of Liberal and Progressive Jewish Intellectuals. The workshop—the main reason I'd signed up for the conference—was titled "Difficulties in Relationships Between Jewish Men and Women." Here was my chance to find out why, in three years at two-thirds-Jewish Brandeis University, not one of the guys I'd been friends with had shown a romantic interest and why every relationship I'd had as an adult had been with a non-Jewish man.

The two psychologists who facilitated the workshop opened with a description of how people bring fears as well as hopes to new relationships and often harm their own cause by keeping people at arm's length. Then they provided a little historical background on some of the stereotypes and prejudices many

Jewish men and women carry toward each other. As soon as they opened the floor for questions and comments, the accusations began to fly. Jewish men aren't sexy. Jewish women are obsessed with money. Jewish men are controlling. Jewish women are intimidating. Jewish men are workaholics. Jewish women are demanding. Jewish men are nerds. Jewish women are bitchy.

The room was full of bright, articulate people thinking out loud, many of them sounding as if they wanted to fight the very stereotypes they were voicing. You could feel them wishing they could break the internal barriers that kept them from connecting with other Jews. They wanted the bashing to stop, but they didn't know how to turn it off.

About an hour into the discussion, I was called on and told the crowd that I'd always wanted to date Jewish men—Jewish guys had always attracted me, my first serious relationship in high school had been with a Jewish guy, and I'd gone off to Brandeis in 1971 assuming that I'd do as well socially as any other nice, smart, amusing girl who wasn't great-looking but didn't frighten small children. Instead, for three long years, I repeatedly found myself a party to the following conversation:

MALE FRIEND: God, I'm horny. I can't take it anymore. I'd sleep with *anybody* at this point. I'd sleep with Godzilla.

ELLEN: What about me? I'd sleep with you.

MALE FRIEND: Uhh . . . no thanks. I mean you're wonderful and I love you, but there just isn't any *chemistry*.

I was 18 years old, naïve enough to think that if a guy was desperately horny and thought you were wonderful and loved you, he'd want to sleep with you. (For the record, only three of the many guys with whom I had this conversation later turned out to be gay.) I knew girls homelier and chubbier than I was who seemed to be attracting men, and I couldn't figure out what terrible crime I'd committed other than to hit the ninety-eighth percentile on the growth curve. Finally, the fog began to lift.

"I looked at these guys, my close friends, and I saw soulmates. . . . As far as I was concerned, any one of them would have been nice to have as a boyfriend," I told the workshop participants. "But even when I tried to look the way they wanted girls to look, it didn't make a difference. They saw their sister, or maybe their mother. I think I was too much like them."

As I spoke, I saw dozens of heads bobbing up and down and started to hear affirming murmurs from other women. The murmurs built as I described the

Gentile men who seemed to experience the "chemistry" my Jewish pals had missed. After the session, several people said they knew exactly what I was talking about/had gone through the exact same thing/had dated non-Jewish men for the exact same reasons. It was all very validating (It isn't just me! I'm not crazy!), and the warmth of that validation stayed with me as I drove home to cuddle with the man who would soon become my non-Jewish fiancé and later my non-Jewish husband. Somebody really oughta write a book about this, I thought.

In demographic terms, my background parallels that of many other American Jewish baby boomers: Brooklyn-born in 1954, raised in suburban New York, graduate of an oversized public high school. High grades, good college, grad school, marriage at 25—I parted company with my yuppie peers only when I went back to school in the early 1980s to earn a teaching credential in secondary English for the most subversive of reasons: to persuade adolescents that knowledge is power.

   I wound up marrying twice. Although I had attended some Jewish singles events and was certainly interested in finding an SJM, as the personal ads say, the man I met at almost-23 seemed too good to pass up simply on the basis of religion. He was sweet, brilliant, funny, and philo-Semitic to boot; in fact, he converted to Judaism a month before we got married. (Five years later, we had what was possibly the most amicable divorce ever filed in Los Angeles County.) Two months after my first marriage broke up, at age 30, I met my second husband. Again, I would have been thrilled if Mr. Right had been Jewish, and again, he wasn't. However, he was (and is) loving, supportive, and wise, and, like my first husband, he had long since walked away from the faith in which he had been raised. Slowly we became a family of two, and in March 1991 we were married under a *chuppah*, by the rabbi of our synagogue.

   Three months later, the major statistics from the 1990 National Jewish Population Survey were released. Suddenly, married to a non-Jew, I was an enemy of the Jewish people—never mind that I'd been sitting on my temple's board of directors for four years and attending Friday night services almost every week. I resented being characterized as a bad Jew when I was the same Jew I'd been before the wedding and a more observant Jew than I'd been during my first marriage. Also, I was still thinking about that workshop at UCLA more than a year earlier and wondering why nobody made the connection between the topic of the workshop and a 50 percent intermarriage rate. By the end of 1991, after six months of survey hysteria, I had seen no sign that anyone was going to make

that connection or to stand up for us "bad Jews" in print, and I started researching, driven by this conviction: I could not possibly be the one and only deeply
committed, holiday-observing, templegoing Jew married to a non-Jew in these
United States.

A schoolteacher knows the value of homework, and at this point there is little I
haven't read or read about that's been published since the late 1960s concerning
interdating and intermarriage, the formation and maintenance of Jewish identity and affiliation, and American Jewish demographic and societal trends.[1] I
also conducted interviews with more than 100 rabbis, demographers, Jewish
educators, communal workers, Jewish journalists, psychologists, and other professionals, and with even more people, Jewish and non-Jewish, who told me
about their lives and relationships.[2]

In planning this book, I had to make some decisions about its scope. I'm not
going to be treading the well-worn path of interfaith marriage's tensions and
pitfalls, ground that has been covered very effectively in scores of books and
articles. Many people have written about how to plan the wedding, how to raise
the kids, how to deal with the in-laws, what to do in December. Since my husband and I have escaped most of these problems, I bow to their greater experience and superior knowledge. My concern is not the conduct of intermarriages
so much as who the Jews are who marry non-Jews, why these Jews marry non-
Jews, who the non-Jews they marry are, how these couples are perceived and
treated by the Jewish community, and how these perceptions and behaviors can
be changed for the better.

With some reluctance, I decided to limit my research to relationships involving heterosexual Jews and non-Jews. Gay and lesbian Jews in committed interfaith relationships face most of the same issues—all, if their families include
children—that many heterosexual Jews must deal with, and I hope Jewish
demographers put some research effort sooner rather than later into studying
the dynamics of inmarriage and outmarriage involving homosexual Jews,
because they are going to be a growing presence in organized Jewish life. To
include lesbians and gay men in this book, though, would have involved twice
the interviewing, without the foundation of existing literature or hard data on
interfaith relationships among Jewish gay men and lesbians, data I don't have the
resources or expertise to gather.

A word about language. Except in quotation, I avoid use of the word *shikse* or
shaygetz in referring to non-Jews. These words, the first feminine and the second
masculine, come from the Hebrew word meaning "abomination" and are pejorative in and of themselves. I also avoid *goy* and *goyim* in casual reference to non-

Jews because although they derive simply from the Hebrew for *nation*, they have taken on a pejorative cast over the years. In speaking of people who are now Jewish but were not born or raised Jewish, I prefer the term *convert* to *Jew-by-choice* (although outside the context of this topic, of course, they're just plain Jews). A lot of people think of *convert* as a negative term, but that's because so many people perceive converts to Judaism as less than fully Jewish, a perception I'm going to try to blow to pieces. *Convert* is rooted in the Latin word meaning "to turn," and the concept of turning toward a life-affirming choice has a lot of resonance in Jewish literature and liturgy. *Jew-by-choice* is a euphemism, and not particularly well-focused, because, as many people have pointed out of late, *all* of us who choose to live our lives consciously as Jews are Jewish by choice.

Why did I write this book?

Certainly not to trash Jewish men. The truth is, having been raised ethnocentrically, I grew up thinking of Jewish guys in a positive light, and I went to school with hundreds of intelligent, witty, and talented Jewish men. What wasn't to like? Nothing I've experienced as an adult has made me think that Jewish men as a group are undesirable as companions or mates. But one reason I got interested in this topic was that, as a heterosexual Jewish woman, I was supposed to find a mate among Jewish men and didn't. When Jewish men are supposed to choose Jewish women as mates, and they don't, and when Jewish women are supposed to marry Jewish men, and they don't, that becomes a Jewish issue, especially when the failure to choose each other is seen as a threat to group survival.

I have been and will be accused of writing this book to justify my choice of life partners, and it's fair to say that if the right Jewish man was ever out there for me, I wasn't available for more than a handful of months out of my entire post-university life, having settled into one long-term relationship fairly young and moving almost immediately into the other after the first ended. And I'm the first to admit that my early decisions were based partly on inexperience and immaturity. The social failures I experienced as a very young woman then looked like the monolithic rejection of an entire population of Jewish male peers; these days, as my forties bring something resembling insight, I realize that I was probably just in the wrong places at the wrong times, meeting the wrong Jewish men. But I settled down with my first husband not because he wasn't Jewish but because he was the first adult man to show an intense romantic interest in me. And I married my second husband not because he wasn't Jewish, but because he's my *beshert*, my destined soulmate. I don't have to write a book to justify *that*.

I wrote this book because I have a passionate commitment to liberal Judaism as a religious faith and a way of life, and it bothers me to see thousands of my peers putting distance between themselves and their Jewishness, with intermarriage as part of that dynamic. Thousands of American Jews are afraid to walk into a synagogue and reclaim their spiritual heritage because they think the experience will be too weird or too familiar—or both. A lot of people have allowed their childhood experiences to define Judaism for them ever since but are still looking, years later, for a source of spiritual energy. I want to encourage these people, intermarried or not, to claim the Judaism they would have liked but never got.

By the same token, I want to encourage interdating and intermarried Jews to create and nurture Jewish lives for themselves and, wherever possible, for their partners and children. Whatever the path that brings a Jew to a non-Jewish partner, there is room in almost any intermarriage for Jewish ritual in the home and for synagogue involvement. Thousands of intermarriages involve non-Jewish partners who are just as alienated from the faiths they grew up with as their Jewish spouses might have been from theirs. That means there are often no obstacles to the establishment of Judaism as the dominant religion in the home if that's what the Jewish partner wants. I want to empower Jews whose partners are religiously disaffected or unaffiliated Gentiles to jump into Jewish life and bring their spouses with them—with the full support of non-Orthodox Jewish institutions.

A few years ago, I led services at my temple and spoke to the congregation about how I had felt exactly twenty-five years earlier as I became a bat mitzvah, and what it means to me now to be a daughter of the commandments. (A lot more than it did at age 13.) The only problem was, now that I had become a fully active, committed member of the covenant, I wanted more. I wanted to be a transmitter of the covenant, to share Judaism's joy and wisdom and soul with others in a way that would help ensure the continuance of the American Jewish community. How do you do that if you don't work in Jewish communal life and you don't have kids?

One of the rabbis I interviewed while pondering this question, a warm and sympathetic man, told me about something he called the butterfly effect. He said the tiny, insignificant breeze created by the wings of a single butterfly can add itself to others and become part of a cumulative force that can circle the globe. The things you do and say today, he told me, may not register in your time and place but may gain in power as they travel and may eventually change minds and lives. It was a lovely image, and it went over great at Friday night services. Moreover, as a teacher, I know it's true.

Still, I prefer the megaphone effect, so I wrote this book.

1

Painting by Numbers

To lend a hand to the sanctification of mixed marriage is, according to my firm conviction, to furnish a nail in the coffin of the small Jewish race, with its sublime mission.

> —David Einhorn, an otherwise radical
> nineteenth-century German Reform rabbi

We focus on numbers because we don't know what else to focus on. . . . There is no agreement on what it takes to make a good Jew, what a good Jew should do, how he should behave, and so on. . . . So, if you can't agree on the dimensions of quality, then what you can agree about is numbers—something you know nothing about.

> —Calvin Goldscheider, sociologist

Throughout Jewish history, intermarriage has been perceived as a threat to Jewish survival, and logically so. Jews, after all, have been a tiny minority in every civilization we've lived in, ancient and modern, with the recent exception of the State of Israel. Although prominent Jews in the Bible, including Moses himself, married non-Israelite women, the writers of the Torah included a strongly worded ban on intermarriage in the book of Deuteronomy. They were well aware that the Israelites were surrounded by pagan tribes and knew that mixing with those tribes would eventually obliterate the nascent Jewish people.

In the fifth century B.C.E., after witnessing the consequences of exile after the destruction of the First Temple, the prophet Ezra not only railed against marriage to heathens but passed on God's order for all Jewish men who had intermarried to cast out their wives and children. With few exceptions, the Hebrew Bible is very clear that the Israelites were not only to marry among themselves but also to keep themselves at a lengthy social distance from other tribes.[1] At the same time, however, Israel had to coexist with other peoples throughout antiquity; the Jews of Greek- and Roman-controlled Palestine, for example, spoke the dominant language as well as Hebrew and Aramaic, and the community contained plenty of Hellenized Jews, while Jewish culture and even teachings drew from the practices and ideas Jews experienced in a multicultural setting.[2]

With the Enlightenment in the eighteenth century, many Jews emerged from their enclaves and sought to make their way in the cities of Europe. Political barriers had been lowered, but the price of true economic success and social acceptance for European Jews often was conversion to Christianity, the ultimate assimilation. The German Jews who founded the Reform movement early in the nineteenth century promoted endogamy, recognizing that Jews who married non-Jews separated themselves from the Jewish community by doing so, but pressures to appear accommodating to the Christian majority led the 1844 Reform Assembly at Braunschweig to acknowledge intermarriage as valid as long as state law allowed the parents to raise their children as Jews. This touched off a debate that lasted the rest of the nineteenth century: Would intermarriage bring about understanding between Christians and Jews and overcome the anti-Semitism ever rampant in Germany, or would it grease the way to oblivion for the German Jewish community's identity as a particular people?[3]

During the same period, in colonial America and the early days of the American republic, Jews did not face social barriers quite as high as those in Europe, but the sheer scarcity of Jews brought about many intermarriages in which the Jewish partners did not necessarily convert but their children were raised as Christians. Jewish women especially who married non-Jews were almost always lost to Judaism, a situation that continued well into the twentieth century.[4] The Sephardic Jews who began arriving in the colonies in 1654 were almost completely assimilated into mainstream American culture by the end of the Federal period, and Jews from many other countries found themselves marrying non-Jews by choice or by default, despite the efforts of the Jewish community to prevent exogamy.[5] Under the vigilant eyes of Jewish leaders and parents, Jewish outmarriage decreased as thousands of German Jews came to America in the mid-nineteenth century. Still, many Jews, particularly men, found themselves in American cities and towns, especially along the ever expanding frontier, in which they had to choose between long-term bachelorhood or marriage outside Judaism.[6]

Everything changed with the great waves of immigration from Eastern Europe. The Jews who arrived in America between 1880 and 1924 came largely from shtetls and ghettos that knew only strict Orthodoxy, and they clustered together, for the most part, in cohesive neighborhoods. There was no shortage of other Jews to marry, and tradition demanded that if you were to rise in America, you would do so with a Jewish partner at your side. Examination of marriage licenses issued in New York City between 1908 and 1912 reveals an intermarriage rate for Jews of 1.17—one Jew in a hundred marrying someone not born Jewish—barely higher than the intermarriage rate for blacks.[7] Vigilance was constant, though. Even as Jews were reaching their peak as a percentage of the American people, Rabbi Mordecai Kaplan, father of Jewish Reconstructionism, warned, "Jews must be prepared to reckon frankly and intelligently with intermarriage as a growing tendency which, if left uncontrolled, is bound to prove Judaism's undoing. . . . If nothing is done to prevent the tendency to intermarriage, Judaism can barely survive another century."[8] This in 1934, when perhaps two or three Jews in a hundred married non-Jews.

Until the early 1960s, most well-established urban Jewish communities in the United States reported cumulative intermarriage rates in single digits; that's the percentage of all marriages in the community involving Jews in which a Jew is married to someone not born Jewish. Jewish leaders began to get nervous, though, when it became clear, right around that time, that the proportion of intermarriages in locations outside major Jewish population centers was much higher than that in, say, New Haven or Baltimore. In addition, demographers studying more recent intermarriage rates discovered that young Jews were marrying non-Jews at a much faster clip than their parents had. Also, Jews were declining as a percentage of the American population, from a high of 3.7 percent in 1937 to 2.9 percent in 1968, a proportion that has continued to drift downward.[9] American Jewish leaders felt another chill down the spine with the 1970–71 National Jewish Population Study, which reported a cumulative intermarriage rate of 9.2 percent but a geometric increase in recent intermarriages: 17.4 percent of Jews in the survey who married between 1961 and 1965 married persons not born Jewish, almost three times as many as in the 1956–60 period, and that figure rose to 31.7 percent for Jews in the survey marrying between 1966 and 1971.[10]

In 1977, Harvard demographer Elihu Bergman declared that if Jews kept intermarrying and reproducing (or, more to the point, not reproducing) the way they had been, the American Jewish population, then estimated at 5.7 million, would shrink to fewer than a million and perhaps as few as 10,000 by 2076. Although the demographers on whose numbers Bergman based his apocalyptic vision refuted his forecast, many Jewish leaders, especially those in the more traditional movements, accepted his dire prediction as a second Book of Numbers.[11] It was followed by a new spate of population surveys that showed cumulative intermarriage rates well into the double digits, with the highest readings in Western cities with young Jewish populations.[12]

Even as the ominous statistics began to pile up, the 1980s were a period of relative optimism for American Jewry. Studies came out showing that mixed couples and their children had an ever more tenuous connection to Jewish communal life and showed little interest in Jewish ritual and practice,[13] but these findings were explained away by sociologists who said that just because people weren't practicing the Judaism of their grandparents didn't mean they weren't Jewish. This optimism was distilled in Charles Silberman's 1985 best-seller, *A Certain People*, a celebration of the huge gains Jews had made in American business, political, and social spheres. Silberman insisted that only about one in every four Jews currently marrying was marrying someone not Jewish at birth, that there was reason to believe that intermarriage was leveling off and might even decline, and that intermarriage gave every indication of leading to a rise in Jewish population.[14]

No wonder all hell broke loose when the 1990 National Jewish Population Survey (NJPS) was made public. The thirty-nine pages of the survey's *Highlights*, which is about as deep as any layperson or Jewish professional gets into the details, kicked the optimists right in the teeth. The survey calculated the "core Jewish" population at 5.5 million, less than 2.5 percent of the American population, and 20 percent of these said they were ethnically Jewish but had no religion. It showed a cumulative nationwide intermarriage rate of 32 percent, if you combined the mixed marriages and the conversionary marriages, and it showed more Jews converting out of Judaism than converting in. The most publicized statistics had to do with intermarriage and child rearing within intermarriage. Since 1985, the survey proclaimed, 52 percent of the Jews who had married chose non-Jewish spouses (with another 5 percent marrying converts to Judaism), and only 43 percent of Jews marrying in 1985 and after had chosen partners who were born Jewish. Among the Jew–Gentile couples, only 27.8 percent reported that they were raising their children solely as Jewish; 30.8 percent said they were raising their children without religion; and a whopping 41.4 percent were reported as raising children with a religion other than Judaism.[15]

The outcry over the survey was loud and anguished among committed Jews, with a big dollop of "We told you so!" from the traditional community and a

certain amount of "Oops!" from the Reform movement, which had taken a welcoming stance toward intermarried families for the past decade. "Those of us
out in the field know that the 'Silent Holocaust' has already most likely claimed
close to two-thirds of America's six million Jews—lost to Jewish life, perhaps
irretrievably," shrilled an Orthodox representative in a letter to *Moment* magazine.[16] A Reform rabbi, a trained sociologist who had published an upbeat, the-
glass-is-half-full summary of the demographic literature in 1985, was singing a
much different tune seven years later in a pamphlet directed at Jewish parents:
"[W]e know that the overwhelming majority of the children of intermarriage
themselves intermarry and evince virtually no meaningful Jewish involvement.
By the third generation of intermarriage, Jewish identity has all but vanished.
The chain, so well preserved over 150 generations, is broken."[17] Silberman
recanted his earlier optimism, and longtime chronicler Arthur Hertzberg
warned that without a spiritual revival, "American Jewish history will soon end,
and become a part of American memory as a whole."[18]

The hysteria was fanned by nationwide coverage in both Anglo-Jewish and
mainstream media; *Newsweek, USA Today,* CNN, and network news broadcasts
were among the press outlets that disseminated NJPS statistics as established
fact, often oversimplifying them in ways that made them look even worse than
they did in the *Highlights* report, while rabbis and Jewish-press columnists sermonized endlessly on the implications of the survey data. Almost no one in the
Jewish community questioned the validity of the numbers or analyzed them to
any extent. "Most rabbis haven't studied the survey," Sylvia Barack Fishman, a
demographer with Brandeis University's Cohen Center for Modern Jewish Studies, said in an interview. "Most rabbis have seen articles in the *New York Times* and
an occasional editorial here and there."

One researcher described the initial response to the 1990 NJPS from Jewish
leaders and commentators as "confused and depressed,"[19] and the confusion and
depression don't seem to have lifted yet. Instead we've had half a decade of
"How did this happen?"

We became Americans, that's how it happened.

The surprise is not that half the American Jews who have married since 1985
may have married non-Jews; the surprise is that it took so long to get there.
Most other white American immigrant groups that arrived since the late nineteenth century had a 50 percent intermarriage rate in the second generation—
half the children of immigrant Germans, Swedes, Irish, Italians, Poles, you name
it, married outside their national or ethnic group. Today only a fraction of
Americans who identify with a specific European ethnic group marry within

that group. Jews didn't reach the "halfway mark" until close to the fourth generation; the children of the immigrants and even most of the grandchildren made endogamous marriages. What we're seeing now is decades of assimilationist behavior finally being played out in marriage patterns.

It started with the immigrants themselves. Although American lore has romanticized the Jews of Eastern Europe as uniformly pious and committed to Jewish learning, most of the Jews who came to America between 1880 and 1924 tended to be the *least* observant and *least* committed members of their communities, the people most likely to disregard their rabbis' warnings that they were leaving Judaism when they left the shtetl.[20] Nor were they necessarily fleeing violent persecution, although that was a factor in many departures. Most of the immigrants were seeking greater economic opportunity in the face of shaky European economies and restrictive laws.[21]

So Jewish immigrants arrived in the New World predisposed to adapt in whatever ways were necessary to get ahead. Most of them were better educated, had more occupational skills, and were more sophisticated than immigrants from other ethnic groups who settled in America at the same time. Although they arrived poor and had worked in proletarian occupations in Eastern Europe, these Jews did not come from a peasant or laboring tradition; they were children and grandchildren of merchants and skilled craftspeople who had been pushed out of their trades and guilds under czarist repression and fully intended in America to recover the middle-class status their ancestors had enjoyed—if not for themselves, then for their children.[22] Moreover, the Jewish immigrants came to stay. Unlike the Italian or Polish men who remained in America just long enough to save money for a piece of land or a business in their native lands, Jewish men were more likely to arrive with wife and children, or to send for them at the first opportunity.[23]

The second generation of American Jews, the children of the immigrants, were the most torn between European values and American ambitions. They wanted only to feel at home in America and saw their parents' foreignness of accent, custom, and attitude as an impediment to that goal. At the same time, they were the ones who left the ghetto as young adults to work in offices and behind sales counters and who had to deal with the ripples of overt anti-Semitism that lingered through the first half of this century. America made an offer huge numbers of Jews accepted: If they would accommodate the dominant culture by scrapping their "foreign" customs, they could become full partners in the American future.[24]

Many Jews of the second generation rejected both their parents' Jewishness and their Judaism, and even those who held on to some form of Jewish culture and religious practice passed on their alienation to their children. Still, very few went to the extreme of marrying non-Jews, a step that generally meant a complete break with family and their own pasts. Jews of the second generation who married non-Jews were really marrying *out*; for them, intermarriage was their escape route from the social and cultural restrictions of the Jewish community.[25]

By 1960, all the doors of economic and social opportunity had popped open for American Jews. The working-class Jew in the United States was largely a one-generation phenomenon; the second generation finished high school and many made it through college. After World War II, the great majority were established in self-owned businesses and professional practices. Restrictive university quotas and residential covenants faded, and Jews began to have career choices in venues from which they had been politely excluded on more than a token basis: large corporations and law firms, advertising agencies, university faculties.

The second generation gave way to the third as American Jews made their wholesale move to the suburbs. Some congregated in "gilded ghettos," happy to stay among Jews as long as the segregation was of their own choosing and in high-status neighborhoods. Many others became a minority presence in predominantly Gentile communities. Third-generation Jews, secure in their identity as Americans, saw no reason to hide their Jewishness and no reason to reject it.[26] Far from disappearing into the Christian majority, suburban Jews entered into an orgy of building synagogues and Jewish community centers, part of the shallow but broad "religious revival" that seized America during the baby boom. At the same time when many American Jews found less "Jewish" places to live, they asserted their heritage and sought the company of other Jews, erecting institutions that could bring them together.[27]

As American Jews achieved ever greater levels of economic and social success, however, the patterns of postwar American life put Jews of the third and then the fourth generation increasingly in contact with non-Jews and at a greater distance from family and other former community ties. Unlike their parents, who established businesses or opened practices in one location and stayed there throughout their working lives, Jews working in academia, government service, or big corporations could be called upon to pick up and move, in some cases every few years, which made it harder to establish communal ties in a particular town and impossible to be with family except on special occasions. The very willingness of young people to move away from their home towns to follow job opportunities, one commentator noted, shows that economic motives are stronger than attachments to their families.[28]

The trend of Jewish migration during the decades after World War II has been away from the Northeast and Midwest and toward the Sun Belt, where Jews are more scattered and less involved in Jewish communal life, especially in the Western states.[29] Highly mobile Jews are more likely to find themselves living in places where the pool of available Jewish mates is small; an assistant professor at Oregon State, after all, is going to come in contact with fewer Jews than an assistant professor at Columbia. Even committed, affiliated Jews can't always marry Jews where there aren't enough Jews to marry. For example, half the members of the synagogue in Anchorage, Alaska, are married to non-Jews, and in the smaller Alaskan Jewish communities, all but a handful are intermarried.[30] "Denver is a very young and very transient and very highly educated community," Rabbi Steven Foster said of his city, which has one of the highest intermarriage rates in the country. "A lot of young people come here for the quality of life, and they're without roots. . . . The high rate of intermarriage has to do with where we live and what we do . . . and as long as we don't live in ghettos, we are going to intermarry."

Most non-Orthodox Jewish youngsters of the baby-boom era, no longer living in homogeneously Jewish neighborhoods, met non-Jewish kids at school, Little League, and Scouts and thought nothing of having Gentile friends. In 1950, young Jews were already attending college at three times the rate of other Americans of similar age. By the late 1960s, college education was almost universal for Jewish youngsters, boys and girls alike, most of whom left home to be educated on campuses that represented, for many, a larger and wider world than the neighborhoods in which they grew up.

At the university, Jews came in constant contact with people of diverse ethnic and racial backgrounds. The atmosphere of the university encouraged open-mindedness, individuality, and personal fulfillment at the same time it put an emotional as well as physical distance between many Jewish parents and children.[31] Nor was the cause of inmarriage helped by Jewish academics, who were married to non-Jews more frequently than were Jews in general and who often were quick to communicate an intellectual disenchantment with the Judaism of *their* youth to their students.[32] All these factors hold true today, with the result that college and postgraduate education have served to broaden what Egon Mayer, the doyen of American Jewish demographers, called in an interview the "field of eligibles" for young Jews at the precise time they're beginning to think about what they want in a permanent partner, even if marriage is a long way off. Among the people I talked with who were or had been involved in long-term interfaith relationships and who told me how they met their partners, most of the relationships developed at school or at work, with school accounting for the largest group.

The higher education years are also a period during which religious involvement is at a low, for any number of reasons: Some kids use the distance from home to break away from what they see as enforced or meaningless observance; some discover intellectual arguments to counter religious beliefs; some find themselves out of step philosophically with the Jewish organizations on campus; and some just get too busy. Hillel organizations, the major source of purely Jewish affiliation on college campuses, never have attracted more than a fraction of Jewish college and graduate students.[33]

Paul Yedwab, a Reform rabbi in Michigan, reminded me of Erik Erikson's chronology of life stages, each of which brings certain developmental tasks or goals. "The tasks when you're twenty-something are to establish yourself in a career and find a spouse. . . . There's nothing inherently religious about those tasks," he said, adding that more spiritual concerns come later, when people are raising children and dealing with their own mortality and that of their parents. People completing their educations and establishing themselves in the workplace are "meeting at a point in their lives when . . . they have a lot more in common now with each other, Christians and Jews, than their parents or their grandparents did," says Ellyn Geller, director of outreach programs for the New York region of the Union of American Hebrew Congregations (UAHC). "They're meeting at a point in their lives, often in professional settings, where they have common goals, and they have a common background in terms of education . . . where, at least in this economy, getting a job and getting settled and [earning enough] to live is primary, and religion's going to kind of wait."

Mayer elaborates: "The average 28-year-old, 29-year-old doesn't walk around with this kind of cloud over his head: 'My people are in danger, I'm a member of an endangered species.' Rabbis would like them to believe that, but they don't. . . . The whole reason we have arrived to this point is precisely because we're like everybody else. We don't look different, we don't talk different, we don't think different, we don't eat different, we're all the same—so what's the problem?"

The intermarriage rate began to take off as America entered a period of tremendous social and political ferment. Almost all the Jewish baby boomers, male and female, were sent to college, and the first of them landed on campus just in time to become caught up in the zeitgeist known as the sixties. Hailing mostly from middle- to upper-class homes, they discovered a student ethic that derided the middle class, to the extent that being Jewish, and therefore middle-class, could definitely be seen as uncool. The most visible Jewish role models in student circles were political radicals like Abbie Hoffman and Mark Rudd, who symbolized a third-generation type of radicalism that alienated kids from their parents. It was a time when all established values were open to question and all institutions were subject to mistrust, when parents saw the fruits of their permissive child rearing, when the watchcry of all youth became "Do your own thing!"[34] The greatest power of the sixties is its coincidence with the coming-of-age of third- and fourth-generation Jews, but that does not discount it as part of a mind set that would allow a young Jew to marry someone of a different background.

The same generation of Jews was the first to experience young adulthood as extended adolescence, with its attendant confusion, rejection, and searching. "It's a real sense of not knowing who the hell you are, that if you're gonna reject what you've known, you don't have anything to replace it with," a 40-year-old Los Angeles psychologist said, acknowledging the heavy presence of Jews in the counterculture and hippie movements. "I think there's a certain sense of us being a lost generation, and definitely a sense of searching for something that held some meaning." Not all these young Jews rejected *Yiddishkeit*—some poured their countercultural fervor into changing Jewish structures—but it was a generation during which a certain number of young people entered college as Jews and left as Buddhists.

The 1960s also saw the flowering of universalism, the idea that we're all one big human family, as a pervasive value in American society. This value, a cornerstone of postwar public education and political liberalism, took root during the 1950s but blazed into the American consciousness with the civil rights, feminist, and peace movements. The liberal party line since World War II has been that no one group of people is better than any other group. For many Jews, commitment to universal peace and justice became as much a part of being a good Jew as professing allegiance to one God. Peoplehood—particularism— went out as brotherhood came in, and evidence exists that many Jews still put universal goals before those of their fellow Jews.[35]

While concern for people of all races and nationalities is not only a laudable ideal but necessary if the peoples of this world are to avoid destroying one another, there has been a definite down side in terms of Jewish particularism. Jews have experienced the loss of their ethnicity as a distinctly perceived tile in the American mosaic, even, for some, in their own eyes. Jewish distinctiveness is being subsumed into the broad category "European American."[36] Parents who raised their children, with the help of schools and even synagogues, to be citizens of the world have had a terrible time trying to explain to their children why they should marry only Jews.

"The dilemma we create for ourselves . . . is that we teach ourselves and our children to respect every human being; after all, our *tikkun olam* efforts are efforts at social action and social justice, working to make the world a better place for everyone," Linda Walker, the UAHC's outreach director for Northern California, said during a workshop. "Having said that everyone is equal and everyone is good, how can we then turn to our child who brings home a non-Jewish boyfriend or girlfriend [and say], 'I'm sorry, this person is not quite good *enough.*' Having established equality, how do we take it away?" The price of "It's a Small World" in 1965 and "We Are the World" in 1985 has been a parade of interfaith couples who think all they have to do to be happy is to be like-minded. Ellyn Geller says: "We've all raised our children to be totally ecumenical, [so] you have the ones that [say], 'I'm a nice person with nice-person values and he or she's a nice person with nice-person values, and we'll live happily ever after with nice-person values.' "

With the triumph of universalism came the near-complete breakdown of any real opposition among Gentiles to *their* children's marriage to Jews. In polls taken during the 1940s, a clear majority of Gentiles disapproved of marriages between Christians and Jews; in 1968, that figure had dropped to 21 percent, and by 1983 to 10 percent. In 1983, only 4 percent of Americans younger than 30 disapproved of interfaith marriages.[37] The acceptance of Jews as marriage partners by members of the dominant culture led some rabbis to view intermarriage with a reluctant equanimity during the 1960s. As one rabbi said, a certain number of mixed marriages was seen as "part of the price that modern Jewry must pay for freedom and equality in an open society."[38]

But as soon as the third and fourth generations of American Jews made it clear that they were not going to keep the intermarriage rate in the low teens, Jewish leaders suddenly were not so calm. Historian Arthur Hertzberg has pointed out at various times that intermarriage rates have always been high in open societies beginning in the third generation, with massive hemorrhaging in the fourth and fifth, going so far as to say, "No Jewish community in Europe which lived four generations in freedom survived." A demographer with the American Jewish Committee wrote in the introduction to a 1979 study that intermarriage has always been more of a danger to Jewish continuity when Jews enjoyed safety and security within a given society, and he quoted a British historian who wrote in 1907, "What centuries of persecution have been powerless to do has been effected in a score of years by friendly intercourse."[39] I sometimes wonder whether the pundits who subscribe to this school of thought believe that Jewish continuity would be aided if American militia groups were to carry out a few well-organized pogroms.

As Jews have become more and more comfortable as Americans, many Jewish parents have found it increasingly difficult to tell their children that they shouldn't marry non-Jews, and many aren't so sure intermarriage is all that bad. The days when parents would sit *shiva* for a child who married a non-Jew are pretty much over. Although people like Deborah Lipstadt, the Emory University professor who has written and lectured widely on Holocaust denial, have exhorted Jewish parents to just say no to intermarriage, much the way they expect their children not to take drugs, a large majority of parents (and more than a few rabbis) are unable to lay down opposition to intermarriage as a strict operating principle.[40]

"Our generation moved away from the guilt ... because we were concerned that we didn't want to give our children a negative attitude toward Judaism, which we had, but we also had the staying power of authoritarian parents who said, 'You *will* marry Jews,'" says Constance Reiter, a New Jersey temple educator. "My generation was brought up to believe as parents that we couldn't dictate to our children. And boy, kids are fast to find that out."

With the relaxation of taboos against intermarriage—and the contemporary erosion of parental authority in general—has come an almost complete breakdown of restrictions, parent- or self-imposed, on interdating. For example, in a survey of Reform Jewish "lay leaders"—people who had attended the 1985 biennial convention of the UAHC—56 percent reported that it would bother them "a great deal" if a child of theirs married a non-Jew, but only 4 percent said they forbade their children to date non-Jews, with another 29 percent reporting that they strongly opposed interdating and their kids knew it. Interestingly, they reported that only 16 percent of *their* parents had forbidden them to date non-Jews—this in a population in which four out of five of the respondents were older than 40.[41] Most young Jews, even those who are religiously committed, see nothing wrong with dating non-Jews, and it's been that way for the past thirty years.[42]

Parental opposition to intermarriage also tends to fade as the unmarried children in question get older.[43] "I hear it over and over again, where parents would have said when a woman's in her twenties, 'I only want her to marry a Jewish guy.' Now, you know, she's in her thirties, and it's like, oy, at least she's married, it doesn't matter who he was, as long as he's not a monkey," says Naomi Levy, a Conservative rabbi who leads a congregation in Los Angeles. In fact, demographer Barry Kosmin says, marriage and child rearing are such important Jewish values—American Jews believe more than any other religious group that it's better to be a parent than to remain childless—that those values may even contribute to intermarriage. "Most Jews want and expect to be married. They also wish to have children and especially grandchildren," Kosmin wrote in a recent article. "If they cannot find a Jewish partner, they will turn elsewhere, and their parents and close family will support them."[44]

Many observers also correlate intermarriage with Jewish parents' failure to provide their children with a strong Jewish education, backed up with consistent ritual observance.[45] "Parents ask themselves, 'Where did I go wrong?'" a Conservative rabbi told *Newsweek*. "The answer often is: by sending their kids to Sunday school while they went to the mall or to the beauty parlor."[46] Rabbi Harold Schulweis, a leader of the Conservative movement, says there is an "absolute Jewish deficit" of experience among young Jews that has fed the trend toward intermarriage. "You cannot exaggerate; I mean it's zilch," Schulweis said in an interview. "I cannot press now buttons of nostalgia. I cannot say, remember when you had a seder? There's no *zayde*, there's no *bubbe*, there's no language; it's really pretty bad." And the parents, whose only participation in Jewish life is the payment of synagogue dues, are no help, he adds.

So we're not just talking about Jews who have taken on American values and customs; we're talking about what one rabbi called "ignorant, marginally attached" Jews whose connections to Jewish observance and institutions are tenuous at best. When some of them *do* get upset when their children form attachments to non-Jews, then, the kids have no clue as to where their parents' anger is coming from. "I cannot tell you how many people I meet who are shocked because their parents are unhappy or even care," one Reform outreach director reports.

Until the 1990 NJPS figures were released, the American Jewish community brought a great deal of denial to the issue of exogamous marriage. Very little was published in scholarly Jewish journals in the wake of the 1970–71 National Jewish Population Study, possibly because the Jewish community had been fixated on what was going on in the State of Israel since 1967. Still, it seems odd that Jewish leaders would pay so little attention to intermarriage at the precise time it was increasing at a more rapid pace than at any time before or since.[47] "The [1990] statistics were surprising to people, but they shouldn't have been," Sylvia Barack Fishman says. "There was nothing in the 1990 NJPS that hadn't been led up to by the population surveys of individual cities that had been done over the past couple of decades. . . . If people were going to be upset, they should have been upset twenty years ago as they saw the trend."

After Elihu Bergman came out with his doomsday prediction for 2076, articles began to appear in which demographers crunched numbers to show that intermarriage had the potential to *increase* the American Jewish population. The basic premise was that if just half the couples in which one partner was born Jewish and the other was not raised their children as Jews, there would be no net loss in Jewish numbers, because when two Jews married people not born Jewish instead of each other, they made twice as many marriages. And it should be easy to attain the goal of at least half those marriages producing Jewish kids, these sociologists argued, given that 25 to 30 percent of the partners not born Jewish had already converted or would convert to Judaism, creating homes in which Jewish child rearing was a near certainty. That meant only about a third of the spouses who remained non-Jewish had to be willing to raise Jewish children for Jewish numbers to be maintained.[48]

Their optimism became less convincing, however, in the face of statistics that appeared to demonstrate the failure of mixed marriages to produce Jewish children and the shrinking proportion of converts to Judaism. Long before the NJPS figures were released, demographers had been conducting studies that showed households headed by mixed couples demonstrating much lower levels of Jewish behaviors than households in which both parents had been born Jewish or one partner had converted to Judaism, with fewer of the children of those marriages identifying unambiguously as Jews.[49]

The year after the 1990 NJPS statistics were released, four demographers at Brandeis University's Cohen Center for Modern Jewish Studies published a monograph that compared the Jewish behaviors of mixed households to those of conversionary and inmarried families and found the mixed households sorely lacking. Their study, based on data gathered from 8,387 responding households (more than three times as many households as were interviewed in the NJPS) in eight large and small metropolitan areas across the United States during the late 1980s, showed mixed households coming up short in every category of Jewish involvement: synagogue membership and attendance, holiday observance, ties to Israel, donation of money to Jewish causes, friendship patterns (about 7 in 10 intermarried Jews in the survey reported having predominantly non-Jewish friends), and Jewish education. For example, only 41 percent of the children of mixed couples polled were receiving Jewish education between the peak years of 10 and 13, whereas such education was found to be almost universal for children of inmarried and conversionary couples.[50]

A large segment of the mixed households in this study identified themselves as "just Jewish," without any denominational affiliation; *none* of those families reported giving their children a Jewish education that led up to bar or bat mitzvah. And more than half the mixed households were what the writers of the report called "dual-identity": they put up a Christmas tree. "Many mixed married households are not environments which are likely to produce a new generation which is connected to Judaism or the Jewish people," the Brandeis demographers wrote in an earlier version of the report. In their final draft, they mourned that "mixed marriage must be regarded as a virtual bar to the achievement of a high level of Jewish identification."[51] Scary stuff; scarier still if you focus on Jews under age 45, the vast majority of whom are third-generation and later. In one analysis of the NJPS data, only about one of six young mixed-married households belonged to a synagogue, with about the same proportion sending their kids to Jewish religious school.[52]

Although Egon Mayer warns against writing off children of intermarriage with tenuous connections to Jewish life, he is concerned that in time there may be too many men and women who identify themselves as Jews without viewing themselves as part of a distinct people. "We are more diffuse, and to the extent that being Jewish has always required a community, not just an individual, that means you need density, you need mass," Mayer said. "And if . . . it all becomes washed out, you will still have a population, but you won't have a community. That's the demographic endangerment. Our population is becoming so diffused that its capacity for community-building and for sustaining community is undercut."

The apparent drop in the rate of conversionary marriages as a proportion of those marriages between persons born Jewish and not born Jewish has also troubled the Jewish establishment. For many years, intermarriage watchers calculated that, at any given time, up to a third of spouses not born Jewish who were married to born Jews had converted to Judaism prior to or during the marriage.[53] The problem is, the incidence of mixed marriage has risen so precipitously in recent years that conversionary marriages comprise a smaller proportion of the total marriages between born Jews and born non-Jews. Converts were close to 30 percent of the born non-Jews who married Jews before 1970, one study reports, but they made up just 13 percent of the same group for marriages contracted during the 1980s.[54]

The fact that conversion has not kept pace with outmarriage is worrisome because, statistically at least, households in which both partners are Jewish, regardless of whether both were born Jewish, do a more consistent job of raising kids who view themselves as Jewish. Conversionary households score higher on every measure of Jewish religious identity and involvement than mixed households do: they affiliate with synagogues, attend services regularly, provide their children with Jewish educations, observe major holidays, and arrange Jewish life-cycle ceremonies for their children. Many rabbis are on record, formally and informally, as saying that converts are better Jews than most born Jews.[55] If proportionately fewer non-Jews married to Jews were becoming Jewish, that meant more children of Jews were being raised without a firm Jewish foundation.

With the 1990s, then, came the end of denial, and with the end of denial came a search for scapegoats: Who or what is to blame for the trouble we're in? Higher education took the fall during the 1960s and 1970s, but by the mid-1980s demographers could point to figures showing that the best-educated Jews, the ones with graduate degrees, entered the fewest mixed marriages, because graduate schools, to be blunt, are where the Jews are. Not only does an advanced degree today provide campus contact with other Jews during prime partner-search years, it opens the door to careers in which other Jews are likely to be concentrated.[56]

Divorce has long been viewed as a predictor of subsequent intermarriage; second marriages have been and are much more likely to be intermarriages than first marriages, and some of the recent rise in the intermarriage rate parallels the rise in the divorce rate for Jews. Until well into the 1980s, Jews enjoyed a significantly lower rate of marital breakup than other Americans did. That gap has been closing because of younger Jews, who, like many other young Americans, are quicker to split up. Divorced Jews are older, less concerned with what their parents think, probably facing a smaller pool of eligible partners than they did the first time around, and possibly projecting resentment toward a Jewish ex-spouse. In addition, considerations of child rearing may no longer be seen as completely relevant in a second or subsequent marriage.[57]

The Reform movement takes a big hit, especially for the dropoff in conversion since the early 1980s. There are a number of reasons why more marriages to non-Jews haven't resulted in more conversions, including increased alienation from religion on the part of one or both partners and less pressure from Jewish spouses and in-laws. But people point more often to the willingness of many Reform rabbis to officiate at weddings between Jews and non-Jews; to Reform Outreach, which since 1979 has made welcoming non-Jewish spouses in the synagogue as high a priority as encouraging conversion; and especially to the Central Conference of American Rabbis' 1983 decision to accept as Jewish the child of a Jewish father and a non-Jewish mother.

Where else can the blame be laid? On the parents of intermarriers? Half of them are already blaming themselves, and the other half are saying, "Hey, I sent them to Hebrew school, and we had a seder every year." What about the synagogues and other Jewish institutions—have mistakes been made? Sure they have, but don't hold your breath waiting for the rabbis and communal workers to describe them. A common refrain among those in Jewish institutional life is, "We're doing the best we can with what we've got." Can't we still blame assimilation? Of course—for all the good it'll do. You might as well try to push the sand back up the hourglass.

"You cannot give sermons about how Jews should live in a ghettoized community and not send their children to regular school and not send their children away to college, [have a] small community and only marry in that community and never go outside and don't travel anyplace," one rabbi told me. "Can [you] pick on assimilation? Oh, you mean my son shouldn't go to Yale or Princeton? Yeah, they're gonna pay a lot of attention. . . . So we can't rail against assimilation, we can't rail against acculturation. But we can rail against intermarriage, so intermarriage becomes a whipping boy for everything that is wrong with Jewish life."

Amid all the outcry surrounding the 1990 NJPS, one of the most interesting factoids in the survey received exactly no press at all: Jewish women now appear to be marrying non-Jews as readily as Jewish men are. It's right there on page 9 of *Highlights*, in the chart that shows the age and sex of Gentile adults living with Jews. "Interestingly, for those under age 45 no strong sex bias is evident suggesting that intermarriage now occurs equally among Jewish males and females," the commentary accompanying the chart reads.[58]

The dominant image of an intermarried couple has long been a Jewish man with a non-Jewish woman (usually blond) on his arm, and coverage of the NJPS did little to dispel this image, even within Jewish institutional life. The comments many rabbis made to me as I researched this book were predicated on the assumption that male Jewish intermarriers outnumbered women by a wide margin. Until very recently, Jewish population surveys clocked Jewish men marrying exogamously much more than Jewish women did, with a two-to-one ratio cited most often.[59] However, some rabbis who surveyed or counseled mixed couples during the late 1960s and early 1970s describe a much narrower gender gap among the populations they worked with.[60] There may have been a significant number of Jewish women "hidden" in mixed marriages twenty-five years ago; one of the practices in conducting Jewish population studies was to look for households headed by people with identifiably Jewish surnames, which means they probably missed quite a few homes of Jewish women married to non-Jewish men.

Assuming there was an intermarriage gender gap, if not perhaps as large as the demographers measured, why have Jewish women finally caught up with Jewish men, and what took them so long? To answer the second question first, most observers point to a lag in opportunity for Jewish women to meet non-Jewish men and the fact that the taboo against exogamous marriage took longer to erode for Jewish women.

This shows up strongly in terms of the biggest single opportunity young people have for meeting potential partners. Jewish boys began leaving home in large numbers to complete their educations around the same time as Jews began their wholesale migration to the suburbs, but the out-of-town college experience didn't become routine for Jewish girls until the mid- to late 1960s. Then, as Jewish women began to earn graduate degrees in larger and larger numbers, they entered professions that exposed them to a wider range of social contacts. Young women who might have become teachers or social workers a generation before were, by 1980, becoming lawyers, doctors, and corporate executives. Jewish parents also exercised a higher degree of control over their daughters than they did over their sons, and kept it longer. "When I went out on dates, I did not show my dating partner to my parents, but my girlfriends showed me to their parents," one fortyish academic reported, adding that the tendency for Jewish men to go away to college before their sisters did paralleled the greater freedom men had overall during the 1950s and 1960s.

"There was a greater negative sanction applied to girls who dated non-Jews than was applied to Jewish men," Rabbi Norman Mirsky, now a professor at Hebrew Union College in Los Angeles, wrote in 1974. "Boys were allowed to 'sow their wild oats' primarily among '*shiksas*.' Girls had to do this clandestinely."[61] In an interview eighteen years later, Mirsky underscored the social pressure Jewish girls experienced to marry endogamously in the "pre-lib" days. "Men wanted to have control over who their daughters and sisters slept with, and marriage for most of the time was where [sex] happened," Mirsky said, adding that today such control is gone: "What right do you have to say to your daughter that she has less right to experience sex with a non-Jew than you have to say it to your son?"

The influx of Jewish women into elite professions has also brought about a sea change in the way some Jewish parents expect their daughters to provide them with *naches*. In generations past, success for sons was measured by academic achievement and economic advancement, for daughters by marriage to "suitable" Jewish men. A son who married a non-Jewish woman might bring pain to his parents, but he still might be fulfilling their expectations in other ways, whereas a daughter who married a non-Jew was "failing" to accomplish the one thing that her parents expected of her.[62] Moreover, gains earned by the feminist movement took away the economic incentive to marry early; Jewish women could support themselves, and many put off even the thought of marriage until their educations were complete and they were settled in careers. Jews went from being the most universally married ethnic group in America to one in which a third of the women during the 1980s did not live in married households. And although the pervasiveness of singlehood for Jewish women has taken some of the sting out of the unmarried state, Jewish parents and Jewish leaders want in no uncertain terms for young Jewish women to be married.[63]

When many Jewish women in the first wave of the baby boom finally were ready to get married, they found themselves in an extremely unfavorable market. Unwilling to "marry down," looking for successful Jewish men who would respect them as equals, many of these thirtyish women, degrees in hand, careers in place, walked right into a demographic brick wall beginning around the mid-1970s: a severe shortage of appealing, accomplished, age-appropriate Jewish men. They became classic examples of the adage, "Good women marry late; good men marry early."[64]

Sylvia Barack Fishman has spoken with many Jewish women who "either because of career or because of schooling, they sort of haven't paid attention to Jewish guys for a long time, and then they're a little bit older, and they just don't meet a lot of terrific Jewish guys, because a lot of the terrific Jewish guys are taken." Egon Mayer warns that waiting even a little longer than most of your friends do to get married can have repercussions. "If your cohort has an average age of first marriage for women of, say, 25, and you're 27 and haven't married, your odds are going to be significantly altered because you're out of synch with your cohort," he says. "If you're out of synch with your cohort, your odds of being 'normal' are going to be diminished, which means that even things like mate selection—you miss a couple of parties, and you're out of it." No wonder increasing numbers of Jewish women stopped filtering out non-Jewish men as possible spouses.

At the end of the 1970s, after hearing story after story from interesting, attractive Jewish women who simply could not meet interesting, attractive Jewish men, journalist William Novak crunched a few numbers himself and reported that, because of the numbers of males and females in the age bracket and especially because so many Jewish men were marrying non-Jews, upwards of

20 percent of baby-boom women who wanted Jewish husbands in the 1980s weren't going to get them.[65] The heterosexual Jewish men their age and a little older who weren't already spoken for wanted younger women who wouldn't pressure them to make babies right away. To their credit, these women were unwilling to settle for Jewish men who lacked the qualities they wanted: sensitivity, intelligence, education, humor, spirituality. To the dismay of the Jewish community, as the 1980s progressed, these women *were* willing to marry non-Jewish men who fulfilled their requirements in all but religious background. When enough Jewish men took themselves off the marriage market by marrying non-Jewish women, the stage was set for thousands of Jewish women to become what sociologist Rela Geffen Monson called "reluctant exogamists."[66]

"I've met a tremendous number of absolutely dynamite Jewish women in their mid- to late thirties who are single," says Rabbi Lavey Derby, a Conservative rabbi with a background in communal work and a congregation in Marin County, California. "They are smart, they are professional, they are funny, they are pretty, they are successful, they have a strong sense of self, and they're single. And not because they want to be. And some of these women have said to me . . . 'I want to have a family, I want to have kids, I can't find a Jewish man to marry, what am I supposed to do? Not get married? Here I've met this terrific guy, everything about him is wonderful, we share all the same values—it just so happens he's not Jewish. Now I shouldn't marry this guy? I want to have a life, too.'"

As Jewish women of the fourth generation—daughters of educated, liberal women and men—earn *their* degrees, the mesh that filters out Gentile men becomes less and less fine; *I looked for a great Jewish guy for years and couldn't find one* gives way to *I would just as soon have married a Jewish guy, but this is who I met.* Women in their mid-twenties are now marrying the kinds of non-Jewish men their older sisters wouldn't marry until they were sure their options were down to *marry a non-Jew* or *stay single forever*, and their aunts and great-aunts may not have been willing to marry at all.

And most of them, and their brothers as well, are marrying non-Jews not out of rebelliousness, not out of self-hatred, not even out of indifference to Judaism, but because the person across the table in the graduate seminar, the plaintiff's lawyer at the deposition, the cousin's friend who just got back from two years digging in Oaxaca, turned out to be a kindred spirit. *This is who I met.* That's what makes Jewish leaders craziest, because you can educate people out of stereotypes, you can dispel their self-hatred with therapy, you can make Jewish worship exciting and compelling—but in this society, you can no longer keep Jews from meeting non-Jews. That ship sailed at least thirty years ago.

•   •   •

"Why does this resonate so powerfully, this intermarriage?" Barry Kosmin asks. "It affects families intensely; it affects every local community and every synagogue in terms of the composition of the people—who's in, who's out. . . . It's so multilayered, and that's why, as far as I'm concerned, of all that information [in the NJPS], the 52 percent figure became so powerful. . . . It's symbolic of other things, but it's the only thing that's relevant to you personally, to every person, to every family, to every little local community, to the national community, to the Jewish people, and to Jewish history. It really is powerful stuff. People have got lots of opinions, and they don't even know why. . . . It's a very emotional topic."

Yet the debate on intermarriage is being run strictly according to the numbers; the sociologists acknowledge only what they can quantify. Everyone in Jewish institutional life uses the numbers to justify how they feel and what they do when faced with mixed couples. The only people who don't seem to have much of a voice in the discussion are the people least concerned with the numbers and most concerned with their own families: the intermarried Jews who want a place in Jewish life but don't know where to find it, or are being told that they don't have one, or are given a place in the last row of the synagogue, or have a place and are tired of defending it.

Some are men who liked Jewish girls okay but met Teresa in med school and that was that. Some are women who got sick of hearing every Jewish guy they knew refer to any successful Jewish woman as a JAP. Some are people who loved Bubbie but couldn't stand Mom; some are people who loved the seder but hated Sunday school. Some married young, some not so young. Some went looking for spiritual fulfillment outside Judaism; others never left. They all came to their marriages from different places, for different reasons. The debate on intermarriage is not truly joined until their stories are heard.

2

I'm Not OK, Mom's Not OK, You're Not OK

At my wedding, one of my mother's friends said [Dina] never did like the Jewish boys, did she? And I didn't, I never did. . . . If they were short and balding and hairy, they reminded me of my brother and my father, and I could not cope with that at all.

—Dina, research chemist, suburban Washington, D.C.

A lot of Jewish women . . . are products of the same kind of family that ruined me. They want to be like their mothers, which is like my mother, and, you know, it's like *grrrrr.*

—Arnie, real estate broker, Los Angeles

Basically, I saw that Jewish men were a lot like me and that they were a bit aggressive and that they were like my dad, and they wanted to have their way . . . and I didn't feel like I could live up to their standards, which I felt were impossibly high. So I determined that that was just gonna be a path for unhappiness for me and I would never date Jewish men.

—Aviva, business consultant, Orange County, California

The antagonism takes root, as it does within all minority groups, because so many of us don't like ourselves.

American Jews have made it as no other immigrant group has made it in this country—bigger, more visibly, and in a shorter time than just about anyone else. But that hasn't made a difference in how many of us view ourselves and one another. We see ourselves as history's weaklings; the Holocaust casts a deep shadow over our psyches. We compare ourselves to the sleek denizens of the dominant culture's cities and beaches and come up, in our own eyes, hairy, dark, and flabby. We're sure that everybody else has better sex and less intrusive parents. Then we look at Jews of the opposite sex and we see them as we see ourselves: unattractive, unsexy, burdened with overbearing mothers and an oppressive ethnic heritage. And we say, That's not what I want. I want something different. Something better.

Not all of us do that, not even close. But enough to make a difference, even among Jews who live and work among other Jews. Enough, now that the taboos have fallen, to tip the scale toward non-Jewish partners for those Jews who don't think being Jewish is anything to brag about.

Self-hatred: Anti-Semitism Turned Inward

"There's no way you can be a member of a despised, persecuted minority without having negative feelings about yourself," says Judith Weinstein Klein, a Berkeley psychotherapist who helped pioneer the field of ethnotherapy, a form of counseling that encourages people to change negative attitudes about their own ethnicity through group interaction and self-exploration. Klein divides Jews, who comprise the bulk of her practice and clinical work, into three groups: positive identifiers, negative identifiers, and ambivalent identifiers.[1]

The positive identifier feels good about being Jewish: has close Jewish friends, is relatively comfortable with himself or herself physically (in the sense of not wishing to look more "WASPy"), enjoys Jewish holidays and observances, and has warm memories of childhood rituals; feels a connection to the State of Israel and to the Jewish past; and sees valued personal traits, such as altruism or love for family, as "Jewish." Positive identifiers accept the bad with the good, synthesizing positive and negative aspects of being Jewish without denying any of them.

Negative identifiers see nothing good about being Jewish: the religion is meaningless, the people ugly and obnoxious. They associate Judaism with the Holocaust and other woeful episodes in Jewish history—many children of survivors are negative identifiers—and recall childhood observances in synagogue and family settings as empty and superficial. Negative identifiers keep other Jews at a distance and blame Jews for their own troubles; some even pass themselves off as Gentiles. They are not, needless to say, interested in marrying Jews.

That leaves ambivalent identifiers, who don't deny their Jewishness but are very much assimilated into (and fascinated by) the dominant culture and unhappy with what they see as the negative aspects of being Jewish. Both valued and despised personal traits are ascribed to the ambivalent identifier's Jewishness.[2] Woody Allen, Klein says, is the quintessential ambivalent Jew; he presents his brains and humor as Jewish but sees anti-Semites in every doorway and runs from the Jewish women of his past to non-Jewish women as erotic partners. Ambivalent identifiers frequently marry Gentiles but run into trouble when their positive feelings about Judaism don't resonate with non-Jewish partners.

Not surprisingly, Klein's work shows positive Jewish identifiers as testing high on scales of self-esteem, with negative and ambivalent identifiers attaining lower scores.[3] A positive Jewish identity, it seems, is good for a Jew's mental health.

So why do so many Jews exhibit self-hatred? Where does it come from?

To begin with, Jewish self-hatred is a product of the modern age. When European Jews were isolated from the dominant culture, they were happy to remain a separate people, interpreting the oppression they suffered as the price of being "chosen" by God. "These religious beliefs, along with feelings of superiority, provided a form of psychological protection for pious Jews, which shielded them from fully internalizing the hatred they encountered, though of course the persecution left profound scars," psychotherapist Estelle Frankel wrote in *Tikkun*. But with the Enlightenment and the political emancipation of Europe's Jews some two hundred years ago, Jews began to enter mainstream society and cast off their religiosity. Wounded by the anti-Semitism of their neighbors but unwilling to return to the shtetl, assimilated Jews put ever more distance between themselves and their Jewishness.[4] This ethnic ambivalence traveled to America with the nineteenth-century waves of Jewish immigration and spread during the twentieth, fed by word of pogroms in Europe that culminated in the Holocaust and by the less frequently violent but psychologically damaging anti-Semitism Jews suffered in this country.[5]

After World War II, the revelation of the Holocaust left deep wounds of guilt, shame, and anger in American Jews that have yet to heal. Keeping alive and honoring the memory of the six million Jews murdered by the Nazis is an appropriate and necessary focus of Jewish ritual and education, but when the Holocaust is presented, as it has been by scores of Jewish clergy, educators, and even parents, as what psychotherapist Doreen Seidler-Feller calls "the central point of our identity," we run into trouble. Our preoccupation with our history of suffering, Seidler-Feller told a Los Angeles audience, impedes us from developing a positive Jewish identity, which must have "celebration at the core," based on achievement, joy, and satisfaction.[6] Meryl Nadell, who counsels mixed couples for Jewish Family Service in New Jersey, says she has worked with a number of adult children of Holocaust survivors who avoid relationships with Jews. "On a very deep psychological level . . . to marry someone not Jewish in some way becomes safe, protective, and I've had some clients who have felt that way, so that not to marry a Jew was some fantasy that they would not have to be subjected to whatever Jews get subjected to," Nadell reports.

Even for young Jews without a direct family connection to the Holocaust, the anxiety of being asked to empathize with Holocaust victims may be so threatening that it may not only affect the health of their Jewish identification but cause some to seek out non-Jewish partners, says Sanford Seltzer, a Reform rabbi who directs the UAHC's Commission on Religious Living. The message that part of the responsibility young Jews have to the memory of Holocaust victims is to bear and raise Jewish children, presumably through marriage to other Jews, Seltzer writes, is a message that contemporary Jewish students do not want to hear and that Jewish educators, clergy, and parents have been increasingly reluctant to teach in recent years.[7]

Some Jews disaffiliate because they simply don't like what they see when they look at Jews as a group or Judaism as a way of life. "My mother often discussed how she would admire a WASP type of person, the way they dressed, the way they conducted themselves," one New Jersey woman said, "and there was always that undercurrent of how some people were so overbearingly Jewish that it was an embarrassment, and that's why people have the stereotypes that they do of Jewish people, because of that grotesque, obnoxious . . . type of Jewish person who's common in New Jersey or any area." Another woman said of her college experience, "I was intimidated by Hillel and the Jewish dating scene; the people that were specifically seeking Jewish culture and Jewish partners intimidated me or turned me off in some way. . . . You know the whole JAP image? I wasn't that; I was a bohemian, I was an artist, a poet. I didn't relate to designer jeans." She wound up marrying a Jewish man who was even more alienated from Judaism than she was, who hung out mostly with Italians and preferred their style to a "Jewish" affect. "He was almost an anti-Semitic Jew, so we got along really well," she said.

In *The Invisible Thread*, a book of highly evocative interviews with Jewish women from all over the United States, one subject, Melody Bowen, describes a Long Island girlhood devoid of any sense of Jewish history, ritual, or faith. Denied a Jewish education by her father, a self-described "cultural Jew," Bowen had no connection to the Jewish past, and what she saw in her community, she hated: "I grew up thinking that being Jewish meant shopping in malls, hating nature, and talking about non-Jews as 'the *goyim.*' . . . The Jews I knew seemed very shallow and materialistic. . . . I associated so many negative qualities with Long Island Jews that I couldn't wait to leave. In college, I was glad my blond hair and blue eyes prevented me from looking Jewish."

In her mid-twenties, after moving to Virginia, she met her husband—Rees Tate Bowen VII—and enthusiastically snuggled into the world of genteel WASPdom, Jell-O salads and all:

> The Bowens represent an aspect of American life that I always felt excluded from. Their family seems like one you'd find on television or in a Norman Rockwell painting. . . . I am now secretly tickled that a daughter I might have could become a member of the Daughters of the American Revolution. . . . I'm happy my future son will be called Rees Bowen VIII. I like the idea of being a chameleon who can blend in with others.[8]

Jewish men have often struggled to see themselves as fully masculine in mainstream American culture, which glorifies qualities in men that Jewish culture historically downplayed. Rather than a swaggering machismo, Judaism teaches men to rely on an inner strength based on restraint.[9] "It's not an easy thing to expect minority men to adopt an aggressive stance with respect to the majority in that culture," Seidler-Feller said at a 1994 forum, adding that the professions into which Jews were historically shunted, such as moneylending, were later used to stereotype them as being possessed of an "economic hunger." "Intellectual work and business success have been the ways in which Jewish men have expressed their aggression, and in a very positive and productive way," Seidler-Feller added. "But it's not something that is ordinarily valued by the majority culture in our society, because, primarily, brawn, physical strength, and the capacity to provide security . . . [are] still very much valued."[10]

Writer-producer Marshall Herskovitz, who presented American television viewers with a strong characterization of the conflicted American Jewish male in *thirtysomething*'s Michael Steadman, also believes that living as an oppressed people steered Jewish men away from aggressive masculine behavior. "I think it served the culture to have men who were obedient, studious, able to solve problems rationally. . . . All sorts of traits that would keep you from getting into a fight with the Gentile landlord or the army and keep you alive were encouraged," Herskovitz said in an interview. The fearfulness that may have been a good survival tactic in Europe doesn't fly in contemporary America, though: "I've seen it in too many instances in Jewish families, where there is an overconcern for personal safety, a fear of letting children be autonomous, be independent, be aggressive, make mistakes." It can all be very anxiety-producing, Herskovitz says, when an American Jewish boy realizes "that what he sees on TV or in the movies bears no relationship whatsoever to [the] messages he's getting from his parents."[11]

Small wonder, then, that a significant number of marginally Jewish men, unwilling to be tagged as wimps, have chosen non-Jewish partners. "In this context the choice of a Gentile wife takes on the character of a counterphobic act; this is how one seeks to prove to himself and to the world that he is indeed *not* afraid of the Gentiles, and that he is *not* afraid of the disapproval of the Jewish group either," Louis Berman wrote in one of the early "big books" on intermarriage. "At the same time, a Gentile marriage partner represents a step toward fuller affiliation with the dominant group, a merger of one's identity, and a mingling of one's germ plasm with the proud majority."[12] To this day, choosing a non-Jewish woman as a spouse has the flavor of a macho act for many Jewish men.

Small wonder, also, that postwar Jewish literature is full of male characters staking out all-American turf by bedding non-Jewish women, with Philip Roth's Alex Portnoy carrying the flag. Describing his relationship with a New Canaan debutante and other Gentile women, Alex tells his therapist, "What I'm saying, Doctor, is that I don't seem to stick my dick up these girls, as much as I stick it up their backgrounds—as though through fucking I will discover America. *Conquer* America—maybe that's more like it."[13]

Some observers see Jewish women as less tainted by self-hatred than Jewish men. A young woman responding to the speakers at a symposium on Jewish male–female relationships said, "What I see among a number of successful Jewish men is that once they've achieved financial success, they seem to have a further need to be validated by the majority culture, and that's why they're attracted to non-Jewish women . . . I don't think Jewish women have the same need to be validated by the majority culture, which is why I don't think they pursue non-Jewish men to the same extent."

But some Jewish women have managed to internalize a very strong message that being Jewish is not a point of pride, whether that message comes from the majority culture or from closer to home. "My parents both felt that they were stifled in their Jewish upbringing and proclaim that they fell in love with each other partially because of their rejection of Judaism," a 42-year-old Los Angeles woman wrote in a letter. "My parents raised us in the Unitarian Church and we were asked not to mention our Jewish roots to our neighbors or childhood friends. . . . Although I'm not really sure why I have not been involved with

Jewish men, I think that the fact that my family has had tremendous ambivalence about their background is the main reason."

"It is a heavy burden, this being hated for being Jewish," novelist Daphne Merkin wrote in a disturbing essay on the self-hatred instilled in her by an observant but deeply ambivalent mother, "and there is no assurance that it will produce in someone as conflicted as myself any overriding sense of community, of oneness."[14]

Mirror, Mirror on the Wall, I Don't Like What I See at All

The other day a friend of mine who sends her children to Temple Emanu-El Sunday school in New York and plans a summer trip to Israel said, "I don't like those Polish-Jewish rat faces, do you? I mean those skinny faces with the long noses and the sunken eyes. I think they're ugly." Her aesthetic is American. The ideal is a Dallas Cowboy cheerleader.

—Anne Roiphe, *Generation without Memory*[15]

Considering the centuries-heavy burden of anti-Semitism and self-hatred that they bear, it isn't surprising that many Jews, even Jews who value their Judaism's teachings and heritage, can't stand the way they—and other Jews—carry themselves, behave, and look. In his book *The Jew's Body*, Cornell professor Sander L. Gilman reels off the long list of physical and behavioral traits that anti-Semites have used to identify Jews: not just the nose, but the shape of the feet, the walk, the voice, the "Jewish gaze." "It is in being visible in 'the body that betrays' that the Jew is most uncomfortable," Gilman wrote. "For visibility means being seen not as an individual but as an Other, one of the 'ugly' race."[16]

Judith Weinstein Klein's doctoral work on Jewish identity and self-esteem among young Jewish adults showed that as far as these Jews were concerned, being Jewish and being beautiful were mutually exclusive. Women saw themselves as too dark, hairy, curly-headed, fat, and big-breasted. Men worried about balding and poor muscular development and saw themselves and their penises as too short. They wanted their muscles and their genitals to be "more WASP," which to at least one respondent meant "stronger and bigger."[17]

Many Jewish men look in the mirror and see a dweeb. "I identified real closely with Paul Pfeiffer on *The Wonder Years*, just the nerdy intellectual," says Brian, age 30, who migrated to the West Coast from Queens. "I was good at sports but not great . . . too shy to even ask a girl for a date . . . the whole braces, glasses, acne package, tall and very thin, very shy." Certainly too shy to ask out the girls he wanted to date: "The girls you wanted to go out with were the cheerleaders and the girls who were in the school plays ... and they were always the non-Jewish girls, because the Jewish girls were usually in the math club and the chess club, and they were the ones with the thick glasses, and they were just not the ideal. I grew up during the *Charlie's Angels* era, and that's the ideal, that's what you were looking for. You're trying to get dates with Farrah Fawcett and Jaclyn Smith, and none of Charlie's Angels was Judy Weinberg."

A rabbinic student who said he never feels unmasculine or unattractive around other Jewish men says he feels like such a nebbish when he's with his sister's blond, muscular, non-Jewish husband, whom he calls "a sweet, sweet guy," that he avoids spending time with him.

> It's not because he does anything that he's conscious of, but because I feel like a Jewish neb when I'm around him. I feel unattractive, I feel geeky ... and [I] don't think of myself in those terms until I'm around him. And I don't know whether it's because he fits the paradigm of what a good-looking American from the heartland who plays football looks like, or because he's sleeping with my Jewish sister ... but for the time being [I] just need to effect some distance.[18]

Jewish women, in this media age, are in even more trouble, held to an extreme—perhaps impossible—standard of beauty. The fashion models and actresses who are put forward as the mark against which other women are measured don't look like most other women: their facial features are more regular, their legs longer, their hair sleeker.[19] "Our societal concept of beauty is not Jewish; it's *Playboy*, it's *Glamour* magazine, *Cosmopolitan*," says Beverly Hills psychotherapist Jonathan Flier. "Those aren't Jews on the cover; they may be Jewish, but they don't look Jewish. They're blond, they have small noses, they have the hips, the body types that are generally not Jewish. So a lot of what becomes the prize ... is defined by our society, and ... it's not Jewish-looking."

Many men, including Jewish men, live by these standards and are unwilling to lower them one millimeter. Irene Seiger, who ran a matchmaking program for the Los Angeles office of the UAHC for about a year during the late 1980s, says men would come in with long lists of nonnegotiable specs: "They want long hair, short hair, no one over five-two, no one overweight. It was amazing. I mean they had all these barriers put up, there was no way they were gonna get married." Elaine and Caren Horvitz, a mother-daughter team of matchmakers in South Florida, know exactly what Jewish men's top priority is:

ELAINE: They want thin.

CAREN: Definitely thin.

ELAINE: It's definitely a pattern with men, more than anything else. Attractive, too, but the first thing is thin.

CAREN: They're very visual; men are very visual.

ELAINE: More so than women. A woman will be more likely to say that a man has a football build. You can't say that about a woman.

Although Jewish women are no more prone to obesity than women of similar socioeconomic status in any other ethnic group, Jewish women are likely to see themselves as fatter than other people, and, conscious of being Jewish in a non-Jewish culture, may be more likely to view their bodies as deficient no matter what size they are. Although hard numbers are difficult to come by, anecdotal evidence suggests that Jews are overrepresented among women with eating disorders such as bulimia and anorexia nervosa.[20]

A 29-year-old schoolteacher—a graceful, lithe competitive runner—says the men she met at the posh Los Angeles synagogue where she used to work "all wanted the perfect little girl, the perfect little tiny petite thing whose hair was perfect, nails were perfect. . . . The girls are dressed impeccably, Stepford wives, from the right outfit to the right length skirt to the hair to everything, and I always feel huge, I always feel awkward, and I always feel ethnic." Daphne Merkin writes, "I'd yet to meet a Jewish girl or woman . . . who didn't take it as the highest accolade to hear it observed that she didn't look Jewish. This wasn't to say that there wasn't, in due fairness, an admission of a genus of Jewish prettiness . . . but not to look Jewish, to look *un*-Jewish—that, it seemed, was to be golden, to be truly desirable."[21]

"The one Jewish girl who I've dated . . . is Jewish, but you wouldn't know by looking at her," says Brian, the ex-nerd from Queens, who says this woman, his girlfriend at the time we spoke, compares favorably to a *Playboy* centerfold. "In fact, I once said that to her; I said, 'This is the best of both worlds—you're Jewish, but you don't look Jewish.'"

In a talk about Jewish relationships, Rabbi David Wolpe, author of several books on Jewish spirituality, spoke of the tendency of single men and women to demand perfection of each other. "We know perfection isn't natural. Go into Mrs. Gooch's [a natural foods store] and look at the stuff that they don't shoot full of chemicals. It looks terrible. I always want the apples that have Alar in them. They look good to me. . . . Our society is pumped full of chemical makeup in all sorts of ways, and there's no way that that can't affect us."

Unfortunately, rather than encouraging the single men among his listeners to adopt more realistic standards for how women should look, Wolpe informed the assembly that men operate a certain way and it was counterproductive to expect them to change:

> The visual is much more important, by and large, to men. . . . There are other things that men have to be; handsome is not as high up on the scale for women as beautiful is for men. What I want to suggest to you is that that won't change. You may find individuals for whom that's not true, but to say, "Why do men value appearance so much? They shouldn't," is not helpful. It just isn't.[22]

In a few sentences, this Conservative rabbi gave his sanction to Jewish men who rank physical beauty as being as important an attribute in a mate as intelligence, warmth, and supportiveness.

Jews and Sex: A Contradiction in Terms?

In the Brandeis University student newspaper, a student-drawn comic strip opens with its protagonist looking at a poster: "Sex Kills!" A word balloon rises from his head: "Then it's a good thing we're at Brandeis!!"[23]

During the summer of 1982, Rabbi Dan Dorfman was leading a study session about sex and sexuality at a Jewish singles retreat, outlining Jewish views on the subject. What he called a "subdued" discussion was suddenly enlivened by a woman who called out angrily, "Why are we bothering with all this? It's because of all this traditional Jewish stuff that Jewish men are so screwed up sexually."[24]

Jews are said to be worriers, and one of the things we worry about, especially since sexual mores loosened up during the 1960s and 1970s, is how good we are in bed. Both Jewish women and men, according to psychologist Esther Perel, often see sexuality and Jewishness as conflicting parts of their identity. "There's a repertoire of sexual language that is missing in how they describe themselves," Perel said. "Jewish men rarely employ the attributes of masculine, sexual, hot-blooded, and virile in describing themselves," nor do women see themselves as "sensual, seductive, desirable, attractive. . . . The sexual part is somehow missing in the way people describe and define themselves, and sex is often a particularly toxic issue with Jewish couples."[25]

Traditional Jewish teachings about sex appear to present a fairly healthy attitude toward sex between men and women. There is no tradition of celibacy in

Judaism, even for clergy; you can't carry out the commandment to "be fruitful and multiply" if you abstain from sex. Nor was sex viewed as appropriate only for purposes of procreation; the rabbis of the Talmudic era saw erotic satisfaction for both husband and wife as an important part of the marital relationship. Rabbinic laws *required* Jewish husbands to have regular relations with their wives and to satisfy them sexually; marital sex was considered a husband's duty and a wife's privilege.[26]

However, a profound ambivalence about sex has run through the past two thousand years of Jewish history. Beginning with the compilers of the Talmud in the second century C.E., rabbinic leaders worried that erotic desire, even between spouses, would distract men from Torah study and serve as a destructive force. As David Biale writes in *Eros and the Jews*, a detailed examination of Jewish attitudes toward sex and sexuality throughout Jewish history, shapers of Jewish thought were influenced by non-Jewish philosophies that preached a greater asceticism than the Bible did. The rabbis of the Talmudic period, for example, who lived in a Palestine permeated with Hellenistic culture, adopted in part the Stoic idea that sex was meant only for procreation and any sex act performed for pleasure only was "gratuitous." Over the following centuries, Jewish individuals and groups from time to time would espouse an ethic that would reduce sexual contact to the absolute minimum necessary to maintain the Jewish people, with the feelings associated with sex to be viewed as a way of uniting with God, not as an expression of desire. Even in the modern era, the Jewish attitude toward sex and sexuality was marked by modesty and restraint.[27]

To this day, most Jews grow up with the idea that we are "people of the book," living life primarily from the neck up, with sexual fulfillment way down the list of priorities, after education, commitment to family, the pursuit of a career, and finding a suitable life partner. Jewish women tend to be viewed as caregivers and facilitators rather than objects of erotic desire. Historically, there is an emphasis on practicality in male–female Jewish relations, and until quite recently marriage was seen as an arrangement by which families (and sometimes finances) were strengthened, with love to develop as the couple lived together.[28] Many Jewish parents are reluctant to discuss sex with their children and are not physically demonstrative with each other, failing to model a loving sexuality.[29]

How loose or uptight, proficient or inept, heterosexual Jewish men are during sex depends on the Jewish man—and the woman he's sleeping with. "They are screwed up, I am sorry," says Dina, a 39-year-old chemist who is married to a non-Jewish man. "I have not met one yet who is hip about sex at all. They don't know what to do, they really don't." Non-Jewish men, Dina says, "don't have those hangups at all. In fact, my mother said that they just think sex with the Jewish girls is sexy."

"Jewish men automatically seem to turn me into their preconceived roles of mother, nag, bitch, or whore, making me feel dirty in sex, because *they* think it is. Or at least clinical. You feel like you're having sex with a gynecologist," another Jewish woman wrote in a letter. Later, in an interview, she said that when she thinks about Jewish men in bed, "I just think of talking too much during sex, and asking how it was afterward, and analyzing it, and making me feel self-conscious and not just going with the moment."

To be sure, plenty of contemporary Jewish men aren't hung up about sex or sheepish about their performance. While many of the Jewish men among my case study informants said they didn't date much as teenagers, most of them pulled themselves together by the time they were out of college and entered the premarital round of serial relationships typical of our generation. ("I'm very, very thankful that I got my fill before the AIDS thing became prevalent," said one man in his early forties. "I feel very sorry for people who are deprived of the opportunity to fuck without any serious consequences.") This is not necessarily a fringe benefit of the sexual revolution, either. Louis Berman, whose research on *Jews and Intermarriage* ended before the 1960s youth culture went into overdrive, cites many complaints from young Jewish women and their parents about sexually aggressive Jewish men. One parent said, "Our son-in-law isn't Jewish but he is a wonderful young man. The truth is, our daughter tried dating Jewish boys, but *dammit* they wouldn't leave her alone; they wouldn't keep their hands off her. The Gentile boys were the only ones who treated her like a lady."[30]

Meanwhile, the Jewish woman is still struggling to overcome a sexual image that swings between fiery insatiability and chilly passivity. From Eve onward, Jewish women are portrayed in the Bible as wielding sexual allure, their only power, to create or destroy, and if the biblical text doesn't condemn them, subsequent commentaries do. Later, the medieval figure of the *belle juive*, the beautiful Jewess, contained a strong hormonal as well as visual element: Rebecca in *Ivanhoe* is tried as a witch because of her sexual allure, and Nazi propaganda always portrayed the Jewish female as an aggressive slut.[31] This image of the sexually insatiable Jewish woman runs counter to the contemporary stereotype of the cold, withholding Jewish American princess, who, when she does deign to have sex with her partner, is so motionless and passive that she drains all pleasure from the act. The reality, of course, is somewhere in the middle.

Of all the Jewish men I interviewed, only one complained in any way about Jewish women's behavior regarding sex, a 30-year-old single man who said he was "tired of Jewish princesses who make you beg and plead." Not one man of any age characterized Jewish women as passive, overly demanding, or otherwise deficient in bed, and several who were married to very Nordic non-Jewish women said that in fact they had always been physically attracted to Jewish women, citing the dark good looks of Jewish women they had known and, in some cases, lived with; their current marriages resulted from meeting compatible partners at the right time, not of any preference in physical appearance or judgment of sexual allure. The younger women I spoke with, too, may have disliked aspects of the personalities and appearances of the Jewish men they met, but they didn't specify sexual performance as a problem area. The women who complained about Jewish men sexually were all older than 35.

Jewish law and folklore have much to say about sex and sexuality, much of it contradictory. Perhaps because sex has been as risky as it's been pleasurable since young non-Orthodox Jews were teenagers, these conflicting messages may be of less concern to them; they may give higher priority to other relationship factors than sexual performance and may have better ways to expend psychic energy than to type Jews of the opposite sex as inferior bedmates. For the second-marriage crowd, however, sexual attitudes are still a potent source of anxiety and judgment.

That Was No Steamroller, That Was My Mother

One time I attended a conference where most of the people were Jewish writers, and they were speaking about the importance of keeping their Jewish identity. And then we had lunch together, and I noticed that four of the speakers . . . were married to non-Jewish women. So I asked them how come this had happened. One of them . . . said, "I would never give a Jewish mother to my children."

—audience member, *Tikkun* conference workshop, UCLA, January 21, 1990

Of all relationships, the one between mother and child is probably the most intense. Mother is our first contact, our first playmate, our first love. Recognition that you and mommy are not in fact one flesh is your first step toward adulthood; every step after that involves further separation. In every culture, some moms and kids handle this process of maturation and growing independence well and some don't. *In every culture*, there are mothers who smother their children with so much unwanted attention that growing up is like trying to fight your way out of a jar of Marshmallow Fluff.

But the mother in just one culture, the Jewish mother, became the American symbol for the intrusive, invasive, overinvolved parent. Sometime after World War II, the Jewish mother became the butt of a national joke, the woman who always knew what was good for you because she knew entirely too much about you. By the 1960s, the joke had been hammered into a hard-edged stereotype, a persona no intelligent woman would want to adopt for herself—and an excuse for thousands of Jews to find non-Jewish partners.

The American Jewish mother's crime? Primarily, being female; also, being Jewish, being isolated from the marketplace, having too much energy and not enough channels in which to direct it, and living in America. Her grandmother was likely to have been born in the shtetl, where, psychologically, she was probably better off.

Shtetl women were resourceful, thrifty, efficient, and tough. They had to be—they were often the sole or primary support of families whose titular heads spent their days studying Torah. They brought their energy and competence to America and continued to contribute to the family income, as the wages of one worker, male or female, were usually insufficient to support a family. But where a Jewish wife in Eastern Europe might have peddled door to door or hawked goods from a pushcart in the marketplace, in the cities of the New World she usually stayed home, perhaps helping out in the family store or taking in piece-work.[32] "[W]omen—working in the kitchen, working in the marketplace, wiping and tending, hovering over sinks and toilet bowls, saving pennies for their son's education—carried the Jewish family into this century on their backs, on their knees," Anne Roiphe wrote.[33]

As the Eastern European immigrants began to pull out of poverty and move into the middle class, these Jewish wives were increasingly confined to their "natural" role of homemaker. After World War II, like millions of others, they established homes in the suburbs and produced baby boomers. No longer needed as an earner, the Jewish mother devoted the competence and energy that had propelled her mother or grandmother across the Atlantic to shaping and decorating her home, her table, her children, and herself—and in so doing, got herself typed as materialistic and smothering. Speaking at a women's conference at Brandeis University, journalist Susan Weidman Schneider laid out the postwar Jewish mother's double bind:

> When your whole world shrinks, naturally you're going to be absorbed in the lives of your children. And in an era where all American . . . women were being accused of momism, . . . Jewish women got a very bum rap. We, in a sense, took the rap

for all American women who were being remanded to the home front. . . . When Jewish women did it and were absorbed in the lives of our children, we became somehow a force for evil.[34]

As a psychological model, the Jewish mother came to symbolize all that goes wrong with the mother–child relationship. (Not just Jewish toddlers go through an Oedipal phase, after all.) "If you think about it along developmental lines, little boys have to form some kind of separation; they have to break away from Mommy, and . . . part of that breaking away and forming their own identity, it is that kind of deep-seated fear of being engulfed by Mommy, and then attaching yourself to Daddy. Looking to Daddy for the male identity involves a certain rejection of Mommy," Los Angeles psychotherapist Patricia Field said in an interview.

In the psychological literature, being Not-Mommy is all-important for boys. Psychoanalysts believe that part of the natural process of separation is to reject and devalue all that is feminine. Analyst Karen Horney linked masculine contempt for the female as indicative of a "dread of women" growing out of the mother's early omnipotence as caretaker. This dread is ambivalent, though; the mother must be rejected, but she is also seductive and attractive. How do heterosexual men reconcile their fear and their attraction? "[They] develop psychological and cultural/ideological mechanisms to cope with their fears without giving up women altogether. They create folk legends, beliefs, and poems that ward off the dread by externalizing and objectifying women," psychoanalyst Nancy Chodorow writes.[35] That's exactly what the rabbis did during the Talmudic period when they came up with *midrashim* to portray every woman in the Bible as sexually driven, and that's what men do today when they stereotype women as Jewish mothers or Jewish princesses.

When a son experiences his mother, accurately or not, as overwhelming, Chodorow writes, he projects his fears onto her and characterizes her as a rejecting, hostile punisher; then, as an adult, he views the world as filled with aggressive, cold, destructive women. "Too much of mother," Chodorow says, "creates men's resentment and dread of women, and their search for nonthreatening, undemanding, dependent, even infantile women—women who are 'simple, and thus safe and warm.'"[36]

The way these processes play out for Jews, of course, is obvious. Psychologist Estelle Frankel sees the "enmeshment" in so many Jewish families as a challenge for Jews seeking partners, particularly for men, whose need to separate from Mother is likely to cause Jewish partners to remind them of their early dependency on their mothers, with an attendant threat to their sense of maleness.[37] Marshall Herskovitz, who thinks Jewish mothers subtly steer their sons toward weakness and neediness, says a man who's anxious about his masculine identity will reject a woman as a partner who displays any particular characteristics of his mother. "If their mother was short, they'll look for a tall woman. If their mother was fat, they'll look for a thin woman. If their mother was Jewish, they'll look for a non-Jewish woman. It has to do with the particular person they grew up with, who they are made anxious by because they are too drawn to that woman. They need the woman too much, and that makes them anxious as men, so they must get away."[38]

Arnie is a real estate broker who, at 48, has never married. His mother stayed home most of the time, doing some college teaching, but when the children were a little older, she took an administrative job in city government. His father stayed pretty much in the background. "Mother was the executive in the family," Arnie says. "[She] was kind of the dominant, child-raising force. She was the discipliner, the authoritarian; I always had to go through her to manipulate what I wanted out of them. . . . She needs to be in control, she needs to be dominating and making things happen her way. Even a few years ago, Mother would be trying to tell me how to run my life."

Since graduate school, Arnie has had one relationship after another with "unsuitable" women, most of them non-Jewish, many of them, in contrast to his mother, distinctly out of control, either sexually or in terms of substance abuse or both. Recently out of the fast lane himself, Arnie is looking for a mate, and although a top requirement is intelligence, he wants a woman who knows her place as a woman. (He extolled one woman of his acquaintance, a Southerner, who, when her husband called her, came in from doing household chores to move an ashtray that was just out of his reach.) "I'm looking for someone who has that kind of a female, kind of the fifties, Donna Reed kind of femininity. . . . A high-powered attorney who just comes home and is a woman would be perfect."

In the eyes of many Jewish women who are dealing with the fallout of these Jewish men's penchant for non-Jewish women, the irony is that these guys all want wives who will mother them; they just don't want *their* mothers mothering them. "They don't want to have sex with their mother . . . but they do want a mother, because as much as they want to get away from her, they want the caring, the caretaking that comes with it," says one 34-year-old Jewish woman. Herskovitz agrees: "I look at so many mixed marriages, and what do I see but the man wants to be mothered anyway. . . . He wants a safe mother, but he still wants a mother."

The overinvolved Jewish mother can have a negative effect on her daughters as well. "I'm sure my mother can never see me enough or talk to me enough," says a 40-year-old Southern California woman who finds Jewish families entirely too intrusive. "I've had to struggle with her for the past twenty years to break away and to have my own life and my own space." "I have a mother that I don't get along with," another Jewish woman says. "She's real domineering and very clinging and gets sick all the time, and complaining. The minute I smell anything like [men in her life] have a family member like that or they're like that themselves, anything, a sinus problem, anything, I turn off."

The Jewish mother stereotype riles many commentators, some of whom would like to know what's so damn wrong with nurturing your children. Zena Smith Blau, writing "In Defense of the Jewish Mother" in 1967, pointed out that the Jewish mother's fierce protection of her children contributed to a low infant mortality rate, even in the slums, and her talkativeness helped her children develop early verbal skills that set them on the path to high achievement.[39] Her shtetl-rooted concern has provided Jewish children with a safe emotional place in a world that has often been hostile to Jews, as historian Judy Timberg noted: "No matter what you do, no matter what happens, she will love you always. She may have odd and sometimes irritating ways of showing it, but in a hazardous and unstable world the belief about the mother's love is strong and unshakable."[40]

Whether or not there's truth to the different components of the Jewish mother stereotype, it is hurtful to the women so labeled, to their daughters who accept the stereotype's validity and allow it to injure their own self-images, and to the potential for endogamous relationships when Jewish men use the stereotype as an excuse to avoid Jewish women.

Dad? What Dad?

In contrast to all that has been written about the *Yiddishe mameh* of the shtetl and immigrant periods, no one ever really developed an accompanying stereotype of the *Yiddishe tateh*. Although the father was the acknowledged head of the household, in most families the breadwinner, and "the court of last resort" in terms of discipline, he tended to be a remote figure, especially to his sons; the mother was the parent who met her children's daily needs. In America, as the Jewish community became more secular, the devotion the Jewish father might once have given to Torah study was turned to his work.[41] The father's pursuit of economic success kept him even more distant from his children than did his father's and grandfather's attention to the sacred texts or the demands of the marketplace.

Nancy Chodorow has written about what happens in families with fathers who take care of their wives and children financially but maintain an emotional distance, an extremely common pattern in American families, including American Jewish families. Without his father as a continuous role model, Chodorow says, a boy is likely to take his marching orders concerning masculinity from the surrounding society, accepting cultural stereotypes as the truth about what it means to be a man.[42] For Jewish boys, this can lead to rejection of their fathers as weak and unmanly when they measure Dad against the messages they get from a macho and anti-intellectual dominant culture.

Although none of the Jewish men I interviewed volunteered stories about growing up with emotionally absent fathers, there is evidence that this is a problem for Jewish men. When Wilshire Boulevard Temple in Los Angeles organized a men's group specifically to explore "the changing boundaries, isolation, joys and burdens of being a Jewish man," each man at the first meeting was asked to describe his relationship with his father. Many of them, a group leader indicated, had spent youthful energy seeking approval from Dad and not getting it. "In one fell swoop," a reporter commented in a newspaper account, "the myth of the overbearing Jewish mother was replaced with more potent and more accurate memories of the emotionally removed Jewish father."[43]

Jewish women did volunteer examples of fathers who were emotionally distant or otherwise unsupportive. A Los Angeles woman married to a non-Jewish man said one reason she was always "put off" by Jewish men was that she "found in them the same coldness I experienced from my father." Her parents had divorced when she was small, and when her mother came close to marrying a non-Jewish man, "the thought formed in my then six-year-old mind that fathers did not always have to be cold, demanding or manipulative. . . . I believe this feeling influenced any further dealings with any man I found cold, etc. and this happened to include most Jewish men I met. I knew that I didn't have to put up with that."

Other Jewish women, uninterested in Jewish men, have found their relationships with their fathers played out with non-Jews. A 43-year-old woman who grew up in Arizona thinking the Jewish boys she knew were too familiar or too unhip thought she was rebelling when she married a tall, blond lapsed Catholic, although her parents, especially her father, thought the guy was great. "He was not familiar, but very much like my father, strong; my father's very controlling. Now that I've done a lot of work in dealing with father–daughter issues, I can see that I really needed to separate myself from my father, and I didn't. I just married my father." A couple of single Jewish women told me that they'd like to marry men just like their fathers, whom they admire—but they'd like non-Jewish versions.

Untangling the Net

The "enmeshment" perceived as prevalent in Jewish families is blamed for producing a number of psychological reactions that may subtly or overtly push sons and daughters away from Jewish life and the selection of other Jews as partners. One is guilt, a staple of the Jewish mother stereotype, which is seen as especially intense among Jews. "Children of a mother who sacrifices everything for them and denies all personal needs may feel bound by guilt, for there is no way to repay her efforts adequately," say Fredda Herz and Elliott Rosen, contributors of the "Jewish chapter" in *Ethnicity and Family Therapy*, a widely used social-work textbook. The need to provide *naches* in the form of success, marriage, and grandchildren—and you can never generate enough *naches*—is a fountain of guilt for Jews, these writers say.[44] This plays badly in an American culture that encourages people to look out only for themselves and may well spur some Jews to detach themselves through outmarriage from a family dynamic that they see as limiting to their freedom and well-being.

Rebellion—against parental authority or family dynamics, the conventions of society, the restrictions of ethnic identity—loomed much larger as a psychological factor in mixed marriage when it was still relatively uncommon.[45] "Jewish males, especially, were in rebellion against their mothers, and therefore they tried to pick a woman as dissimilar as possible from their mothers," said one New York rabbi, whose older brother, now past 70, did exactly that. "When he intermarried, he was typical of his time; he was rebelling against Mama, and we had a strong mama. He picked that way to rebel because he couldn't find any other way at the time." Today, this rabbi says, things are different. "It's not just the luck of the draw, but there's certainly less of this male Jewish rebelliousness and more of the factor of assimilation."

Still, the urge to rebel against parents or community turns up from time to time in discussions of Jews' current decisions to marry non-Jews. "A lot of people in [Southern California] seem to be the rebellious child," says Jonathan Flier, who facilitates counseling groups for prospective converts to Judaism. "I find that for a lot of the people that were born Jewish, a lot of it is like, 'I'm not gonna do what my parents want me to do,' the whole smothering Jewish family." A young Brandeis alumna says, "The thing that gets me is like a lot of Jewish guys will be like, 'Oh, you're exactly what my mom wants me to marry; therefore, I can't go out with you. You're my parents' wet dream, and I want to be rebellious.'"

Of all the psychological undercurrents swirling through Jewish families, the sky-high expectations Jewish parents have for their children probably engender the most resentment—resentment that many Jews are quick to project onto potential dates and partners. During a program led by Judith Weinstein Klein on relationships between Jewish men and women, the participants were given charts and instructed to fill in what it means to be a Jewish woman or a Jewish man from their own perspectives and the imagined viewpoints of siblings, parents, and grandparents. One guy left behind a chart on which he had answered the question, *What does it mean to be a Jewish man?* almost completely in terms of money and success. In the spaces for himself and his brother, he wrote, "You've got to be successful." He listed his sister's perspective as, "You've got to be perfect." In mom's space, he wrote, "My son the doctor"; in dad's, "Oy, I get such naches from the boy." And for all four grandparents, he wrote that to be a Jewish man means "He's got to be a good provider."

"As a Jewish male, I had a negative reaction to what I grew up with in my Jewish community, which was that my worth as a male was based on performance, specifically what grades you get, what you'll do for a career and living, and how successful you are at it financially, what kind of family you marry into," Herb Goldberg, a psychology professor and author of several books on relationship-building, said at a Los Angeles symposium. "A sense of failure, self-hate, shame, and guilt was always lurking in the shadows of the first misstep."[46]

What happens, of course, is that Jewish men and women who grow up with what they perceive, often accurately, as astronomical or unrealistic expectations from their parents project them onto each other, and to the degree they feel they can't live up to the expectations, they project their frustration and rage as well. A college student commented, "Whatever Jewish men call us—cold, hot, leech, bitch—it's all the same thing: They're afraid they can't live up to our standards." A male student said, "Lashing out at Jewish women . . . is a way to get back at the entire high-expectation, high-pressure Jewish family. You can lash out by becoming an academic failure, or you can become a doctor—which is less self-destructive—and then simply refuse to marry a Jewish woman."[47]

The Smell of Incest Wafts through the Air

As I leaf through the interview transcripts, it comes up again and again: *The Jewish boys who were in my synagogue, I didn't like 'em. They were like brothers; I mean we'd been together since nursery school. . . . There is in my mind a fundamental unresolved thing; I felt almost as if it would be incest with some Jewish women, almost as if they're more family than anything else. . . . You know the things that are awful about Jewish men; you've grown up with*

them. . . . They became so much like your friend or your brother that you couldn't look at them as
someone to date.

A significant number of Jews experience their opposite-sex counterparts as siblings—perfect as friends, unacceptable as romantic partners. Combined with all the other issues of self-image and family dynamics, the sheer familiarity of a Jewish man or woman as a potential love object makes it hard to "eroticize" the other person, to use Klein's term, to project onto him or her the attributes you find sexy. In addition, Klein says, the tension and excitement of getting to know a romantic partner often collapse quickly between Jewish men and women, who make so many assumptions based on shared cultural histories that they create too much good buddy–type intimacy too soon. Traditional Jewish society knew how to maintain the mystery between men and women—they were kept apart, out of physical contact, and, in places like the synagogue, out of each other's sight. In American society, except among the very Orthodox, the figurative *mechitzah* is gone, and so is the mystery, spurring some Jews to look outside the social circles of their youth for a partner they don't know so much about.[48]

"The Jewish girls were a little more predictable in the way that they were. I mean they all sort of seemed similar . . . [though] they were all very nice," says a Massachusetts man who dated both Jewish and non-Jewish women and is now married to a Protestant. "The non-Jewish girls I think I was a little more intrigued with; there was a little less known about them, a little more mystery."

Much of the literature on intermarriage mentions the incest taboo, the injunction against sex with close blood relatives, which in this century has been very strong for Jews, possibly in reaction to the fact that for many generations, Jewish society didn't have a problem with such marriages. "Jewish culture was artificially endogamous," says Hebrew Union College's Norman Mirsky. "Most other cultures survived by going outside of their groups, bringing in other people. Jews made what we would consider incestuous marriages legitimate in order to maintain endogamy. You could marry your first cousin, niece, things that were forbidden [in other cultures]." Reaction to this enforced intimacy fed the young Jew's search for a "contrast choice."[49]

Although the Oedipal wish generally doesn't cut the same way for girls as it does for boys, and more Jewish women than men may be comfortable with family intimacy, the whiff of incest influences partner choices for plenty of Jewish women. "It's really a kind of uncomfortable feeling I have when dating Jewish men, of looking in a mirror," a 52-year-old Los Angeles woman said. "I've had that with non-Jews, too, but it's the positive side of the mirror." Dan Dorfman recalled a woman's comment from his work with Jewish singles: "She said dating Jews was like dating their brothers . . . that non-Jewish men are exotic, they're not familiar, and therefore there's a certain attraction. . . . Familiarity breeding contempt, as opposed to warmth. I think that's still happening."

Which means for some Jews, their top requirement in a mate is simple: otherness.

The phrase "forbidden fruit" comes up quite a bit in my interviews. "I think for some Jewish men there is literally an attraction to the, if not blond female goddess, at least the *shikse* per se," says Jeffrey Marx, a Reform rabbi who has worked extensively with mixed couples in his Santa Monica, California, congregation. "A lot of Jewish men grow up with some strictures in the household about dating non-Jews; I think a lot of them are seen as . . . exotic and loose and attractive that way. In a number of the couples I see, I really see the men's future partners as their conquests."

It isn't just male, either, although it does seem that Jewish women who prefer non-Jewish men are usually able to articulate reasons beyond "they're different." That is, they're able to contrast what they like about non-Jewish men to what they don't like about their families, themselves, or the Jewish men they've known. "I would have crushes on these terrible hoods, who were of course not intellectual and totally the opposite of Hunter," said a New York woman who attended Hunter High, one of New York City's elite high schools. She says she never liked Jewish boys: "I guess I felt that they were too much like my parents, and I didn't want to be anything like them. My father would always want me to go out with these safe little Jewish boys, and we would have these terrible fights, and I would sneak out of the house. . . . I was always attracted to people the opposite of me. I always wanted these WASPs. We lived near Columbia, and we would go to these frat parties and totally demean ourselves . . . but these WASPs were who we wanted."

As Daphne Merkin struggled to come to terms with her own self-hatred as a young woman, she noticed a phenomenon that she called

"shiksa hunger": the longing for the non-Jewish, the crystallinely Christian, woman on the part of Jewish men. And what Jewish men they were! All the best, most creative ones—Woody Allen in his movies, Philip Roth in his novels— steered clear of the besmirched, mother-polluted Jewesses in their midst and cast yearning eyes upon the blond, Aryan fantasy. In a toss-up between having Anne Frank or Eva Braun . . . as a date, it was clear to me whom these men would choose.[50]

Put It All Together, It Spells GET LOST

I am a fairly attractive Jewish boy, age 25, and I date only non-Jewish girls . . .
If someone would teach Jewish girls how to use makeup and look attractive,
teach them some manners and how to be feminine instead of feminist, the
intermarriage rate would plummet. Since there is no chance of that happening,
I'm off to see my beautiful Korean girlfriend.

—respondent to *Moment* questionnaire on mixed marriage, 1977[51]

Taken together, the factors described in this chapter have created an atmosphere
of intense hostility and hypercriticism among many Jewish men and women,
hostility that has petrified into the Jewish American princess, prince, and nerd
stereotypes. For thousands of contemporary Jews, everything our culture and
our parents taught us becomes something not to like in a potential Jewish
partner.

The hostility shows up in the Jewish male's fear of competition. Young Jewish women learn fast that a large proportion of Jewish men have serious trouble
with the idea that their sisters are just as intelligent and articulate as they are.
One unmarried woman in her early thirties said, "My mother says to me, 'You
may have a mind like a steel trap, but not every man you go out with wants to
get caught in it.'"[52] Another single woman, age 40, told me that her father
pushed her to complete a Ph.D., only to express concern that she'd educated herself out of the marriage market. A student told her class in "Contemporary
Issues in Jewish Existence" at Colgate University about two friends at another
school who got *JAP* spray-painted on their dorm room door. "[N]ow I wonder—which one of the girls was being called a JAP? The one with the dozen
Benetton sweaters, or the one who'd gotten 750 on her L-SATs?"[53]

"We really grew up at a time when in some ways the women's movement was
making an impact in terms of women going into careers side by side with us,"
says Jeffrey Marx, who remembers—admiringly—many women during his years
at Brandeis and Hebrew Union College who he says were just as smart or
smarter than he was. But among Jewish men who come into his office with non-
Jewish women, it's a different story: "I sometimes see that their choice of partners are not 'not as bright,' but seemingly not as threatening to the male. There's
a certain amount of security in not having to compete."

"It doesn't matter what profession they're in, sometimes they're in great professions making oodles of money, and still they're afraid," a Los Angeles matchmaker says. "They want, I hate to say it, but maybe they want a dumb blonde.
It makes them bigger."

One man told columnist Marlene Marks that he never goes to see movies starring Barbra Streisand or Bette Midler. "He has his own good reasons, but it's not as a film critic that he's responding," Marks wrote. "[He] doesn't like Barbra and Bette because he doesn't like to see Jewish women enlarged to 50 by 125 feet."[54]

Even among men you'd think would know better, the rage comes through. In an April 1994 forum at UCLA, "Jewish Men and Women: Love or War?" psychology professor Herb Goldberg described his work with a number of Jewish men, "successful professionals in their thirties and forties who have never married":

> While most of them, ideally, wanted to have a relationship with a Jewish woman, the relationships they did manage to sustain were often with non-Jewish women, the *shikse* goddess or the Gentile queen, as I have termed them. As these men saw her, compared with the Jewish women they knew, the Gentile woman was noncritical, nonblaming, noncontrolling, adoring, easy to get along with, and sexually accommodating. His perception was that she rarely, if ever, made him feel guilty, did not pressure him for marriage, and was not preoccupied with status.
>
> Our city is filled with Jewish men and women who . . . consciously or unconsciously seem to avoid, fear, and even resent each other. The problem is very much, I think, a two-way street: a polarizing dynamic between the generally workaholic, ambitious, self-absorbed, self-protective, often sexually preoccupied, driven, and even wary and fearful Jewish male, and the status- and marriage-focused, guilt-engendering, manipulative, and blaming Jewish female who nevertheless sees herself as very loving and giving, often as a victim of this Jewish male.

After the speaker for the women's side of the question, Doreen Seidler-Feller, spoke about the inability of Jewish men to accept aggressiveness in Jewish women, Goldberg said he admired aggressive women, he just didn't like critical or controlling women, and when Seidler-Feller suggested that a Jewish man's experience of a Jewish woman wasn't necessarily the truth, Goldberg replied, "If I have a certain feeling about you, it doesn't matter whether it's true or not. I have that feeling, and if you don't pay attention to it, we don't have a relationship."

Jewish Journal columnist David Margolis, trying to find out whether Jewish men reject Jewish women "for cause," had one college-educated 30 year old tell him, "American Jewish women are crass, materialistic, neurotic," as opposed to non-Jewish women, who are "immediate, uncomplicated, unlayered, easy-going, fun-loving . . . the Girl in the Beer Commercial."

"The search for the uncomplicated, easy-going Girl in the Beer Commercial suggests, I have to say, what is wrong, not with Jewish women, but with American Jewish men," Margolis wrote. "The tragedy of the Jewish single is perhaps to be so often mired in fantasies which engender hostility and suspicion between those men and women, Jews, who should most naturally be drawn to one another in love."[55]

Demographers insist that migration patterns and market opportunities explain everything about spiraling intermarriage; the rest of us know better. Look to the open society, by all means, but look also to how we see ourselves and our families, and how we treat each other.

As long as Jewish women see Jewish men as "fat-assed mama's boys," as one woman characterized them; as long as Jewish men, as one rabbi put it, would rather go home to Kim Basinger than a challenging conversation,[56] Jews are going to look outside the Jewish community for partners. "Why is the intermarriage rate in this country so high?" Jeffrey Salkin, a young rabbi, asked in 1983. "It is not only the result of living in an open society in which ethnic groups mix and mingle at will. It is surely rooted in the inability of Jewish men and women to see each other behind the barbed wire fence of stereotypes and clichés."[57]

3

Rush to Judgment

ABOUT JEWISH WOMEN	ABOUT JEWISH MEN
JAP	JAP
pushy	aggressive
very demanding	egotistical
whiny	wimpy
manipulative	nerdy
too critical	needy
want men with $	rich
Nordstrom's all the way	yuppie
lots of jewelry	shows off "toys"
spoiled	spoiled
too serious	mama's boy
flashy	poor dressers
fat legs	short
nonathletic	nonathletic
not blond	noncommittal
want someone better than Dad	has Jewish mother
expect men to be super achievers	assume Jewish women are JAPs

—from comments posted at a Jewish Federation-Council session
on relationships between Jewish men and women,
Orange County, California, January 5, 1992

It wasn't a pretty sight: a broad swath of brown paper running half the length of a hotel ballroom covered with the collective judgments of Jewish women and men about one another after participants in a workshop were invited to express their feelings about Jews of the opposite sex as graffiti. Some of the comments were positive, but the negative stereotypes outnumbered the compliments three to one. Although the workshop was informative and constructive, I recorded the graffiti with a heavy heart, realizing that these people were their own worst enemies when it came to finding Jewish partners.

Perhaps no more—but certainly no less—than people in other American ethnic groups, contemporary Jewish men and Jewish women judge each other by external criteria without exploring individuals' hearts and minds, perpetuating stereotypes and using those stereotypes, in many cases, as excuses to seek out or accept non-Jewish partners. Jews are arguably the best-educated group in America, yet some lack the imagination to look beyond a date's clothes or fingernails before dismissing the person as a potential partner. We have participated in every twentieth-century movement that strives for social justice, yet thousands of us use epithets to denigrate fellow Jews in a way we wouldn't dream of applying to people of different races or ethnic groups. We are notoriously willing to avail ourselves of psychotherapy, yet our singles events and dating services are filled with people who cannot move past the memory of the boys and girls they grew up with or knew in college.

I can't stand JAPs, and that's all I meet. . . . The Jewish guys I meet, their mothers taught them that they were like God's gift to Earth. . . . I hate women that bitch, and Jewish women are just famous for that. . . . I'm just not attracted to Jewish men. They're very nebbishy. . . . They're like Daddy's girls, driving big cars, lotta credit cards, lotta makeup, and everything is buy me, buy me, give me, give me.

Where did these stereotypes come from? Why are they so pervasive? When and how did we allow them to become weapons in a guerrilla war between people who should be at peace and in each other's arms?

By Her French Tips Shall You Know Her

Let's get one thing straight right away. Just as every ethnic culture contains overbearing, overinvolved mothers, every American ethnic group has its princesses: young-to-youngish women who spend an excessive amount of time and money on makeup, hair, and clothes; who are overly materialistic, measuring their own worth and that of others by their possessions; whose world view fails to extend much past their circle of family and friends; who go through life assuming that the men in their lives, especially their fathers, will solve any problems they may have without requiring more of them than a kiss on the cheek.

There are WASP princesses (does the term *Southern belle* sound familiar?), Cuban American princesses (ask anyone in Miami), African American princesses (as depicted in Spike Lee's *School Daze*, television's *The Fresh Prince of Bel Air*), and

Italian American princesses (I've heard of Italian wedding receptions that make the wedding scene in *Goodbye, Columbus* look like a trip to City Hall). Asian men are known to make some very cutting remarks about how nothing's ever good enough for ABC (American-born Chinese) women, and you don't know from Daddy's girl until you've met some of the Armenian teenagers I've taught.

Every ethnic group has its princesses; such women exist in every culture. But during the past twenty years, the *Jewish* princess has become the national poster girl for *all* American women who exhibit certain appearance and behavior characteristics. If a college girl judges every boy she meets by the car he drives and where he gets his clothes, no one says, "God, what a Southern belle," but many people have no trouble labeling such a girl—no matter what her ethnicity—a JAP. Worse, the willingness to stigmatize a Jewish woman as a JAP has fanned out from labeling the relatively small number of women who really are materialistic, shallow, daddy-dependent, and whiny to include any Jewish woman who asserts herself or takes good care of herself physically or would rather marry a man who earns a solid living than one she'd have to support. Thousands of Jewish men have found a way to bolster their egos when faced with a Jewish woman who makes them feel threatened in any way: Just dismiss her as a JAP. Also, the epithet has been taken up by the general culture, adding anti-Semitism to the sexism and self-hatred that allowed it to flourish among Jews. The spray paint on the university wall has spread to tag any woman whose attitude displeases contemporary American males.

Jewish men have been complaining about spoiled, materialistic Jewish women since antiquity, although the contemporary Jewish princess is very much a twentieth-century creation, the product of Jewish economic attainment, parents who are at once indulgent and perfectionistic, the baby boomer's sense of entitlement, and an American culture that still measures a woman's worth by how well she maintains her home, her children, and her own physical appearance.[1] The first expressions of overt resentment against the Jewish princess, which began in the mid-1970s, coincided with the beginning of America's economic decline; Jewish women, viewed as consumers and not producers, became a convenient target for the economic and psychic frustration of Jewish men and eventually a symbol of parasitic self-centeredness in the population at large.[2]

I first heard the term *JAP* at Brandeis in the early 1970s, much more from other women than from men. The label was used as a simple descriptor; we didn't approve of their values, but they were often friendly and generous. JAPs certainly didn't want for social life, since many guys at Brandeis had no problem with girls who put lots of time and effort into looking good. We didn't think of the JAP stereotype as anti-Semitic because only Jews told JAP jokes back then, and we didn't think of it as sexist; if anything, the JAP herself was antifeminist, with her obsessive attention to physical appearance and her lack of interest in politics and social issues, and plenty of folks in the women's movement felt the same way. A 1971 issue of the feminist magazine *Off Our Backs* ran a comic strip featuring "Felicia," a Jewish princess with all the trimmings: nose job, lawyer daddy, dentist husband, three kids, a split-level house in New Jersey, a powder-blue Mustang, and a bridge game every Thursday.[3]

Even feminist psychologist Phyllis Chesler bought into the JAP stereotype back then. In an interview for *Lilith* magazine, she declared, "Jewish women under 30, with many exceptions, of course, are still involved in country-club life, sorority life, and travelmania, and have an obsessive concern with appearance," which she found "distressing, appalling, and shocking." Asked why so many young women, including Jews, pursued this lifestyle, Chesler replied, "All women are ashamed of revealing their emotional and economic vulnerability, their inability to be strong. They prefer, instead, to rattle their chains high in the air and say, "Look! Mine are made of gold; yours are only silver. I am therefore better than you; my master has more slaves than your master.""[4]

This increasingly sour undercurrent running through the Jewish community during the 1970s became more turgid in the early 1980s, when a lurid murder case put a particular Jewish princess in the headlines. In May 1981, entrepreneur Steve Steinberg stabbed his wife, Elana, 26 times in their Scottsdale, Arizona, bedroom, killing her immediately, while his terrified daughters listened. Steinberg went on trial for first-degree murder but was acquitted when his defense attorney and a forensic psychiatrist, both Jewish, established to the jury's satisfaction that Elana Steinberg was so extravagant, shrewish, shallow, demanding, and sexually withholding—in other words, such a JAP—that she drove her husband temporarily insane. "Though defense attorneys saw no reason why Steve Steinberg should not return to a society to which he posed no further hazard, they left jurors with little doubt that society was safer minus the woman whose post mortem diagnosis their paid forensic psychiatrists obligingly produced: Jewish American Princess," one commentator wrote.[5] It was around that time that many non-Jews as well as Jews began to tell JAP jokes.[6]

For a while, many American Jews behaved as if the best way to handle the spread of the JAP stereotype to the dominant culture was to buy in and play along. *The Jewish American Princess Handbook* and *The Official J.A.P. Handbook*, paperbacks modeled after the best-selling *Preppy Handbook*, were published in 1982, giving tongue-in-cheek credence to every aspect of the JAP stereotype as they tried to portray the princess in the most positive light possible. "Jewish American Princesses are warm, coddling, funny, smart, and achieving," *The Official J.A.P. Handbook* trumpeted. "They are wonderful, dedicated mothers. Among the last of the traditional women, they are the consummate homemakers. They know how to make a man feel smart and appreciated and loved. . . . The true JAP *always* looks great. . . . A JAP has a flair for living and entertaining unlike almost anyone else."[7] Other "joke" items that first appeared during this period include greeting cards (one with set-up lines to ten JAP jokes on the front and a series featuring the unattractive, shopping bag–laden "Bunny Bagelman") and the much-displayed "Are You a JAP?" poster.

Meanwhile, many Jewish women continued to show "pride" in their JAPitude, buying T-shirts proclaiming themselves "JAP" or "Princess" or "Born to Shop" from catalogs, specialty stores, and temple gift shops. *Lilith*, possibly the only Jewish magazine to publish commentary on the stereotype during the late 1970s, ran an ad in the "Oy Vey!" feature of its first issue in 1976 that showed a young woman wearing a tiara, perched on a chaise longue, and modeling a T-shirt emblazoned with "JAP" in Hebraic lettering under a crown. The copy read, "You don't have to be Jewish to be a Jewish American Princess. You just have to expect . . . everything." The consumer was encouraged to "LET THE WORLD KNOW" her status as a JAP with these items.[8]

But laughing it off didn't work. The jokes became increasingly nasty, comparing Jewish women to vultures, labeling them as sexually inert, and, finally, wishing them dead. By the mid-1980s, American college campuses with high concentrations of Jewish students were rife with overt expressions of hostility toward JAPs, including T-shirts and posters sporting abusive slogans and ubiquitous graffiti—some of it not just anti-JAP but blatantly anti-Semitic—spray-painted on walls and scratched into library carrels. At Syracuse University, some student hangouts were identified as "JAP-free" zones; any girl dressed in what was considered JAP attire would be greeted by someone yelling, "JAP alert!" followed by a crowd of kids pointing and chanting, "JAP! JAP! JAP!" If a similarly dressed woman walked in front of the student section during a lull in a basketball game at the Syracuse Dome, upwards of four thousand students would pick up the chant—led by the campus pep band.

At one college, a student carnival featured a game where contestants could "prove she's not a JAP: make her swallow!" by throwing sponges through the mouth of a large cut-out board painted with the face of a coed. Campus newspapers and humor magazines began to publish cartoons and "satirical" pieces reinforcing the stereotypes and encouraging readers to avoid, punish, or even murder JAPs. The Cornell humor magazine ran a feature entitled "JAPS-B-GONE: A Handy Info Packet for the Home Exterminator."[9]

The promotion of the JAP image beyond all reality may be the ugliest slander of Jews since the Nazi era. University of Maryland professor Evelyn Torton Beck points out that only when anti-JAP graffiti began to contain swastikas did people begin to see the connection between "JAP-free zones" and Nazi Germany's creation of *Judenrein* (Jew-free) areas.[10] "If it had been all Jews," Susan Weidman Schneider said, "if it had been Jewish men that had been portrayed in that way, we would have noticed: 'My God, this sounds just like *The Protocols of the Elders of Zion!*' . . . But nobody noticed, because it was only women."[11]

So why have we allowed this slander to be perpetuated, especially by Jews? Because we believe it.

While researching this book, I asked almost everyone I interviewed what characterizes a Jewish American princess:

- Selfishness. Everything had to be just right, your hair had to be just right, the way you looked had to be just right. . . . Money means a lot to them.

- They're all spoiled little brats. . . . They don't have enough to do, that's what it is. They starve themselves and binge and purge, because they have to look perfect.

- She's had everything her whole life, drives a nice car, wears really nice clothes, and always is like really pristine about what she's wearing.

- [The attitude that] you're only as good as how you look. There's no sense of any values being important.

- The overdone makeup, the very loud clothing, and just very whiny. Especially at this dance I went to, I'm like no wonder guys don't want to marry Jewish women if this is what the women are like. I mean the scowls on their faces, it just doesn't make them attractive, both outside and in.

Just another bunch of guys bitching about Jewish women, right? Sorry. Those remarks were made by Jewish women, ages 23 to 40, and they represent a fraction of the women I interviewed who perceive the Jewish American princess as a real, identifiable type of person. Several informants said, without undue pride but without sheepishness, that they themselves had been raised to be JAPs or currently possessed characteristics they associated with JAPs. Almost every single person I asked—professionals as well as my case study people—affirmed in one way or another that the Jewish princess exists. Many respondents loaded their statements with qualifiers, deplored the abuse of the stereotype, reminded me that princesses are found in every ethnic group, refused to let the acronym pass their lips. But no one really said, "Nope. No such person." Most Jews— some in sorrow, some in anger—buy into the image of the Jewish princess, even though women who truly fit the stereotype are a small minority of American Jewish women.[12]

At the height of the college JAP-bashing phenomenon, Rabbi Larry Edwards, Hillel chaplain at Cornell University, sermonized against the stereotyping, with its combination of anti-Semitism and advocacy of violence against women, at Rosh Hashanah services. "But later in the sermon . . . I sort of listed what I thought were kind of common elements of the stereotype," Edwards told me. "I said, 'It's offensive to stereotype people, but if you recognize yourself in any of these stereotypes, then you should think about some of these other issues, in terms of values and living one's life and expectations of material possessions.' So I guess since I did that, it must mean that I think there are people who at least value some of those things personally." Other Hillel chaplains I spoke with, while they took pains to note that these character traits were not specifically Jewish, subscribed to the "kernel of truth" school of thought on the JAP stereotype.

Many Jewish men can quote you chapter and verse from their real-life versions of the *J.A.P. Handbook*. There's the obnoxious fastidiousness: "I like a person that can flow, roll with the punches," says a 30-year-old single Jewish man. "You spill chocolate sauce on your pants, so what? You wipe it off and you eat your ice cream. You don't sit there and say, Oh, my God, I gotta get these to the cleaners, I just bought them, oh, my God, it's not gonna come out."

"The unwillingness to do things that might involve getting one's hands dirty or being uncomfortable, if they're gonna travel, they have to have such and such of a room," is what grates on one attorney. "There's an experience I've had with a number of Jewish women, and I don't think I've ever had it with a non-Jewish woman, of being in a restaurant and getting ready to order, and having them do a third-degree on the waiter. 'Can I have it this way, and how does it come, and does it come with this?' I've sat there and just wanted to disappear."

Other men cite an undue emphasis on money. "Jewish women, I think . . . especially the Jewish women I grew up around, grow up expecting diamonds and cars," says Eli, 35, who was raised in New York and now lives in the Midwest, where he does very well in advertising. "To me, if that's as deep as it goes, I can go out and rent a whore and pay them money, which might be a little easier than to marry somebody who has no interest in other things than clothes and diamonds and jewelry and stuff." Men with incomes in the civil servant range often feel they don't measure up. A schoolteacher, calling himself "Romeo Minus Bankroll," wrote a bitter letter to the Los Angeles *Jewish Journal* complaining that Jewish women won't date him solely because he doesn't have a fat wallet or drive a Porsche.[13] A librarian told me that on a date his job scores against him: "There's still unfortunately the doctor-lawyer syndrome. They look for somebody who has a little bit of gelt in the pocket."

These negative judgments are compounded, says psychotherapist Esther Perel, when a man, perceiving a woman as being JAPpy in one way, assumes she's signed up for the full package. "If I am a Jewish man and I see you as very materialistic, I may immediately say that you're a JAP, and if I say you're a JAP, I include in that 15 other attributes which may have nothing to do with you," Perel told *Lilith* magazine.[14]

But these perceptions don't come only from men. In 1969, a book called *The Jewish Wife*, based on a poll of married Jewish women in and around several U.S. cities, with quotes from 70 follow-up interviews, made much of the fact that many of these women were very caught up in their physical appearance; a large chunk of the poll sample wouldn't be caught dead running out for milk without putting on makeup. They were obsessed with being or becoming thin; few were content to look like the stereotypical chubby Jewish mother of yore. They were found to value small luxuries; to the Jewish wife, the authors said, roughing it meant "staying in a motel without a heated pool, driving a car without power steering, eating tepid food in the corner cafeteria, or missing her weekly appointment at the local beauty salon." Several who had worked in offices—the authors devoted two pages to this—would have to have a gun at their heads to make them change a typewriter ribbon.[15] These wives represent the mothers of many Jewish women now in their twenties and thirties.

As for materialism, any glance at the personal ads or chat with someone who runs a dating service will tell you that some Jewish women are in fact determined to find partners with healthy financial portfolios. "Men are supposed to be money machines, and women have extremely stringent expectations about how much a man is supposed to earn," said a female psychotherapist based in New York. "There are women who have told me point-blank, 'He's gotta make at least $60,000 a year, or I'm not interested.' . . . They judge men by where they take them on dates. If they're not spending at least $50 to $100 on a date, it's not enough; they won't go out with them a second time." Irene Seiger told of a successful journalist who refused to meet a man in commercial real estate, at the time making upwards of $70,000 a year, because the market was subject to too many ups and downs; he might not make $70K the following year.

Several women I spoke with say they want to meet men who make at least as much money as they do and to live in the comfort they knew as youngsters.

Asked if she wanted a prospective husband to make a certain amount of money, an insurance executive said, "To be perfectly honest, I probably do. I grew up very comfortable, and in a way, when you grow up living very nice, you get used to that at an early age." One 34-year-old New Yorker rising rapidly in the entertainment industry told me that she'd be happy never to work again if she met a man who was willing to support them both.

And so it goes, even unto the next generation. Amy, 35, identifies her sister as a JAP. "She feels that the world does owe her something. . . . She has to have the right bathing suit to wear to the JCC, and she calls me and . . . complains about the maid and the kids and the car, and it's just not having enough to do." When her 12-year-old niece came for a visit, Amy recalled, "she says, 'Auntie [Amy], I'm gonna live in California some day,' and I said, 'You are?' and she said, 'Yeah, I'm gonna marry a rich man and live in California.' Well, where does that come from? Obviously, it comes from your training."

The forecast for endogamous marriage gets pretty bleak when people buy into the princess characteristics as specifically Jewish—when the guy, instead of saying, "I have a problem with acquisitive (or demanding or self-centered) women," says, "I have a problem with Jewish women because they're acquisitive (or demanding or self-centered)," when even rabbis blame Jewish women for being so materialistic that Jewish men don't want to marry them. One rabbi identified "Jewish girls seeing themselves as the center of the universe" as symbolic of the Me Generation narcissism visited upon the Jewish community, while another called Jewish princesses a sign of social decay; solving the JAP problem, he asserted, would "get our house in order."[16]

Eli, the ad executive, whose wife's background is Catholic, makes a definite distinction between the acquisitive Jewish women he knew growing up and the non-Jewish women he met beginning in graduate school. "I've hit it big, real big. I make a lot of money. It's nice to know I can have anything or buy my wife anything, but at least I know she will never request it. Probably it would be a little different if it was with a Jewish woman." When he met his wife, a teacher, Eli says, "There was a spiritual sense that we connected on that I probably did not connect with many people, especially who were Jewish. There was a depth, that there's something deeper on this earth than a Mercedes or a million-dollar house." To Eli, Jewish women will always seem shallow and grasping, while non-Jewish women will always appear to be independent and supportive.

Susan Weidman Schneider mentioned a Jewish man whose date, a Jewish woman, complimented him for having a nice, shiny car and then, on seeing the odometer, commented that it wasn't that new. "He felt, he said, absolute revulsion and was embarrassed by the force of his own reactions," Schneider said. " 'I thought what a total JAP she was; all she cared about was how new the car was.' He conceded that had this been a non-Jewish woman, he would have thought her remarks quite benign, that she was making comments about the car just to make conversation. But because she was Jewish, he immediately judged her to be materialistic."[17]

"Jewish women have been programmed to marry men with money," a female talent agent said. "And I think Jewish men sense that. I see some of these Jewish women, and they are disgusting. They're horrible. If I were a man, I would shy away from that too. . . . I think that's why they're more attracted to women in the business that are not necessarily Jewish."

Swirls of denial marble the discussion of the JAP stereotype, including denial that there's anything wrong with being a princess. "The level of consciousness is still not very elevated," feminist activist Julia Wolf Mazow told *Newsweek* in 1988. At one gathering, Mazow said, "a woman stood up and said, 'I'm a JAP and I'm proud of it.' She was wearing a JAP T shirt and a bracelet with 'Bitch' spelled out in rhinestones. They just don't see what the fuss is about."[18]

Some Jewish princesses take the approach that the people who don't like them are just jealous. "The kids who feel they can't keep up, that they don't have the cars, that their clothes aren't stylish enough, they're the ones who resent JAPs the most," an American University student said.[19] The jealousy can come from Jews or non-Jews: in the words of an Irish Catholic student at Colgate, "People hate JAPs because they seem to have everything: money, confidence, style."[20]

When Gary Spencer, a professor of sociology at Syracuse who has done extensive research on the princess stereotype and has been in the forefront of the effort to defuse JAP-baiting, asks young women who display the appearance characteristics associated with JAPitude how they feel about being called JAPs, he says he gets a few different responses:

> One group says, and I find this the most disturbing, "Well, this is the way I like to dress, but I'm really not a JAP because I don't have a JAP attitude, and if they took the time to get to know me, they would know that I'm really not, but I know women who are." These women themselves accept the stereotype; they just say they're not one. And . . . they don't quite understand how stereotyping works when they say, "if they took the time to get to know me." We use stereotypes as a way of *avoiding* getting to know people. . . . There's another group that says, "Yes, I think of myself as a JAP, and my father calls me a JAP and my mother calls me a JAP, but we don't mean it in the bad way, we mean it in the good way," meaning, "I like to look nice," that kind of an idea. . . . We often take negative labels that other people give us, and we find a way of thinking of them as positive.

Denial that the JAP stereotype is anti-Semitic is endemic among men and women, Jews and non-Jews. Most students who complain about JAPs insist that the term doesn't imply anti-Jewish sentiment, Spencer says, because they can identify princesses of other ethnic groups. Conversely, people will deny that *JAP* is an ethnic slur because Jews tell the jokes themselves.[21] ("I'm not insulted by [JAP jokes]," a woman who calls herself an "ex-JAP" told me. "The ones that I've heard, they're true.") Evelyn Torton Beck writes, "I have repeatedly heard young Jewish women admit that they would be offended to be called 'too Jewy,' but claim not to mind being called 'too Jappy.' "[22]

For much too long, institutional leaders denied that stereotyping was a problem they needed to deal with. In April 1987, Spencer and other Syracuse personnel brought the JAP-baiting issue into the public arena when they held an open forum on the subject. They expected 50 people; 500 showed up. At the same time, Spencer sent an information packet containing his findings on JAP-baiting to Syracuse faculty and administrators. The response from the administration was "absolute, total silence," Spencer said.[23] The not-so-benign neglect of Jewish organizations is mirrored in their house organs' coverage of the JAP stereotype. During the eighteen months after *Lilith* devoted much of its fall 1987 issue to JAP-bashing and the state of relationships between Jewish men and women, the publications of several national Jewish organizations (American Jewish Congress, UAHC, Anti-Defamation League, B'nai B'rith) ran an article apiece about the ill effects of the stereotype. Before and after: silence. Others, if their publications give an accurate reflection, have never specifically addressed the JAP stereotype.[24] Writing in 1986, Anne Roiphe charged, "That Jewish organizations and Jewish spokespeople have not vigorously protested the jokes that are told about their daughters and sisters tells us that they are agreeing with the general cultural anti-Semitism. They are cooperating in a disguised mockery of themselves. The Anti-Defamation League does not count Jewish women as Jews."[25]

"I think there are Jewish people who are not brought up to dislike each other, but I think there are Jewish people who *are* brought up to dislike each other," says Rabbi Bonnie Steinberg, who leads a Reform congregation on Long Island. "The burden of that falls on girls and women, because it's convenient and because of sexism. So there was a whole generation that was empowered to make fun of Jewish women."

But it isn't fun. It is devastating to self-esteem. You can see the damage in the shame and fear of Jewish women who are scared that they'll be identified with these loud, spoiled people. Donna, 27, an executive in a New England corporation, was a Syracuse undergraduate during the period that JAP-baiting began to get out of control. She had grown up with what she calls "JAPpy tendencies," which she buried quickly when she got to Syracuse. By not dressing in the way associated with Jewish princesses at the time, Donna avoided any abuse directed at her, but the images she took in hung over well into adulthood.

The week before I spoke with her, some five years after graduation, Donna was visiting her parents with a bunch of friends from college, and they went out to a local Chinese restaurant. "I'm the only Jew in the group, and we walk in, and there is a husband, a wife, and their daughter. And the mother and daughter have the bright red nails out to there, the dark eye shadow, the daughter had the big, curly hair; she kept checking herself out in the mirror. . . . The father just sat there like a shlump. All of my friends made a comment about it. It was almost embarrassing, like I don't want you to think that's how I grew up, because that's not how I turned out."

In *The Invisible Thread*, a Long Island teenager, although she believes there's nothing wrong with being visibly affluent, says she's becoming careful about the image she projects. "When I attend college next year, I plan to dress conservatively. But I'm worried that even if I wear well-tailored, nonflashy clothes, people might still label me as a JAP," she said. "I'm nervous that when I walk into my dorm, my future roommate might look at me and think, 'Oh, no, a Jewish girl from Long Island.'"[26]

Because we have allowed non-Jews to define us, the argument goes, we have swallowed the larger culture's contempt and let it poison ourselves and our relations with each other. "I think within any oppressed, marginalized group . . . you find this hostility among members," says Harry Brod, professor of gender studies at Kenyon College:

> In the Jewish community, sexism is the way we internalize the larger community's anti-Semitism. [The Jewish mother and JAP stereotypes] are in origin, I think, anti-Semitic criticisms of Jews for taking care of the families, for striving for economic security and success, that then get scapegoated, deflected onto Jewish women. It provides men a counterproductive, seeming safety valve for the pressures of anti-Semitism from the society at large.

In fact, says Marlene Marks, the problem for Jewish men is not that Jewish women use them as providers but that they don't have to: "Jewish men have lost their monopoly on the role of protector [and] caretaker," she wrote in a 1994 column. "While many men complain that Jewish women only look at them as a meal-ticket, in fact the opposite is true. Jewish men have lost their sense that they can indeed provide a meal-ticket, and feel diminished in their own eyes."[27]

In an interview, Letty Cottin Pogrebin, author of *Deborah, Golda, and Me*, suggested that the stereotype will fade when Jewish life overall has less to do with money:

> The self-hatred has nothing to do with the self. The self-hatred in my daughters' generation has to do with the acquisitive, bourgeois, middle-class Jewish world they see all around them. . . . And I see it too; I travel all over the country and I see women who are comparing diamonds and women who are talking about caterers, and these are people who aren't involved in their community except to raise money and spend money. . . . In certain communities in this country, and we had better be honest about it, in certain communities the women that men are seeing and the men that women are seeing are very—materialistic is the only word that comes to mind. I don't blame them, because I think it's a phenomenon of second-generation immigrant behavior, and third-generation immigrant behavior, and when they get more comfortable, they won't have to do it this way, I hope.

So much wrongheadedness surrounds the JAP stereotype that it's tempting to refuse to dignify it with counterarguments. But two points need to be made before moving on:

1. Nothing about the princess persona is intrinsically Jewish.

Elisa New, writing about Elana Steinberg's murder, makes this clear when she points out that there were American princesses long before Eastern European Jews began to burrow into the American middle class. Years before the Jewish wife started visiting the beauty salon once a week, Daisy Buchanan was admiring Jay Gatsby's shirts; years before Brenda Patimkin strode from tennis court to swimming pool in *Goodbye, Columbus,* 1920s flappers were spending their daddies' margin gains. The Jewish princess came much later—"only as narcissistic as the Yankee Princess she imitates . . . and only as trapped."[28]

As for the single Jewish woman's notorious search for Mr. Gelt, that appears to be cross-cultural. In a poll of single adults in Orange County, California, more than half said most of the singles they meet of any ethnicity are interested in material wealth. "Women want to check your financial statement," one man complained. "When I date, we go out in my old truck, and it ends after one date." A psychologist who counsels singles says looking for the best-feathered nest just makes good evolutionary sense: "For a billion years, females have been programmed by evolution to seek out the strongest mate with greatest resources."[29]

2. Much of what is labeled materialism is simply a desire for security or for shared middle-class values.

It's gotten to the point that a Jewish woman can't ask a guy what he does for a living without being accused of wanting to pick his pocket. All that says is that there are a lot of Jewish men who either aren't getting out much or are getting out to the absolutely wrong places. The vast, overwhelming majority of American Jewish women do not bring a Las Vegas mentality to dating. They are not out to hit the jackpot.

"In my experience, you men, having to be successful and having to have a great job and everything, I don't think that's an expectation that comes from Jewish women; I think that's an expectation that comes from Jewish men of themselves, and then it's sort of projected onto Jewish women," a woman said at a Jewish relationships forum. "I think Jewish women and women in general want to be involved with someone who has a reason for getting up in the morning, whether that's to teach tennis or to go to a successful law practice or to go to a successful bicycle shop. But this whole notion that women want someone who's ultra-ultra-successful is something that men have imposed upon themselves, and it keeps them from becoming vulnerable and connected."

"I don't think most people say they want someone real, real, real financially secure. They want them stable, that they have a steady job," says Miami matchmaker Elaine Horvitz. "I think most people realize in today's world, many times it does take two people to work." Horvitz's daughter and partner, Caren, adds, "They want to know that if they have children one day, they can take that year off and be with the child."

An analysis of personal ads supports the idea that Jewish women who specify a desire for a man with a successful career may simply be looking for men whose ambition, accomplishments, or values are comparable to their own. From November 1991 to December 1992, women placed about 1,200 personal ads in the *Jewish Journal of Greater Los Angeles.* I counted 336 different ads, 28 percent, in which terms like *professional, financially secure,* or *successful* appeared, sometimes in combination. The other 72 percent didn't list any qualifications for a man that explicitly dealt with money or success. Of the 336 ads that did, 116, about 10 percent of the total, specified only that the woman was looking for a "professional," without any mention of financial success. In almost every one of those ads, the woman described *herself* as a professional, as did most of the women, especially those under age 50, who explicitly sought a financially secure man.

What this says to me is that women with careers want to meet men who are at a similar level of education, sophistication, and success, not that they're casting about for a meal ticket. It tells me that the majority of Jewish women value intelligence, education, commitment, love for family, and *menschlichkeit*, all specifications that turn up frequently in women's personal ads, ahead of financial success in their men. It says that while most Jewish women aren't interested in supporting a husband or starving in the proverbial garret, a relatively slender percentage consider a fat wallet to be an important qualification for a partner.

This piece of the stereotype crumbles further when you look at the mothers of women 45 and younger. For all their love of comfort and small luxuries, Barbara Wyden and Gwen Schwartz report in *The Jewish Wife*, their subjects were not preoccupied with material goods. When asked what possessions they prized most, the Jewish women polled were markedly less likely to list household goods than were the non-Jewish women in a parallel poll. And when mothers were asked what qualities they'd tell a daughter to look for in a husband, "future financial prospects" made the top five only among the *non*-Jewish mothers; the Jewish mothers' list ran, in this order: health, religion, education, family background, and humor.[30]

So all contemporary Jewish women have *not* been programmed, some commentators notwithstanding, to marry rich men. Most Jews under fifty in this country grew up in relative affluence. Is it unreasonable that they seek to maintain some measure of that affluence as adults? Is it materialistic and selfish to look for a partner who's willing to pool two incomes so that maybe, as a team, they can get close to the standard of living their parents managed with one? If that's what makes a JAP, then there are a lot of male JAPs out there.

But then, we knew that, didn't we?

Have You Seen This Man?

Let's call him Lance. He's the scion of a wealthy Los Angeles family, and at 30 he's president of a company doing business in the "multimillions of dollars." He is divorced from a Jewish woman and is the father of two small sons. I met Lance at a standard-issue Jewish singles event in 1992 and thought he was pretty good-looking in a standard-issue sort of way—full head of wavy dark-blond hair, regular features, trim build—but at the beginning of our phone interview, Lance said he'd just had plastic surgery: a chin implant and liposuction. "Like I needed it, right? I just wanted to fix myself up."

> Since I got divorced . . . I've dated a lot of goys. They're kind of 10's—the ones with the big boobs and the long legs, tight butts, the whole nine yards. Body is

very important to me . . . somebody with large breasts, small backside, long legs. I just don't settle for anything. I don't feel I need to or should have to.

What's that girl who . . . just got pregnant in Greece, the princess—Stephanie. That's the kind of girl for me. She's rich, wild, rambunctious, does what she wants to do, probably loves sex, loves having a good time, doesn't care what people think about her. That's the kind of girl I would want in my life.

I like being fixed up on blind dates. . . . Whenever I go on a blind date, I always have somebody in my office, I always make him do it or I'll kill him, page me on the pager. And I'll say I have an emergency or something, I have to make it an early evening. . . . But I'm never an asshole, I'm never like rude to 'em. Even if I'm not getting along with them, I'll still walk them up to their door.

You saw me in a pair of jeans, but—how do I say all this without coming across too ostentatious?—I dress to a T, I wear custom-made suits, I have a beautiful Porsche, beautiful Mercedes, I carry myself extremely well. I was in Neiman-Marcus today; there's a million beautiful women in there, [and] I felt that a lot of them were looking at me. . . . I've had girls come up and give me their phone numbers. I've had literally 10, 12 phone numbers in one day.

I don't know if I'll go to one of those [singles] parties again. They're all losers. The guys just look like they're all losers.

Ladies and gentlemen, I give you His Royal Highness, the Jewish prince.

"I hear, frankly, more Jewish females complaining about males than I do males complaining about females," says a Los Angeles–area rabbi:

> Jewish women view a lot of Jewish men as Jewish princes: spoiled, primarily. . . . I don't know if I know any Jewish princes. I see a lot of Jewish men as somewhat superficial, as very much wanting to make it, wanting to make money . . . I see a couple preening around, overly concerned with their looks and their car. I certainly see them wanting to be in control, to be right and not be contradicted. . . . Narcissistic, self-centered, in some ways not able to truly view their current mate [or] projected future mate as an equal. . . . Maybe that's what the Jewish women mean.

Yes, that about sums it up.

The Jewish American prince, who displays the same characteristics as the Jewish princess and is just as universally acknowledged as a type of person who really exists in our society, has never come in for the same sexist abuse as the Jewish princess because the qualities the princess displays, which are considered odious in women, are accepted and even admired in men.[31] There are fewer jokes told about him. In fact, only a couple really have endured over the years, and unlike JAP jokes, they tend to be told exclusively by Jews. Oh, all right, here they are:

How does a Jewish man masturbate? By talking about himself for two hours.

How do we know Jesus was Jewish? He lived at home until he was 30, he went into his father's business, and his mother thought he was God.

Nasty? A little. But don't look for those jokes spray-painted on a wall at Syracuse.

"Why, since Jewish sons are raised with material advantages comparable to those of their sisters, is there no comparably widespread 'prince' stereotype?" Susan Weidman Schneider asked:

The answer is that the daughter is still a two-dimensional object, whereas the son has a real, authentic life. It's acceptable for a Jewish young man to think well of himself, to feel worthy of all that he possesses or achieves. . . . The core anxiety for his sister, often victimized by the demanding princess stereotype, is that she is only the sum of her parts: what she possesses or wears or achieves, or whom she marries. There is no parallel objectification of her brother.[32]

But make no mistake: Jewish princes are not admired by their sisters. They are not Great Jewish Guys, the warm, funny, wise, responsible men that Terrific Jewish Gals long for. Most contemporary Jewish women get fed up with Jewish princes at an early age and have been fed up with them for years.

Dina described the rigid social divisions observed by the Jewish guys she grew up with. "Starting in high school, you were pretty much judged by the neighborhood you lived in and the clothes you wore. So if you were a rich Jewish girl who had Villager clothes and Pappagallo shoes . . . then you were okay. If you . . . didn't have those clothes, then there was a whole group of guys that didn't look at you." Later, in college, Dina lost interest in Jewish men altogether. "Jewish guys were like, they were gonna run everything, and you were just something on their arm. Most of the ones I met [dated] very madeup, very jeweled, very Star Search-looking Jewish girls. . . . They liked girls with money, girls who got their hair cut every six weeks. . . . That's what women were to them."

"The guys I went to college with were very concerned with money and who they knew, and what they were worth and what their parents were worth, and they didn't have their own identities," says a 30-year-old New Jersey woman who dated non-Jews almost exclusively in college (at a "very JAPpy school") and recently married a non-Jew. "They didn't have to work for anything; everything was handed to them. They had no character." An Arizona woman was less than enchanted with the Jewish men she met after her divorce. "I had a few dates with Jewish men, but I found them to be . . . the stereotype of very money-oriented, very chauvinistic, not the kind of people that I wanted to spend any time with." She is now remarried to a non-Jewish man.

The novelist and screenwriter Nora Ephron probably gave American culture the ultimate comic riff on the Jewish prince in her novel *Heartburn*, in which she shows a Jewish man asking questions like "Where's the butter?" or "Is there any butter?" or holding up a piece of dry toast and asking, "How do you think butter would taste with this?" in an attempt to get his wife to wait on him. "I've always believed that the concept of the Jewish princess was invented by a Jewish prince who couldn't get his wife to fetch him the butter," Ephron wrote.[33]

Most annoying to Jewish women is the prince's absolute conviction that he is God's gift to the world, let alone to women—and for that they blame his mother. "The Jewish Prince is the boy whose mother made his favorite dinner every night and brought him an extra sweater whenever there was a chill in the air. . . . She fussed and protected and hovered and admired until he developed an opinion of himself that mirrored hers," Anne Roiphe writes. "He grew into a man who expects women to stop whatever they are doing and worry about him."[34]

Los Angeles matchmaker Gloria Karns thinks tensions arise between Jewish men and women "because Jewish women bring their daughters up to be wives and their sons up to be sons. A Jewish woman . . . [was] brought up to be a wife, to nurture, to be a caretaker, and Jewish women bring their sons up and leave them sons; they're never brought up to be a husband."

Although the Jewish princess has received much worse press than the Jewish prince, it can be argued that, pound for pound, the prince is in fact more damaging to Jewish continuity than the princess because he exhibits, even more publicly than the princess, qualities that feed into classic anti-Semitic stereotypes and because he is more alienated from his Judaism than his female counterpart and much more likely to marry a non-Jew. The true Jewish princess wants to marry a Jewish man and raise Jewish kids, period. And to this day, that's exactly what she does, perhaps settling, if she goes unmarried long enough, for a man less good-looking or polished than she might have required in her early twenties. Whatever her faults, the Jewish princess is highly visible and active in synagogues and in Jewish community organizations.

But the parallel for Jewish men hasn't held. In years past, the Jewish prince usually married the Jewish princess, at least the first time around; it was expected of him, and she and their kids always looked good. (He could and often did divorce her later to acquire a non-Jewish trophy wife.) More recently, as the taboos have fallen, the young Jewish prince often has gone straight for the Gentile gold, spurning both the Jewish princess, who is pretty and appreciates his earning potential but is seen as too demanding, and the stronger, more down-to-earth Jewish career woman who might challenge his superiority. "The Prince has no stomach for another strong woman, even if her power is channeled into a profession," one journalist commented in an early takeout of His Royal Highness. "[He] might marry a sweet, docile, rather uninteresting woman, possibly a rich Jewish girl who doesn't look Jewish, or a non-Jewish girl who advertises the fact of his assimilation."[35]

One sign of the prince, in fact, is a commitment to Judaism about as thick as a pledge card. They'll donate money, but don't look for them when it's time to pick up the kids from Sunday school. These are guys who often, out of ego and guilt, require their non-Jewish wives to convert to Judaism without lifting a finger to help them make Jewish homes. They *want* Jewish homes, but that's her responsibility. Take our friend Lance: "I wanted a Jewish mother for my children when I got married, and I have it. Now I want a wife and a mother, if she's Jewish or non-Jewish, she does what she's gotta do when she's gotta do it. If the kids are there, she'll be the good Jewish mother, and she'll go to temple and be involved with them in activities. And since I only have the kids part-time, if I don't have the children, she'll be herself."

"I think that a far more serious problem for the Jewish future than the American Jewish princess is the American Jewish prince," says Mark Winer, senior rabbi of a Reform synagogue in suburban New York. "American Jews are rearing their girls predominantly in an egalitarian fashion, but they're not rearing boys who can marry girls who have been reared in that fashion. We're still rearing princes. . . . We're rearing boys who are really not very capable of making the only kind of marriages that [Jewish] women will settle for." The boys can't handle the girls' independence, Winer said, and the girls won't defer to the boys—nor should they, he says.

Okay, you say, I'm convinced. Jewish princes are just as repugnant as Jewish princesses, and by rejecting them, Jewish women are showing how truly smart they are. But aren't princes, like the princesses, just a small subgroup? If most

Jewish women are intelligent, down-to-earth, warm, caring people imbued with solid, life-affirming values—Terrific Jewish Gals—then aren't most Jewish men Great Jewish Guys? And shouldn't those guys be desirable to Jewish women?

Well, yes—but it's more complicated than that.

Sheldon, Courtier to the Prince

In terms of personality and values, the Jewish American prince is the direct male counterpart to the Jewish princess. In terms of sheer misapplication and abuse, however, the male counterpart to the JAP is the nebbish, the nerdy, neurotic Jewish guy who combines the sex appeal of a wet dog with the emotional maturity of a 14-year-old. I call him Sheldon.*

You know who I'm talking about. He can't dress, can't dance, he's lousy at sports, he's a hypochondriac—Woody Allen in his first eight movies. If he's intelligent, he bores you to death with the arcana of his work; if he's not, he has nothing to say at all. Forget about good sex; Sheldon is so out of touch with his body, let alone yours, that the games of spin-the-bottle you played in sixth grade compare favorably. He's often sweet-natured, but that's usually paired with emotional neediness—if you're his girlfriend, you're also his mom and his shrink. He has the career ambition of a box turtle, little imagination, and no idea how to have fun.

Sheldon is real; many of us have him as a brother or cousin. He is omnipresent in high school honors programs, and he's a permanent wall fixture at singles dances. But just as a lot of Jewish men call any Jewish woman a JAP who isn't a self-effacing, adoring doormat, a lot of Jewish women characterize almost any Jewish guy who doesn't beat women with a club and drag them off to his cave as a Sheldon.

Donna thinks of Jewish men as "very nebbishy. They're very pushy, they're very insistent. You know, go out with me, go out with me, go out with me." A young public relations executive reports, "Most of the Jewish men I meet have not

---

*Let me say immediately that I got the name Sheldon from the movie *When Harry Met Sally*: Sally tells Harry toward the beginning of the picture that she had great sex with her boyfriend, Sheldon, and Harry replies, "No, you did not have great sex with Sheldon," explaining that Sheldons are accountants and dentists, not lovers. I hereby apologize to anyone actually named Sheldon and ask you not to take it personally. I happen to be acquainted with two very personable, very attractive men whose parents named them Sheldon. Like almost all men named Sheldon who are not really Sheldons, however, these men are called Shelly in all but the most formal situations.

developed the social skills that I find attractive (e.g., outgoing, take risks, enjoy dancing). Most of them I meet just don't seem to have a lot of personality."

"One of them, his mother made his bed, I mean he was a man, he was in college, and my thought was, 'Oh, God, I don't want to replace this woman.' I didn't want to become someone's mother," a television camera operator said of a boy she dated in high school. Others "just were not self-sufficient; they were like little babies. It was not very appealing." Another Los Angeles woman described her brother as "an archetypical type of Jewish guy that I now avoid. He was pampered and hypochondriacal and neurotic. He was a lot of times cowardly to the point where, though I was younger, I was the one that had to go on the daring errands and call out the old man in the haunted house, stuff like that. That's where I get the wimp thing from."

Writing "with some shame," a Massachusetts psychologist reports in *Lilith* magazine how her own Jewishness colored her reactions to her clients. One depressed man brought out all the unflattering images she carried about Jewish men and how they relate to women:

> He is wonderfully emotional, a characteristic that I usually am delighted to find in men. But he focuses on his weakness, his dependence on his lovers. Under stress, he whines. . . . As he bemoans the fact that he feels embarrassed when he works out at a local gym, I feel both empathy and irritation.
>
> Much as I care for him, I am impatient. Not simply as a therapist, but as a woman. And not just as a woman, but as a Jewish woman facing a Jewish man. How I wish he could retain and cultivate the sweet loyal emotional side of him, yet toughen it with aggressive self-assurance and passion.[36]

Men buy into the stereotype, too. A New Jersey man said, "I had gone to one of the Jewish singles functions. It was like nebbish city. If I know a Jewish guy who's separated, I'll tell him, go to one of these things, you'll feel great about yourself."

When Dan Dorfman asked one woman where the stereotype of Jewish men being clumsy and unphysical came from, she replied that it was a matter of attitude; Jewish men just presented themselves in a way that communicated discomfort with sexuality and physicality. Dorfman asked her who had an attitude she admired, and she replied that Jack Nicholson and Marlon Brando did. "They have an air of mystery and power to them," she told him. "They don't have to say anything in particular. Nicholson just turns his head and gives you a sideward glance, and you know that he understands everything about sexuality."[37]

American Jewish men, caught between an ethnic culture that, at least in its European mode, historically downplayed physical prowess and encouraged verbal agility and emotional expressiveness, and a dominant culture that glorifies violence and wordless action, resent being typed as Sheldons just because they'd rather cruise the Internet than go club-hopping, or because they drive a Honda Civic instead of a Harley. I've heard several Jewish men complain that while Jewish women *say* they want to meet gentle, emotionally available men, the guys they really lust after have a touch of the "bad boy" to them.

Contemporary Jewish women also may not be willing to put in the time and effort some of their mothers did to make their partners more sociable and, in some cases, presentable. "The women of my generation did it all the time, because we thought we could change everybody," one grandmotherly matchmaker said, adding that she works with a lot of "nerdy men" who are not as attractive as the women she matches. "I don't know if the women want to do it now. They don't put out the work it takes." Rather than recognize the potential in a Sheldon and work to realize it—broaden his world view, teach him how to make love, take him shopping—many women pass him by and look for someone who meets more of her requirements right from the first date.

Now there are plenty of Jewish women—accomplished, pleasant Jewish women—who weren't scooped up by Great Jewish Guys in the first, mid-twenties round of Let's Get Married and who are in fact more than willing to deal with or overlook a man's Sheldonesque tendencies. They really do want a sweet, gentle man, especially if he's smart and funny, and if some of the superficial stuff isn't as appealing, if he has a couple of psychological kinks to smooth out, that isn't as important as a good heart and a sharp mind. You'd think Sheldon would leap at the chance to marry such a woman, but often, it doesn't work that way.

For one thing, intelligent, accomplished women scare Sheldon silly. "Some of the women are 'outbrighting' themselves. They're just too bright," says matchmaker Shirley Albert. "They've got too much going for them. These girls are really there, they know who they are. . . . I don't know if they're sharper than the men, I hate to say that, but . . . they do frighten the men terribly." A rabbi who grew up in the 1950s said the pretty, sharp-tongued Jewish girls he met during his teens scared him to death. "There's a certain kind of competence . . . it's a feeling that you're not going to measure up to the expectation of these people," he said.

Even men who are doing well in the business world can turn their own neuroses against the women they meet. A 30-year-old male attorney says,

It's easiest for an insecure guy to grab onto something that he feels will be validated, which is, "Well, I've got a good job. I might not have my shit together in other parts of my life, but I work at Sibley & Austin, or this accounting firm, or for Spelling Entertainment." So I think they look to that first, and then I think a lot of them project themselves onto women and decide, "Well, you're the one who's being judgmental," as opposed to, "I'm judging myself harshly."

The other barrier between Sheldons and Jewish women is perhaps more maddening to women because it's behavior in which they don't, by and large, indulge. Almost all Jewish women who are not Jewish princesses—and that's all but a fraction—hold the princess in contempt. They don't like her and they don't want to be like her. Many Sheldons, however, are Jewish prince wannabes. They may not have the clothes, the cars, the high-profile jobs, or the cocky stride, but they can be just as picky as His Royal Highness and believe they can get away with it. After all, they're Jewish men, in short supply and high demand.

"They view themselves as some kind of rare commodity for which they can, in their minds, demand a goddess," says a single Jewish woman in her early forties. "The Jewish men I meet are all leftovers," a 38-year-old woman told Sylvia Barack Fishman. "They are seriously flawed people—bitter, self-hating, self-centered, or just plain strange. And each one thinks he's God's gift to women because he's Jewish. Like he's this prize and you're nothing."[38] "Don't forget," another woman said to me, "Sheldon's mother gives him as many strokes as the prince's mother gives the prince, and that intense adulation can outweigh whatever messages he gets about marrying a Jewish woman." If he can't find a Jewish woman to feed his fantasies, in other words, he can find a non-Jewish woman who will, and if he's criticized for intermarrying, he can blame it on Jewish women for being too JAPpy or too pushy or too ugly.

This sense of "Why should I settle?" allows Jewish men, regardless of their looks or behavior, to walk into dating services and demand a mate who is model-thin, cheerleader-cute, well-educated, earning her own living—and ready to work the swing shift attending to his every need. "Aside from very young, men wanted the women to be . . . independent and successful—and nurturing," Irene Seiger said of her matchmaking experience. "They wanted what they thought of as this old-fashioned, nurturing wife, but she should also work and make her own money. That's what they said, over and over."[39]

The extent to which Jewish men have controlled the dynamics of Jewish male–female relations—the seller's market they have created, to put it crassly—has been devastating to a generation of Jewish women, especially those committed to marrying Jewish men and those women whose imperfect bodies, frizzy hair, unglamorous jobs, and quirky personalities make them Sheldon's female counterpart. "We're just not physically the type they're looking for," says Margie, a chubby, lively 28-year-old who works in a Jewish day school.

> They're looking for blond hair, blue eyes, thin . . . not what you picture as Jewish-looking. And they want girls who are neat and quiet, and they don't picture Jewish as being that. Well, I'm not. I'm a brunette, I wear glasses, I'm busty . . . and quiet is not my forte. Nor is it for any of my friends. The guys seem to be wanting to get away from the stereotype of what they picture as Jewish, which is kind of upsetting, because the girls seem to want a stereotypically Jewish male. So the girls are looking for the guys, but the guys are looking for other women.[40]

Enough, thousands of Jewish women have decided, is enough.

Psychotherapist Patricia Field sees an escalating number of Jewish women over 30 in her practice who are willing to marry non-Jews. "They are accepting a certain reality . . . the cliché that Jewish men don't want Jewish women as much, and so it's like a self-perpetuating prophecy, because they . . . give up quicker and are willing to start looking and expand their horizons sooner. . . . They want to get married, and they'll deal with the intermarriage stuff when it comes up. But they're not willing to put up with the dwindling pool and the rejection they get from Jewish men."

Do Jewish women indulge in stereotyping? Sure. Are there Jewish women who are too quick to label all the Jewish men they meet as insufferable princes or shlumpy Sheldons? You bet. Do some Jewish women attack Jewish men without provocation, blame them for all their problems, crush them like bugs at singles events? Absolutely. Are there Jewish women who use stereotyping to justify the choice of a non-Jewish mate when their agenda from age 14 was to marry a Viking? Of course. But Jewish men do it more, and with more profound effect.

The stereotypes with which Jews batter one another serve no one, certainly not the Jewish community as a whole, and people must be persuaded to set them aside if Jewish men and women are ever to enjoy the full measure of pride and fulfillment we have earned in this country—and to turn to each other in love. It won't be easy.[41] The stereotypes are resistant to rabbinic homily, to intellectual discussion, to therapy, even to parental example. Gary Spencer, academic tilter at JAP-bashing, has a son in his twenties "who tells me, 'I can't stand these JAPs; I'd like to appreciate your research, but you know, they're all bitches.' We have these big long discussions, and I always disagree with him, and he more often than not ends up with an Asian woman who walks half a step behind her man."

The Jewish princess is real, the Jewish prince is real, and the neurotic Jewish nebbish is real, but added together, they are not numerous or pervasive enough to account for an entire Jewish dating population, and Jewish men and women must learn to stop using stereotypes to mask their own lack of self-esteem and lack of pride in being Jewish. "I would like to confront what people mean when they [employ Jewish stereotypes], confront the characteristics that are being decried, and to deal with it in our communities, through the kind of consciousness-raising that I think is necessary to save our souls," Letty Cottin Pogrebin told me. "I'm not just looking to save us from intermarriage, but to save our souls."

4

That's Entertainment

Good Christ, a Jewish man with parents alive is a fifteen-year-old boy, and
will remain a fifteen-year-old boy till *they die!*

—Alex Portnoy in *Portnoy's Complaint*

I made the big mistake about five days ago in New York. And when I say
big, I mean Radio City Music Hall big. She's a nice girl, but just not really
my type. . . . So I'm going to get out . . . get rid of my mistake.

—Lenny Cantrow, talking about his new wife in *The Heartbreak Kid*

Very often I'm doing roles that were written by a man who tends to write
a mean-spirited character because he's working something through with his
mother.

—Fran Drescher, actress

By media standards, I am not an attractive woman. My hair is dark and
kinky, impossible to control unless cropped short. My eyes are too small
and a little too close together, my nose straight but a shade too long. Even
at 40-plus, my skin still breaks out. And, most grievous sin, I'm big: just over
five-foot-ten without shoes and, after a chubby childhood and a chubby adolescence, still fat. Throughout adulthood I have ranged anywhere from 10 to 50
pounds overweight.

None of these physical shortcomings worried me too much when I left for college a couple of weeks after my seventeenth birthday. I was coming off a romance that had lasted most of senior year and all summer, so I arrived at Brandeis knowing that *someone* had found me desirable. The university seemed to be full of brainy, quirky, bespectacled Jewish guys much like the one from whom I'd just parted; I didn't require or even want an Adonis. Surely, among the thousand-plus available undergraduate guys on campus was *one* who valued character more than slenderness and a mane of straight hair.

When, after a year or so, that guy had not appeared, I did some work on myself: lost weight, put on makeup, wore skirts instead of sweats—I even bought a wig. Also, I tried to come on a little cooler than I naturally was, to be a little less intense, speak more softly, laugh less easily. But nothing worked; no matter what I did, I failed to put out the chemistry that attracted men. Unfeminist and irresponsible as it seems now, I mourned, because among my wide and horny male acquaintance, not one guy wanted to take my clothes off, and I couldn't figure out why.

Finally, something of a clue presented itself. The movie *The Heartbreak Kid* had opened that December, and when I caught up with it in a downtown Boston theater, I watched with growing horror as the young Jewish protagonist became disenchanted with the plump, silly, unattractive girl he had just married and enamored of the beautiful, slender blonde, played by Cybill Shepherd, whom he met on the beach during his honeymoon. The horror for me came not so much from watching a newlywed dump his bride as from the realization that the Jewish men I wanted to be with probably looked at me and saw someone like that overbearing, goofy young woman, even though I was smarter, funnier, even cooler. They looked at me and saw her, and how could I compete with Cybill Shepherd?

It was that kind of experience that made me quit wearing the long wig and put back the weight. (What was the point? I would never look like Cybill.) It made me choose Stanford's dinky, unknown cinema program over NYU's renowned film school, explaining that I wanted to go someplace for graduate school where I'd be a little exotic—and it made me think I'd better not count on marrying a Jewish man. These were not mature decisions; they were made with all the wisdom of a 19-year-old girl who thought her entire romantic career might have ended before she left for college. But they did influence the rest of my life.

I'm not saying *The Heartbreak Kid* made me head in a direction I wouldn't have chosen otherwise. I don't think any entertainment medium has the power to counteract the forces that forge family relationships and put us in contact with potential mates. But I do think that American popular culture, the novels, films, and television programs that permeate American life, as they portray Jews, have the power to reinforce existing stereotypes in a way that can underscore, if not determine, the choices we make in our romantic lives.

Fiction: Out of the Ghetto and Through the Looking Glass

American Jewish fiction holds up a sharp-edged mirror to the Jewish experience in this country, from the great waves of immigration onward. The striving newcomer eager to take his place in upwardly mobile American society leapt onto the page as soon as those driven to write for a mass audience mastered English. Exemplified by Abraham Cahan's *The Rise of David Levinsky* (1917), immigrant Jewish literature established the themes for the next two generations: the all-consuming desire to assimilate; the spurning of "higher" values for the accumulation of wealth; the repressed sexuality experienced by many Jews raised within traditional bounds; the allure of non-Jews as potential social equals and romantic partners.

Second-generation writers portray much of the insecurity and sometimes rage experienced by Jews caught between the values of their immigrant parents and their own desire to be fully, unquestionably American, often in self-hating language.[1] Sexuality is out in the open in these novels, a weapon used to beat back Jewish tradition, and non-Jewish women are not only desirable but marriageable, although until about 1960 such marriages were often portrayed as ultimately shaky or unworkable.[2] Second-generation Jewish fiction is marked by characters pulling away from their families, often out of embarrassment over their immigrant origins, yet exhibiting a nostalgic attachment to place, perhaps reflecting the authors' sense of emotional dislocation.[3]

Jewish writers of the third generation, like third-generation Jews in general, have been secure enough as Americans to embrace their cultural identity while casting off whatever tribal aspects they see as inhibiting or irrelevant, and have incorporated into their fiction, both high-brow and popular, the assimilatory processes, psychological issues, and stereotypes that inform the lives of many baby boomers and younger American Jews.

Family Relationships

Jewish literature from the first to the third generation clearly charts the deterioration of the Jewish mother from woman of valor to abject stereotype. Yiddish writers of the late nineteenth and early twentieth centuries portrayed the

Jewish mother as indomitable and soldierly, enduring every hardship—some-times sharp or shrewish, but capable of keeping families together in the face of incompetent husbands and rebellious children.[4] Transplanted to America, this immigrant Jewish mother is still portrayed as the center of the family, but also as dislocated and powerless. Much first- and second-generation literature deals with the huge gulf between the immigrant Jewish mother and her Americanized children, making her at best a figure of not-so-gentle fun and more commonly a source of embarrassment and resentment.[5] The gap continues into the third gen-eration, as postwar Jewish writers turn on the second-generation Jewish woman and expose her in all her bourgeois, appearance-obsessed, food-monitoring, often sexually provocative glory. Trashing the Jewish mother became a growth industry in literature by the end of the 1950s, as the nurturing immigrant mother evolved into a domestic terrorist.[6]

Sophie Portnoy in *Portnoy's Complaint* (1969) is the mother of them all, of course, Philip Roth's guilt-inflicter *par excellence*. But for all her outrageous behav-ior, Sophie is just one member of a large and toxic sorority in both popular and literary fiction, a veritable legion of know-it-all, marriage-obsessed, overprotec-tive meddlers.[7] For years, she has made her daughters feel inadequate and has infantilized her sons, turning out generations of "boy-men" by smothering her sons with more love than they are likely ever to find from peers and spoiling them for romantic attachments to women their own age.[8]

Jewish fathers have never received as much ink as the Jewish mother, although each generation has its standout Jewish father as would-be Terminator. More often in contemporary American Jewish fiction, the Jewish father comes off as subordinate to the mother, often ineffectual. While third-generation Jewish liter-ature contains plenty of unsupportive and even abusive fathers, novel for novel, Mother tends to be portrayed as the parent who metes out most of the *schmerz*.[9]

Other Female Stereotypes

Women, Jewish and non-Jewish, have not fared particularly well at the hands of the male Jewish writers being taught in our universities, including Nobel lau-reates Isaac Bashevis Singer and Saul Bellow. Philip Roth, whose fiction strad-dles the high-brow and popular categories, has long been accused of drawing almost all of the female characters in his novels as stereotypes: the Jewish women either as spoiled suburbanites or variations on Sophie Portnoy; the non-Jewish women as sex objects.[10] Roth also can take credit for bringing the postwar Jewish princess to a mass audience with the publication of *Goodbye, Columbus* in 1959.[11]

Brenda Patimkin, the princess in question, pretty well embodies the stereotype: a girl who expects her every wish to be granted without any effort on her part. Unlike the JAPs lampooned since the early 1970s, Brenda does exert herself physically and enjoy passionate sex, but in every other way she is the woman her parents have raised her to be. Her sweat is the sweat of leisure, her only responsibility to please herself and her parents. When her mother complains that she has invited the protagonist, Neil Klugman, as a house guest just before her brother's wedding, Brenda goes on the defensive:

> "I need a houseful of company at a time like this?" "My God, Mother, you'd think we didn't have Carlota and Jenny." "Carlota and Jenny can't do everything. . . . When's the last time you lifted a finger to help around here?" "I'm not a slave—I'm a daughter." "You ought to learn what a day's work means." "Why?" Brenda said. "*Why?* Because you're lazy," Mrs. Patimkin answered, "and you think the world owes you a living." "Whoever said *that?*" "You ought to earn some money and buy your own clothes." "Why? Good God, Mother, Daddy could live off the stocks alone, for God's sake. What are you complaining about?" "When's the last time you washed the dishes?" "Jesus Christ!" Brenda flared, "Carlota washes the dishes!"

Eventually, class differences break up Brenda and Neil—his salary as a librarian won't provide the good life in Short Hills, New Jersey, that is Brenda's due.[12]

Male Stereotypes

His Royal Highness and Sheldon turn up fairly regularly in popular fiction written by (surprise!) Jewish women. In her 1972 novel *Sheila Levine Is Dead and Living in New York*, Gail Parent presents a title character who dates, for eight years, one Norman Berkowitz, a badly dressed, boring schoolteacher whose sexual technique never progresses from his very first experience. Sheila can't stand Norman, but as she approaches 30, her mother constantly on her back about marriage, she presses Norman for a commitment, ready to settle—and he dumps her.

Parent nails the Jewish prince in *David Meyer Is a Mother* (1975), the story of a very cute, utterly sexist man who, as he rounds 30, finds that because of the women's movement, he can no longer get laid because women are making completely unreasonable demands of him, such as respect. David learned the perks of the throne at Myron Meyer's knee:

When I was eight years old, my mother reprimanded me for leaving my under-wear on the floor. Myron said, "Leave him alone. He's a boy." For twenty-five years I didn't pick up my underwear. . . .

When I was eighteen, Myron sent me off to college with a checking account, a red Corvette and seven words: "Schtup all you want, but be careful." . . .

When I was twenty-two, I joined Meyer and Meyer. . . . I fucked the recep-tionist and thought that was what she was there for.[13]

By the end of the novel, David has renounced his obnoxious ways for the sake of his baby daughter, which is obviously why they call it fiction.[14]

Possibly in reaction to the image of the Jewish man as nonphysical and unsexy, for the past generation American readers have seen a slew of what one writer referred to as "Rambowitz" novels, some written by Jews, some not, in which Jews have been portrayed as spies, soldiers, pioneers, and tough cops. The books include accounts of historic battles such as Masada, multigenerational sagas, spy thrillers, and police procedurals. Everywhere you look, tough Jews are holding off the Romans, blowing up German ammunition dumps, infiltrating Arab terrorist cells, and combining brains and firepower to catch murderers.[15] However, among the novels with contemporary settings, the heroes' Jewishness is often incidental to the story; the modern American Jewish hard guy has not become a staple image in popular fiction.[16]

Self-hatred and Self-image

Self-hatred in third-generation Jewish literature is something of a red herring, an accusation made every time a Jewish writer portrays Jews in a less-than-flattering light.[17] Conflict over self-image, on the other hand, pervades contem-porary Jewish literature. In many novels by and about Jewish women, characters ranging well beyond the standard princess are preoccupied with what Betty Friedan called "female economics—beauty and physical appearance," which is seen as a down side of growing up female and Jewish.[18] Shelly Silver, a curvy, handsome caterer in Gail Parent's *A Sign of the Eighties* (1987), feels constantly inadequate:

Shelly was a brilliant woman who knew what all brilliant people know: Looks count. She had nothing against beauty. She would have been perfectly happy to let beautiful women live in a roped-off part of the city with their own stores and restaurants. Then she would only have to see them in magazines, where they were flat and glossy and not able to steal plainer people's boyfriends. . . . She knew the gorgeous young women who smiled at her from the pages of *Glamour* were not necessarily happy, but she couldn't help thinking that their perfect hair and baby-blue eyes insured party invitations and marriage whenever they wanted.[19]

To be sure, many of the female characters unhappy with their looks are reacting as women, not as Jewish women, but the ethnic element does creep in from time to time, especially when noses come under discussion.[20]

Jewish men are not immune to insecurity about self-image. Bruce Gold, in Heller's *Good as Gold* (1979), lusting after a Washington political appointment and a ditzy but leggy and well-born Washingtonian, worries that he's too Jewish for either, and struggles to maintain his dignity while fending off his girlfriend's outrageously anti-Semitic father. Alex Portnoy, dreaming as a teenager of passing himself off as a Gentile to the blond ice skater he lusts after in Irvington Park, has his bubble burst every time he remembers what has sprouted in the middle of his face.[21]

Sexuality

Roth, of course, put the *id* back in *yid*[22] as the sexual revolution gathered steam, but, interestingly, most of the unfettered heterosexuality in contemporary Jewish literature comes from women novelists, with Erica Jong carrying the flag. Closely preceded by Sheila Levine, who used promiscuity as a hedge against loneliness, and Sasha Davis in Alix Kates Shulman's *Memoirs of an Ex-Prom Queen* (1972), who believed she was beautiful only if she'd gotten a man into bed, Jong's Isadora Wing famously went in search of the "zipless fuck" in *Fear of Flying* (1973) and proceeded to carve notches in her bedpost through two more novels. Among contemporary female novelists, good sex is a cause for celebration, bad sex a source of resentment and often infidelity. Third-generation Jewish novelists seem to have put behind them whatever cultural hang-ups about sex they were raised with; the main difference between male and female writers is that the men present male characters who lust primarily after non-Jewish women, whereas the women are as likely to develop sexual relationships between two Jews as they are to show a Jewish character, especially a Jewish woman, sexually involved with a non-Jew.[23]

The Allure of the Other

"Look, I'm not asking for the world—I just . . . want to be the boyfriend of Debbie Reynolds—it's the Eddie Fisher in me coming out, that's all, the longing in all of us swarthy Jewboys for those bland blond exotics called *shikses*," Alex

Portnoy tells his psychoanalyst, adding that plenty of these blond beauties are panting for Jewish men, either because they're more exotically sexy than the men they grew up with or because they have a reputation for making loving, dependable husbands.[24] The assimilated third-generation Jewish author, free of the taboos of previous generations, will step over all the familiar girls of his youth to achieve the golden object of desire. While teaching at the University of Iowa in the 1950s, Roth had no fewer than three Jewish students in one seminar who turned out stories about young Jewish boys with doting mothers and distant dads who learn about the joys of the flesh through friendship with a more sophisticated Gentile neighbor or schoolmate. "The Jewish women in the stories are mothers and sisters; the sexual dream—for whatever primal reason one cares to entertain—is for The Other," Roth wrote in a description of the class.[25]

Jewish female writers of fiction are more of a mixed bag in portraying the desirability of non-Jews as opposed to Jewish men. Erica Jong pairs Isadora Wing with Jews as well as non-Jews, although in her "post-Isadora" novel, *Any Woman's Blues* (1990), the protagonist, Leila Sand, is obsessed with a great-looking, years-younger, well-endowed WASP. "He was my shiksa, and I treated him accordingly, the way my rich English uncle Jakob from Odessa, East End furrier turned country squire in Surrey, treated his chorine," Leila says early in the novel.[26] Gail Parent wants her Jewish characters to be with Jews, but her male characters don't exactly constitute good PR for Jewish men.

In other popular novels, a Jewish woman's choice of a non-Jewish partner occurs by chance. R. J. Misner, a 37-year-old widow in *'Til the Real Thing Comes Along* (1987), reluctantly goes out with a non-Jew she meets at a party after some disastrous experiences with Jewish men; he ends up on the *bimah* at her son's bar mitzvah. In each of Susan Isaacs' Long Island murder mysteries, *Compromising Positions* (1978) and *After All These Years* (1993), the protagonist becomes involved with a non-Jew who represents a decided contrast to a pretentious, hypercritical Jewish prince of a husband. It's not that these women are looking for non-Jewish men—all things being equal, a sane, loving Jewish partner probably would have been preferable—but the message comes across: The wrong guy was Jewish; the right guy is not.

Film: Becoming American in the Dream Palace

If American Jewish fiction reflected the process of assimilation during the first half of this century, American movies pushed assimilation with the enthusiasm of a used car dealer. While the average Jew living in America during the first few

decades of this century was staunchly opposed to intermarriage, movie producers clearly believed in the melting pot, and a number of films show children of
immigrant Jews overcoming their parents' objections to their marrying non-
Jews. Some early pictures, especially those written or produced by Jews, show the
Jewish son or daughter realizing his or her error and returning to the fold, but
many others, culminating in *The Jazz Singer* (1927) and *Abie's Irish Rose* (1928),
depicted intermarriage as a desirable means toward the end of Americanization
and the objecting parents as beloved but irrelevant obstacles to their children's
happiness and success.[27]

Considering who the people were who were making these movies, the positive portrayal of intermarriage and the desirability of assimilation are no surprise. The men who built the film studios and controlled the industry until the
1950s were Eastern European immigrants, uneducated but savvy businessmen
who had made considerable money in fields such as the garment industry and
film exhibition. When they went into film production, it was wide open; there
was no Gentile power structure to stop them. As a result, by 1930 men like
Louis B. Mayer, Harry Cohn, Adolph Zukor, William Fox, and the brothers
Warner had attained wealth and success they could not have dreamed of had
they or their parents not decided to make the crossing to America.[28]

These men "were absolutely the most passionately in love with America that
you can imagine," says Stanford University professor Joyce Penn Moser. "They
were immensely ambitious, tremendously hard-driving, [with] a sense of their own
worth, but also a profound sense of insecurity. They were gonna out-America
America. [They] were not particularly nice people as a rule, and there's a ruthlessness about the way they did business which had an impact on the way Jews
are portrayed." This ruthlessness extended to their family lives; they had a tendency to run from their own Jewishness, and several of the moguls divorced the
Jewish wives of their youth and married more glamorous or socially advanced
Gentile women.[29] "It's possible that they associated Judaism and Jewishness with
the shtetl and with failure and with poverty," Moser said. "The early message is,
intermarriage, success, freedom, and assimilation were all connected to each
other."

For decades, the studio heads were convinced that the American public did
not want to see Jewish faces or hear Jewish voices in their movie theaters. When
Jews were portrayed as major characters, they were more often than not played
by Gentile actors, a situation that continues to this day. As a result, for more
than thirty years, American Jews did not, for the most part, see themselves on
the big screen except to the extent that they could identify certain actors, con-

cealed behind Anglicized names, as Jewish.[30] Letty Cottin Pogrebin, who grew up going to the movies on Saturday afternoons during the 1940s and 1950s, writes, "Other than life experience, nothing left a deeper imprint on my formative self than the movies":

> Movie women entered, good and bad, with their grating voices and their funny lines, their kind eyes, round bosoms, and oversized gestures; skittish women, brown-haired usually, women with the contours of a cello; screamers and whiners, women who give the anti-Semites plenty to write home about, and women who could have been my grandmothers. . . . As a child, I used the movies as a litmus test and lesson plan to guide my growing up . . . I studied the Jewish women: Is that how I'm supposed to behave? Is she what I can hope to become? Am I like that? Is anyone? Above all, the movies helped me define the Jewish women I did *not* want to be.[31]

Not until the late 1960s, when a younger set of studio executives had replaced the first-generation moguls and what we now call multiculturalism replaced the melting pot ethos, did identifiably Jewish actors with Jewish names, Jewish voices, and Jewish faces begin to appear in starring roles, often playing Jewish characters. Studios then were willing to make films geared to smaller, urban audiences, and many executives were third-generation Jews who didn't worry about offending Gentiles. At a time when alienation was a crucial gear in the youth movement's psyche, Jewish novelists whose protagonists were high priests of alienation were widely read and hipper than hip. The Jew was no longer a quaint ghetto denizen; he was Everyman. For the next ten years, studios did not worry quite as much that a given performer or project was "too Jewish."[32]

However, the higher visibility of Jewish characters on the big screen came at a price: a steep toll on the self-esteem of Jews who saw themselves depicted as negative stereotypes. The ghetto films of the 1910s and 1920s regularly portrayed young Jews in revolt against their parents, but their problem was with the parents' outdated parochialism, not mama and papa themselves; these films almost always ended in reconciliation. Forty and fifty years later, the attack against the parents was ad hominem: Dad and especially mom were *personally* depriving the protagonist of autonomy and an adult identity, and a happy ending meant booting mom and dad (and any relatives or partners who represented mom and dad) out of their lives. To make the audience root for such an ending, the characters who represented obstacles to the protagonist's happiness had to be made so unattractive that the audience would consider the protagonist well rid of them.[33]

The almost all-male cadre of writers and directors who created these films reserved most of their contempt for female Jewish characters; during this period, the Jewish mother stereotype reached its most grotesque heights. Blown up 20 feet high on a movie screen, she left nothing to the imagination and was portrayed during the late 1960s and early 1970s across a spectrum ranging from *nudzhedik* but loving and well-meaning through meddlesome, shallow, and judgmental to floridly, humiliatingly nuts. "She's practically feeding her kids strychnine with the chicken soup," Susan Weidman Schneider, describing the more toxic examples of Jewish motherhood, told a conference audience.[34]

In more recent films, the Jewish mother's punch as a negative stereotype has weakened. For one thing, she appears less often as a major character. You may not like her, but she isn't on screen long enough for you to walk out of the theater hating her. Mothers in period pieces like *Brighton Beach Memoirs* (1986) are seen in a softer light as well, and even meddling grandmothers, most notably the matchmaking *bubbe* in *Crossing Delancey* (1988), are treated lovingly. The only flamboyantly awful Jewish mother to dominate the screen (literally) in recent years is the one who hovers in the sky and torments her son in Woody Allen's *Oedipus Wrecks* (1989). Incredibly, this is the one and only film Allen has made to date in which his protagonist leaves a demure Gentile girlfriend for a down-to-earth, very ethnic Jewish woman.

Younger Jewish women have also suffered at the hands of male Jewish writers and directors, although the specific stereotype of the Jewish princess has not been that much of a problem. In the best-known film portrayals of the Jewish princess before 1980, *Marjorie Morningstar* (1958) and *Goodbye, Columbus* (1969), she was played by well-established non-Jewish actresses (Natalie Wood and Ali McGraw, respectively), desirable women by almost any guy's standards, which took much of the sting out of the portrayal. For the most part, classic JAPs have not appeared in films all that often since Jewish characters started turning up regularly, and they're usually in secondary roles along the lines of the protagonist's bitchy sister-in-law.[35]

When a Jewish princess does have a central role, the story is usually one of redemption; she's no longer a JAP at the end of the movie. The best example of this is *Private Benjamin* (1980), in which Judy Benjamin, a spoiled, childish 29-year-old who conforms in every way to the stereotype, joins the Army and grows up. She's a complete washout at first, but when, at her lowest point, her parents come to bail her out, she squares her shoulders and tells them to get lost. After that, she triumphs in basic training and begins to carve out a career niche for herself. (Judy is assigned as a purchasing specialist: "the one job I've trained for all my life.") She meets and is about to marry a gorgeous French-Jewish doctor, but when she realizes that life with him would return her to abject JAPitude, she leaves him at the altar. (I distinctly remember cheers rising from the audience when Judy decks her fiancé after he's called her stupid.)[36]

Much more troublesome than the JAP stereotype, as far as persistent film images of Jewish women go, is what Patricia Erens calls the Jewish Ugly Duckling, whose heyday was the early to mid-1970s.[37] Although Jewish women had acted in films from the earliest days of the genre, actresses who looked Jewish were not considered romantic-lead material or even very attractive. When Cecil B. De Mille was casting the 1949 epic *Samson and Delilah*, he demanded a real "Jewish Jewess" for Miriam, the girl Samson spurns in favor of the Philistine temptress, but Paramount didn't have any Jewish actresses under contract. Finally, one of the writers, Jesse Lasky, Jr., found Olive Deering, who had worked in Jewish theater. De Mille interviewed and cast her but complained to Lasky that Deering was "the one actress in the world who could not be photographed from *any* angle."[38] Many latter-day movie moguls have remained under the impression that, as one actress was told all too recently, "Jews don't play."[39]

The best-known movie to feature a Jewish Ugly Duckling is *The Heartbreak Kid*. The picture opens with Lenny Cantrow's marriage to Lila Kolodny, who doesn't have one redeeming quality other than her obvious adoration of Lenny: she's clingy, tactless, and none too bright; she's a lox in bed; she's already running to fat; she sings loudly and off-key; and she has terrible table manners. Reviewers and columnists felt sorry for Lila, but none of them defended her as a more appropriate spouse than the cool yet radiant Kelly, whom Lenny pursues for most of the picture. The film ends with Lenny and Kelly's wedding after Lenny faces down Kelly's grim, anti-Semitic father. At the reception, Lenny is left alone; it's clear that this new marriage is empty and that the moral of the story is, "Be careful what you want, because you might get it," but by then, the damage is done. "I am sure that no Jewish woman felt good about hailing from the same tribe as the pitiful, loathsome Lila," Letty Cottin Pogrebin commented.[40]

In an article blasting filmmakers for purveying negative images of Jewish women, 16-year-old Diana Bletter noted, "This film has audiences. In each audience are Jewish boys who might buy the stereotypes, who might begin to believe that Jewish girls are not ideal marriage partners and that gentile women are. Who would want to marry someone who might be labeled a 'Lila'?"[41] "I think it reinforces negative stereotypes about what Jewish women are like," Joyce Penn Moser agreed. "I find it after all these years one of the most painful movies I have ever seen, because the woman is humiliated, and because the guy is a jerk and he in some sense gets away with it." Even Charles Grodin, who played the protagonist and tried to put Lenny in a sympathetic light in interviews during the film's initial release, eventually became less than comfortable with the messages the movie sent beyond its theme. "[I]t was supposed to be funny," he wrote of the film. "Well, it could be funny to a lot of people, but I felt that to many others—mostly young women—it could be something other than funny. How about scary or hateful?"[42]

Perhaps the most insulting aspect of *The Heartbreak Kid* is how shamelessly it stacks the deck in favor of Lenny. "The film is set up for you to go with Charles Grodin," *Los Angeles Times* film reviewer Kenneth Turan said in an interview. "You're supposed to be on his side, so you make the wife an extreme stereotype. The film doesn't want you to think, at least not at that point . . . that maybe he's making a mistake. You're supposed to think he's well away from this person. And the way you do that is to make her . . . into a caricature." The film also portrays Lenny as a much more attractive Jewish guy than Lila is a Jewish woman and makes Lenny look like a hero for outsmarting the blond jocks who surround Kelly, jumping through sexual hoops for her, and turning down a massive bribe from her father.[43]

"It's a very tricky movie because you're rooting for him on some level, especially if you're Jewish, not because he's been so shitty to his Jewish wife; you're also sitting there as a Jew and you're saying, go ahead, outwit those horrible Gentiles," television producer Richard Rosenstock muses:

> I don't necessarily believe . . . that the movie is generous in spirit to anyone. The WASPs are fairly horrible; the character Cybill Shepherd is playing is beautiful but kind of vacuous. . . . It's a laceratingly self-critical piece about that particular kind of Jewish guy that's never satisfied. . . . The issue, however, that he does leave his ungainly, unattractive Jewish for this *shikse* goddess is unfortunately built into that structure. . . . And I have always thought, from a Jewish woman's point of view, that it's horrible and unfair. You can't get around the ethnicity . . . I think it's a great movie despite that, but that's a big despite if you're a Jewish woman.

Has the American Jewish woman been able to see a more attractive reflection of herself in film during the past twenty-odd years? The glib answer is absolutely—if the woman is Barbra Streisand. The picture isn't completely bleak: apart from Jewish actresses such as Debra Winger and Ellen Barkin, who are attractive by media standards but rarely play Jewish characters, Bette Midler, Jennifer Grey, Julie Kavner, Amy Irving, and, most recently, Sarah Jessica Parker have portrayed appealing, desirable Jewish women.[44] Even more refreshing is news of a romantic comedy greenlighted by Warner Bros. that has a witty, over-weight Jewish woman in her 30s as its protagonist.[45] But for Jewish women who want to see themselves portrayed on the big screen as viable alternatives to the Gentile goddesses, it's generally a long wait between pictures.

It took quite a while for Jewish men to come into their own in films. As with Jewish actresses, Jewish actors who looked good (or at least tough, in the case of actors like Edward G. Robinson) by all-American standards played non-Jewish roles, while more Semitic types were relegated to small character parts. The Jewish male in movies through the 1950s was rarely portrayed as heroic or sexually alluring (during the silent era, a number of films were made in which lovely Jewish maidens would be rescued from pogroms—by dashing Russian noblemen), and when they were, they were played by non-Jewish actors.[46] But as American Jewish fiction made the Jewish intellectual a culture hero, actors like George Segal, Dustin Hoffman, Woody Allen, Elliott Gould, and Richard Dreyfuss began to have box office appeal as leading men, often playing explicitly Jewish characters. Woody Allen's ascendance as a romantic lead in the films he scripted during the 1960s and 1970s tells the story of Sheldon turned pistol; Allen began his acting career as a randy heir to Chaplin's Little Tramp and wound up able to pick and choose his golden girls.[47]

Whether played by Jewish actors or non-Jews, male Jewish characters who show the tiniest bit of sensitivity and maturity have done very well attracting women on the big screen, and they are almost always paired with Gentile women. Between the books and articles I read on Jewish film history and my own moviegoing experiences, it took me about 10 minutes to list almost 40 films made since the mid-1960s with such matches, and those are just the movies in which the guy is explicitly identified as Jewish. The near-complete exclusion of happily endogamous Jewish relationships from the big screen may not be a conscious influence on contemporary Jews, some of whom are, after all, married to or marrying other Jews, but it is considered such by the Jewish establishment: "This distortion of contemporary reality sends a particularly pernicious message to younger Jewish viewers as to what constitutes a romantic ideal," critic Michael Medved complained in 1991.[48]

The phenomenon, moreover, is largely without parallel on the distaff side. While there have been several movies (a fraction of the total featuring Jewish men) that pair Jewish women and non-Jewish men romantically, and while the allure of the Other is significant in those pairings, there's one big difference: *The relationships don't last.* In *Dirty Dancing* (1987) and *Baby, It's You* (1982), class differences break up the romance between a bright, sheltered college girl and the proletarian hunk she attracts. In *Crossing Delancey*, Isabelle loves the glamour of the publishing world and is tempted by the suave Gentile author who represents it, but in the end she listens to her Bubbie and goes with the pickle man. Streisand's Katie Morosky in *The Way We Were* (1973), a character I experienced as soothing balm after being rubbed raw by *The Heartbreak Kid*, can't hold on to her "gorgeous *goyishe* guy"—the intensity he admired so has worn him down and become a threat—but in the final scene, she has a Jewish husband who presumably supports her leftist activism. And in *The Prince of Tides* (1991), Streisand leaves her snotty non-Jewish husband and sends her summer lover back to his wife in South Carolina, saying (as her character does in Pat Conroy's novel), "I've got to find me a nice Jewish boy. You goys are killing me." You don't need all the fingers of one hand to count the portrayals, even in secondary roles, of permanent, successful big-screen relationships between Jewish women and non-Jewish men.

Writing about the films of the 1970s, movies that appeared as thousands of baby-boom Jews were thinking about marriage, Patricia Erens wrote, "The Jewish son is presented as a Neurotic Man-Child—dependent, self-centered, over-sexed and immature. Only in his professional accomplishments does he achieve a degree of dignity. The Jewish daughter in the comedies and light dramas of the seventies is even more inept than her brother—awkward and gross, obsessed with marriage and sex, the consummate Ugly Duckling."[49] These images hardly reflected the majority of young American Jews, but they were presented as if they did. How many young Jews were influenced by them (rather than angered, as many have been) is anyone's guess.

A few years ago, a woman wrote to *Tikkun* wishing someone would make a movie about non-Orthodox Jews with "a likeable, smart, beautiful Jewish female" as its protagonist. "None of the Jewish characters would whine. They would be comfortable with, not self-conscious about, their Jewishness. . . . And they would have parents who imparted to them meaningful traditions, ethical values, and a proud sense of their history, and didn't fill them with guilt about everything."[50]

Steven Spielberg, are you listening?

Television: Sheldon Triumphant

The first thing you should know about the Los Angeles man is that he doesn't look even vaguely like Tom Cruise. . . . In his high school back east . . . he was the class nerd. . . . Back in those miserable teen years, when all the cheerleaders were fawning over the athletes and laughing at the nerds, our future L.A. man promised himself one thing: that someday, he would make a lot of money off those stupid, handsome jocks. And now he does.

—Claire Scovell, "The Los Angeles Man," *Gentlemen's Quarterly*, October 1989

Right around the time I went to that workshop at the UCLA *Tikkun* conference, I began to notice the growing presence of a new television character: men who looked and behaved exactly like the guys I went to college with, but grown up; short, quick-witted, sorta-cute-but-hardly-hunky Jewish men of 30 and 35 and 40, well-established in high-powered professions but insecure, even neurotic. The female characters with whom they were paired were, almost to a woman, not Jewish—no surprise there. But what struck me as notable was that although most of these men worried about their relationships and their performance as lovers, they didn't have to; their partners adored them, and they were uniformly portrayed as, shall we say, stand-up guys in bed. Sheldon had become a sex god in a Brooks Brothers suit.

I went looking for a corresponding female character: a wisecracking Jewish gal with a mane of curly hair and great legs, who could sway a jury *and* make great lasagna; a woman whose vulnerability was as endearing as her warmth and sensuality. Result of search: as a series regular, this character was, and remains, close to nonexistent. So one of my research inquiries became: Why are there so many neurotic-but-sexy, explicitly Jewish men (played mostly by Jewish actors, no less) on series television, and why don't these guys have a female counterpart?

While television presented very few Jews as series regulars during its first thirty years in people's living rooms,[51] it also kept negative Jewish stereotypes to a minimum. The tube didn't give us a really obnoxious Jewish mother until Rhoda Morgenstern's mom, introduced on *The Mary Tyler Moore Show* circa 1971; Jewish mothers on TV have rarely been presented as the harpies who have filled the big screen. The first nasty caricature of a JAP I can remember was during an early season of *Saturday Night Live* —Gilda Radner posing in "Jewess Jeans." But while primetime TV has portrayed scores of princesses, only a couple I can think of have been Jewish. Jewish princes, classic Sheldons, and female Jewish ugly ducklings have been few and far between as well.[52] The problem on television hasn't been that Jews are stereotyped; it's that they're invisible, and when they're not invisible, they're being presented as poster children for assimilation.

Take *Bridget Loves Bernie*. (Please!) This sitcom, a kind of updated *Abie's Irish Rose*, premiered in 1972 and elicited such an outcry from the Jewish community that it was canceled at the end of one season after the producers received bomb threats; to this day, it gets dragged into every article written about media depictions of intermarriage. The thing that got everyone so exercised was not that it portrayed an interfaith relationship (such relationships had been scripted repeatedly on anthology dramas of the 1950s) but that it was portrayed so cavalierly. The young lovebirds had the same values and world view; neither was more American than the other—why shouldn't they be happy? What about raising the kids? No problem! They'd have twins and raise one Jewish and one Catholic. Adding insult to injury, Bernie's family, the Steinbergs, were portrayed as loud and vulgar.

The show was woodenly written and acted, but it made one good point. After Bernie and Bridget dropped their bombshell about getting married, the highly assimilated Steinbergs suddenly started making Shabbat and telling jokes in Yiddish. "Why all of a sudden is everyone being so Jewish?" Bernie asked. In one line, the writers nailed thousands of Jewish baby boomers' parents who never gave a thought to being Jewish until a son or daughter brought home a Gentile partner. When Bernie's parents objected to the intermarriage, he was mystified; mom and dad were accusing him of turning his back on something he was never given. The same situation was played out seventeen years later, with a much older mother and son, on the short-lived series *Chicken Soup*.[53]

In their ethnic-only approach to Jewishness, the Steinbergs set the tone, with very few exceptions, for how episodic television presented its Jews. *Brooklyn Bridge*, a 1992 series as acclaimed as *Bridget Loves Bernie* was vilified, gave viewers an extended family from 1957 not one bit more observant than the Steinbergs—a family whose Friday night ritual was to watch the fights on TV. "The Jewish community glorifies *Brooklyn Bridge*, which is exactly what has caused our problem," says Rabbi Lavey Derby. "It was lovely then, but what we taught our kids is that we'll go shopping on Shabbos rather than go to shul." Only during the past few years have several episodic programs shown Jewish series regulars asserting themselves as Jewish, and even then, the identification is more likely to be ethnic than religious.[54]

Network executives still worry that mainstream Americans can't relate to overtly Jewish characters on television. "I still hear that Jews only play well over the Coasts," an Anti-Defamation League official said. "And even though Jews supposedly run the business, I think in some ways they are a throwback to the Goldwyns and Warners of the movie business. Those guys ran away from their heritage by changing *their* names. These people change their characters' names." A *Los Angeles Times* reporter called such personnel "The New Assimilationists," Jews who have made it in the biz by balancing stories that reflect their own cultural identities with the need to reach a wide audience.[55]

"Even now, even with the preponderance of shows [featuring Jewish characters], if you go in to a network, and . . . you say, I want to do this show about a Jewish guy, your pitch is over right there," Richard Rosenstock, who has produced two sitcoms based on Jewish characters, said in an interview. "They use all these television euphemisms like 'too ethnic' or 'too New York' or 'too urban' when they come back with their testing results on your pilots and on your series." Rosenstock brought up, as many people have, *The Golden Girls*, a show in which "two spectacularly Jewish characters in conception" (played, no less, by Jewish actresses, in a show set in Miami) became Italian. "If you go in and say, it's about Sophia Petrillo . . . nobody bats an eye," he said. "If you go in and you say, 'This is a Jewish woman and her mother,' they shut down."

Marshall Herskovitz recalls that when the Jewish head of the studio where he and Edward Zwick made *thirtysomething* (1987–91) saw the series pilot, which opens with Michael and Hope Steadman's wedding, he asked if it was necessary for Michael to wear a *kipah* in the first 30 seconds of the episode. "He was concerned that people would turn off the show when they saw the main character was Jewish. I mean we were still dealing with that level when we put the show on the air [in 1987]. And we said, 'Yeah, we have to show that.' " Comedian Jackie Mason once suggested that mainstream Americans don't have a problem watching Jews on television because they see the world of entertainment as the proper venue for Jews. "You don't have to like someone marrying your sister to enjoy watching them on television," Mason commented. "As a matter of fact, you're happy to watch them on television because you know where they are. They're not moving next door. They're not coming to your house. . . . *They stay in the box.*"[56]

The reluctance to portray romantic relationships between Jewish characters amounts almost to an industrywide phobia. "There's such a preponderance of intermarriage that it would give one the impression that no Jews are marrying Jews," says Judith Pearl, who, with her husband, Jonathan, founded the Jewish Televimages Resource Center, which publishes a newsletter on how Jewish characters and situations are presented on television. The Pearls wouldn't have intermarriage disappear from the air, which would be a denial of reality; in addition, they applaud the sensitivity and depth with which series such as *thirtysomething* have realistically portrayed the tensions and pitfalls of marriages between Jews and non-Jews. "But . . . to have [intermarriage's] exclusive appearance on television is just as false," Jonathan Pearl said in an interview. "It gives the impression to particularly young people . . . that there's no other way," Judith Pearl added. "It's the 'in' thing, it's on television, this is the cool, with-it way, and to do otherwise has no virtue, has no benefit, has no importance or significance."

Why are Jews shown in relationships almost exclusively with non-Jews when endogamy is standard for other minority groups depicted on television? The first explanation is usually that the writers are intermarried Jewish men and are simply reflecting their own lives in their work; they're writing what they know. Marshall Herskovitz says he had no agenda when he conceived Michael and Hope as a mixed couple: "I was simply dealing with an issue that interested me because it was in my own life, and I thought it was dramatically interesting." Another series producer said, "If you're intermarried, you have a vested interest in being convinced that you've done something in which there is no harm, and I think they then express that point of view in the scripts that they write for the shows that they create."

Other producers have incorporated their relationships in their shows. Stephen Kronish, creator of the recent cop series *The Commish*, turned around his own marriage to a woman who was raised Catholic to present a union of long duration between the title character, an Italian American, and his Jewish wife. Their mixed household was the only one on television in which an unambiguous choice for Jewish ritual and child raising was made, to the exclusion even of a Christmas tree, which is also reflective of Kronish's family. Several people who have worked with (non-Jewish) producer Diane English (*Murphy Brown, Love & War*) note that English likes Jewish men in general and has written more than one character after her husband and partner, Joel Shukovsky.

Another explanation for the preponderance of TV intermarriages is the claim that an endogamous Jewish relationship lacks the dramatic tension that a Jewish–Gentile partnership provides. This argument is spurious on its face: "Have you ever heard anyone complain that there wasn't enough 'conflict' between two Christian characters?" a casting director asked in a seminar on images of Jewish women in the media.[57] "If the legitimate demands of dramatic tension preclude romance within one's ethnic or religious group, then why wasn't Claire Huxtable [of *The Cosby Show*] a white woman?" a columnist asked in the *Los Angeles Times*.[58]

More to the point may be the idea that in the eyes of the Hollywood powers-that-be, two Jews in a relationship comprise at least one Jew too many. "Whether people will accept Jewish couples on TV is irrelevant," says University of Pennsylvania professor Joseph Turow, who teaches and writes about television. "The point is that the Hollywood lore [and] the Hollywood myth of what's acceptable or not acceptable construct a certain notion of how you portray Jews on television." Elias Davis, who worked on *Chicken Soup*, said in an interview, "I'm cynical enough to believe that any executive, Jewish or not Jewish, who believed there was viewership, there were ratings, there was money in the depiction of a Jewish family on television would do whatever he or she needed to do to bring that about."

> Q: Why do so many sitcoms feature short, quirky Jewish men who serve as sex gods to non-Jewish women?
>
> A: That's easy. They're written by short, quirky Jewish men who want to marry *shikses*.
>
> —a sitcom producer who prefers to remain anonymous

How many Jewish guys do you know who fit any of the following descriptions?

- A short, dumpy attorney in his mid-forties who (thanks to a new sex technique) turns up his tall, WASPy girlfriend's passion from medium-high to *Oh, God!*

- A fortyish writer who, during his first night with his gorgeous, 30-year-old friend-turned-lover, makes love to her five times, causing her to compare him to Oliver Twist: "Please, may I have some more?"

- A divorced book editor in his late thirties, cute but not especially well built or handsome and not terribly sensitive or deep, who has sex with half the nubile women in New York City.

- A skinny, nerdy 23-year-old, living with his parents on Long Island, who becomes the boy-toy of a hip young New Yorker so beautiful that strange men run up to her and declare their love.[59]

You don't know a lot of Jewish guys like that? But they're all over the tube.

"It's wish fulfillment to a certain extent," says a senior staffer for a sitcom featuring a typical neurotic-but-sexy Jewish guy. "It goes all the way to something like *The Heartbreak Kid*, the myth of the *shikse* goddess; these [shows] are variations on that myth." A 30-year-old man who worked for a while in program development agrees that The Biz is a magnet for East Coast Sheldons, of which he was one: "The Jewish guys were the nerds . . . you're not one of the cool kids in high school, but when you get to be 30 and you come into your own looks-wise and intelligence-wise . . . you say, okay, now it's my chance to be one of the cool kids." A talent agent describes the Sheldons-turned-Los Angeles-men as "the kids that were beat up on the playground in school, and now they're running studios. . . . I think it's a way of getting back at the people who treated them very badly as kids, and that could have been the very attractive girls."

I wish these characters well—they've been a refreshing change from the brawn-before-brain Nordic hunks who inhabit a much larger number of TV shows—but I still want to know: Where are their female counterparts?

In 1991, a *Jewish Journal* article asked, "Where's Rhoda Now?"[60] but Rhoda Morgenstern, in retrospect, was a lousy role model for young Jewish women during the mid-1970s. As a foil to Mary Tyler Moore's Midwestern primness, she had been feisty and clever, but given her own arena, she came off as a loser. Desperate to marry at 33, Rhoda strong-armed a reluctant (non-Jewish) boyfriend, a rather dull, uncommunicative guy with whom she had little in common, to the altar after an all-too-brief courtship. The marriage did little to improve her self-esteem or emotional security, and when it fell apart, so did Rhoda. She spent the rest of the series in what the network obviously thought was her "natural" role: wisecracking, unloved Lonely Gal. Her kid sister, Brenda, presented as a textbook ugly duckling, had an even lower self-image; she constantly denigrated her looks, regarded herself as boring—which she was—and let the men she dated walk all over her. Both characters were frequently pushed around by their overbearing, guilt-inflicting mother. They were given unattractive clothes and hairstyles, even for the 1970s, and were extremely skittish about sex. Neither Rhoda nor Brenda had gone to college; in Rhoda's case this was within the bounds of verisimilitude, but Brenda was a middle-class Jewish girl born in the early 1950s. Even if her high-school grades had been mediocre, a realistic portrayal of such a young woman at the beginning of the series would have made her a student at some branch of SUNY or CUNY, not a bank teller at 21.

In fact, Rhoda and Brenda set the tone for how Jewish women past college age were presented on episodic television for the next twenty years, when they were presented at all: undereducated, financially marginal or dependent, not conventionally pretty, and generally no threat to the men in their lives. (The best-known exception to this characterization was psychologist Lilith Sternin Crane on *Cheers*, but her intellect, severely restrained beauty, and refusal to defer to men were often turned against her by the other members of the ensemble.) Jewish women, who poured into the legal and medical professions beginning in the 1970s, have seldom been portrayed as doctors or lawyers on prime-time television; they are overrepresented in those professions today but are all but absent from television's hospital corridors and courtrooms.[61]

To women who work in the business, the failure to feature Jewish women as equals to men is no mystery. "Jewish men who work in television don't marry Jewish women, they don't care about the problems of Jewish women, and many of them won't even work with Jewish women," a female film executive said. "What makes you think they're going to put Jewish women on a television show?"[62]

In recent years, television series have presented some attractive, appealing Jewish female characters, but for the most part, Jewish women on episodic series tend to stand out less than their brothers, showing up much more frequently as part of an ensemble than as central characters. They are usually unavailable as partners to the Jewish men they might come across, either because they are already married (always to non-Jewish men) or are guest characters, not sticking around long enough to become involved.[63] Interestingly, the two Jewish women recently portrayed on episodic television who have come closest to being true counterparts to the New Anti-Sheldon have found themselves targets of stereotyping and misrepresentation in the press.

Melissa Steadman, Michael's cousin on *thirtysomething*, was repeatedly labeled as "neurotic"—not cute neurotic, like a Jewish guy, but pathetic neurotic—by reporters and columnists. Series creators Herskovitz and Zwick had conceived Melissa as "fat and full of problems," and actress Melanie Mayron, who had begun her career playing ugly ducklings in the mid-1970s, had to fight for her character's dignity. Writer-producer Richard Kramer admitted mid-series that "in the beginning, it might have been our impulse, if not our desire, to make Melissa pathetic," and credited Mayron with pushing the character in a positive direction.[64] Herskovitz said that Melissa's much-criticized offbeat clothes and hairstyles came strictly from Mayron herself. Keep in mind, also, that while Melissa enjoyed increasing career success as a photographer during the series, her degree from NYU put her on a lower rung than the Ivy League–educated Michael and Hope, and her work in an "artistic" field rather than a spot on the doctor-lawyer-executive matrix meant she didn't threaten Michael's superiority; in fact, she often worked for him.

Melissa was often described as unable to sustain a relationship, but she did just that with Lee Owens, a much younger man, through most of the third season of the series. (They broke up over their age difference but showed clear signs of getting back together as the series wound down the following season.) To this day I haven't read one word about the show's truly neurotic female character, Ellyn Warren, who drove away a longtime lover with her self-destructive behavior and lack of trust, then took up with a married man. But of course Ellyn dressed for success, Ellyn got married at the end of the series, and Ellyn wasn't Jewish.

Another Jewish female character who has taken more than her share of shots is Fran Fine of *The Nanny*, which premiered in 1993, the first sitcom since *Rhoda* to have a Jewish woman as its central character. Played by Queens native Fran Drescher, who created the show and produces it with her husband, Fran is loud, tactless, and garishly dressed, and her voice could cut diamonds. She is also, as one development executive described her, "perceptive, caring, empowered, self-aware, a truth-sayer who has all the good punchlines." Like Rhoda, Drescher's character has more street savvy than formal education. The preppy children she takes care of adore her, and their widowed father, a patrician British theatrical producer, enjoys her outspokenness and her penchant for Spandex dresses.

The show was an immediate hit; CBS research showed that the title character, whom Drescher based on her mother, herself, and other people she knew growing up in Forest Hills, appealed to a wide range of viewers. But Fran cuts too close to some American Jews' working-class, outer-borough roots for them to see any but her negative qualities. One Jewish columnist called her a "vulgar, crass, loudmouthed opportunist"; another expects her to start wearing plastic slipcovers over her clothes: "Why can't she be Jewish without these offensive stereotypes?" she complains.[65]

Jonathan Pearl, who notes that the voice Drescher uses in the show is the same voice she uses when she picks up the phone, says, "I don't think she's a bad reflection on Jews or Jewry or Judaism. She's got a good heart, she's nice, and she's pretty, so is that . . . a threat to Jewish survival?" Casting director Andrea Cohen agrees: "I don't have a problem with Fran Drescher's voice or how she presents herself. People like that exist. . . . This big melting pot idea that we all have to talk like we came out of Yale is just ridiculous."

Drescher got the last word with the woman who made the plastic-slipcover crack, asserting in a reply column that her character is "carving inroads for other Jewish characters—particularly women—who will not have to apologize for who or what they are," adding that the writer had apparently been influenced by television into believing that only soft-spoken, assimilated Jews should be portrayed by the entertainment media. "That shut her up," Drescher told a reporter.[66]

"Why aren't there attractive Jewish women on television? I don't think there are enough women in show-running positions to put this mandate over, and I think if there were, and I feel that's a failure of the business, of sexism in the business, I think they could," Richard Rosenstock says, suggesting that if creative powerhouses like Diane English and Linda Bloodworth-Thomason were Jewish, they probably would have created a few compelling Jewish female characters by now. Although the number of Jewish women working in television has increased during the past twenty years, they are still very much a minority; Marta Kauffman, co-creator of the sitcoms *Friends* and *Dream On*, says no more than a third of the scripts she and her colleagues read are written by women. And women in the biz are often unwilling to make waves. "Networks control the shows, and the networks are controlled by men," a sitcom scriptwriter told the *Jewish Journal*. "When a woman finally gets a job with any clout, she only wants to blend in. Our hold on power is so tentative, we'll be whatever the power structure wants us to be."[67]

Also, young Jewish women as characters don't seem to show up on TV radar. "There are certain kinds of things that mean Jewish to the mainstream American; they usually mean Yiddishisms, male intelligence, and a certain kind of humor . . . and Jewish mothers, of course," Joseph Turow said. Kauffman thinks the fate of Jewish women on television is tied up with the perception that they are too intelligent and gutsy to be appealing. "I mean look at the country politically," she said in an interview. "People are terrified of working women, bright women. . . . I don't know how much can change in television until it changes in the country."

"[The men in the business are] into the dream, the ideal woman, and that's what they want to see, and that's what they think other people want to see; they don't really relate to what a woman wants to see," agent Josh Schiowitz said. "These men are embarrassed and threatened by Jewish women," an angry writer said at a seminar. "When society's sexy prize of a woman is a blond, Gentile ice princess, Jewish women don't stand a chance."[68]

Americans are glued to the tube: the typical household has the set turned on seven hours a day, and 95 million people watch TV during primetime hours every night. By the time the average American teen today gets to college, he's watched 18,000 hours of TV—that's more than two solid years, twenty-four hours a day, seven days a week.[69]

If the message, year after year, is that *Charlie's Angels* and the *Baywatch* babes represent what is desirable in women; that being an aggressive, driven female divorce lawyer is great—if you look and sound like Mariel Hemingway; that Jewish women exist only on the periphery of American society, what does that do to the way young Jewish men see Jewish women and the way Jewish women see themselves? "The very negative message that American Jewish women are not good enough for American Jewish men is going out to anyone watching television," screenwriter Andrea King said at a 1994 conference.[70] "I should have seen the influence of the media when my misled, but happy, brothers would bring home *shikse* beauties to our family celebrations," said actress-scriptwriter Arleen Sorkin. "At Passover, I always wanted to ask 'The Fifth Question': 'How come my brothers don't go for Jewish girls?' "[71]

"I certainly had my Gentile period, where a six-foot-four blond guy looked real good to me," said one woman-in-the-biz, who at 37 yearns for a Great Jewish Guy. "So yeah, I think absolutely that those images that are plugged in front of you every day have an influence. And I think maybe that's why the real Paul Reisers of the world, the people who are actually in the pool of available men, suddenly become desirable."

"The actual impact of these shows is very powerful, even on educated, sophisticated people," scriptwriter Elias Davis said at a Hillel-sponsored forum. He sees programming that portrays interdating and mixed marriages to the exclusion of relationships between Jews as "a powerful message to teens who are starting to get involved in relationships. . . . This kind of propaganda is going to lead to an even quicker decrease in the numbers of Jews."[72] Joseph Turow is more cautious about the influence of Jewish portrayals on relationship decisions: "What I would say is that it reinforces [intermarriage] and gives it credibility. I wouldn't say that it is the primary cause by any means, but I think that it sort of rationalizes it among people who do it."

"I think television and movies are enormously, almost unbelievably powerful," Rabbi David Wolpe, a baby boomer, says:

It has a big effect on me personally. I think, like most people who grow up in a culture that constantly presents fantasies, I find myself all the time fighting a fantasized picture of other people and trying to deal with people as people. Even realistic movies and TV present fantasies of people. And when you have a society where people watch television several hours a day . . . it can be very destructive.

If contemporary Jews have been harmed by their absence or by negative images of themselves in the popular media, how might Jewish self-esteem—and the perception of other Jews as attractive—be enhanced by being able to find themselves on the screen? The portrayal of young Jewish women and men as attractive, the occasional Jewish couple turning up in a movie or TV series, might not turn around the intermarriage rate, but no one can say media images aren't influential. We know it from our own experience; I certainly know it from mine. You see, I married a man whose idea of an appealing film actress is . . . Julie Kavner.

5

Thirteen and Out

I'd like to take some course that would teach me what I never learned as a teenager about Judaism. . . . It never opened itself up to me in any inviting way, and I never saw anything in it that filled . . . those gaps in my adolescent personhood—you know, feeling accepted and feeling I had a place and something to contribute and a mind of my own.

—Paula, 34, bat mitzvah and confirmand

I still have this resentment toward Judaism. Putting a yarmulke on, you might as well put a thousand-pound weight on my head.

—Brian, 30, bar mitzvah

Just before I started junior high, our family moved, and my parents joined a small, newish Reform congregation. The rabbi was young, typical of many that Hebrew Union College was ordaining in the 1960s: liberal but passionate about Judaism, with a pronounced social activist bent. I had been politicized by televised reports of the civil rights struggle and the Vietnam conflict, and this guy suited me to the ground. He assumed every girl in his temple would become a bat mitzvah at a time when not all Reform rabbis made that assumption. He made us happy to stay in religious school through confirmation. He had the youth group create a public worship service for the Vietnam Moratorium. One Yom Kippur, he held up a gag gift of the day, a can of "Instant Jewish," and spent the next thirty-five minutes haranguing the adults in the congregation about wanting a September shot of Instant Jewish when they should be participating in genuine Judaism all year round. After graduating from high school and leaving home, I spent fifteen years looking for another congregation with a rabbi like that.

I was lucky.

I didn't know *how* lucky until I started interviewing people for this book. My Jewish case study informants differed in many ways, but most of them had one thing in common: failure to experience religious life in a way that engaged them as youngsters and inspired them to remain involved in Jewish life for its own sake as adults. Most of their parents provided them with a strong ethnic identity but gave little attention to home ritual and observance. Sunday school and Hebrew school were a drag, worship boring and empty of meaning. Today they identify as Jews, generally with pride, but most of them are not interested in synagogue life, nor do they practice any kind of Jewish ritual they didn't experience as children.

Of all major American religious groups, Jews are the least likely to establish a formal connection with a house of worship and the least likely to attend services even when they do affiliate.[1] Over the past generation, American Jews have come to view themselves less and less in religious terms and increasingly as an ethnic or cultural group. Minimal observance and experience of Jewishness purely as ethnic identity are one more undercurrent in the riptide of intermarriage—if being Jewish is as portable as a *chanukiah* and a bag of bagels, if what you want to pass down to your kids about Moses and the Maccabees is no more than the pride a Latino might feel about kinship with Simón Bolívar or someone of Scottish descent with Rob Roy MacGregor, why bother looking for another Jew to marry? What's the point of marrying "within the faith" if you have no faith?

As discussed earlier, the Jewish immigrants from Eastern Europe who came to America between 1880 and 1924 tended to be the least devout of their former communities, and the veneer of religious customs they brought with them, such as keeping the Sabbath, was easily pierced by the requirements of making a living in America.[2]

Eager to see their children acculturate and often possessing little formal Jewish education themselves, they put a higher priority on their children's studies in public school than on religious education. From the first decade of this century through the 1930s, only a quarter of Jewish children of elementary school age received any Jewish education. Nor were American Jews consistent worshipers during the first half of the century. Although immigrants established numerous synagogues, they often existed more as social clubs than houses of worship. Not surprisingly, by the mid-1930s, the vast majority of young Jews, the children of the immigrants, didn't attend services at all.[3]

You didn't need to go to temple to feel Jewish—most Jews lived in homogeneous urban neighborhoods where *Yiddishkeit* was in the very air they breathed. "To the extent to which people thought about Jewishness, their concern was not how to ensure its survival but how to escape its all-embracing grasp," historian Charles Silberman wrote.[4]

Many of the immigrants had been caught up in the antiauthoritarian social and political movements of the period, and others arrived in active rebellion against what they saw as the meaningless constrictions and hypocrisies of shtetl Orthodoxy. In America, some of these people found a secular Jewish identity in continuing study of Yiddish language and literature, some in socialist movements such as Labor Zionism, producing a wide array of schools, publications, and community activities. "My family's shul was the union hall of 1199, the Drug and Hospital Workers Union that my father, a pharmacist, helped found," one man recalled. "My sense of *aliyah* came from fetching hot coffee in leaky styrofoam cups for picketing strikers. It didn't matter *that* we were Jewish; but things mattered *because* we were Jewish."[5]

The secular Jewish movements were largely unable to sustain themselves during the decades after World War II, however, and Jewish political activism became channeled mostly into multiethnic movements.[6]

Everything changed when American Jews flocked to the suburbs after World War II. The 1950s saw a tremendous revival of institutional religion, both Christian and Jewish, across America, and with the decline of overt anti-Semitism, Jews felt comfortable building synagogues and sending their kids to religious school. During the first half of the century, being American to many Jews meant assimilating to the point of submerging one's Jewishness. In the 1950s and 1960s, joining a synagogue and/or a Jewish community center was as American an act as chairing a PTA committee or coaching Little League. Temple membership and religious school enrollment figures shot up exponentially during this period.[7]

But the real agenda for postwar Jews was to fit into the dominant culture while maintaining an ethnic identity. "It was important [to my parents] to be American and to assimilate and to belong to the country club rather than the shul, although they did belong to a shul that we went to for Rosh Hashanah and

Yom Kippur," says Erica, 52, who grew up in Eastern suburbs and now maintains a kosher home with a non-Jewish husband. "There was no observance of Shabbat, no holidays at home; it was more important to be American than Jewish. Corned beef and pastrami was being Jewish."

A woman in her late twenties grew up in a family that "kept up some Jewish connections," but the attitude toward observance her parents passed down was more negative than positive:

> My parents both came from Brooklyn, what they would refer to as a "Jewish ghetto." And they definitely wanted out of that. Wherever they lived—in Long Island, New Jersey, or Washington, D.C.—they purposely moved to non-Jewish neighborhoods. . . . We would go to Seders at my grandparents and to cousins' bar mitzvahs. In our own house, we had a menorah for Hanukkah. . . . For a while, we even observed Yom Kippur; we would fast and go to temple. That is, my mother would. My father wouldn't. He was an atheist, and he always told me the whole thing was bullshit. . . . The issue of bar mitzvah [for my brother] never came up. My father just got him a dog for his thirteenth birthday.[8]

Is it any wonder that half these young people marry non-Jews—and that their parents put up little or no resistance when they do?

What turned off contemporary Jews to Jewish ritual and worship? What made them walk out of the synagogue at 13 or 15, and what keeps them away as adults?

Much had to do with the temple itself. The synagogues built during the 1950s and 1960s were large and grand, befitting the Jews' newly secure status in American society, but the layout showed who the clientele really was. The temple was given over to pediatric Judaism—Judaism for the kids. "Synagogue buildings tell the story," Rabbi Lawrence Hoffman, professor of liturgy at Hebrew Union College in New York, told a lecture audience:

> Very tiny sanctuaries which nobody went to anyhow. Huge school wings and busy, busy, busy Sunday mornings when people dropped their kids off. But the adults did nothing religious themselves. . . . Religion, therefore . . . emerged out of the 1950s and 1960s as something you did when you were a child . . . something you do until you are 13 or 14, but certainly nothing you did as an adult, because [your] parents didn't do it.

The synagogue served children of the third generation through religious school, youth groups, and recreational activities and provided their mothers with a social outlet through Sisterhood. Adult men faded out of the picture as Judaism's target population.[9]

During this time, non-Orthodox Jewish worship broke away from the European model and began to look and sound more like that of their Christian neighbors. Especially in the Reform movement, which had followed the Protestant model since its inception in nineteenth-century Germany, but also in Conservative synagogues, services were highly structured, controlled, and decorous. By the 1960s, the kind of worship most Jews experienced (when they went at all) was dull and unmoving, using a prayerbook in which the Hebrew was incomprehensible to most adults and the English translations clunky and unpoetic. Most synagogues shied away from addressing controversial subjects or even God; they depended on the rabbi's oratory and the musical skill of the cantor and choir to attract worshipers and succeeded only in creating a religious experience as grandiose and empty as the buildings they were housed in.[10]

Mainstream Christian denominations were facing the same problem, as Hoffman underscored when he spoke of a survey conducted to find out why Americans were religiously unaffiliated. "A Methodist woman said, 'There's a huge Methodist church on the corner. I don't go because it is so impersonal and inhuman that we call it Fort Methodist.' What she did not say was that it was across the road from Fort Jewish, but I guarantee you that it was," Hoffman said.

None of this sat well with the young people, third- and fourth-generation Jews, who came of age beginning in the mid-1960s. The more involved students (of any religion) became with the touchstones of the counterculture—rock music, drug use, and political protest—the more likely they were to drop out. They were also quick to note ethical inconsistencies between the religious teachings pushed by their parents' generation and the way members of that generation operated in the world.[11] To this day, baby boomers remain the least trusting of all age groups in America regarding social and political institutions, less trusting even than Americans younger than themselves.[12]

At the same time, young people thirsted for sources of meaningful spiritual expression, and just as they were encouraged by the counterculture to experiment with drugs and sex, so too did they sample, and sometimes adopt on a long-term basis, religious systems based on meditation and Eastern thought. Jews were overrepresented not only among hippies and political activists but among the growing ranks of American Buddhists, practitioners of Transcendental Meditation, and adherents of other Eastern religions.[13]

Although liberal Jews began to bring a more contemporary spirit into liturgy during the 1960s, institutional Judaism got sidetracked from any consistent attention to spirituality by issues of ethnicity and peoplehood. The Six-Day War in 1967 touched off an explosion of nationalistic pride in American Jews just as particularism became popular in the United States and people of many ethnic groups began to celebrate their traditions. The State of Israel became the filter through which all Jewish experience passed: only Israel, it seemed, represented the promise of Jewish redemption after the Holocaust; only Israel provided a society in which Jews could live without danger of assimilation into an alien culture. The spiritual lives of American Jews took a back seat to preserving Israel, supporting Israel, getting Soviet and Ethiopian Jews into Israel. Congregational rabbis were preaching on the same topics they had twenty years earlier: Israel and peoplehood. They let the Orthodox worry about devotion to God and the liberal Christians take on issues of poverty and discrimination. So another generation of American Jews grew up with the message that being Jewish was about what you ate and how much money you gave to the UJA, not about your heart and soul, let alone your relationship to God.[14]

At home, many young Jews, including some of my informants, experienced Judaism as something lived on the surface of their parents' lives, not as deeply felt beliefs, even when parents appeared to be involved in synagogue life or ritually observant. Several people complained to me that the Judaism their elders practiced seemed to be more of a social activity than a spiritual outlet. A 45-year-old man raised in Chicago, whose parents held leadership roles in their temple, described his bar mitzvah in terms of "social obligations . . . the social celebration of everything that is Jewish in middle-class America. . . . We were a family that was together on Passover always encouraging my Zede to speed up the seder," he wrote in a letter. "Other holidays were always an invitation for a family assembly celebrating my mother's cooking abilities. The Jewish holiday and its religious significance were . . . lost in the family's social shuffle."

Other Jews grew up resenting the mixed signals they got from their parents. One woman in her forties, whose grandparents were Orthodox and who was raised in a kosher home, became enraged when her widowed mother remarried a less observant man and stopped keeping kosher. "Her reaction was vehement and, as she herself recognized, irrational: how could my mother do this?" the woman's friend wrote. "After so many years of demonstrating to her children her commitment to tradition, her mother could turn it over in an instant? She was in a rage at her mother for her inconsistency." The reason for her anger, the writer explained, was that the ritual her friend grew up with gave her a sense of belonging to the Jewish people, but it didn't carry with it a love of being Jewish or a strong element of pride. The fact that her mother would give up *kashrut* for a man told this woman that being loved and being "too Jewish" didn't go together, and if you had to choose, it was better to be loved.[15]

For some younger Jews, with parents more removed from tradition, the sense of connection was even more tenuous. "Even my grandparents weren't that religious," said one 30-year-old, adding that the only complete seders he attended while growing up were made by friends of the family, not his own parents. A 23-year-old woman who got turned on to Judaism at Reform summer camp told me, "I would come home feeling warm and fuzzy about Judaism and Shabbat every time I'd come home from camp, and I'd get home, and there's nothing, and it was really like culture shock for me." Her sister was a camper, too: "We'd both come home and say, 'Let's do Shabbat!' and we'd dress up in white, and make my mom make chicken and the whole bit, but it just wasn't there."

Some young Jews took direct issue with Jewish doctrine, lore, and theology, especially when no one bothered to explain them properly. Kids who are products of a universalist society can have trouble with the whole "us versus them" aspect of Jewish identity and the flat assertion that Jews are the chosen people (which is how it comes down to many of them). This is particularly true of youngsters who have already committed themselves to the well-being of all people. They are easily put off by the parochial attitude that Jews should donate time and money only to Jewish causes and that the survival of the State of Israel has a higher priority than that of the homeless and hungry on their own streets. "I grew up in the time of the Watts riots, with black people saying they wanted equal rights. So were women and Chicanos," said a Buddhist nun who grew up Jewish in Los Angeles. "That made a lot more sense to me than this Jewish protectorate. I moved into the sphere of social action, taking what I learned about suffering from my Jewish background but going well beyond the narrow Jewish limit to which it was applied."[16]

Some Jews may be unable to reconcile the concept of a just and merciful God with God's mandate to the Israelites to eliminate all non-Jewish residents of Canaan or unable to accept the idea that a just and merciful God would allow the Holocaust to happen. Others reject the miracles that appear in the Bible and in rabbinic lore, believing only what can be proven empirically.[17] Some, including many raised in observant households, believe that rabbis and often parents are more concerned about whether the meat and dairy dishes are kept separate than whether we live in a humane and caring society. One young woman told a journalist that as far as she was concerned, "Judaism is an old man saying no."[18] Young Jews also find themselves alienated by the materialism they perceive as rampant within Jewish life: the obsession with what to wear to holiday services, the *gantzer macher* (big shot) syndrome in synagogues and other organizations in which the ability to raise funds is valued over the ability to connect people to God.[19]

Another common complaint is that American Jewry is obsessed with Jewish suffering to where it crowds out any potential for joy and celebration. "Our generation, this crisis Judaism doesn't attract us," Rabbi Neal Weinberg, who runs a burgeoning Introduction to Judaism program in Los Angeles, said in an interview. "It's all negative. I'm not gonna be a Jew because six million Jews died in the Holocaust. I'm not gonna be a Jew because Israel's threatened."

"You can't build loyalty completely out of the sense of martyrdom," echoes HUC professor Norman Mirsky. "You go to school, you learn about the Holocaust, you see *Night and Fog* and everything like that, and you find out what's the reward, what's the payoff for being Jewish? You get murdered. And you're powerless."

Carla, a member of two synagogues, speaks of a Jewish friend, married to a Jew, who refuses to include any Jewish ritual or education in her son's upbringing. Urged to send her child to religious school so he would have at least a sense of Jewish history, the friend replied, "What's Jewish history? We lived in a lot of places where people tried to kill us." Carla is irked with her friend but has the same criticism of her own Jewish education: "Quit showing me movies about the Holocaust, and quit telling me that if I'd grown up in Germany I'd be dead. This is not a reason to be Jewish."[20]

As the feminist movement gained momentum during the 1970s, women of all ages across the Jewish spectrum began to voice the alienation so many of them felt because they were shut out of so much Jewish ritual and worship and made to feel, at every turn, like ciphers in their own congregations. Jewish tradition does not allow women to be members of a prayer quorum or witnesses to a Jewish legal proceeding, nor can they be called to read from the Torah or to chant the blessings for its reading. Women who grew up attending Orthodox services spent their time in shul behind a partition or up in the balcony, unable to participate fully in the men's worship. The literature is full of stories of women who were forbidden to mourn their own parents aloud in a traditional setting.[21]

Letty Cottin Pogrebin, whose ejection from her mother's *shiva* prompted her to stay out of organized Jewish life for fifteen years, cites novelist Cynthia Ozick: "In the world at large I call myself and am called, a Jew. But when, on the Sabbath, I sit among women in my traditional shul and the rabbi speaks the word 'Jew' I can be sure that he is not referring to me."[22]

A woman in her thirties who has lived almost all her life in Brooklyn regrets that her parents sent her to traditional synagogues without providing the knowledge for her to appreciate the worship. "In Brooklyn, there was not one temple that I could go to that I would understand what was going on," she said. "I resented that growing up, because I had to sit separate from men or behind a curtain, or it would be completely in Hebrew, and I would walk out of there, and I would say, I'm Jewish, but I don't know what the hell is going on." On weekend visits to a friend in the suburbs, she would be taken to Reform services: "I used to tell my parents, I loved it so much—why can't we have a temple like that in Brooklyn?"

The Reform and Reconstructionist movements began to ordain women as rabbis and invest them as cantors in the early 1970s, but only now are even those movements degenderizing their English liturgy. As recently as 1978, fewer than half of Conservative congregations counted women for a minyan or allowed them to lead services, although this has improved since the Jewish Theological Seminary began to ordain women in 1985.

Traditionally, Jewish education for girls has not been given the priority it has had for boys. Girls in the non-Orthodox movements have been encouraged in recent years to stay in religious and Hebrew school and become *b'not mitzvah* and confirmands, but their Jewish education still lags behind that of their brothers, although they are catching up.[23]

"Women have been excluded from Jewish educational opportunities, from Jewish leadership roles, from the inner sanctum of Jewish organizational life, and yet we expect women to not only make Judaism an important part of their own lives but to bear the brunt of the responsibility for making Judaism an important part of our children's lives as well," Donna Berman, a Reconstructionist rabbi, told a conference audience. "This is not to say that many women haven't tried and tried valiantly to do this, but we haven't given women either the proper tools or, some might argue, sufficient reason to want to expend the energy to do this. . . . Most of the women who are now raising children grew up as invisible members of their synagogues."[24]

Perhaps the biggest single turn-off to American Jews in their development as Jews, what one writer called "the castor oil of Jewish life," has been the most prevalent: the religious education to which, in some communities, up to 90 percent of Jewish kids are exposed during their school years.[25] In concept and execution, it stinks, and it has stunk for the past seventy years.

The reviews are in:

- They never teach it right, so you end up hating it. They teach you to read Hebrew, but they don't teach you to understand it. . . . To have to go to after school and on Sunday morning is more of a hassle than a wonderful learning experience. So you come out at 13, you're bar mitzvahed, and you really don't know that much about Judaism. (Eli, 35)

- It seemed like it took a lot of time: every Tuesday and Thursday afternoon, Friday night I had to be in temple once a month, three Saturdays out of every four, Sunday school every Sunday. . . . The rabbi that officiated at my bar mitzvah had me sign a document saying that I'd continue on in Hebrew school, otherwise he wouldn't attend my bar mitzvah. . . . I went the other year, but I resented being there. . . . I hated being put in that position. (Dave, 42)

- I just never felt any kind of connection, and I didn't like going to Hebrew school. I got sent down to the office, so I started climbing out the bathroom window, or challenging my teachers to the point where it was kind of useless, and I just didn't feel anything for it, so I [told] Mom and Dad, "I really don't want to go through with this. It means nothing to me," and they said, "Well, you'll regret it some day." That day hasn't happened yet. (Valerie, 31)

- I would ask these questions, I was one of these, not smart-alecky, just inquisitive [kids]. . . . I asked a question about Jesus once: Why, if the Jews are waiting for a messiah, why didn't they accept Jesus as their messiah while most of the world has? And my rabbi hit me. That's one of those things that can turn you off from religion. (Brian, 30)

One problem with the rise of pediatric Judaism was the accompanying abdication by many parents of any responsibility not only for their children's Jewish education but for their children's very identity as Jews. These parents were mostly children of immigrants with little or no religious education, unequipped to answer their kids' questions or even prepare for most holidays with any degree of comfort. Born in the 1920s and 1930s, many had experienced Jew-baiting firsthand during their youth and had lived through the period of the Holocaust, reaching their childbearing years seeing participation in Jewish life as an obligation ("don't break the chain") but not a pleasure.[26] In effect, these parents looked to modern synagogues and their personnel to do what they were unwilling or unable to do themselves: make Jews out of their children.

Synagogue classrooms filled quickly after the war, but by 1960 studies were beginning to demonstrate that supplementary schools were turning out adolescents who knew little of Hebrew, Jewish history, Jewish texts such as the Bible, or synagogue and holiday skills, charges that would be repeated over and over by academics, rabbis, parents, and the students themselves over the next thirty-plus years.[27]

The schools' failures have generally been ascribed to the meager amount of time children spend in class (rarely more than six hours a week and often as little as two) and to poor instruction. A recent study of Jewish education in three American cities showed that although Jewish educators are, by and large, committed and dedicated to Jewish learning, fewer than 20 percent of teachers in programs including supplementary schools and Jewish day schools had training both in education and in Jewish studies. Among supplementary school teachers, almost 80 percent have no formal certification in Jewish studies. Thousands of Jewish children are being taught by people whose own formal Jewish education ended at age thirteen.[28]

Jewish education is also plagued by a sense of vague goals and standards, a lack of consensus on what a graduate of a supplementary school is supposed to know. Many Jewish parents are perfectly happy with what their kids are learning in religious school. They expect creditable performances at their children's bar or bat mitzvahs and usually get them. Other than that, they just want the years in religious school to make their kids "feel Jewish," that is, give them a solid Jewish identity. There's some evidence that part-time Jewish education is helpful in achieving that end, but the lack of backup at home—the failure of parents to reinforce what their children learn at temple by incorporating ritual and service attendance in their own lives—undermines what the children are taught and makes any gains short-term.[29] Once past bar or bat mitzvah, a rite of passage for three out of four Jewish children, not many teenagers find much to keep them in religious school. Half of them drop out within a year after the ceremony.

"You can't just have a bar mitzvah for your kid," Rabbi Jerome Epstein, executive vice-president of United Synagogue of Conservative Judaism, said in an interview.

> You can't create the Jewish life you want if you're only educating for *der Kinder*. The kids . . . come home and what do they see? They see, well, this is okay, this is play-acting what we learned at the synagogue level, and the home isn't really serious about it. . . . I think we send tremendous signals to our children when they have to go to services until they're 13, and after 13 they don't have to go anymore and their parents don't go. . . . It cheapens Judaism.

Comments from some of the young women profiled in *The Jewish Wife* about raising children in the late 1960s underscore just how ambivalent a lot of Jewish parents were (and are) about their kids' Jewish identity and leave little doubt as to why so many Jewish children of the time grew up to feel comfortable about the prospect of marrying a non-Jew. Some pushed the universalist approach, like this Queens mother: "I would let them have the privilege, when they are older, of accepting their religion or not. Many of the same basic concepts are taught by all religions. . . . I don't want to overstress religious training. This can also make a person intolerant." Another said, "I would not expect my children or grandchildren to accept Judaism as a practicing religion. . . . But if they did not respect their *lineage* deeply, I would feel very badly."[30]

Supplementary school enrollment fell by 60 percent during the twenty years following its 1962 peak, only partly because of the smaller pool of Jewish children after the baby boom ended. Other factors included, and continue to include, intermarriage and adult apathy to Jewish life.[31] "You may see a rise in kids who have never been in a synagogue," says Rabbi Alan Bregman, director of the UAHC's Chicago region. "There used to be a formula that said, we have 60 percent unaffiliated in Chicago, but 80 percent of the kids have had some Jewish education. I would surmise that you're going to see a fall-off in that 80 percent, because there may be people . . . who are beginning to say, 'I'm not gonna put my kids through that, especially for fifteen hundred dollars a year, two thousand dollars a year. So they don't have a bar mitzvah, so what? I didn't like mine.'"

In the minds of some educators, the failure of Jewish education has less to do with poorly trained teachers or sketchy curriculum than with the unwillingness of school personnel to involve students in discussion of the topics that engage them the most: what it means to be Jewish in America; what it means in Jewish terms to be human; what or who is God. "I felt that there was a lack of this whole area of religious experience," said Sherry Blumberg, who now teaches education at Hebrew Union College in New York. Blumberg was a temple educator in the Bay Area during the mid-1970s, when the bottom dropped out of the aerospace industry. "In our congregation, several of the kids' fathers committed suicide. So here we were talking about Jewish history and holidays and celebrations, and what these kids needed to know was, What gives life meaning? Why do you survive a crisis? Why find meaning in life when everything else you thought you had was crumbling?"

"We teach you . . . can be Jewish without understanding God," says another longtime educator, Constance Reiter.

What [young Jews] do not know, and what their families (who also did not know), and their synagogues and schools never taught them, was a God concept which underpins their identity as Jews. The educational philosophy was based on the belief that if our youngsters were taught our history and the essentials of Bible, and if they were taught enough Hebrew to make their way through the basic worship service, and if we taught the skills of observing the holidays . . . then our students stood a good chance of remaining "committed Jews." It didn't work. We simply taught them the cultural underpinnings of a particular group, not the deeply meaningful life-philosophy of why we behave in this way. . . . Only now are Jewish educators and institutional leaders beginning to realize the harm that this failure has caused.

The repercussions in terms of alienation, both short- and long-term, are obvious. Students who don't become familiar with traditional liturgy and Hebrew texts, especially when they come from minimally observant homes, are likely to shy away from college organizations like Hillel, whose chapters often are dominated by traditionally religious students. "I really feel shortchanged," a sophomore from a Reform background commented. "I feel like my religious school cheated me. When you come to college and you meet Jews with a more solid education in Jewish tradition, you feel stupid. On campus I meet a lot of kids who have been confirmed, but they realize that they know nothing. They can't stand up for themselves as Jews, and they question their Jewish identity."[32] On the practical level, the unwillingness to spend time in a campus Jewish organization cuts students off from the one sure source of potential Jewish mates.

"I don't even go into [Judaism] with the same politeness and openness, not even close to it, that I would go into a stranger's [religion]," said a Northern California man in his early thirties who left religious school—and, for all practical purposes, Judaism—a year after bar mitzvah. "I mean if I go to someone's home, or into someone else's culture, I would respect all the religious practices and be absolutely polite and respectful. But I don't even give that same slack to my family and that structure. Even if I feel that some of these things don't hold meaning for me, it's like the least that I could do is have the same respect that I would have toward strangers. There is obviously an animosity there."

As adults, many Jews are still put off by the lack of spiritual depth in the synagogue experience. The prayerbook is uninspiring; services are impersonal and devoid of real emotion, and the congregants themselves rarely form anything resembling a community. The style of preaching and approach to prayer is often coldly hyperrational: "It is as if we Jews have never danced, sang, told stories, laughed, or cried," one psychologist commented.[33]

On the other hand, worship can be all too subject to the requirements of pediatric Judaism. After urging an audience of mostly single people in their twenties and thirties to reexperience synagogue life, Mordecai Finley, a Reform rabbi who leads an independent congregation in Los Angeles, acknowledged that they might not get their souls stirred the first time they walk into temple. "You go to shul, and what might you find? Sixth-grade family night, right? 'I'm ready for soul, I'm ready for depth, I'm ready for Torah to come into me, and I'm ready to expose myself to God,' . . . and instead you get little Josh Goldstein: My Trip to Tel Aviv."

The Jewish prayerbook is dull and uninspiring, Lawrence Hoffman says, because it was never meant to be read in any language other than Hebrew. "A goodly number of our prayers, it turns out, are really written for the sake of the affect, the sound of the Hebrew language, not for the meaning. . . . It was almost like a Jewish mantra." Accordingly, he says, prayerbooks should provide less literal prose translation of Hebrew prayers and more poetry that gets across the spirit of each prayer in a way that is both emotionally moving and relevant to our time. In general, Hoffman believes, Jewish services need to move away from what creates social distance to a more intimate style and organization of worship.[34]

A number of factors that keep Jewish adults out of the synagogue are based in their own psyches. Some people see prayer as a surrender of the self and avoid situations over which they feel they have no control. "Something about prayer can often feel awkward and make one self-conscious," psychologist Michael Bader told a lecture audience at the 1994 *Tikkun* conference. "The kinds of self-effacing expressions of love and God that fill our prayerbook can, if taken seriously, feel embarrassingly submissive." This is especially true for people who had problems in their childhoods with love expressed in terms of idealization, wonder, and surrender, Bader said; to employ such emotions in adult worship can seem regressive and childish. The surrender to love and praise of a force greater than oneself also represents a challenge to the cynicism that pervades our society, Bader added.

Many Jews also stay away from temple because they think they'll feel stupid—they'd like to be part of the community, but they think their Hebrew isn't good enough or they won't know what to do. Highly educated, successful young professionals "don't like to put themselves in places or positions where they feel ignorant," says Steven Z. Leder, a young rabbi who runs study groups for this constituency. "And the synagogue is just such a place. They simply avoid environments that make them feel ignorant because they're so capable." Nor are most of these people able to acknowledge their feelings of Judaic inadequacy. Rather than confess what they don't know, they simply say they don't want to be religious.[35]

Susan Weidman Schneider extends this reasoning to home observance and connects it directly to intermarriage itself:

> A religion that has located much ritual in the home requires its lay practitioners . . . to be fairly expert, or at least competent. . . . One needs to be familiar enough, competent enough, and confident enough to perform these blessings or rituals in front of others. For Jews who feel uneasy about their skills it may be easier to opt out and not have to be the competent [head] in a Jewish household. . . . [T]here is an additional burden on underachieving [Jews] that isn't there for their Christian counterparts for whom, if any religious expression is required of them at all, might be no more than saying a grace before meals (and in their own language, too).[36]

Nor are all Jews in search of God or interested in spiritual experience. "I always felt so distant from it," says Valerie, a designer in the Pacific Northwest. "I can understand it, but I don't feel it. Culturally, that's where I came from, it's what I'm part of, but religiously I have a whole different feeling about existence and whatnot, and it doesn't really fit in with Judaism." "I think by the time I was three years old I knew that religion was a crock," a 46-year-old psychologist told me.

Then, too, a lot of the reasons Jews stay away from shul seem rooted in the perpetual adolescence and sense of entitlement that characterize baby boomers, making them as picky about their encounters with Jewish life as they are about whom they date.

Mordecai Finley complains about "consumer Judaism," in which someone samples a temple, decides he hasn't had his needs met, and walks out, never to return. "That's immature," Finley says. "No [romantic] relationship can ever withstand a person saying, 'I didn't get my need met today, so I'm walking out of here.' You have to work and you have to be patient. . . . Acknowledge that it can be tough to walk into the right synagogue on the right night and have your soul addressed. But . . . take a step in spiritual responsibility and maturity and stick with it."

"I don't think the problem is the synagogue," Steven Leder says. "The problem is a total lack of understanding that effort is required. These are people who will rent videos, pay lots of money, get a private instructor, get out of bed early on Saturday and Sunday morning, all to improve their tennis game, but don't understand that a similar sort of energy is required to get something out of Judaism." Many Jews, including dozens who told me their stories, seem to assume that the way they were raised is the only way to be Jewish, and if that way didn't work for them, they weren't about to explore others. "It's pathetic," a New Jersey rabbi said. "If you go to college and you have one bad professor, it doesn't mean you quit college and you never want to study again."

On a more mundane level, a lot of people don't join synagogues or enroll their children in religious school because they can't afford to—or because they don't attach a high enough priority to Jewish life to spend a good chunk of family income on it. Some Jewish leaders note that plenty of couples will pay $100 a pair for their kids' tennies or think nothing of dropping several hundred dollars on a ski weekend but will cry poverty at the thought of spending $1,000 to join a temple. "If a family balks at this level of membership dues, then it regards Judaism as just another recreational activity that is measured or 'valued' in relation to other forms of voluntary association or activity," demographer Barry Kosmin wrote recently. "Most Jews, even among the minority . . . who are members of synagogues, see the religious institution as the place that renders services to them rather than a place where they give service to God."[37] Migration is also a factor; people take a long time to feel settled in a community, and those who never do put down roots in a town are usually unwilling to commit to any financial outlay for a communal affiliation.[38]

But, in fact, active participation in Jewish life *is* expensive. Basic dues at many mainstream synagogues are $800–1,000 or more, and most temples assess an annual contribution to a building fund. If you have kids, add preschool or religious school tuition, and your annual commitment can easily run to more than $2,000. That doesn't begin to address the cost of "intensive Jewish experiences" such as summer camp and travel to Israel, along with smaller items such as subscriptions to Jewish publications, inviting people for Shabbat dinner and seder, and donations to Jewish organizations.[39] Two thousand dollars is not an insignificant amount for people who may be underpaid or underemployed, worried about job security, or facing an ongoing or unexpected financial burden. There's a strong correlation between synagogue membership and household income; the more money a Jewish family makes, the more likely it is that they belong to a temple, and the perception among many Jews is that synagogue membership is only for the rich.[40] Such a perception can make it difficult for an intermarried Jew to justify the expense of temple membership to a non-Jewish partner.

Assuredly, fewer Jews would begrudge membership dues if they viewed the synagogue as a true community, an extension of their families, rather than a place to which they bring a shopping list: "bar mitzvah for my kid, rabbi on call in case I get sick, High Holiday seats," Lawrence Hoffman says. "And if the kid gets bar mitzvahed or bat mitzvahed, they say, stroke it off, no need to belong any more. . . . And they leave, the way they leave a supermarket when they've got enough bread and milk."

When synagogues appear to devote themselves only to the shopping lists of affluent parents with children at home, other constituencies—childless couples, singles of all ages, empty nesters, the elderly—may leave or never show up. While the great majority, perhaps as high as 80 percent, of American Jews belong to a synagogue at some point in their lives, no more than a third nation-wide are currently affiliated.[41]

The phenomenon in American religious life that has the most profound impli-cations for Jewish continuity is the trend toward religious privatism, the idea that one's faith is based on personal choice and inner feelings, rather than loyalty to one's family, ethnic group, or community. Based on the American heritage of church–state separation, religious pluralism, and individualism, privatism takes religion out of the public world and keeps it at home, or even within one's own heart. "What one believes in private is one's own personal matter, and hence off limits to religious institutions. With *believing* disjointed from *belonging*, it amounts to a 'portable' faith—one that a believer can keep in the inner life and take along in life, having little contact with a religious institution or ascribed group," Wade Clark Roof wrote in his study of religious faith among baby boomers.[42]

In Roof's survey, 53 percent of the subjects said their preferred mode of spiritual expression was to be alone and meditate, while only 29 percent said they preferred to worship with others. Among people who were disaffiliated from their childhood faiths, almost three out of four said they would rather be alone to pray.[43] If these figures are true for Jews, that's an ominous sign for syn-agogues, because community is the foundation of Jewish life and has been since the Israelites stood together at Mount Sinai. Of course, normative Judaism does accommodate private, meditative communication with God—but the people who aren't going to temple are also unlikely to be laying tefillin and chanting morning prayers.

One Northern California man said he quit going to High Holiday services in recent years because he was put off by the local rabbi's pulpit manner. "I started taking the day and heading out into nature, which I find a much more religious experience. . . . Do I want to, since we're not affiliated, spend a lot of money and hope that I'm gonna get into the mood, or do I go off somewhere, take some time and have kind of a meditative day, which is very much the point of it anyway?" Another man, living in the Southwest, said his life is too hectic to put much time into Jewish practice right now. "I have my own concept of religion, which is more or less inside me now, and it's my concept of prayer, and it's just something I've adopted and cultivated over twenty years of little tidbits of information and little bits of Jewish prayers."

Both men see the value of community—the California man says "spare time and energy, and kids who would behave" would get him back into synagogue life; the other credits having his butt dragged to the local JCC, where he was intensely involved for several years, with saving him from possible delinquency. "I think the time is gonna come where I'm gonna want to express it more," he said, "and I think a lot of that will be through my children. . . . I don't know how formal I'll want it to be; I'll have to see what the community has to offer." Under a system of pediatric Judaism, the presence of children in the home is the one variable that can get some individualistic Jews into synagogue life.

Religious privatism certainly feeds intermarriage. If your faith is strictly personal, it shouldn't matter whether you marry someone of a different religion, as long as you're ethically compatible. "That's why so many of them can make their peace with an interfaith marriage," says Constance Reiter, who leads workshops for interfaith couples. "Several of [the Jewish partners] said, 'I could never have married this girl if I believed that my Judaism was at stake, but I am so committed as a Jew that nothing is going to turn me away from that. And if she wants to do her Christian thing, that's fine, that doesn't affect my Jewish identity. . . . That's *my* identity; it isn't going to be our identity, and it isn't going to become a household thing."

But that's just the problem. Leaving aside the *cri de coeur* "But what about the children?", Judaism, by definition, *is* a household thing. Harry Danziger, senior rabbi of a large Reform congregation in Memphis, is willing to officiate at weddings involving Jews and non-Jews, but he makes sure to counsel each couple as to what it means to make a Jewish home.

> I teach them that in chemistry, the smallest particle that contains the traits of the whole is the molecule. In Christianity, the molecule is the individual person, who's in relationship to Jesus, [but] in Judaism, the molecule is the household. . . . While individuals are Jews, they are like a single atom of oxygen. . . . You can have a Jewish household in which there's a person who's not Jewish, but the molecule has to be the household.

The idea that your religious identity is private also makes it harder for a Jew to explain to a non-Jewish partner why he or she wants elements of Judaism in their household. Someone raised in a Christian denomination is likely to see religious practice as church-based, since that's where Christians express their connection to God, not through home ritual. The Gentile who doesn't believe anymore shows it by never going to church. Accordingly, the non-Jewish partner whose Jewish spouse never sets foot in a temple is thrown when that Jewish spouse insists on having a *brit milah* for their new son. Also, the various expressions of Christianity are based solely on belief, while being Jewish, of course, is as much a matter of peoplehood as faith. Even the disaffiliated Jew is likely to retain associational ties, however childish or nostalgic, to language, food, family, friends, and holidays.[44] Danziger said that the average intermarrying Jew, asked to explain to his partner what Jews *believe*, will within 30 seconds be telling the partner what Jews *do*. "It's because Jews don't learn theology; Jews tend not to be trained in the meaning of their religion," he said. "They just sort of know what their family does."

Unwilling to admit their shortcomings, *Tikkun* editor Michael Lerner says, Jewish institutions transfer the blame for Jewish decline to intermarrying Jews. Intermarriage "wouldn't be a problem if the people who were marrying or dating a non-Jew were themselves exposed to a Judaism that was spiritually nourishing, intellectually challenging, politically progressive, ethically alive," Lerner said in an interview.

> In that case, they would themselves feel that they wanted to bring their partner into that Jewishness.... The Jewish establishment cannot understand this because it is the problem. It itself has created the problem and then wants to project the problem onto individuals who are trying to search out and make some kind of life choice for themselves, and for whom their Jewishness isn't that important because the Jewishness they were exposed to didn't turn them on. [The leaders] want to blame the little 12-year-olds who got turned off and then grew up to be people who would be open to other people.

•   •   •

These are gloomy times for institutional Judaism. By a number of measures, Jews are less religious than other Americans. Ritual performance, synagogue membership, and religious school enrollment have dropped steeply among Jews, both intermarried and inmarried; religion in terms of both belief and ritual has become a minimal part of the lives of a wide swath of American Jewry.[45] If the baby boomers among them are like others in their age cohort, they are all too open (in the minds of Jewish leaders) to exploration of other faiths and all too comfortable combining Judaism with bits and pieces of other religions.[46] Communal structures have become so obsolete and affiliation so tenuous, one Stanford University professor reported, that an elite of no more than 25 percent of American Jews, many of them Orthodox, can be considered "serious" in their practice and in their commitment to the Jewish community.[47]

But there are rays of light poking through the clouds. Almost no one born into a Jewish family, almost no one raised as a Jew, no matter how estranged from active Jewish life, denies being a Jew as an adult. "Repudiators" are estimated at no more than 5 percent of the American Jewish population.[48] A Jew might decline a friend's invitation to go with him to shul, but he'll probably come to the friend's seder; ethnic ties and enjoyment of holidays remain strong. Four out of five Jews, after all, *do* believe in God. And while most Jews disengage from organized Judaism at some point in their lives, many, like other Americans, are likely to be looking for an institution-based source of spiritual fulfillment later on, when they become parents, or their own parents get sick, or they turn 40 and realize the Lexus and the corner office aren't enough.[49] The Jewish community's challenge is to be there with something they need when they come looking.

Demographer Steven Bayme says the knock on contemporary American Judaism as spiritually arid is a "legitimate criticism":

> The Jewish community has to take itself more seriously as a spiritual community. . . . The notion of Judaism as addressing the ultimate questions of the meaning of life and the meaning of death, of addressing where religion can play a role in our consciousness. . . . What we don't transmit is that this is an incredibly rich heritage that has much to say about personal ethics, about relationships, about personal meaning.

Disaffiliated Jews will not, most of them, come back to an organized Judaism that operates like the one they left at 13 or 15. They will not come back to a place where they don't feel welcomed, or where their partners don't feel welcomed. They need what they don't think they got as kids: a place that helps them shape a coherent concept of God; a place that gives them language to tell someone else why being Jewish is important; a place that accepts them *on their terms*, as exactly who they are. Most American Jewish institutions are not yet this place.

6

Don't Tell Us Who We Are

This is an amazingly complex thing. It's a thousand shades of gray. . . . We live in a fast, complex society where we want everything to be simplified. . . . We simplify it because we don't want to deal with the people. And if you don't want to deal with the people, the easiest thing is to have a system [that keeps them out].
 —Barry Kosmin, codirector, 1990 National Jewish Population Survey

There are three kinds of lies: lies, damned lies, and statistics.
 —Benjamin Disraeli

In 1948, Israeli philosopher Simon Rawidowicz published an essay, "Israel: The Ever-Dying People," in which he listed the many Jewish thinkers from the Talmudic period onward who were sure their generation of Jews was the last. "There was hardly a generation in the Diaspora period which did not consider itself the final link in Israel's chain," Rawidowicz wrote. Not only our tribulations at the hands of invading tribes and murderous tyrants, but our failure to live up to God's commandments, our inadequacies as passionate upholders of peoplehood and faith, have threatened our existence since our inception as a people. Accordingly, the Jews have considered themselves to be terminal for four thousand years.[1]

Intermarriage has been targeted as the latest virus eating away at the last shreds of flesh on the corpse of diaspora Judaism, making Jews who marry non-Jews the demographic equivalent of Typhoid Mary. Because intermarriers have become a convenient scapegoat, Jewish leaders have felt free to treat them as people have always dealt with scapegoated populations: characterizing them as identical in motive and behavior; castigating them regardless of whether they exhibit undesirable traits; and, in the modern age, using statistics to prove their inferiority. Just as many Gentiles through the centuries have been comfortable vilifying Jews as evil-minded, money-grubbing parasites, so have Jews become comfortable stereotyping those of us who choose to marry non-Jews as self-hating, antireligious destroyers of our people.

It has to stop.

The Numbers Can't Begin to Tell the Whole Story

At the junior high where I taught for nine years, every spring the ninth graders would gather on the P.E. field and have a group picture taken. Looking at this photograph of several hundred kids, you could sort them by race and sex and, by looking at the individual faces, could form some idea of who was happy that day, who was solemn, and who was bored. But if you didn't know the kids, you couldn't tell just by looking who was an A student and who was failing; who was a fourth-generation American and who had arrived from El Salvador the previous fall; who would give birth before eleventh grade and who was on her way to Stanford. The photo captured those kids, that day—it told you nothing about where they'd been or where they were headed.

The demographic studies of American Jewish populations over the past forty years, on which Jewish leaders have based so many fears and so much policy, are snapshots, each one of a given group of people at a given moment. Leaving aside the fact that the methodologies employed in some surveys can render such a snapshot too dark, too light, or hopelessly out of focus, even the best technology and the most expert photographer can't put more information into a picture than what meets the eye, let alone construct the past or predict the future. The compilers of the 1990 National Jewish Population Survey knew that: in the introduction to the *Highlights* booklet, they stressed that their data presented "a still frame photograph taken in the late Spring and Summer of 1990. . . . The evidence suggests that very little is fixed in the dynamic community formed by contemporary American Jews."[2] Yet rabbis and communal leaders have continued to use the figures of that survey and many others as if they had been revealed at Sinai.

Before subject-location techniques such as random-digit dialing became standard, population surveys depended on techniques that caused many Jews to be left out of the response pool. A number of local surveys, along with the 1970–71 National Jewish Population Study, employed a list called the Distinctive Jewish Names Index to help locate neighborhoods with high concentrations of Jews in which investigators could focus their resources. Such a focus made it likely that researchers would miss many Jews who lived in areas with sparse Jewish populations, as well as Jewish women who had married non-Jewish men. Some surveys based their samples on local mailing lists from Federation or other Jewish organizations, excluding Jews without communal ties. Some asked subjects to answer a lengthy series of questions (the average interview in the 1970–71 study was an hour and a half), which a disaffiliated Jew would be less likely to spend time on than someone active in the Jewish community. If anything, these factors make it likely that population surveys of a generation ago *undercounted* Jews married to non-Jews.[3]

Sociologists also have had a tendency to make large-scale pronouncements based on study of population samples that are not only skewed but are too small to be representative. The findings of the 1970–71 survey concerning intermarriage were based on a sample of 344 respondents; the scary intermarriage rate of almost 32 percent for the years 1966–71 was based on 83 cases.[4] Egon Mayer based the findings in his 1983 monograph *Children of Intermarriage*, in which he asserted that only about a quarter of the offspring of mixed marriages grew up to identify as Jews, on 117 subjects ages 16–46, which means their parents had married during a time that intermarriage was more likely to represent a rejection of Jewish identity on the part of the Jewish spouse and therefore less likely to result in a transmission of positive Jewish identity to children.[5] I must have come across half a dozen journal articles in which academics and rabbis confidently extrapolated general trends based on analyses of populations no larger or more representative than my own pool of case study informants.

A good example of a tiny local study that mushroomed into so-called proof that intermarriage is a death knell for Jewish identity is a Philadelphia survey published in 1984. Of 1,424 respondents, 63 were children of intermarried couples. Of those 63, 50 were not married, had no children, or were married to Jews and raising Jewish children. That left 13 children of intermarriage who were married to non-Jews *and* had kids. Of those 13, none identified their children as Jewish by religion. You know what that means, don't you? *When children of mixed couples, any place, at any time, marry non-Jews, they're guaranteed not to raise Jewish kids!*

Never mind that the question to these parents was not, "Are your children

Jewish?" but "What is your children's religion?" to which most answered, "None." Never mind that of those 13 households raising "non-Jewish" children, 6 said they celebrated Chanukah, 5 attended a seder the previous year, and 4 reported fasting on Yom Kippur. Never mind that this conclusion was based on a sample of *13 households*. In 1986, Israeli demographers U. O. Schmelz and Sergio DellaPergola cited the study in an article entitled "Basic Trends in American Jewish Demography." Three years later, Steven Bayme of the American Jewish Committee expanded the Philadelphia survey into multiple "studies" that showed "that in the absence of conversion, the grandchildren of intermarried couples simply cease to identify as Jews." In 1992, Jewish spokesperson Stuart Eizenstat cited this sample of 13 households as proof that a large segment of American Jewry was "bankrupt, dispirited, and alienated."[6]

As for the 1990 NJPS, many of its findings have been challenged, most publicly by demographer Steven Cohen, now at Hebrew University. Without denigrating the survey's value as "the richest, most comprehensive . . . research data set on American Jewry ever collected," Cohen asserted that the researchers who analyzed the data misclassified the religious identities of a significant number of respondents, their spouses, and their children. Instead of simply asking, "Are you Jewish? Is your spouse Jewish? Are your children Jewish?" the questions asked of the 2,441 respondents concerning their religion and that of their family members were more open-ended, giving respondents opportunity to give ambiguous answers. More than one in five said they had no religion or identified with a religion outside the Jewish-Protestant-Catholic matrix, although that group probably included a good number of nonreligious Jews, nor did the researchers ascertain the religious identities of the parents of most of the respondents.[7]

Other factors in the data analysis, Cohen said, inflated the rate of recent intermarriage to the 52 percent that gave the Jewish community a collective heart attack. Any respondent with one Jewish parent was counted as Jewish, even if raised in another religion, so when these people said they had married non-Jews, those relationships were counted as intermarriages. More than 20 percent of the recently married listed their spouses' religion as "other" or "none," which made it impossible to know whether they were married to born Jews or Gentiles. The researchers arbitrarily labeled almost all spouses with "other" religions as Gentiles and almost all the "nones" as Jews, Cohen said, although an "other" could have been a born-Jew-turned-New-Ager and a "none" could as easily have been a lapsed Catholic as a disaffiliated Jew. Cohen found a significant discrepancy between his identifications of the "others" and "nones" and those of the

NJPS team. Weighing these and other factors, Cohen came up with a recent intermarriage rate of closer to 40 percent—not good, but not a majority.[8]

The NJPS, Cohen said, also misrepresented the number of people who had left Judaism for another religion. The category "Jews by Choice," in which the NJPS researchers counted a total of 185,000 people, consisted, as one might expect, of people who were raised in a faith other than Judaism, rejected that faith, and embraced Judaism. But the NJPS definition of people who had "converted out" was much broader than the parallel "Jews by Choice": along with people who had been raised as Jews, rejected Judaism, and adopted another religion, the "converted out" category included thousands of Jews who had one Jewish parent and had been raised in the other parent's religion. In fact, almost two-thirds of the people listed as having converted out of Judaism had simply remained in the faith in which they were brought up. Cohen calculated the number of converts to Judaism as more than 50,000 higher than the NJPS figure and estimates that converts to Judaism outnumber converts out of Judaism by a three-to-one ratio. The misrepresentation was so egregious that the CJF staff now includes an errata sheet with the *Highlights* booklet.[9]

Other demographers have criticized the 1990 NJPS for its small sample, its failure to analyze more closely the religious practices of people who identify culturally but not religiously as Jews, its failure to ask questions about life-cycle events, its rigid adherence to fixed-choice, easily quantifiable questions, and its overly broad definition of who was Jewish enough to be included in the survey.[10] Steven Bayme agrees with Cohen that including the children of mixed couples, regardless of their actual upbringing, as Jews for purposes of the survey inflated the incidence of reported intermarriage. "They married out at rates of over 90 percent, because there were no constraints whatsoever. . . . If you look at children of two Jewish parents and see what their intermarriage rate is, it's less than 50 percent, meaning that there's still a Jewish communal preference for inmarriage. So therefore I would not read those statistics as absolute," Bayme said in an interview. Several sociologists have called for in-depth follow-up studies to the NJPS to explore the qualitative issues of Jewish life and for longitudinal studies that can follow people over a number of years to see how their relationship to Judaism and their requirements of Jewish institutions change over time.[11]

Statistics are enormously useful, often serving as a compass for the agencies and institutions that serve specific populations. But at bottom they always contain a political element; anyone can spin them to make a point, push an agenda, shut someone up. The danger for American Jewry is that too many Jewish leaders are using statistics to read all too many people out of Jewish life. Egon

Mayer, noting that there are 150,000 Americans (and counting) who are descendants of two generations of intermarriage *and* who consider themselves to be Jews, asks, "[W]hy the eagerness to write off possibly hundreds of thousands of people who may well think of themselves as Jewish or have the potential to do so? And why is this being done by the very people who claim to be so concerned about the quantity as well as the quality of the Jewish future?"[12]

In an article decrying the Jewish community's obsession with survivalism, Steven Cohen said he had a chance to speak with Elihu Bergman, the researcher who electrified Jewish leaders in the late 1970s by announcing that there could be as few as ten thousand Jews in America by 2076, and asked him why he hadn't been more scrupulous about presenting accurate statistics. "He said that getting the facts straight wasn't all that important," Cohen reported. "What was important was provoking Jews to sit up and take notice."[13]

An Unfair and Counterproductive Stereotype

At the time of my second marriage, I had been a member of a synagogue for more than four years, had edited the temple's monthly newsletter, was a member of the ritual committee, sang in the temple choir, and was completing my first year as vice-president. I attended Shabbat services at least twice a month, had taken a course on the biblical prophets, and had served numerous times as lay rabbi or lay cantor on Friday night. After I got married, I finished my term as vice-president, remaining on the temple's board of directors, served for a time on the temple's prayerbook revision committee, and learned the rudiments of Torah cantillation. In addition, my husband and I began to observe Shabbat, attended the biennial convention of the UAHC as delegates from our temple, and continued our tradition of gathering friends for a full-*haggadah* seder every Passover. I know lots of intermarried Jews who operate at the same level of involvement, but in the minds of many, it means nothing, because we married Gentiles.

"Several times a year we receive an invitation to the wedding of Lieberman and Kennedy, Goldberg and MacIntyre. We feel that knot in the stomach— another Jew lost," writes *Moment* magazine's managing editor. Another pundit pronounces, "If Judaism is important, no arguments against intermarriage are necessary. If Judaism isn't important, no arguments against intermarriage are effective." From historian Ruth Wisse: "Any Jew who lives a meaningful Jewish life will not marry a non-Jew because he would no longer be able to live a meaningful Jewish life." And my personal favorite, from a Conservative rabbi in

Southern California, "The only cogent barrier to intermarriage is the conviction that it is an abdication of the will of God, an abandonment of our central purpose as Jews."[14]

Interesting—I always thought our central purpose as Jews was to study, worship, and perform acts of lovingkindness. And let's leave aside the logical idea that if you believe things happen because of the will of God, then perhaps it was God's will that we intermarriers met and married our spouses. I got Rabbi Abandonment of Central Purpose on the phone, and toward the end of a long interview asked him whether he really thought I abandoned my central purpose as a Jew when I got married. He sighed. "I'm saying you're going to need to work extra hard to get back to it." When I told him I never left it, he changed the subject.

"I suggest that we add one more stereotype to the list of those we must exorcise—that of the self-hating, confused Jew who has betrayed her or his people by intermarrying," an irate reader wrote to *Tikkun*:

> When I hear people . . . explain the twisted reasons why Jews marry gentiles, I feel that I am being called names. . . . People like me would like to participate in the activities of our Jewish communities. We would like to take our spouses and children with us. But the promulgation of these stereotypes about Jews who intermarry . . . often forces us to stay clear of Jewish organizations.
>
> Perhaps the vast majority of the Jewish community would prefer that Jews like me who have intermarried take our tainted families and keep out of the Jewish world. . . . The Jewish community, whose survival is of such great concern to many, will have a much brighter future if it could only learn to support all the Jewish families who would like to feel welcome within it.[15]

Look at the vicious circle described here: The people who stereotype intermarriers as willfully alienated from Jewish life create a climate of unwelcome in Jewish institutions, and, understandably, many intermarried Jews and their families stay away—allowing their antagonists to point to their lack of involvement.

Another consistent charge is that intermarried Jews cannot make truly Jewish homes and raise unambiguously Jewish-identified kids. The reasons they give are legion, ranging from the halachic through the sociological to the psychological, and are well covered in the literature.[16] Moreover, the recent statistics on this subject, which are somewhat more comprehensive and convincing than those on intermarriage in general, are hard to counter.

But I fail to see the value of a black-and-white, two-Jewish-partners-or-forget-it attitude, especially when it involves gross exaggeration or even untruth. A woman who runs a matchmaking service in which parents of Jewish singles list their children told a reporter that one of the reasons she started her business is that "the numbers show that children of mixed marriages *invariably* receive no Jewish education [emphasis mine]."[17] Come on, lady! Even the NJPS said 28 percent of mixed couples were raising their kids as Jews. I don't see the purpose it serves to tell an intermarrying couple that any efforts they'll make to instill Jewish identity in their children are futile. "How can I be expected to embrace a religion when its leaders say my marriage and my family contribute to a bloodless holocaust?" asked a Jewish woman who married a Catholic man in rural New England. "I'm a Jew. My children are Jews. And that kind of attack is inexcusable."[18]

The pundits who label intermarried Jews as uniformly uncaring and antireligious often mistake lack of knowledge or difficulty in articulating feelings about Judaism for alienation and lack of commitment. "There's a range . . . that always fascinates me, because there's no relationship between how much people want a Jewish family and what they do in their life," says Arlene Chernow, the UAHC's outreach director for Southern California and the Southwest. "I can't tell you how many people say to me, 'Can you explain it to me? Can you help me understand? . . . I can't walk away from this; it's important to me, but I don't know what it is.' Very, very deep attachment to Judaism with very little practice and very little knowledge."[19]

Some Jews may have perfectly strong ties to Jewish life but not such healthy self-esteem. They worry, however prematurely, that if they hold out for the right Jewish man or woman, they'll be out in the cold. "Someone said, no one ever sets out to marry a non-Jew," says Dennis Ross, rabbi for a Reform congregation in Pittsfield, Massachusetts, citing a report he heard claiming that 90 percent of people born Jewish say they want to marry another Jew. "Sometimes these kids are so worried that time is running out and they want to get settled and they want to get on with their lives and be married . . . they'll marry the first decent person who walks through the door." Others have absolutely no agenda at all. "I'm meeting Jewish people of every possible Jewish background . . . their parents care, they care, it's not like they hate being Jewish or don't want to talk about it or hate Jewish people or Jewish women. For many of them, it was a real surprise that this is what they ended up doing," says the UAHC's New York outreach director, Ellyn Geller.

Although it's true that many Jews don't bring religious commitment or even a strong sense of ethnic heritage into mixed marriages, the very fact that intermarriage is on the rise even among Jews with solid Jewish backgrounds means that when these strongly and positively identified Jews marry non-Jews, the Jewish community is going to have more mixed couples living Jewish lives. "As mixed marriage becomes more prevalent ... more Jewish Jews are going into mixed marriages," Steven Cohen said in an interview. "So long as more and more observant parents have kids marrying non-Jews ... it'll turn out that those kids will in turn be more committed to being Jewish."

Such couples are already present in growing numbers in American synagogues. "Someone who comes in with a strong identity ... gives a message in their marriage that this is a value that they really want to be essential in their marriage," Michael White, a rabbi at a large Los Angeles synagogue, said at a UAHC regional conclave. "I've seen couples who are intermarried where one partner feels very strongly about being Jewish ... It infuses the whole relationship with, 'This is important; our children will learn about Judaism, and we will honor that by participating with them.'" Another rabbi who occasionally officiates at weddings for mixed couples says she can spot from the first meeting which couples are committed to making Jewish homes. One clue, she says, is that they have already established Jewish ritual and holiday celebrations as part of their relationship. Two different Conservative rabbis, while declaiming loudly and at length that committed Jews are the least likely to intermarry, conceded that there are committed Jews who marry non-Jews and make Jewish homes; both have such families in their synagogues.

Many American Jews are tired of "the language of reproach, evaluation, and ultimately accusation" that they hear from rabbis and fundraisers, Steven Cohen says. They don't like being scolded for being bad Jews.[20] Carla remembers how angry she was when the Reform temple her parents had belonged to for twenty years wouldn't let them use the social hall for her wedding, a battle that went to the temple's board of directors. "I was pissed off because I felt that what the rabbi was basically saying, what the board was saying, what the community was saying, was that if you marry this guy, you can't be here anymore, you've left us. And I thought that was terribly unfair, because we had said very clearly that the children would be Jewish," she said. Carla saw the situation as especially unjust because her fiancé was a Parsi from Bombay who had no religious commitment of his own. "It's not like I [was] marrying a Christian. In fact, I don't know if I could have married a Christian. I felt very strongly that what I was doing wasn't going to impede being Jewish."

Jeri, who grew up in Conservative synagogues and had leadership roles in Jewish organizations during high school and college, recalls the cold shoulder she received when she and her Catholic husband settled where they live now.

I made it well known that I was Jewish. I joined the JCC, I got involved in the parenting center, I joined Hadassah … because I have always affiliated myself with the Jewish community. The other Jewish couples that came when I came were given free temple memberships and free JCC memberships. . . . I was offered nothing. . . . If I weren't so involved with the Jewish community, I probably wouldn't notice. But I am.

Jeri and her family were welcomed by the local Reform temple, but a new rabbi has made for a cooler climate. "I think if you ask him, he would say no, he has no prejudice against interfaith marriages, but in fact he does," Jeri said. "Any time there's a problem with a child or preparation for bar mitzvah, confirmation, whatever, he blames it on the fact that the one parent is not Jewish."

Jeri doesn't understand why organized Judaism seemed to go out of its way to make things hard for her, her husband (a regular temple-goer), and their three kids (two bar mitzvahs and one in the pipeline). "Had my commitment to Judaism not been so strong . . . to this day I wonder why I bothered to stay with it. At every turn in the road in our married life, it seems like Judaism has tried to make it more difficult."

I don't get it either. How did trying to alienate a committed Jew serve the Jewish community? What did it accomplish?

Needed: A New Taxonomy for Intermarried Couples

The 1990 NJPS made it easy—too easy—to type how mixed couples were raising their kids: 28 percent were raising them as Jews; 31 percent were raising them without religion; and 41 percent were raising them in a religion other than Judaism. In the wake of the survey's release, the media, and many Jewish leaders, made it sound like every kid in the 41 percent was being marched to church every Sunday, returning home to a house devoid of Jewish ritual objects, and eating a big Honeybaked dinner seated under a picture of you-know-who. Such a characterization completely misrepresents the actual composition of the "other religion" households.

Look at the description in the *Highlights* booklet: "The 'other religion' category includes children being raised as Protestants or Catholics as well as combinations of various types of religions, *including syncretic Judaism* [emphasis mine]."[21] Syncretic Judaism is Judaism plus something else, which means that 41 percent includes not only households in which children are given religious education as Christians but households in which children learn the doctrine and celebrate the holidays of both Judaism and Christianity, households in which the family makes a pass at observing a couple of major holidays in each faith, and households in which children become bar and bat mitzvah and the only way you know there's a Gentile in the house is the presence of a Christmas tree every December.[22]

Because the NJPS "other" and "none" categories are so amorphous, I would like to propose a new taxonomy for classifying households headed by a Jewish/non-Jewish couple.

- *Jewish-only.* These families operate as if both partners were Jewish, observing only Jewish holidays and raising their children unambiguously as Jews.

- *Jewish-dominant.* The partners agree that it is best to raise the children as Jews and work toward that end, although the non-Jewish partner may retain contact with his or her birth religion.

- *True dual-identity.* Both partners have a sincere commitment to their faiths *as religions* and are willing to put in the time and effort to teach their children about both traditions.

- *Dual-minimal.* The watered-down version of true-dual. These families celebrate the major holidays of both religions but generally give their children little input on either.

- *Christian-dominant.* The Jewish partner bows to the Christian partner's more intense religious commitment but maintains some cultural observances.

- *Systematic secular.* The partners choose to teach their children ethical values in a nondenominational or nonreligious context, possibly through a philosophical system such as Unitarianism.[23]

- *Christian-only.* The Jewish partner does not distract the religious orientation of the household from Christianity with any Jewish observances.

It's impossible to say exactly how much of the mixed-married population is contained in each of these categories. Recent hard data suggest that the Jewish community can count on about a third of current intermarried households being unambiguously Jewish in character, enough to send the children raised in those households into adulthood with a strong sense of their own Jewishness.[24] Several of the other categories are very small; for example, systematic secularism takes as much time and commitment as raising children conscientiously in the religion of one parent or the other, and in most families, at least one parent has an emotional attachment to a childhood faith.[25] The true-duals comprise a tiny fraction of the whole as well, because what they're trying to do is very hard to pull off successfully.[26]

The Christian-dominant category is also small, and the Christian-only group, which used to include a lot of Jewish women who allowed their identities to be subsumed in marriages to Gentile men, is miniscule and fading fast, because these days, even disaffiliated Jews balk at the idea of raising their children in church, let alone convert to Christianity themselves.[27] "I'd want [a child of mine] to be raised as a Jewish child simply because I don't know that I could identify with a kid who was anything else," a 34-year-old New Jersey woman said. "I mean if some kid in my house was walking around telling me that Jesus did all kinds of wonderful things, and Jesus was the Savior, I don't think I could relate." A man in his twenties who grew up on the fringes of Jewish life surprised himself when Jewish feelings surged forth after he and a more devout Catholic girl-friend began talking marriage. "I got very confused . . . because if it really meant nothing to me, I could have converted and I probably would have been married by now. But . . . there was something there that said no, that's not right."

That leaves the Jewish-dominant group and the dual-minimals as sizable pluralities among intermarried households. The best-case-scenario Jewish-dominant families are those in which the non-Jewish partner is active and involved with Jewish life, with the only manifestation of a Gentile in the house the presence of a Christmas tree in December. To be sure, not all Jewish-dominant households are that committed; some have that character only because the non-Jewish partners are uninterested in religion. In fact, some Gentile partners don't participate in Jewish life on the grounds that all religion is nonsense, an attitude that can easily make its way to their children. Another widely documented situation involves a non-Jewish wife, willing but untutored, assigned sole responsibility for making a Jewish home by an insensitive Jewish husband. Rabbis often point to the chaos created when a mixed couple breaks up and the non-Jewish parent retains custody of the children. No matter how conscientious the Gentile partner has been in raising the kids as Jews, they say, without the presence of the Jewish spouse, that partner may be too upset, angry, or overwhelmed to maintain Jewish rituals and affiliations, and if the Gentile partner retains any connection with another religion, he or she may switch the children to that faith.

However, most mixed couples who make the commitment to raise Jewish kids stick to it, if not as conscientiously or completely as some would like. When

rabbis and social scientists are made uncomfortable by families that call themselves Jewish but haven't made unadulterated Jewish choices, they miss the fact
that these couples felt it was important to negotiate how they're going to conduct their religious lives and raise their children. "There are a lot of people like
that," says Rabbi Rachel Hertzman, outreach director for the UAHC's South-
east region.

> They had to communicate and they had to work it out, and they had to be happy
> with their compromise. . . . A lot of times we see them . . . later, when, because
> they're so into Jewish life, one of them chooses to convert. . . . And then, of
> course, there are also those who just live within the dual-identity kind of situa-
> tion, but many of those do raise Jewish kids, even within the dual identity.

A frequent comment of intermarried Jews is that marrying Gentiles made
them become more involved with Judaism than they would have been with Jewish spouses because their partners' questions and interest made them quit taking
Judaism for granted and learn more about it.[28]

In fact, when one of the Jewish choices a mixed couple makes is to affiliate
with a synagogue, it's likely that half the battle is won right there. "Households
that are members of congregations, whether mixed married or in-married, may
be much more similar to each other (and much more Jewishly identified) than
they are to Jews who are religiously unaffiliated," one communal leader wrote.

> In fact, the division in American Jewish life between mixed married and in-married
> Jews may be less important than the division between religiously affiliated and
> religiously unaffiliated Jews. Affiliated, mixed-married households have made a
> commitment to Jewish life. Though the intensity of this commitment may vary,
> the act of affiliation itself provides an opportunity for the congregation and the
> community to deepen the household's involvement and encourage conversion.[29]

"I come from an intermarriage; my dad's not Jewish," a 17-year-old camper
at UAHC's Camp Swig told me.

> My mom said from the very beginning: We're gonna raise our kids Jewish, that's
> the way it is, deal with it. And he was like, "Okay." We have a very Jewish house-
> hold. . . . My dad is incredibly involved. He's very supportive. He helped build
> the sukkah for the synagogue. He helps put on the carnivals that Sisterhood puts
> on, he goes to the congregational meeting even though he doesn't get to vote. He

goes to Friday night services when I do. He's always there. I have a very Jewish household, and I don't see us as being a detriment to the Jewish population in America.

The dual-minimals—the couples Harold Schulweis calls the "interfaith-less"—pose the biggest problem for Jewish continuity, in part because of their numbers; they may be the single largest constituency among the intermarried. They, too, represent a range of religious lifestyles. Some, not ready to sever religious ties completely, depend on their parents to provide the religious backdrop for their children's lives, so they go to Nana Sylvia and Grampa Maury for seder and to Grandma Kate for Christmas. Many, with the best of intentions, talk the true-dual talk, but life and their own ignorance get in the way: The Jewish parents have neither the language to explain how their God is different from Jesus nor the skills to make Shabbat; the non-Jewish parents, unaccustomed to going to church, would much rather lounge with the newspaper Sunday morning than take less than enthusiastic children to services. Each parent is unable, by and large, to answer children's questions about the other parent's faith, and neither understands when their 16 year old announces that all religion is stupid or when the same kid, at 20, is taken up by a cult.[30]

Many dual-minimals who profess common values and world views cannot understand that the religions to which they feel a vestigial but real allegiance have doctrinal differences that cannot be reconciled. Christians, who find little if anything to quarrel with in Jewish theology, liturgy, or ritual, often don't understand why their Jewish partners can't show equal "tolerance." Especially in this era of privatized faith, they don't see how their holidays and life-affirming beliefs could threaten anyone. But they are threatening; Christianity is more pervasive than Judaism in our society, Jesus more concrete than an abstract God, Christmas more seductive than Chanukah. Households in which each partner demands a small amount of "equal time" are unlikely to produce children with strong identities as Jews.[31]

So the time bombs explode. The wedding plans cause endless wrangling. The non-Jewish husband announces, a week before his wife's due date, that he thinks ritual circumcision is barbaric. The first grader asks his Sunday school teacher who made him, the Christian God or the Jewish God? The 15-year-old girl lies in bed at night wondering how she can choose one religion without being disloyal to the other parent. The 30-year-old man, told throughout his childhood and adolescence that his religion was his choice, announces to his widowed mother that he's making a formal conversion to Judaism and is stunned when she explodes in rage.[32] The potential for time bombs exists within other types of marriages between Jews and non-Jews; religious reawakening can occur at any time and disrupt a previously negotiated arrangement. There are no guarantees that a non-Jewish partner, facing the death of a parent or the birth of a first child, won't look to his or her early faith community for answers. The dangers are greatest, however, for the dual-minimals, who don't make the effort to negotiate the religious character of their households. Most of their children will be lost to Jewish life, not so much because they choose to become Christians but because they choose to live without an organized faith.

The American Jewish community has an internal problem much bigger than what to do with religiously minimalist mixed couples, though: the fact that the tensions over religion residing in many intermarried families can be found in households where everyone is Jewish. Plenty of Jews married to Jews won't go to temple with their spouses. Plenty of Jews married to Jews tell their kids that religion is a crock. Plenty of Jews married to Jews "can't distinguish a menorah from a matzah," as one intermarried woman put it.[33] Plenty of marriages between two Jews are rocked when one partner becomes more observant, stunning the spouse who was perfectly happy with a little spasm of Jewish activity a few times a year. Some endogamous Jewish couples couldn't care less if their kids turn out to be Jews, Buddhists, or Lutherans, as long as they stay away from drugs and finish law school. We don't hear as much about these tensions, because if Jewish leaders were to look at the problems within all-Jewish households that endanger Jewish continuity, they wouldn't be able to spend as much time blaming intermarriers for the decline in American Jewish numbers.[34]

When her Catholic sister-in-law was pregnant, one Jewish woman said, she offered to convert to Judaism:

> She had the attitude, "I'm a religious person, but it doesn't matter to me what religion I'm religious in. . . . I'd be happy to be Jewish." And my brother just shrugged his shoulders and said, "Why would you want to do that?" . . . Why? Because my brother is not Jewish! I mean he's born of two Jewish parents, he's 100 percent genetically Jewish, but . . . Judaism is not at all part of his life. . . . So his wife said, "Gee, I'd be happy to convert, but if you don't want me to," [and] she baptized the baby, because she wanted to be in a religious family, and if he didn't care about it being a Jewish family, well, then, she would just stick with the religion she had.
>
> It's the Jews who are "lost to the faith" long before they ever intermarry, or even if they don't intermarry. If my brother had married someone who was Jewish in

the same way he is, their kids wouldn't have been raised Jewish, they wouldn't have necessarily had a Jewish family. It's just too easy to point toward intermarriage as a cause of all of this.

A Christmas Tree Does Not a Christian Make

Personally, I have never been threatened by the annual pervasiveness of Christmas in our society. I see it as a largely secular phenomenon, the music and decorations of which I can enjoy without the hassle and guilt some of the non-Jews in my life have to go through every year. By the same token, I have never had a problem with Christmas trees, historically a pagan symbol of the winter solstice.[35] When I have lived alone or with another Jew or Jews, I have not had a Christmas tree. Whenever I have lived with non-Jews, I have lived with a Christmas tree for two weeks of the year, a tree decorated with shiny balls, twinkling lights, strings of gold stars, and other more idiosyncratic but definitely non-Christological items: no Santa, no angels, no nativity scene. The presence of a Christmas tree in my home has always been a minor accommodation to a roommate or partner who grew up with one; it does not have the power to make me feel less Jewish.

Now I'm well aware that many Jews, along with many Christians, do view the Christmas tree as a religious symbol; to them, it has the same impact as a crèche or a cross.[36] Plenty of my intermarried informants have required their partners to do without a tree, and plenty of the singles can't feature having one, even if they marry Gentiles. "I'm really not a fan of Christianity, to put it politely," a 34-year-old Jewish man said. "It would just churn my guts to have a Christmas tree in the house." I respect their views. I've had friends I didn't invite over at Christmastime because I knew the tree bothered them. To me, it's a live-and-let-live kind of issue.

Unfortunately, the Jewish establishment doesn't see it that way. To many Jewish leaders and most Jewish demographers, the Christmas tree is the overriding symbol of religious Christianity, the one and only object that defines a dual-identity family. In every demographic survey, a question about the tree is the only one that determines the "Christian culture" of an intermarried household. This practice reaches the height of absurdity in the American Jewish Committee's 1992 report compiled by demographers at Brandeis's Cohen Center, *Jewish Identity in Conversionary and Mixed Marriages*, which refers to multiple "Christian symbols and practices" as indicative of ambiguous Jewish identity when in fact it measured only one: the tree.

Although the researchers acknowledged that the single question of the tree "does not indicate whether it is an isolated practice or the tip of the iceberg— part of a more extensive incorporation of Christian symbols and values into the home," they felt comfortable using that one question to divide the population of mixed and conversionary households into "single-identity" and "dual-identity" categories. Since they found that 22 percent of the conversionary families in their sample put up Christmas trees, they characterized all those households as dual-identity, ignoring the illogic of such a label for a family in which both partners, after all, are Jewish. Even conversionary households with "high Jewish identification" (based on a rather arbitrary index of Jewish behaviors) that continued to display the tree were deficient: "The value and identity transformation is still not fully achieved, since Christian *symbols* [note the plural] show themselves."[37]

The ethnocentric arrogance of such a characterization is mind-boggling. No shades of gray here: no allowance made for the idea that the tree may be the one vestigial accommodation to the inner child of a partner not born Jewish, or that the born-Jewish partner may have grown up with a tree, too, or that the born-Jewish partner may be using the other's non-Jewishness as an excuse to have the tree he or she was denied as a child; no inquiry among the mixed-married into truly Christian symbols, like a cross around the neck or on the wall, or blatantly Christian practices, such as church attendance.[38] To the Cohen Center researchers, it's very simple: If you put up a Christmas tree, there's a self-identifying Christian in the house.

I also noticed that the researchers did not characterize *inmarried* Jewish households with Christmas trees as "dual-identity." Most Jewish leaders conveniently forget that there are some families headed by two born-Jewish partners that have Christmas trees—not as many as there used to be, but enough to show up on the charts. Lots of third-generation Jews who were raised in mixed suburbs by assimilationist parents grew up with trees. "It's pretty rough on the children when you live in a non-Jewish neighborhood and everyone has a big tree and presents but you," said one of the late-1960s moms in *The Jewish Wife*. "We don't make too much of Christmas, but there is no reason why we should skip it and make it a big problem."[39] Leslie Epstein, who writes novels on Jewish subjects, said, "We always had a Christmas tree. Christmas is a fabulous thing for kids; I remember presents piled up under the tree. I'm not going to take something so beautiful away from them."[40] While the Cohen Center researchers reported that only 2 percent of the inmarried couples in their surveys said they put up Christmas trees, contemporaneous studies count 10–18 percent of inmarried Jewish couples doing so.[41]

The Christmas tree in Jewish homes makes Jewish leaders nervous for a number of reasons, generally pertaining more to the decline of Jewish particularism than to encroaching Christianity. "Christmas is a wonderful national holiday which Americans love, children love," says Steven Bayme. "By having the Christmas tree, [Jews] are not saying that they believe that Christ was born on this day. . . . It's a statement about the inclusiveness of America that almost anyone can feel comfortable with Christmas. But the reality is that Christmas is a disaster in terms of Jewish identity, that that home celebrating Christmas is also making a statement that the Jewishness simply isn't powerful enough," Bayme says. "As Jews have become so comfortable with the Christian ethos, even when it's not terribly Christian, such as a seasonal tree, then are they still able to define what specifically is the content of Jewishness that makes it distinctive?"

Not having a tree, Hebrew Union College demographer Bruce Phillips says, is one of the ways you get across to Jewish kids that we're a particular people: "When Jewish kids don't have a Christmas tree, it's like a real strong physical reminder that they're different. It has no religious content whatsoever, it's just saying, 'You don't have this because you're different from them.'" At the same time, Phillips acknowledged in a UCLA lecture, the Jews who allow their non-Jewish spouses to put up trees don't always see the tree the way demographers and rabbis do. "We tend to equate the Christmas tree with assimilation," Phillips said, but in his research, "it became apparent that for intermarried couples, a Christmas tree symbolizes family. As one person said, 'You know, it's a Jewish household 364 days a year, and on one day of the year we have something of mine,' and it just happens to be the most alarming symbol to all other Jews."

"I don't consider [the tree] to be necessarily an indication that it's a dual-faith family," said David Fass, senior rabbi of a large Reform congregation outside New York City. "I've got 50 families minimum in the temple who are married this way." "The Christmas tree is a really bad criterion [for dual identity]," Rachel Hertzman said. "It has nothing to do with the way the people live their religious lives throughout the year." In one household, the annual appearance of a tree has not kept one Jewish woman's older son from putting a mezuzah on his bedroom doorpost and laying tefillin.[42]

Are you really telling me, I asked Cohen Center director Gary Tobin in 1992, that the Christmas tree that sits on our dining table two weeks out of the year means my husband and I don't have a Jewish household? "It's less than unambiguous," Tobin said, "because it's still linked to cultural, familial, and religious behaviors around that holiday." But without knowing the cultural, familial, and religious behaviors of every mixed and conversionary family that puts up a tree, how can anybody make that judgment?

In many homes, with Jews and without, a Christmas tree is simply a seasonal decoration. It is not an appropriate seasonal decoration for a synagogue, nor should a Jewish parent put one up just because the kids whine for one. But the tree does not necessarily symbolize Christianity. Jesus was not nailed to a Christmas tree. The Crusaders didn't march into battle behind Christmas trees. I'll be persuaded that the tree is a universal Christian symbol when I see Gentiles wearing them around their necks. Until then, I wish people would stop using it as an reason to read mixed families out of Judaism.

A Smaller but More Cohesive American Jewish Community

So whose children are going to be Jewish? How many Jews are there going to be twenty, fifty, a hundred years from now? Can at least 50 percent of America's Jewish-Gentile families produce offspring who identify as Jews and conduct themselves as Jews throughout their adult lives? Nobody knows, really. On paper, the 50 percent mark seems attainable, depending on how large the Jewish-dominant category is and who trickles in from the other groups. In reality, when you consider how disaffiliated so many of the Jews are who are raising children with non-Jewish partners and how badly many Jewish institutions are serving their constituents, the outlook is less rosy.

The model of American Jewry that seems to be taking hold as we head into the next century seems to involve a firm core of committed Jews surrounded by a wide, mushy ring of Jews who are more and more alienated from Jewish life the further you get from the core. Think of a matzo ball in a big plate of chicken soup. The matzo ball is the American Jewish community, and the soup is American society. The middle of the matzo ball is dense and chewy; you'd really have to attack it to cut it apart. The outside of the matzo ball is fluffy—too fluffy. Little bits keep breaking off and floating into the soup. The question becomes, how big and how firm is our matzo ball?

Steven Cohen, who a few years ago didn't see a problem maintaining a majority of children of intermarriage who identify themselves as Jewish, has more recently come around to a more down-to-earth position, saying that many grandchildren of today's intermarried Jews will wash out of Jewish life but that the core of committed Jews may be growing. Younger adults are no less ritually active than their elders, and the ones who aren't intermarried are more likely to be providing their kids with a meaningful Jewish education and intensive Jewish experiences. Jewish studies programs on college campuses are booming, denoting an interest in Jewish knowledge among young adults. So, Cohen says, although many Jews may have to live with the pain of seeing their grandchildren lost to Jewish life, and the American Jewish population may be pared down a bit, "the future of American Jews is not imperiled, but challenged."[43]

To other demographers, the matzo ball may get spongier, but it won't shrink. "It's clearly going be a much more diverse community and it'll be a paradoxical community, because at least at this point, based on the data from the NJPS, people who presumably should assimilate altogether maintain at least some kind of Jewish links," Bruce Phillips told his UCLA audience.

> Whereas [among] Jews by religion, a large proportion will say, yes, being Jewish is very important to me, a huge chunk of [more secular Jews] say, yeah, being Jewish is at least somewhat important to me. So we are going to be a much more diverse community, with people who some of us might wish to go away, but I think will not be going away, and will remain sort of moving in and out of the community and in a funny way in dialogue with us, with the core Jewish community.[44]

Steven Bayme, on the other hand, thinks the matzo ball is going to dissolve into the soup.

> When you have a Jewish community whose boundary lines are so blurred, it's next to impossible to come up with anything distinctively Jewish. . . . For a minority to survive in a democratic majority culture, that minority has to find ways in which it sharply distinguishes itself from the majority culture. When the Jews look like everyone else, then you can't expect Jewish identity to be sustaining.[45]

However, others believe that even a much-shrunken Jewish population can be vibrant enough to carry the Jewish community forward. "Essentially, we are on the edge of systemic collapse," educator Joel Lurie Grishaver said in an interview:

> I believe very sincerely that Jewishly, the age of the Road Warrior is coming. . . . The national movements are going to fall of their own weight. . . . There's no second generation of leadership. In a universe where young leadership is 45, things are scary. I think in ten or fifteen years, when all this stuff falls and collapses and the dust is left to settle . . . it's gonna be the seven years of skinny cows that we haven't set aside any grain for, [and] what's gonna be left are small, practicing communities.

But, Grishaver says, that's not the end of the American Jewish world. "The shtetl [was] never more than 10 percent of the Jewish population," he says. "When the creators of the Talmud were running around doing their shtick, most Jews were busy pulling their circumcisions down so they could go to the gymnasium. Judaism has always been sustained actively and really by a core of 8–10 percent." Is that enough to sustain American Jewry? "It was a hundred years ago. It was fifty years ago."

Jewish Women and the Dynamics of Intermarriage

The conventional wisdom about Jewish women who marry non-Jewish men has generally been that (a) they're vastly outnumbered by Jewish men marrying non-Jewish women, (b) they're running away from Judaism and therefore not interested in making a Jewish home and raising Jewish children, and (c) even if they want to make a Jewish home and raise Jewish children, they can't, trapped as they are under the thumb of the brutish Gentile oppressor. Clearly, it's time for a reality check.

Although Jewish men probably did intermarry at a higher rate than Jewish women until the mid-1980s, the 1990 NJPS has established that Jewish men and women are now roughly at parity, and, as mentioned earlier, there is evidence that Jewish women married to non-Jewish men may have been grossly undercounted in years past. The idea that intermarried Jewish women were uniformly disaffiliated from Judaism comes mostly from a study conducted in Washington, D.C., a highly assimilationist community, in 1956 and published in 1963, which found that only 13.6 percent of mixed couples in which the wife was Jewish were raising their children as Jews, an even lower proportion than couples in which the husband was Jewish. These numbers were still being quoted as a cautionary finding in articles published during the *mid-1970s*, twenty years after the survey was taken.[46]

By the early 1970s, outmarriage for Jewish women was no longer deviant behavior, and they were marrying non-Jews, if not at the same rate as Jewish men, for pretty much the same reasons: they were meeting non-Jews in school and at work; they didn't find Jews particularly attractive; they were disenchanted with organized Judaism's materialism and lack of spirituality. But they weren't breaking the chain: the 1971 National Jewish Population Study makes it clear that Jewish women who intermarried had every intention of raising Jewish children. In an early-1980s survey done in New York, Steven Cohen found three out of four couples composed of a Jewish wife and a Gentile husband raising or planning to raise their children as Jews, with one in three reporting Jewish child rearing when the husband was Jewish and the wife Gentile. A 1986 study of college freshmen found that students with a Jewish mother and a non-Jewish father were more than twice as likely to identify as Jews than were students with a Jewish father and a Gentile mother.[47] In my own anecdotal research, out of the hundred-plus informants I met through correspondence and/or interviews, only one woman raised Jewish, married in 1970, severed all ties with Jewish life to raise her children completely in another faith.

Feminism, which has taken a lot of shots from folks who say uppity Jewish women have chased away Jewish men, may in fact be one of the societal trends that helps preserve the saving remnant. Columnist Marlene Marks says she doesn't worry about the dire predictions in the 1990 NJPS when she sees how individual Jewish women are embracing Jewish ritual and study. "[P]erhaps the time for worry was 30 years ago, when studious young Jewish girls of my generation were told that their bat mitzvahs were ceremonially meaningless or ridiculous, and not to bother," Marks writes. "But no one worried then that such angry young girls would become angry young women, who might turn off, marry non-Jews and then find it hard to feign enthusiasm when passing on a heritage to their own children."[48]

"I actually think that Jewish feminism works against intermarriage, because Jewish feminism works to make women feel more heavily involved with Jewish life," Sylvia Barack Fishman says:

> Because of Jewish feminism, Jewish women now get Jewish education in equal numbers with Jewish men. This was not true of the children of the seventies. They have a much more active role in the synagogue, they feel more personally invested, it's a religion that they feel belongs to them, it's not a private men's club.
>
> And my guess is that women like that are also going to take a more activist role in terms of making sure that they have Jewish households. Even in the context of intermarriage, I think that they will be more willing to insist that children be raised as Jews and to advocate for conversion. I think that they feel more pride in themselves as Jews, that they're much less likely to have the phenomenon of feeling lucky that somebody wanted them, which I think used to happen a lot with Jewish women because of the negative picture of Jewish women in the media. I think that Jewish feminist activity really gives them a sense of pride in self.

This is one area in which the Americanization of Judaism benefits Jewish continuity. In this country, women are the engine of religion in the home, and as male dominance loosens its grip on Judaism, more and more Jewish women are bringing not only commitment to but knowledge of Judaism to their marriages.[49]

And there is evidence from people in the field that many Jewish women actually bring a different emotional dynamic to a mixed marriage than a lot of Jewish men do. "I think that their motives are different," says Los Angeles educator Janice Alper. "I think men's motivation is really almost a rebellious kind of thing underneath, you know, I love my mother but I don't want to marry someone like her. The women, I think, feel okay in their identity and feel that they can overcome any obstacle because they're strong in their identity. I don't think Jewish women go out and look for non-Jewish men; I think it happens."

Outreach counselor Meryl Nadell adds that the Jewish women who come to her

feel it very important to continue their Jewish heritage despite the fact that they've intermarried. It might have been latent at the time of their marriage, or it might have been set aside . . . or [they] underestimated the intensity of their feelings about Judaism. . . . I've seen women who had really wanted to marry Jewish, but they had other demands, and some of them were pained by setting aside their religious requirement, but the reality of wanting to couple and falling in love with someone, they're the ones who are really working very hard to try and make it work.

These are the "reluctant exogamists" whose presence was first brought to light in the late 1970s: the women who, facing a crunch in the Jewish marriage market that has continued to this day, strike "and he's got to be Jewish" off the checklist. One rabbi told me that she started officiating, very selectively, at mixed weddings because "I was extremely sympathetic to Jewish women who would have preferred to marry Jewish men but find themselves in their thirties and this is who they've got. . . . I felt a wellspring of anger at the denial of [their] plight," she said. Had she not been a rabbi, she says, she might have made a similar choice. "It would [have been] very conceivable to me, if I found someone who was loving and kind, to really try to work out the possibility of having a union in which they basically abdicated religious involvement and cultural involvement to me and were willing to kind of learn as they went along. I would not have needed the kind of commitment which comes with conversion to contemplate such a union for myself."

Thousands of Jewish women, in fact, are married to such non-Jewish men. Almost all the young single Jewish women I spoke to were willing to contemplate intermarriage for themselves, but they were very specific about how they foresaw the religious dynamics of their households: *At this point, I would marry somebody who wasn't Jewish, but I would only want to get married by a rabbi and raise my children Jewish. . . . [It's] important to me that my kids are brought up Jewish, so I could marry someone who wasn't Jewish as long as he wasn't adamant about another religion. . . . The only way I could marry someone of another faith is like if Jewishness rules.* Overall, the single Jewish men among my informants sounded a little less firm about imposing Jewishness on their partners and future homes: *I'd like to have Jewish kids* rather than *We will have Jewish kids.*

"I'm very, very involved in Judaism, and I interdate," said Talia, a 17 year old who holds a leadership position in her region of the Reform youth movement.

> I think people more have the commitment to raising our kids Jewish rather than marrying. That's my feeling. As long as I continue my Judaism with my future generation, then it doesn't matter what my husband is. . . . I have more of a bond with Jewish guys, so that's what I see myself marrying. But if I find someone that I'm equally compatible with that happens to be of another religion, as long as he lets my kids be raised Jewish, I don't see a problem with it. And I think a lot of people feel the same way.

Is this what Jewish leaders want to hear? Hardly. Is it a commitment Jewish institutions can build on? Maybe—if they take what kids like Talia say at face value and hold them to it.

Likewise, more of the intermarried Jewish women I interviewed had established going in that their homes were going to be Jewish-only than had their male counterparts; in fact, the only all-Jewish, no-tree-no-nothin' households headed by male informants who had married women not born Jewish were the ones in which the female partner had become interested in Judaism and converted. Although I can prove nothing, after three-plus years of research, I'm convinced that Jewish women who are willing to intermarry have better radar than Jewish men for Gentile partners who have nonexistent or vestigial religious ties. The vast majority of intermarrying women who *are* Jewishly committed manage to find nonreligious Gentile men, and these days, I would venture, most intermarrying Jewish women who are *not* Jewishly committed find nonreligious Gentile men, because they are no more interested in raising Christian children than committed Jews are.

A thirtysomething woman in suburban Washington told me that *no Christian observance* was part of the verbal pre-nup.

I said . . . that if we had children, they would be raised Jewish, with no wavering, like, "Well, we'll just have Christmas but we'll call ourselves Jewish"—nothing like that. I said we will be Jewish, the children will be Jewish, and that's that, that's how I want it. I didn't have a desire to have a halfy-halfy family, to do both. And he was agreeable to that because, well, one reason, he never really got a good background in Christianity. The only time he'd ever been at a church was for his grandfather's funeral, and he found it creepy.

She added that, as far as she can see, the woman always holds the reins of religious power in the home: "Maybe it's because she prepares the meals!"

Plenty of outreach counselors and demographers won't acknowledge any gender difference in how Jews approach intermarriage. The demographers say that there's nothing in the numbers to support the idea that intermarried Jewish women create more unambiguously Jewish homes than intermarried Jewish men do. All the rise in female intermarriage has done is to create more interfaith households, they say, not to mention bring down the conversion rate, since Gentile men don't convert to Judaism as often as Gentile women. The communal workers insist that the religious dynamic of a mixed household is individual to each family. "It has to do with the power balance within that relationship, how they negotiate," says Dru Greenwood, the UAHC's national director for Reform Outreach.

Again, let's apply some logic:

First of all, the demographers *can't know* that Jewish women in mixed marriages aren't raising more strongly identified Jewish children than Jewish men are, because they haven't studied whether or not they have. The numbers for Jewish involvement by mixed households in the Cohen Center's report are certainly abysmal, but I'd be interested to know whether the numbers for mixed households where the Jewish partner was female were a little less abysmal. If the Jewish partner was the wife, was the family less likely to have a Christmas tree? More likely to light Shabbat candles? More likely to join a synagogue? We'll never know, because the researchers never asked, just like they didn't bother to ask whether the non-Jewish partner went to church. Barry Kosmin did say, however, in so many words, that among the 28 percent of mixed families in the 1990 survey in which children were being raised unambiguously as Jews, they were "much more likely to have a Jewish mother than a Jewish father."[50]

Second, it's too soon for the impact of committed Jewish women marrying non-Jews to show up in the statistics. Most of them covered in the 1990 NJPS probably show up in the 1985–90 group—a little early, I would think, for many of them to have children, let alone be able to report how they're raising them. The earlier marriage cohorts (1975–84, 1965–74, pre-1965) are likely to have fewer Jewish women among the intermarried, fewer Jewish women with solid religious educations, and more second- and third-generation Jewish women of a secular or assimilationist bent. Will the outcome be different in the 2000 NJPS? It will be interesting to see.

Third, outreach counselors tend to see the people with problems: the hitherto marginal Jew who can't articulate to the Gentile spouse why he or she has experienced a surge of Jewish feelings with the arrival of their first baby; the "spiritual" Christian who doesn't understand why the "ethnic" Jew objects to Christianity as the house faith if Jewish culture remains in the home; the concerned Jewish wife whose Gentile husband doesn't want *any* religion in the home; the true-duals trying to negotiate one home with two deeply felt religions. The committed Jewish man with a religiously unaffiliated Gentile wife needs outreach services, too: finding a Reform *mohel* for the *brit milah*; arranging a formal conversion for the children, if unambiguous status is a concern; Jewish education for the wife so she can function as a competent, if not official, conductor of Jewish identity.

But the committed-Jewish-wife-supportive-Gentile-husband partnership doesn't have these problems. If the wife wants to light candles, they'll light candles. When she says it's time to join a synagogue, they join. She's no less "spiritual" than he is, and their children have no status problems. The only roadblocks they might have in Jewish life tend to involve rabbis rather than communal workers: finding an officiant for the wedding, and participation of the non-Jewish husband in synagogue life. Thousands of these couples are present in the American Jewish community, but outreach counselors don't see them, so many don't acknowledge their existence.

More than fifteen years ago, psychologist Edwin H. Friedman turned "the myth of the *shiksa*," the Gentile woman who lures Jewish men away from faith, family, and community, on its head:

> The most blatant aspect of the myth of the shiksa today is that she will, or even wants to, attract a Jewish man away from his origins, no less destroy his family. In my experience that is the last thing she wants, generally being attracted herself to that very rootedness that she often lacks. Indeed, if there does exist a "shiksa" today, she is to be found, of all places, among Jewish women. . . . When the focus is confined to those [mixed] marriages in which the Jewish partner is female, then I have to add that I have almost never seen such a union where the non-Jewish

male will be the less adaptive partner in family matters. . . . [The] preservation instinct in Jewish women who marry non-Jewish men generally puts them in the very position that the term *shiksa* was originally intended to describe, that is, a woman who will seduce her man away from his background.[51]

To be sure, Friedman overstates a bit. There are certainly marginal Jews of both sexes who will acquiesce to the stronger religious identification of a Christian spouse, and Friedman makes it sound as if Jewish women, in the name of continuity, have been all but brainwashing Gentile men into aligning themselves with The Tribe. Usually, these men were estranged from their religious backgrounds long before they met their Jewish spouses. But in essence, Friedman is correct: Committed Jewish women present a faith and culture more attractive to their non-Jewish mates than the ones in which they grew up, and the men respond by separating themselves from their early indoctrination in the name of love and family unity, often adopting the new traditions as their own.

If you don't believe Friedman, talk to my mother-in-law.

Jews who intermarry are no longer necessarily lost to Judaism, and even Jews who intermarry to lose Judaism sometimes come back. Remember Melody Bowen, who ran screaming from the Jews of her Long Island youth to the Virginia horse country and a Roman-numeraled husband?

> Ironically, being away from a sizable Jewish community has given me a deeper appreciation of both the cultural and religious aspects of Judaism. . . . There are only one hundred Jews in Bluefield, but they seem to be the best and brightest people in the community. . . . There must have been people like them on Long Island—I didn't see them. . . .
>
> I went to the temple out of curiosity. I expected to find the religion to be a lot of mumbo-jumbo, but it has great wise teachings about justice, charity, community, and God that make a lot of sense to me. . . . Being far enough away from Long Island enabled me to strip away many images and cultural stereotypes I had held about Jews. . . . Letting go of this bitterness has helped free me to find a religious Jewish identity for myself.[52]

Jewish leaders are so busy worrying about the Jews they've lost—or think they've lost—that they're not seeing the Jews they never lost and the ones who are coming back. They'll see us when they pay a little less attention to the numbers and a little more to the people who may or may not be represented by those numbers. The statistics have been given lives of their own, but those are not the lives from which Judaism has evolved over several millennia.

"I really believe that God did not put us in this world to disappear," Rachel Cowan, a Reform rabbi and coauthor of *Mixed Blessings*, said at a recent University of Judaism lecture. "We have survived for thousands and thousands of years, and now we have a new challenge, and . . . I'm sure we'll meet this one also." Reminding her audience of one of the images suggested by the Hebrew phrase that means "to heal the world," Cowan said, "We create *tikkun olam* by picking up the sparks that are scattered around. We just have them scattered wider now than they have been before."

7

Who's Marrying In?

A lot of the things I like in women are so-called Jewish characteristics.
The stereotype is being direct, not bottling things up, being active, being
verbal, just a lot more Tabasco in the sauce, so to speak. I hate bland little
Southern belles who never tell you the truth about anything.

—Andrew, Los Angeles

I think I always liked Jewish men because they seemed more sensitive.
They were certainly more intellectual than the non-Jewish men that I
knew. . . . There's a kind of intellectual discourse, a kind of questioning,
and a sort of living for the moment, a positive attitude. . . . They're
basically sort of high-integrity people, and they also just happen to be
really loving.

—Kathleen, Washington, D.C.

aron Christensen became a bar mitzvah in the spring of 1994 at his
temple in Hopkins, Minnesota. His great-grandfather handed the Torah
to his grandparents, who passed it his mother, Shelly, who handed it to
Aaron with the assistance of his proud father, Richard Christensen. Richard,
raised a Baptist, isn't about to convert to Judaism, saying that he gets his spiritual nourishment from a variety of traditions. But he participates in synagogue
worship and in the Jewish life of his family. "I just want my boys raised as good

little Jewish boys and to understand there is a God and what it means to be Jewish," Richard says.[1]

You can say that Shelly Christensen is married to a Gentile; you can, with some limited accuracy, call the Christensens' union an interfaith marriage, or, to use the sociologists' jargon, an exogamous marriage. But you can't say that Shelly married out. You *can* say, on the other hand, that Richard Christensen married in.

Multiply Richard Christensen by thousands, add thousands more men who, turned on to Judaism by wives and partners, have converted, and multiply several times more to represent Jewishly involved Gentile women married to Jewish men, and you have hundreds of thousands of people not born into Judaism who, formally or informally, have *married* into Judaism. They and their partners may not be a majority of the intermarried—yet. They may even be outweighed for the moment by the Jews who have married out into nothing much at all. But they greatly outnumber the Jews who have married all the way out to another faith for themselves or their children. At the very least, non-Jews who have married in comprise a sizable segment of Gentiles living with Jews. They are in every non-Orthodox synagogue, they are making seders and lighting Shabbat candles, they are raising Jewish kids, and they too deserve to be viewed as individuals, not as members of some marauding horde bent on stealing our children and smothering our future.

I am well aware of the horror stories: the secret baptisms, the spiritual custody suits, the divorced dads who won't get up early enough to take the kids to Sunday school when it's their weekend, the undermining Christian grandparents and stepparents, the *pro forma* converts who whisper that Jesus is still in their hearts, the promises broken, the agreements violated, the pushed-and-pulled children who finally, as adolescents, call down a plague upon both houses. Yes, intermarriage means that some children of Jewish parents will be raised as Christians, while others will be lost to religious apathy or their parents' *mishegoss*. But I can tell you also of devoutly Christian grandparents taking their orphaned Jewish grandchildren to Hebrew school, keeping the promise their daughter made; the Gentile mother making the tallit she drapes around her daughter's shoulders at her bat mitzvah; the man surprising his wife, just returned from several months at an out-of-town job, with the news that he has begun and completed his conversion studies.

So who marries in? Who—quietly, willingly, conscientiously—take their places, with or without conversion, with or without attachment to another faith, in Jewish life and devote a good chunk of their energies to raising Jewish children? We think we know so much about marrying out—but who marries in?

• • •

When women comprised the bulk of non-Jews who married into Jewish life, the stereotype of the Gentile partner of a Jewish man was something of a trophy wife: a woman who knew her main functions were to look good and adore her man. At a time when many young Jewish men considered romances with Gentile women as "practice," a lot of intermarriages were hatched when these guys realized they had fallen in love with the girls they were practicing on.[2]

The sexy-blonde tropism hasn't disappeared, of course. Eve, a tall blond woman who met her Jewish husband in the early 1970s, recalls one of the two times he addressed their differences in background, years into their marriage. "We were walking down the aisle of the temple arm in arm on Rosh Hashanah," she wrote in a letter. "We were a bit late, the temple was full, and I felt every eye was upon me. I muttered in his ear, 'Are you embarrassed to be prancing into this temple with your obviously shiksa wife?' He smiled and squeezed my arm and muttered back, 'Hell no; it's a status symbol.'"

But Eve is no submissive *objet d'art*. She and her husband met in law school, and one of the things that brought them together was shared delight in their intelligence. "I was attracted to the relationship because he was extremely smart, extremely funny, honest, kind, and very competent at running his life," she wrote. "Also—and this is very important—he was not intimidated by me, either by my being smart (most men had been) or my emancipated lifestyle." The women I interviewed who have married into Jewish life include attorneys, social workers, an economist, a nurse-practitioner, and a corporate executive. They're as well educated as their husbands, and they did not sign on to play a subordinate role to anyone.

While "otherness" is still a draw for many Jewish men, there are many kinds of "others," of every race and ethnic background; look around any big-city Introduction to Judaism class to see the variety. Rabbi Allen Maller, who has conducted innumerable Intro classes at his synagogue in Culver City, California, estimates that no more than 10 percent of the non-Jewish women in his classes fit the stereotype of the cheerleader-cute or model-beautiful blond girl; most are ordinary-looking women whose common attribute is that they're involved with Jews. And while there are plenty of Jewish guys whose rallying cry is, "*Shikses* look up to their men," there are others who take pride in sharing their lives with women whose intelligence and accomplishment equal theirs.[3]

Likewise, while some Jewish women, as mentioned earlier, have a taste for what stand-up comic Elayne Boosler has called the Happy Viking—the well-built, cheerful, blond masculine ideal—case studies of intermarriages from an era that put more emphasis on manners show Jewish women becoming attracted to Gentile men who presented a contrast to the brash, loud Jewish men they knew. The adjectives that come up over and over in early literature to describe non-Jewish men marrying into Jewish life are *polite, shy, gentlemanly, quiet,* and *mature*.[4] This dynamic may not have changed much over the years. "When I talk to Jewish women about the non-Jewish men, what they say about them is that they're gentle, caring, and accepting," Arlene Chernow says. "There is a kind of gentleness to many of them that is really quite special." In other words, even a Jewish woman harboring a severe aversion reaction to the Sheldons of her youth is unlikely to go for a beer-swilling heavy-metal maniac with naked girls on the mudflaps of his 4x4.

Many Jewish women have been pleased to be valued as warm, earthy, exotic, and sexy by non-Jewish men, although they also see the danger of being objectified as a sexual type. Psychologist Phyllis Chesler once commented, "Non-Jewish men treated me the way white men treat black women—as more sensual, earthy, sexually accessible," while another woman recalled her first encounters with non-Jewish men at college: "I knew that they saw me as an exotic, and were surprised to discover that I was human too."[5] One dark-eyed woman with a brunette mane told me that her WASP husband used to call her his "Indian princess."

But most of the Gentile and formerly Gentile men I talked with who had an ongoing affinity for Jewish women expressed their attraction in terms of personality rather than physical attributes. A Los Angeles woman raised in a highly assimilated family was incensed when her future husband, after meeting her relatives for the first time, said her mother struck him as "a typical Jewish woman." When she asked for an explanation, he replied that her mother was warm-hearted, spontaneous, sensual, and funny. "It was the first time I had seen a non-Jew . . . stereotype Jews in this very positive way," she said. Pete, who grew up in Los Angeles and has dated many Jewish women since the 1950s, valued "their openness, and their warmth, and their sense of humor" as a young man. "Jewish girls were a lot more hip, more aware. . . . Their grandparents had come out of the pogroms and everything, so they were sharp. A little defensive, but still sharp." Today, Pete thinks of Jewish women as "sensitive and loving and kind and sympathetic . . . I've noticed it all my life. It's kind of written in their faces."

Certainly the allure of the Other is part of the attraction for many Gentiles who become involved with Jews. For a few, there's an element of Jews as forbidden fruit. "I thought I was doing something exciting—in a bad sense—when I began to go out with a Jewish attorney from a big city," one Nebraskan said. "It was everything I wasn't supposed to do."[6]

"During my childhood some of the brightest young people I met were Jews, and some of them were interested, as I was, in art, literature, politics, philosophy—more so, on average, than the somewhat dull WASPs," a man who grew up in Texas wrote in a letter. His first marriage was to a Jewish woman from New York. They had met at a university far from both their homes to which, he said, both had fled. "I think we each found the other refreshingly different from those of our contemporaries we had met while still younger. Certainly she had none of the brassy false femininity of the tough young Texas would-be cheerleaders and gold-diggers I was used to."[7]

The product of an insular small town outside a large Midwestern city, Paul, a 40-year-old technical writer, had a taste for exploration of the larger world that most of his high school classmates did not. "I always wanted to know what it was like growing up Jewish in New York, or Catholic in Chicago, or as a punk rocker in East London. I just flat out *wanted to know*," said Paul, who moved to Los Angeles at 25 and married a Jewish woman four years later. "A lot of Midwesterners aren't smitten with that same sort of curiosity."

Andrew, a Los Angeles-based set designer, felt so out of place growing up in the South that he got rid of his regional accent while still a teenager. "Assumptions I was supposed to have just didn't seem to be self-evident to me," he said, explaining that his consuming interest in theater and film set him apart from everyone else he knew. "Also, just being that dreaded thing, the loner. You can be a mass murderer or anything, that's cool, but if you're a loner [in my home town], that's considered very peculiar." Andrew eventually met a Jewish woman who shared his interest in the arts and found an embracing community at her synagogue.

In addition, many of the non-Jews who burrow into Jewish life see Jews and Jewish families as warm, communicative, and supportive, often more so than the neighbors and relatives with whom they grew up. "One of the things that's very attractive to the Jewish male about his mate's family is they're not like his family, that they stay off his back. It's in the literature, but I see it constantly," Rabbi Jeffrey Marx says. "The male will say, 'I love her folks, they're nice to me, they respect me, they don't pry into my life.' And *she* says, 'I love his family. Unlike my cold parents, they're interested in everything I do.'"[8]

"I grew up in a family where you hid every emotion," says Greg, an ex-Catholic who converted to Judaism several years into his marriage.

> You painted the fence white and pretended that the inside was just great. You hid all the ugliness and all the bad stuff at all costs. And [my wife]'s family is just the opposite. They're just as crazy as my family, but it's on the surface, and they yell

and scream, and that's okay. And then they get over it, and it's done, and it's history. And I think if I have to choose a way to live, I'd rather be crazy on the outside, because the stuff on the inside's what eats you up.

•   •   •

The non-Jews who marry into Jewish life often feel comfortable with Jews because they come from similar socioeconomic backgrounds, from which they received education and values not unlike those of the Jews they marry. Many of the "practice" relationships young Jewish men used to pursue involved working-class women, and the literature on intermarriage cites many case histories of educated Jewish women with blue collar Gentile men—a popular image thirty years ago was the bohemian Jewish woman married to an African-American man. But sociologists point out that such stories are isolated cases found mostly in the psychological literature and don't reflect the year-in, year-out reality of most intermarriages.

"The predominant pattern is class inmarriage," Egon Mayer says. "Always was, always will be. Nobody wants to marry down." In other words, most people, including Jews, marry people of more or less their own social class, ensuring that they will bring at least some shared values to their marriage.[9] "Very few people make major leaps in life," either up or down, Mayer says. "It very rarely happens that way. In isolated cases it does, and it usually becomes part of folklore, and then because it's part of folklore, everybody tends to think, well, this must happen a lot." Today's middle-class Jewish woman, then, is unlikely to run off with a biker or become consort to the Norwegian crown; a Jewish doctor paying off his med school loans with service in a rural area is more likely to marry the woman who teaches third grade in the local school than the mother of three who lives down in the hollow.

It isn't difficult in today's society to find Gentiles who feel an affinity with Jews. Liberal in their world view, they come from parents who, if not liberal themselves, at least raised them free of anti-Semitism.[10] "The type of family that doesn't like Jews doesn't want a Jewish son-in-law or a Jewish sister-in-law," Barry Kosmin says. "You end up with the liberal Jewish people marrying the liberal Gentile people and mixing on their kinds of terms," a statement that rather undermines the standard warning about not marrying Gentiles because the first time you fight, your spouse will turn around and call you a dirty Jew. (Among my older informants, an undercurrent of anti-Semitism broke up several marriages, and among the younger ones, the faintest whiff of anti-Semitism stopped relationships in their tracks. Just as the vast majority of young contemporary Jews will not submerge their Jewishness in favor of the faith or culture of a Gentile partner, they will not tolerate *any* anti-Jewish prejudice from a spouse.)

These are also people likely to have had Jewish friends growing up and whose circles of friends as adults included Jews. Chances are good that their marriages aren't their first romantic involvements with Jews, either; in one early 1980s study, Mayer found that half the non-Jews married to Jews had dated other Jews before meeting their spouses, a proportion Mayer found remarkable given the numerical disparity between Jews and non-Jews in the American population.[11]

"All my good friends were Jewish, and all my parents' good friends were Jewish. I've been in more Jewish functions than Christian functions, weddings and bar mitzvahs and the like," said Terrie, who was raised more or less Presbyterian outside Washington. "Growing up, [Jewish guys] tended to be the more intellectual ones, which was kind of where I was at, so I had Jewish guys who were friends." It wasn't a stretch, then, when she arrived on the West Coast for graduate school, to strike up a friendship with the man she eventually married. "We had an uncanny amount in common," Terrie says, praising her husband's assertiveness, "wacky" sense of humor, focus on education, and respect for other people. Literature concerning well-educated Gentile women, disaffiliated from their own backgrounds and drawn to what they consider the greater authenticity, cohesion, liberality, and intellectual tradition of Judaism, began to appear in the early 1960s and continues to appear today.[12]

The non-Jewish men who demonstrate an affinity with Jews and who are drawn to Jewish women have received less attention, probably because, until recently, they've been less numerous, but they may be one of American Jewry's best hopes for continuity, because they bolster the commitment of strongly identified Jewish women and have been known to bring less observant Jewish women firmly into Jewish life. These men have a lot in common with each other.

Allen Maller goes so far as to recite a demographic profile of the men he considers to be Gentiles with "Jewish souls." They often come from communities where people are under pressure to conform to certain values and behaviors and grew up feeling out of step with their peers and parents. Their interests tended to be wider, different, or more intellectual; they were more liberal politically, more involved in social activism. If they went to school with Jews or had Jewish neighbors, they were likely to have had Jewish friends, and they were probably impatient with the non-Jewish girls they knew, valuing women of independence and spirit over conformity and self-effacement. Not surprisingly, they have tended to gravitate as adults to urban centers, where they were likely to meet Jewish women.

A non-Jewish man in one of Maller's Introduction to Judaism classes once told him that all his friends when he was growing up in Atlanta in the 1960s were Jewish. Maller remembers being skeptical at that statement. "All of them?" he asked.

"Yeah," the man said.

"How many people went to your high school?"

"About two thousand."

"And how many were Jewish?"

"Maybe a hundred."

"So your school was about 5 percent Jewish and *all* your friends were Jewish?" Maller said incredulously.

"Sure," the man said. "They were the most interesting kids. They were the kids involved in civil rights."

These men display a healthy feminism, sometimes in reaction to the women they knew growing up. "I really wanted to marry a girl unlike my mother," said one man raised in a fundamentalist Christian denomination. "My mom was very submissive, very country-girl. I wanted a companion equal to me, not somebody I could lord over," he said, adding that most of the girls in his church community were also retiring and deferential. Andrew, the set designer, found that the male-as-minor-deity principles he was raised with weren't borne out in the world of work. "If you're a guy in that section of the South, everything you do is an example of God-given genius. . . . And you see women being put down or treated as totally irrelevant," he said, adding that his theater experiences, beginning in college, gave the lie to that mind set.

> You needed somebody who wasn't flaky and could do hard work and would deliver the goods. . . . An awful lot of the guys . . . were just trying to see what cute actress-types they could hit on. You have a running relationship with women being competent, in many cases more competent. . . . My work experience has paralleled that. [In my business,] the women who are there are very low on the B.S. and just try to solve the problems of getting the [work] done. . . . When you get guys, even in something as unmacho as [the arts], there's just an outrageous amount of dick-measuring.

Most refreshingly from the Jewish woman's point of view, these men with "Jewish souls" appear to find attractive the very qualities in Jewish women that seem to turn off many Jewish men.[13]

"I get the impression, on an extreme level, of the Jewish men looking for non-Jewish spouses, that they look for very mealy, spineless women who are not going to challenge them and in fact will wait on them," said Greg, who recently finished a term as temple president. "I have several friends who I like as friends, acquaintances in the synagogue, and . . . they're almost abusive to these [non-Jewish] women, how they take advantage of them. . . . These are the same kind of guys who could never handle one of these powerful Jewish women. They avoid them [socially] and they confront them [as adversaries] in temple politics, at board meetings, in any situation that comes up."

By contrast, Greg values his wife's outspokenness and her ability to cut to the heart of the matter. "Her strongest point was she was somebody who I could trust and that she was an extra set of eyes in this world," he said. "[She's] a great friend and a great partner."

The bottom line is that while many Jewish men (and many non-Jewish men, for that matter) seek to marry women who represent a departure from their own ethnic backgrounds, most Jewish women seem to want men who embody the "Jewish" qualities they were taught to prize: intellect, humor, kindness, devotion to family, social conscience. They want men whose values correspond to their own, which often are values informed by their Jewishness. Far from intermarrying as an act of rejection, they are marrying or willing to marry non-Jewish men who are, in essence, the Great Jewish Guys who appear to be in such short supply these days.

"It's almost always men who fit this stereotype of what a Jewish man is supposed to be, but isn't Jewish. That's . . . the funniest part, is these gentle, soft men," says Rabbi Jane Litman, who officiates at carefully chosen weddings for mixed couples. Litman worked for a couple of years at a large Los Angeles synagogue that didn't permit its rabbis to officiate at intermarriages, and when she told a colleague that she would probably perform such weddings once she left the temple,

> he said, "How can you do that? I see these guys come in with these blond women on their arms who haven't a thought in their heads, and all they can talk about is how bad Jewish women are," and I said, "You know, I never see anybody like that. . . . What I see is these searching, passionate Jewish women who bring in these guys who I think would make great Jews, and who I'm hoping that intermarriage will be an act of welcome to bring them into the Jewish community."

•   •   •

If that isn't enough to convince you that non-Jews aren't necessarily trying to lure the Jews they marry away from Judaism, try this:

They're not all Christians. Believe it or not, not all non-Jews are Christians.

Most speakers and writers on the subject of intermarriage assume that anyone who isn't Jewish is religiously something else and filters any Jewish experience through his or her identification with another faith. You can see this assumption in the subtitles of books on intermarriage—*Mixed Blessings: Marriage between Jews and Christians; The Intermarriage Handbook: A Guide for Jews and Christians; Intermarriage: The Challenge of Living with Differences between Christians and Jews.*[14] "The non-Jew does have a religious identity," one rabbi stated confidently at a UAHC regional convention. "A non-Jew is someone who is not Jewish, but a non-Jew is someone who is something else, who is Catholic, who is Baptist, who is Christian, who is Muslim, who is Buddhist." He went on to suggest that someone who isn't part of the tribe couldn't possibly derive any spiritual meaning from Jewish ritual or even comprehend what it was about: "The way I as a rabbi understand Jewish rituals, Jewish rituals are Jewish. They were written by Jews, for Jews, for Jews to do, and carry with them Jewish meaning, Jewish value, Jewish understanding."

Which is more arrogant—this rabbi's assumption that all Gentiles are idiots, or his disregard for the non-Jews who are praying in his synagogue? He seems oblivious to the thousands of non-Jews that his own movement calls "religiously nonpreferred," the ex-Baptists, former Congregationalists, and disaffected Catholics who vein American religious life, as well as the non-Jews who were raised without religion. One recent survey reported that 30 percent of Americans age 18 and older define their outlook as completely secular; they are atheist or agnostic, or retain only "trace elements" of religion in their lives. Since 98 percent of those people aren't ethnically Jewish, that's a big pool of nonreligious Gentiles.[15]

If you hunger for cheerful statistics, know that American Jews stay Jews more than American Christians stay Christians; mainline Protestant denominations especially have been hemorrhaging followers since the 1970s. At a time when 45 percent of people brought up as Presbyterians no longer identified themselves as Presbyterians, only 15 percent of people raised Jewish had ceased to identify as Jews; even the Catholic Church had a lower retention rate. While many people raised in liberal denominations have gone into more conservative Christian groups, the mainline churches have also lost substantial numbers to the "no religious affiliation" category. A recent study reported an 86 percent increase in that choice.[16] Millions of liberal Protestants and Vatican II–era Catholics, the Gentiles whose religious training and worship style are most like that of non-Orthodox Jews, have walked away from Christianity. The vast majority of Jews, while many will intermarry, retain their identification as Jews. Whom do you think most exogamous Jews are marrying—Pat Robertson and Tammy Fay Bakker?

Rabbi Harvey Goldman, who leads a suburban congregation in New Jersey, says he encounters many Christians who have dismissed the notion of a divine Jesus as a point of faith but share ethical and moral values with a Jewish partner. "Many postmodern Christians basically have given that faith up. To them, it's about as much of a myth as it is to us," Goldman says. "You have usually, I find, Christians in mixed marriages who really say, 'Look, I don't have any religious-centered values at all; I just believe in the same values as [my wife] over here, and her values are my values, and I don't have any hang-ups about Jesus.' . . . So basically you have a drift into secularity on the part of Christians."

"I was a rather defiantly agnostic sorta guy in the mid-1970s, so it was unlikely that I would have started dating a devoutly Christian woman," said Paul, who was baptized at age 12. "I didn't want to date somebody who talked about Sunday school or how terrific Reverend Schuller's sermon had been at the Crystal Cathedral that week." Frank, an ex–New Yorker who became Jewish after several years of marriage, was harsh in his criticism of Catholicism. "I didn't like the priest, nor did I like the nuns, nor did I like what I knew of the structure of the Catholic Church. I felt that they were not open, they were not warm. . . . They used to basically preach, if you don't do this, this is gonna happen to you; if you don't do that, you're gonna burn in hell."

"I was kind of caught up in the spirit of the time, where everybody my age assumed that everything the adults were telling us was total crap anyway," says Andrew, who says he assimilated many positive messages in Sunday school but started pulling away from church attendance around the time of the invasion of Cambodia. "I said [to my parents], 'Listen, if [the pastor] came out strongly against war in general, everybody would take that to be against the Vietnam war, [and] how many people in the congregation would give him a lot of trouble about this? How dare he be unpatriotic—and un-Christian? And yet it's very clear in Scripture that war is wrong.' All these hypocrisies, it doesn't mean anything to them." Sound familiar? Remember, every complaint Jewish kids brought home during the 1960s and 1970s about what went on in temple being irrelevant, boring, and politically incorrect was echoed in Protestant and Catholic households across America.

Yet non-Jews who have disaffiliated from their childhood faith communities often participate happily in Jewish life; their disenchantment with their parents' religion doesn't carry over to Judaism. Writer and school psychologist Josie Levy Martin says her husband, the agnostic son of a Nazarene minister, has celebrated every Jewish holiday she has chosen to observe over a quarter-century of marriage. "He is the one who takes out the silver candlesticks on Shabbat when I'm ready to 'let it go . . . this once,'" she wrote. "He is the one who quietly makes donations to Jewish causes, sometimes unbeknownst even to me. He has supported all expressions of Jewishness in our home, and encouraged the Jewish education of our son."[17]

There are, of course, religiously disaffiliated non-Jews who are antagonistic to *any* religious involvement, often in reaction to their own repressive religious upbringings, and among the Gentiles who *don't* marry in, they may be the most destructive, because their antipathy may not show itself until well into a marriage. A couple of fairly chilling examples appear in *Mixed Blessings*, including one man who bragged about his attempts to undermine his wife and daughter's growing involvement with synagogue life through sarcasm and insults and said he would "try to sabotage" his wife's plans to teach Sunday school.[18] Among my own informants, I did not come across any currently intermarried Jews whose spouses derided or would not support Jewish involvement, although I did speak to a few Jewish women who had divorced such men.

"We talk about intermarriage as if there's one undifferentiated mass of Gentiles," Barry Kosmin says. "In fact, of course, there isn't. Some of them are more compatible, more acceptable." One of the things Jewish leaders don't want to admit is that, in large part, Jews who intermarry these days manage to find those more compatible, acceptable Gentiles. Since Jews are no longer marrying out to lose themselves in the dominant culture, they are less interested in having their Jewishness subsumed by a partner's stronger faith. Marginal Jews tend to marry marginal Christians—that's why there are so many "interfaithless" couples— and strongly identified Jews are not about to spend their lives in pitched battle with someone who really is an adherent of a competing faith. Given the choice, even marginal Jews would prefer a non-Jewish partner who will marry in, which is why, from what I can gather, only a tiny fraction of Jews marry practicing Christians from evangelical backgrounds. That doesn't mean positively identified Jews never marry conservative Christians, and it certainly doesn't mean Jews don't date such Christians. But it does mean those relationships are less likely to reach the altar than relationships with nonreligious Gentiles or those from mainline denominations.

Rabbi Dennis Ross says he has counseled a number of mixed couples in which a Jewish woman is dating a strictly observant Christian. "What happens is she starts going out with him, but she's not connected to Judaism. Then he starts to pull her into Christianity . . . and she freaks out and begins to return to Judaism and finds things in there that she likes," he said. "So this guy, on the first date, he asked out an assimilated Jew, and by the time they're talking about marriage, this is a person with a growing Jewish commitment," a situation, he says, that is likely to end the relationship. Constance Reiter, who has led interfaith workshops in New Jersey for a dozen years, says, "If the Christian partner is a practicing Christian, chances are there's going to be trouble, and over the twelve years I have seen many split up. Most of them are when the partner has a strong Christian commitment."

So who marries all the way in? Who converts to Judaism?

Among the people I've come across in my research for whom a relationship with a Jew was the catalyst for a formal conversion, there seem to be four categories (with some overlap): *searchers, switchers, family unifiers,* and *long-term intermarrieds.* The searchers are people whose adult life includes some degree of spiritual experimentation before they discover Judaism through a partner. The switchers take the spiritual energy they put into their religious life as youngsters and transfer it to Judaism. Family unifiers feel it's important that everyone in the household have the same religious identity and convert before the wedding or before children are born. Long-term intermarrieds, on the other hand, live more or less as Jews for years before deciding to formalize their commitment.

People who come to Judaism after a spiritual search often were raised without much religious identity or by parents from two different Christian denominations. Tired of being shunted between two churches, confused by conflicting messages, or given little instruction beyond "be good to others," searchers feel a spiritual gap that Judaism eventually fills. One woman's mother had married to escape her strict Mormon background. "[S]he did her best to raise us as nothing, to teach us to be accepting of everybody. So, depending on what neighborhood we were in, that's where we went to church," she said. "My father was a teacher at a Congregational school, and he studied Christian Science for a while. And I guess that it was really very easy for me to convert. There was nothing involved in the conversion that went against anything I believed in."[19]

Jennifer, raised without religion in Northern California by an "artsy craftsy" mother and a physicist father and stepfather, brought an ultrarational perspective to her search:

My mom . . . always told me I could believe in whatever I wanted to. . . . I had some Jewish friends when I was in grammar school, and I was intrigued by it. . . .

I used to torment my friends in college . . . especially the born-again Christians and the very Catholic . . . and say things like, "Do you believe that the Jews are God's chosen people?" and they'd say "Yes," and "Do you believe that Judaism is a valid religion?" "No." Okay, well, how come not? How come God's chosen people don't have a valid religion?

I grew up in a very logical household. So if I was gonna believe in God, I guess it had to be in a logical way.

Jennifer's husband wasn't much help; at the time they met, his Jewish connections were all cultural. But the curiosity she had about Judaism was ignited by their partnership, and she took some classes at a Reform synagogue. Reform Judaism, Jennifer discovered, was a good fit on both the logical and philosophical levels: "I decided, hey, this kind of goes with what I already feel." Workshop leader Jonathan Flier finds that many converts approach Judaism warily from an intellectual standpoint after leaving a religion they found illogical. "They study Judaism, and they're fascinated by the fact that Judaism makes sense to them. A lot of them have very much an 'aha!' kind of experience, like *This is what I've been looking for.*"

For many searchers, conversion is a homecoming. One woman, who grew up Southern Baptist with a decided preference for the Old Testament, identified with the Israelites to such a degree that she was shocked, as a child, to find out she *wasn't* Jewish. She reached adulthood having pulled away from the restrictions of her childhood church, and after sampling Catholicism and Buddhism, tried to go without religion. But she missed the worship experience, and besides, "[e]ver since my childhood, I had *known* I was a Jew." She was brought into Judaism by her fiancé, delighted to find out that Judaism is not a closed society.[20]

Switchers are the folks who make conversion look easy. They were perfectly happy being lapsed Whatevers, or maybe not-so-lapsed Whatevers, then they fall in love with Jews, and the next thing you know, they become Jewish.

Dru Greenwood, now national director of the UAHC's Commission on Reform Jewish Outreach, had fallen away from Christianity as a teenager and was drawn into Judaism by her future husband early in their relationship. She realized right away that "[t]his is who I am but I didn't know it had a name" and converted prior to her marriage in 1970.[21] Layne Drebin's very Catholic husband-to-be understood that although her Jewish education was sparse and her connections to Judaism tenuous at best, Layne would never be able to accept Christian doctrine for herself or as a family faith. She was determined to give their children the religious instruction and ethical foundation her childhood home had lacked, and both agreed to raise their children as Jews. That question settled, her fiancé, John Murphy—who had considered becoming a priest and who was writing his doctoral dissertation on the idea of purgatory in Middle English literature—became more and more immersed in Jewish studies before and after their wedding, while Layne found the sense of belonging she had always missed through synagogue life. John's conversion took place just after the birth of their son.[22]

Another man's passage to Judaism in his early twenties was something of a roller coaster ride. Ethan, the son and grandson of Baptist preachers, was expected to follow his forebears into the ministry, but in college two things happened: he began to explore his religion for the first time; and he met Miriam, a strongly identified if not strictly observant Jew. For her part, Miriam appreciated Ethan's commitment to his own faith. "I liked that he cared about religion, even if it wasn't my religion," she said. "You could talk about important things. He could respect my religion, where . . . maybe a Jew who's more self-hating wouldn't respect any of my beliefs."

At the beginning of their relationship, Ethan considered his Christianity much stronger than Miriam's Judaism.

[She] was reading in one of the Jewish books about how the person with the lesser faith should bow to the person with the greater faith. And I was saying, "Well, look, it's me with the greater faith! Your family doesn't even go to shul, you don't do anything Jewish at all. . . ." But what I didn't realize was that her religion wasn't like, she wasn't wearing it on her coat sleeve; it was much deeper than what I could see.

And then I started to explore her religion. And that was a difficult time, because I remember thinking to myself, hey, if my faith is strong enough, I should be able to explore this with a completely neutral mind and come away with the right conclusion. [I read one book] by a rabbi a couple of hundred years ago talking about the flaws in Christianity. I said, "You know, if my faith is strong enough, I should be able to refute some of these arguments." And the more I read, the more I thought, "Gee, my faith is not holding up to this." And then once I lost my faith . . . the entire Christianity just crumbled beneath it, because that's all Christianity was. Christianity was based on faith, and once I lost the faith, then it was all gone.

There was a time there where I certainly wasn't Jewish at all, I was sort of like between religions, I wasn't anything, and that position was much more uncomfortable for me. Growing up religious all my life, to not believe in God was completely unheard of. I couldn't go back to my former religion, so I was really pushed more towards Judaism.

After a full year's cycle of holidays, which brought him firmly into Jewish life, Ethan was ready for the final steps of an Orthodox conversion, but what his rabbi didn't know was that he had never been circumcised.

The rabbi says, here, go see this mohel for the ritual circumcision. . . . So I'm expecting some kind of clinic or something, I figure the guy's done this before, no big problem. So I go there, and it's this man's house. It's this old man, about seventy-five, eighty years old, and I'm like, Oh, my God. So the mohel says, "Why don't you step back in my study?" and I'm like, he's gonna do it in his study! Oh, my God! The mohel grabs his little satchel and he says, "Okay, well, why don't you drop your drawers?" I'm like, "Oh, God, I'm gonna bleed to death right here in his office." It was really a test of faith, but I was sitting in there trembling. The mohel turns around and says "NO, NO, NO, NO, NO, NO, NO!" Sent me to the hospital. . . . I had it done surgically, and then after the hospital, a few weeks later, I had to go back to the mohel for the ritual [symbolic circumcision].

Okay, it isn't the binding of Isaac, but who could doubt a guy's sincerity after something like that?

Non-Jews who convert so that everyone in the family will be Jewish are often accused of superficial commitment, but their decision often leads to spiritual fulfillment down the road. "I wanted my child to be unambiguously part of the Jewish community," said a New Jersey woman who now leads interfaith workshops. "I thought it would be good for the family; there would be a place for the three of us. And I thought there would be something in it for me; exactly what, I didn't know." That "something" turned out to be an emotionally satisfying chain of rituals and a sense of community. "The Jewish holidays give me a fresh way of looking at things, which offer a whole range of emotions that people can live out together throughout the year. There is something very psychologically sound about that."[23]

A woman sitting on a panel of converts said that although her conversion was possible in part because she felt the values she identified with Jews were her own, "the most important reason was that I did not want my children, in shaping a sense of identity, to have any feelings of conflict. That reason alone would have been enough."[24] Although there is less pressure on men to convert for the sake of family identity, a Queens rabbi remembers one man brought into Judaism by his son's delight at starting religious school. "His son was so enthusiastic about being in temple—he was in first grade at that time—that [the father] wanted there to be unity in the family, and he wanted to be called as an *aliyah* to the Torah at his son's bar mitzvah," the rabbi said.

Perhaps the least visible converts are the Gentiles, up to now primarily men, who formalize their commitment to Judaism years into their marriages to Jews. They are comfortable with Judaism, they get involved in temple life, and they're often as much a part of their children's Jewish educations as their partners are. But for whatever reason—usually it has to do with personal autonomy or a skittishness about allegiance to an organized religion after having rejected one already—they don't convert when the rabbis, and sometimes their in-laws, would like them to convert: before the wedding. Then one day they wake up, realize how they've been living for the past five or ten or fifteen years, and decide the time has come. There may be a "transforming experience," such as a death in the family, a weekend retreat, a fortieth birthday, or—I've heard this one over and over—the eldest child's impending bar or bat mitzvah. But for many, it just happens when it feels right.

"Before I converted . . . the big question for me [was]: If something happened to my marriage, would I continue on leading a Jewish life? If the answer wasn't yes, then I wasn't willing to convert," said Greg, who had two small daughters and was already serving on the board of his small Reform synagogue before he took the plunge. "When I got to a point in my life that the answer was yes, then I felt comfortable converting."

When one couple, a nonreligious Jewish man and a woman who rejected the Catholicism of her youth while in college, lived in the Northeast, they had no religious involvement. But when they moved to a small city in the South, they found themselves in a place where religious institutions were the basis of social life, and they joined the Reform temple. That drew them into religious observance and membership in other Jewish communal organizations. In addition, their older child was receiving a Jewish education and asking questions about religion. After several years of Jewish involvement and almost a decade of marriage, the wife converted.[25]

Renee, who facilitates interfaith workshops in Los Angeles, had been married to a non-Jew who enjoyed Jewish rituals at home but balked at joining a synagogue and enrolling their children in religious school. When that marriage broke up, she swore that if she ever married again, she'd marry someone Jewish. She broke that vow, but only temporarily.

In Texas I met a guy, just a fun guy, and we dated for a long time, very innocently and just for fun . . . and things started getting more serious in our relationship. I told him one thing I do regularly is go to temple on Friday nights. Well, he decided to check it out . . . and even before we were married, he was shlepping kids from the youth group and serving on committees, and as [he] became more and more active in the Jewish community and in the congregation, people really started giving him a time about when are you going to convert, and he kept saying no, no, no, I'm not gonna do it.

[Then] we went to the UAHC biennial . . . and my guess is that that was his transforming experience. I was out here with my new job; he was still in Texas. When I returned . . . he and the rabbi had cooked it all up, his conversion ceremony, and surprised me, I mean absolutely blew me away. He had been studying the whole time I was gone; they didn't require a lot of study because he already knew everything.

•   •   •

There's a very thin line between the "converts who wait" and the nonreligious Gentiles who are practicing Jewish rituals and raising Jewish kids, a line often consisting of nothing more than a principled atheism or the wish not to upset a devoutly Christian parent. For every story rabbis like to tell about an unsupportive or religiously subversive non-Jewish partner, there's at least one other about a Gentile spouse who has been an enthusiastic fellow traveler, often revitalizing a Jewish partner's connection to Jewish life. "I think that number is huge compared to the horror stories," Robert Schreibman, a rabbi from suburban Chicago, said, "but I don't think that you find those talked about, because people are so frightened, and then if you talk about these [intermarrieds], you start having to recognize them as Jews and their children as Jews."

Many rabbis don't want to talk about the Jewish woman whose husband is so caught up in study of Hebrew and liturgy that she's afraid he and their son are going to leave her in the dust. Or the woman whose husband resolved his ambivalence about raising Jewish children after reading a book about the Holocaust.[26] Or the stepfather who convinced his wife's middle child, as his wife could not, that it was her responsibility to be in temple instead of school on Rosh Hashanah—if he could miss a staff meeting and rearrange interviews, she could miss class.[27] Or the Jewish woman who did much better the second time around after her first husband, a Jew, left her and their two children. "It is only since my remarriage that my family has joined a temple," she wrote to a Jewish weekly. "My husband and I and my children attend services and temple functions together, and my children attend religious school. I feel a stronger commitment to Judaism now than I did when I was married to a Jew."[28]

Although making an unambiguously Jewish home with a non-Jew is probably easiest when the non-Jewish partner professes no strong religious identity of his or her own, there are many cases of non-Jews who bring a different faith to their marriages yet are able to help raise Jewish children. A Christian partner who believes that individual salvation is more important than peoplehood is likely to be willing to compartmentalize his or her faith and let Judaism stand as the household religion. "It appears that those individuals who know the most about their own faith are the ones who can tolerate with greatest equanimity the situation where their children are being raised in another religion," Susan Weidman Schneider writes, citing Baptist theologian Harvey Cox, who raised his son as a Jew with his Jewish wife, as one of many examples.[29]

Not every Gentile partner is comfortable giving up a large chunk of his or her religious role for the sake of family unity, of course, and there are many stories in the literature of non-Jewish spouses who stall or renege on promises to raise their children as Jews. Sometimes the pressure is external: "There are plenty of Jewish guys who married women who said they never walk into a church, they don't care about it, and then when that first kid is born, the Catholic grandmother says, 'You don't raise that child as a Catholic and I'll disinherit you and your children.' And all of a sudden, these kids are getting catechism," Sylvia Barack Fishman said.

However, a great many people raised as Christians, even those who maintain an attachment to their childhood faith as adults, are able to accommodate Judaism as the dominant religious force in their households and maintain their own religion as an adjunct culture. Jewish leaders don't want to admit that there are people living meaningful "two-track" religious lives, but they're out there: the Catholic woman who fasts on Yom Kippur and scours the house for *chametz* with her five-year-old Jewish daughter and brings home a Christmas tree for the Catholic kids from the first marriage, and the former seminarian who gets a kind of Christian fix with his family at Christmas and a couple of Sundays a year in an Episcopal church but also has served as chair of the fundraising and scheduling committees at his synagogue.[30]

Chuck, a Roman Catholic, is immersed in his wife's Conservative Jewish world. "I still got Christ in there somewhere, and maybe it's because I was brainwashed [in parochial school] for twelve years," he says. Yet he cried when their local JCC was vandalized and called a rabbi he and his wife had studied with so he could talk about it. "[She] said, 'You know why you had this reaction to this JCC incident? . . . Because you're one of us. You really are one of us.' . . . They all think, hey, he's going to be [Jewish], it's just a question of when."

Maureen, who grew up in an Irish Catholic community so insular that to marry an Italian boy would have been viewed as leaving the fold, met her husband, Sam, in law school, and offered to raise their children as Jews when their relationship got serious. Now she's a Christmas-and-Easter Catholic: "Even though I have objections to things that Catholics teach these days, I think that there's a lot of good in it, and there have been many times when it has really comforted me to be in a church service at different times of my life." Maureen spends a lot more time in synagogue than in church, though: most Friday nights, along with the holidays and committee work, plus Passover and Chanukah at home (and yes, they have a Christmas tree as well). "We do it in a way that seems serious to us. I function much more as a Jewish person, but I'm not."

To remove any ambiguity about their children's Jewish status, Maureen and Sam took them to the *mikvah* for formal conversion. All went smoothly with the first two *bet dins*, the panels of rabbis who approve conversions. With their third child, however, two of the rabbis on the panel began to give them a hard time, especially about their Christmas observance.

> I didn't really care, because I knew I had the winning card. All I had to do was stand up and say, "I am Catholic, and if you guys don't shut up right now, this child will be, too." . . . I mean, what could they do? Then our rabbi kind of stepped in and started saying nice things about us . . . so then the other two just quieted down and went on with it. But as we were leaving, one of them like takes a shot at me; he goes, "Really, you should try to get rid of that Christmas tree."

Victor, a doctor in a small Mid-Atlantic city and father of three teenagers, broke with the Catholic Church for a time in college, disenchanted with what he thought were the "dippy" changes wrought by Vatican II. While in medical school, he met Jeri and was attracted by her intelligence, her strong personality, and her good looks. "I was partly attracted to her because she was different from other people that I had known, and part of that was probably the fact that she was Jewish, too; I think that had an attraction to me," Victor said. Neither set of parents objected to their marriage, although Jeri's mother did say to her, "Leave it to you to find the one medical student that isn't Jewish."

> We didn't really discuss much what we were gonna do about religion. I wasn't going to church, she really wasn't going to temple or doing anything, and then all of a sudden both of us felt that religion is worthwhile, and we both sort of drifted back to it in our own ways. Then the thing came up with the children, well, what are we gonna do about them? . . . It just didn't seem right that the child[ren] had no religion, especially since we each had religion.

I didn't know much about Judaism, and there's a lot of things that I didn't understand looking at it externally. . . . But then when we started going to the temple, and the kids started being raised and I would pray and I would see what it was all about, and learned about the Torah and learned about the history of the Jews, and the spiritual side of Judaism, then to me it was a whole new awakening. . . . Frequently on Friday nights we'd go as a family, because I thought it would be good to go as a family to the temple. But at the same time I did the Catholic part, and still do.

In some ways I get more of a boost with going to temple [than mass]. It's more of a meaningful experience. . . . I would say that at this point, although I still am Catholic and I still believe in most of the things in the Catholic Church—you know, I recognize the roots of Catholicism in Judaism. It's so clear how much of Catholicism has come from Judaism. I see the same prayers, I see the same manner of talking to God, of dealing with God, the contracts, everything—it's just more eye-opening and a more spiritual experience at the temple.

I don't want to see Judaism die out, certainly. If anything, I'm contributing in the other direction, because I'm raising Jewish children.

•   •   •

Out of fear, we erect fences made of our assumptions. We assume that any practicing Christian married to a Jew is up to no good. We assume that even nonreligious Gentiles will undermine their children's Jewish lives. We assume the stranger can have nothing in common with us, even though many of them learned the same values we did. We assume we are unknowable, when some Gentiles have known us all their lives.

We assume no one else can understand the pain of our history, no one else can understand what it means to live as a particular people in a sea of others. Are we the only minority group in America? Are we the only people in the world with a history of suffering? Are we to assume, conversely, that all Jews who find partners from among America's privileged groups have chosen to love ignorant clods incapable of empathy?

We assume we have nothing the strangers want, yet we lock it away, lest they come in search. We build stout fences with narrow gates around our community and then wonder why all those people are climbing over the fence into our compound. We still cannot believe that we are respected, honored, loved. Well, thousands of people who have married into Judaism are here to tell you: *Believe it.*

8

So You Want Your Kids to Marry Jews

I think rabbis and synagogues have to get into the matchmaking business. I don't mean just having singles groups and dances where people come and drool all over each other. I mean we have to actively get into the matchmaking business. Those rabbis who are kicking and screaming about interfaith marriage—what are they doing to help young Jews meet each other? Are they doing things to bring in hip, disenfranchised Jews?

—Rabbi Steven Z. Leder, Los Angeles

I'm like Goldilocks: I go to all these services, and this one has too much Hebrew, and this one is too New Age. I'm looking for the one that's just right.

—Amanda, San Francisco

In 1986, after fifteen years without synagogue affiliation, I found a temple that was just right: warm and friendly, politically progressive, egalitarian, inclusive, nonjudgmental, eclectic in its liturgy, geared toward adult worship, and affordable. Within two years after joining, my life was transformed. Not only could I be Jewish there on my own terms, but it gave me an outlet for Jewish learning, friends around our seder table, a place to sing, a place to get married. To find such a synagogue, a temple where I fit in after years of falling through the cracks of Jewish institutional life, seemed like a miracle.

It should not take a miracle for Jews to find synagogues in which they feel comfortable. If the Jewish community wants Jews to marry Jews, or to develop strong enough *Yiddishkeit* to engage Gentile partners in Jewish life, Jewish institutions have to make themselves much more relevant and welcoming. And if individual Jews want their children to marry within the tribe, they need to take responsibility for their own Jewish lives. At this moment, the institutions—synagogues, schools, JCCs, summer camps—actually may be doing a slightly better job of holding up their end of the bargain.

Jewish Education, Formal and Informal

Synagogue-based Religious Schools

The time has come to quit trashing supplementary schools, which are, after all, still the predominant medium through which non-Orthodox children receive Jewish education, and instead work toward their improvement. While no one is about to argue that two or four or even seven hours a week is enough to deliver a complete working knowledge of Jewish holidays, Jewish history, synagogue skills, and Bible, educators are beginning to make better use of the hours they have. The trend lately is toward "informal" educational experiences such as field trips, camp weekends, retreats, *shabbatonim* (celebrations of a full Friday-through-Saturday Shabbat), and holiday celebrations that provide intensive Jewish experiences outside classroom hours.[1] Many temple-based programs involve parents in home activities and parallel learning sessions while their children are in the classroom; through these "family education" efforts, many Jews are getting the Jewish knowledge—and the excitement in that knowledge—that they missed the first time around.[2] The major Jewish movements are also starting to hire better-trained instructional leaders, encouraging educators to use innovative materials and learn new skills, and training volunteers to function as caring, competent teachers.[3]

Parents can begin to hold up their end, first of all, by enrolling their kids in religious school—the percentage of Jewish children given formal Jewish education has been drifting downward for years—and, once they're attending, by keeping the kids in school as long as they possibly can. The enhanced value of Jewish education that takes place after bar and bat mitzvah is well documented. Educator Joel Grishaver suggests that, rather than shy away from being the ogres who force their children to continue in Hebrew school when other parents don't, parents in the same religious school make a pact not to be the first to let their kids drop out. It's not as hard as it sounds, Grishaver asserts, because a lot of teens are willing to continue, if only to hang out with their friends.[4] For their part, synagogues are employing strategies to keep teenagers engaged, often by training them as teachers' assistants and making them role models for younger kids.[5] Parents should also commit, without excuses or complaint, whatever time their synagogues ask of them for family education; the more they learn, the less embarrassed they'll be by how little they know.

Beefing up supplementary education and drawing in new students are important because the much-touted alternative, Jewish day school, simply is not an option for most Jewish families. Day school tuition is astronomically high—understandably, because the schools hire double staffs for secular and religious subjects—but the schools justify the expense, somewhat disingenuously, by claiming to be the last defense against intermarriage. (It's easy to produce statistics showing low rates of intermarriage among day school graduates when the vast majority of day school students are Orthodox.) Ignoring the fact that day school teachers are badly paid and often poorly trained, and conveniently forgetting that many non-Orthodox students in day schools go home to parents who fail to reinforce what they learn in school with ritual observance or synagogue attendance, Jewish leaders have no trouble trying to guilt-trip Jewish parents, three-fourths of whom make less than $60,000 a year, into spending half their pretax income on day school tuition.[6]

Rather than harangue parents about day school, the Jewish community would do well to address the families for whom even part-time Jewish education is a burden and make it possible for them to join synagogues and enroll their children in religious school. Supplementary schools may not deliver what day schools can in terms of the sheer amount of Jewish knowledge, but they've produced thousands of Jews who have continued their educations and wound up as rabbis, cantors, communal workers, Jewish educators, and lay leaders. We treat these schools with contempt at our peril.

Youth Activities

The components of informal Jewish education—retreats, summer camp, youth group, travel to Israel, fine and performing arts programs—loom larger than classroom study as Jewish kids reach adolescence. They are viewed as highly effective in cementing teens' Jewish identities and in making Jewish peer relationships a normative part of those teenagers' lives, therefore providing a possible deterrent against intermarriage and, at minimum, setting the stage for their involvement in Jewish life as adults.

Informal experiences usually have a number of strengths in common. First, they're voluntary; even when parents require their children to participate, the sales pitch is more along the lines of "You'll like it," rather than "You have to," which is how many parents present experiences like bar mitzvah training. They're unpressured and not explicitly goal-oriented. They provide immediate gratification: We're enjoying Shabbat *now*; we're kicking Southwick JCC's butt in basketball *now*; I can sing this song I just learned *now*. They're group-oriented, interactive, and participatory (as opposed to all too many classrooms). While not fixated on specific goals, they do contain structure and direction. Finally, they're fun.[7] They provide "the extended time, the role models, the social reinforcement, and, in Eric [sic] Erikson's terms, the 'locomotion,' the sense of movement and activity that preteens and teens need to learn and grow in a positive and joyful way," one communal leader wrote.[8]

Participation in a temple youth group puts Jewish teens in contact with other Jewish kids on a regular basis throughout the year; demographer Bruce Phillips identifies it as one of three factors (along with formal Jewish education through high school and having mostly Jewish friends) that seem to be linked with choosing Jewish partners as adults. Much depends, though, on how seriously a synagogue takes its youth program. Some are content to have the youth director schedule social events, while others support efforts to engage teenagers in intellectual, spiritual, and communal pursuits such as social action projects and the creation of worship services.

Summer camp can provide a sense of connection to kids who may not have access to Jewish peers where they live. "At school, I was one of ten Jews in a class of five hundred, so being at camp was wonderful. I finally felt I was part of a whole instead of an oddity," said a veteran of a UAHC-sponsored camp.[9] Los Angeles rabbi Steven Leder calls Jewish summer camp

the one place that gave us a totally organic Jewish experience, where we could live a Jewish rhythm, a Jewish life, without being Orthodox. . . . And Israel, with all of its problems, is a profound experience for any Jew, especially an adolescent Jew. Will it guarantee the creedal identity of every kid who goes? No. But if a hundred percent of our kids went to Israel one summer and went to Jewish summer camp one summer between the ages of ten and eighteen, you would see a tremendous difference.

College Organizations

The university campus can be a reasonably comfortable place to be Jewish and meet other Jews—if you're already observant. A number of universities have thriving Hillel centers or their equivalent, although the national Hillel organization and most of its 105 members are perenially strapped for funds. The current Hillel leadership has ambitious plans to double its financial base and revitalize its institutional structure.[10] In addition, the Conservative movement has established KOACH, a network of programs that allow students to extend into their college years the kinds of worship, study, holiday, and social action activities they enjoyed as teens in youth group and at summer camp.[11]

As discussed earlier, marginal Jews tend to stay away from Jewish campus organizations, and even committed Reform Jews find themselves out in the cold. Few campuses, even those with Hillel directors from the Reform movement, are able to sustain a regular schedule of liberal worship services. A little self-help might be in order here. For example, it seems to me that if someone were to promote a reunion of former campers and counselors from Camp Swig, say, on a large California campus with a signficant Jewish population, that person might get a healthy turnout—and the critical mass for a liberal minyan. (Attention, Reform movement: Where's our KOACH?)

However, most Hillel directors are resigned to the fact that for many kids the college years are a time of resistance to religious life. "They're away from home for the first time, and they've got a lot of stuff to explore, and they're very busy with other things anyway, so it seems perfectly logical, normal, to me that people would drift away," says Cornell chaplain Larry Edwards. "I don't at all believe that that means they're lost to Judaism or the Jewish community. They're just doing other things right now."

As for interdating, if it's going to happen anywhere, it's probably going to happen in college. Even Brandeis has plenty of Gentile students. At the Claremont Colleges in Southern California, Rabbi Devorah Jacobson works with a very small Jewish population. "The only students that I meet who don't interdate are the ones who have really not left home emotionally," she says. "They talk about the terrible anxiety that they live with if they think about dating a non-Jew, because they know exactly what their parents' reactions are gonna be . . . and they're really quite fearful of those reactions, so they're the ones who emotionally have a harder time leaving home."

A note to parents (and this should not be news): No matter how strongly identified your children are as Jews, there is a much greater chance of them bringing home significant others named John Jr. and Kristin if you send them to St. Olaf's College in Railsburg, Illinois, rather than, say, Washington University. If you want your kids to be where Jews are, locate campus guides to that effect and use them as you start college-shopping.[12]

Adult Education

One of the tragedies of our community is that, for most Jews, their religious education ends at the precise moment—early adolescence—when they could begin to get something out of it. "Imagine if there was a profession that the knowledge ended when they're thirteen," J. Simcha Cohen, an Orthodox rabbi in Los Angeles, said in an interview. "Judaism is not for juniors. It's for adults, and therefore many of them have to learn as adults, have to be retaught as adults. And they have to be motivated once again." If the non-Orthodox movements want to create more solidly Jewish families, one thing they have to do is to make lifelong learners out of their young adults, starting the minute they emerge from grad school.

Opportunities for adult Jewish education are growing across America in both formal and informal settings. Every year, more Jews are attending retreats, workshops, and courses of study running from four weeks to two years, sponsored by synagogues, foundations, local Jewish colleges, and JCCs. People want these experiences and are willing to put time and money into becoming more Jewishly educated.[13] There's a catch, however: The vast majority of the Jews flocking to educational programs are folks who have already raised their families or committed themselves to Jewish practice and learning; they're the people historian Deborah Lipstadt calls "the lay elite" of the Jewish community.[14] (An ongoing exception is the Brandeis Collegiate Institute, which for more than fifty years has offered a 26-day summer camp to Jews in their twenties and has reignited the Jewish identity of many disaffiliated young people.)[15]

Of course, Jews of all ages should be encouraged to immerse themselves in Jewish learning, but once the programs are in place, leaders may want to focus their attention on the age group least likely to take advantage of them. The mid-twenties to mid-thirties have become the years during which American Jews are most likely to choose spouses, begin having children, and make other decisions that will determine the Jewish direction of their households, but they are also the years in which they are too overwhelmed by job and family responsibilities to go to a movie, let alone sign up for a course.[16] The Jewish community would do well to put resources into convincing singles that Jewish adult classes are where Mr. and Ms. Right hang out, into persuading couples without children that learning together is sexier than a week in the Bahamas, and into telling young parents what they want to hear most: Child Care Will Be Provided.

Institutional Life

A number of problems cling stubbornly to Jewish communal organizations. To many Jews, the synagogue and other institutions still appear to be unfriendly, forbidding places, where if you don't conform to the dominant demographics and lifestyle, you'll be snubbed, shunted aside, or even turned away. Some Jewish leaders claim that the synagogue can't be all things to all people, but, demographer Gary Tobin argues, it should be most things to most people if it's to play an important role for Jews at all stages of life, which is supposedly what the Jewish establishment wants. "The synagogue has to be more than a religious institution . . . but also must be a community center, an education center; it has to be the conduit for Jews to serve the community at large," Tobin told a UAHC regional convention audience. "It has to be an extended family and a nuclear family. It has to be a place that provides essential human services to Jews such as day care and Meals on Wheels. It has to be a place of worship, and it has to connect worship to all of these other activities."[17]

Much of the problem people have with the synagogue centers on money; the perception that you have to "pay to pray" engenders enormous resentment. "Only Jews define unaffiliation . . . as not paying dues to a congregation," Tobin said, adding that among Christians you're basically a member of a congregation unless you disappear or make a formal declaration of disassociation. Money can be a barrier to participation in other venues as well. For example, a friend complained that he was not allowed to help staff the phones for Federation's annual fundraising Sunday because he couldn't afford the minimum donation Federation required.

Tobin also indicates that leaders are forever expressing their concern over the survival of the American Jewish community but are not willing to admit that current mainstream institutions no longer meet the needs of many constituencies within that community, including singles, divorced and blended families, the intermarried, and older Jews who are relocated. (Add gay and lesbian singles and couples, not all of whom live near gay congregations and who increasingly are parents, with the same needs as heterosexual parents.) Some institutions are struggling to redefine themselves, he said in a University of Judaism lecture, but others are going to fall by the wayside through their stubborn insistence on looking to the past for answers, and synagogues have the greatest responsibility of all: "If [they] fail to adjust to the realities of contemporary American life, the probability that American Judaism can thrive in the ways it should thrive in the next century are fairly remote."[18]

Among the Jews underserved by Jewish institutions, the most ink has probably been devoted to unmarried adults. Since it became apparent that single adulthood was becoming more than a brief waystation between college and marriage, commentators have been pointing out the need to provide programming for singles and decrying the Jewish community's relegation of singles to the fringes of Jewish life.[19] "To the extent that Judaism is a family-centered tradition, people who do not see themselves as part of a family have no models to express their Judaism," two women wrote twenty years ago. "Since single people are no longer primarily defined as their parents' children, and are not—or at least not yet—defined as part of a couple and a new family, they do not fit into the Jewish community," they said, adding that the family-oriented activities and social groups within the synagogue marginalize and alienate single adults.[20]

One woman reported not long ago that after the end of a relationship she attended six different synagogues to meet new people and to explore the religious side of Judaism, which had been denied her by a secular upbringing. "I have smiled and said hello to many people; most ignored me," she wrote. "The one person who chatted with me was almost immediately carted away by his wife, who came running and attached herself to him like a remora when she saw him talking to me. Hey lady, I don't want *your* husband; I want my own."[21]

Single parents have it just as tough, even though mom-dad-and-kids households are now a minority among American Jews and more than one out of eight Jewish children are growing up in single-parent families, children whom Jewish leaders presumably want educated as Jews. They buy into the family orientation of the synagogue, but their needs as singles are not met, and they, too, often feel like outsiders among all the couples. They're also more likely to face financial and child care issues, which often get an insensitive response from institutions.[22] Marlene Marks wrote about one working single mother who couldn't find a Jewish preschool open until 6 PM. "Our mothers don't work," one administrator told her. "Or if they do, they send their drivers."[23]

One Northern California woman told a UAHC workshop audience that after her divorce she had struggled to keep up her temple dues, which were not lowered when she became single, and to keep her children in religious school. After several years, she remarried, and she and her new husband, per temple policy, received a year's free membership. "When I was struggling and by myself with kids, everyone knew it, and nobody helped," she said. "What really bothered me was that people my own age, people who had never been married and were out having a great old time while I was going to Shabbat services all those years, got to go to the High Holidays free with their parents once a year, and no one ever saw them again."

At times, institutional rigidity becomes self-destructive. A man in the same workshop said that after his son and non-Jewish daughter-in-law separated, the daughter-in-law, the custodial parent, wanted to enroll their five year old in religious school at the local Reform temple. The son, who was disaffiliated from Judaism, refused to join the temple, and the mother couldn't because she wasn't Jewish. When the son's parents tried to join the temple so they could enroll the child, they were told that only parents could enroll children in their religious school.

Synagogues, JCCs, and other sites of Jewish connection that alienate Jews through rigidity, bigotry, or simple obliviousness to potential members' needs are not only shooting themselves in the foot but are blowing it for the rest of the organized community, because people who are shined on by one institution often are loath to try another. The institutions that do business the way they did forty years ago may think they're preserving traditional lifestyles and values, but all they're really doing is fossilizing a Jewish community that no longer exists.

On the plus side, options for worship and Jewish involvement have expanded during the past decade or so.

Synagogue membership has slid to a postwar low, but a large swath of Americans, including many Jews, have found themselves searching for spiritual outlets that transcend the institutions in which they grew up and synthesize a desire for community with their needs for personal fulfillment and, in many cases, a feeling of connectedness to God.[24] Although many Jews, remembering their childhood experiences, are skeptical that they can find spiritual fulfillment within Jewish structures, the range of opportunities in which Jews can establish spiritual and interpersonal connectedness as Jews has grown enormously since most baby boomers were children.

Recognizing that American Jews are thirsting for spiritual connectedness but unwilling to accept the restrictions and sexism of Orthodoxy, the other major Jewish movements have begun to put some emphasis on making worship more appealing and accessible. In the Conservative movement, this has come about primarily through the inclusion of women in most situations as full participants in worship and service leadership (although many Conservative institutions offer parallel traditional and egalitarian services rather than unifying worship under the egalitarian banner) and through a new generation of leadership that has no ties to Orthodoxy.[25] Although not all Conservative synagogues have progressed with the times and most do not promote social activism in the larger community, the official movement position includes a respect for religious pluralism that makes it a good choice for Jews who seek traditional worship within a modern context.[26]

"Spirituality" is the buzzword for the 1990s in the Reform movement. Although some Reform leaders dismiss the idea of more "spiritual" worship as a fad, dismissing it alternately as supernaturalistic and an attempt to suck up to the more traditional movements, the UAHC, at least on the national level, seems sincere in its efforts to translate what could be an empty concept into warmer, more interactive, and more inclusive worship that brings God into the room rather than keeping the Divine Presence at an unreachable distance. This trend moves away from the classical Reform aesthetic and sensibility to one that encourages congregations to use more Hebrew and traditional prayers in the service, to institute Shabbat morning worship and Torah study, to include a variety of musical styles, and to make God a focus of discussion and connection. At the same time, Reform remains faithful to its principles of social action, gender equality, rational thought, and pluralism. While many temples and congregants are comfortable with the old model, the Reform leadership appears determined to shake off the movement's image as a default mode for lazy, assimilationist Jews who define themselves by the traditions they *don't* have to follow and present itself as a movement in which practitioners are encouraged to choose the traditions and observances that are relevant to their lives and that make them feel connected to God and to each other.[27]

The newest of the major movements, Reconstructionism, is less familiar to most Jews, having become institutionalized only during most baby boomers' lifetimes. A rapidly expanding breakaway from the Conservative movement, Reconstructionism is based on the teachings of Rabbi Mordecai Kaplan, who rejected the concept of a supernatural, controlling God (defining God rather as the power or process that leads to human fulfillment) and the concept of the Jewish people as chosen by God. The movement sees the rabbi as a facilitator and teacher rather than an authority figure and shares the egalitarian and progressive principles of Reform Judaism.[28]

Another consortium of small, progressive fellowships, one whose members combine elements of Eastern religion, New Age thought, meditation, and mysticism with traditional and not-so-traditional Hebrew worship, is found in the Jewish Renewal movement, loosely organized under the banner of ALEPH: Alliance for Jewish Renewal. Founded by Rabbi Zalman Schachter-Shalomi, a former Lubavitcher Chasid who was deeply influenced by the 1960s counterculture and studied psychology and Asian religion during that period, the Renewalist movement focuses on prayer in all its aspects: whom it addresses, whom it includes, what it means, how it sounds, and how it affects each person. There is also an emphasis on dance, song, and motion in worship. Jewish Renewalists are also devoted to the precepts of inclusivity, diversity, gender equality, and *tikkun olam*, the healing of the world, with a special emphasis on environmentalism.[29]

Among Jewish congregations organized along demographic rather than philosophical lines, there are communities devoted to interfaith couples, congregations for single adults, and synagogues with an outreach to gay men and lesbians.[30] Gay and lesbian congregations around the United States vary widely in size and liturgical style, but they tend to be progressive and innovative, as well as welcoming and nonjudgmental communities. Many heterosexuals, especially couples who are at ease with gay men and lesbians, who don't need a Jewish religious school, and who feel out of place at mainstream synagogues, may find themselves very much at home in a gay shul. In addition, the feminist movement within Judaism has produced formal and informal institutions that are not congregations but that offer classes, festival celebrations, and women-oriented activities such as Rosh Chodesh observances that connect Jewish women with new skills, knowledge, and connection to Jewish practice. They also serve as think tanks for new rituals that celebrate the cycles of women's lives.[31]

The structure within organized Jewish life that is beginning to exert what may be a lasting effect on Jewish institutions is the *chavurah*, the small fellowship community. In 1968, a group of religious but countercultural Jews in the Boston area, out of patience with the complacency of mainstream synagogue life, founded a group, Chavurat Shalom, to provide the autonomy, democracy, intimacy, and focus on prayer that conventional temples did not. Other *chavurot* sprang up around the country as Jews discovered what one writer later called "a Judaism of scale." The early *chavurot* followed the traditional liturgy more or less, but they comprised one of many movements to give *halacha*, Jewish law, a vote but not a veto.[32]

The *chavurah* influence is felt today not only in the Jewish Renewal movement but in the independent *chavurot*, sometimes called minyans, and small independent synagogues that dot the Jewish landscape; in the congregations that have broken away from large, impersonal synagogues; and in the many synagogues that have organized *chavurot* among their own members on the basis of demography, interest, or social needs. Synagogue-based *chavurot* have allowed members of large congregations to study together, socialize, celebrate holidays, and form extended families in settings that make possible the intimacy and participation the larger venue cannot always provide.[33]

In making synagogues welcoming communities, liberal Jews can learn from the Orthodox, who forty years ago were supposed to be dying out. When a New York Orthodox rabbi noticed that Jews weren't going to shul because they didn't know the service, he instituted a "beginners' service" (sometimes called a learners' minyan), in which participants could go through the prayers slowly, have them explained, and ask questions; now Reform and Conservative temples have instituted them, too.[34] The liberal movements are just beginning to study what the Orthodox are doing to welcome Jews into their communities and to adapt those activities for their own institutions; this should be a priority.[35]

Finally, if Jewish leaders want less intermarriage and more strongly identified Jews, then Jewish institutions need to go where Jews are and provide what Jews need. Large urban synagogues need to open satellites in suburbs where not so many—but some—Jews live. Struggling small congregations need to link up to provide programming they cannot afford solo. And they all have to get the word out: We're here, we're open, walk in.

So who pays, and how?

It's become clear that synagogues are going to have to move away from their rigid definitions of what constitutes temple membership and how much people should pay for it. We are a society of consumers, and American Jews bring the same consumerist mentality to the synagogue as Americans bring to most institutions. No matter how much hot air Jewish leaders expend scolding American Jews about their responsibility to join synagogues, most people simply will not spend a large chunk of their disposable income on year-in, year-out membership in an institution they see as relevant to their lives only at certain discrete moments in the life cycle. "It's not that dues are too high," Egon Mayer has said. "The full sentence is, 'For an institution I'm not using, that's a lot of money to pay.'"[36]

Accordingly, many synagogues have instituted reduced-fee and even free memberships for young singles and couples, generally people under 30, with graduated increases in fees after the cut-off point until they're paying full dues. By allowing people to experience the full range of synagogue life for little or no money, these institutions have created a large group of Jews who see temple membership as multifaceted and worthwhile for the long term, and their programs have an excellent retention rate after the "young adult" phase.[37] And although the idea of offering a la carte life-cycle services is anathema to many congregational rabbis, fee-for-service structures may be another way to bring families into synagogue life by making available what they need when they need

it. "I provide the unaffiliated with life-cycle services, and I don't particularly rel-
ish it, but those ritual moments are the times you can really touch people," says
Rabbi Steven Foster, leader of Denver's largest Reform congregation.[38]

In the short term, though, making synagogue membership and Jewish education affordable is an expensive proposition, and many Jewish institutions are too
strapped for cash to provide all the programs their members call for, let alone
subsidize temple dues and school fees for households with limited disposable
income. In recent years, there has been a steady call for a closer and more equal
partnership between Jewish Federations, the central agencies that provide a variety of services and program funds to the Jews of large and good-sized American cities, and synagogues.[39] But there are obstacles to such aid. One involves
Federation politics and its mandate to work with the full range of Jewish constituencies, which in real terms sometimes means that a local Federation will
fund the programs of one denomination at the expense of others.

The other involves the amount of money Federations have to spend; donations are in decline, with the biggest givers dying off and younger Jewish households with discretionary income more likely to give to non-Jewish charities than
to Jewish causes. (The single bright spot in Jewish philanthropy is the growing
role of Jewish family foundations.) In addition, less than half the money raised
by United Jewish Appeal/Federation drives stays home; at least half of it goes
overseas, mostly to Israel. Between 1990 and 1992, Operation Exodus, the
effort to resettle Jews of the former Soviet Union in Israel, raised almost $600
million, an outpouring that HUC sociologist Gerald Bubis says is unlikely to be
repeated.[40] Lately, Israeli leaders have been telling American Jews to keep their
money at home,[41] but rather than providing more money for programs here in
the States, donors have simply given less or given elsewhere; domestic programs
aren't as compelling as building the Jewish state.

When Neal Weinberg of the University of Judaism told the UJA that the
Jewish community needed an American Emergency Fund analogous to the Israel
Emergency Fund to subsidize scholarships and help upgrade Jewish schools,
synagogues, and camping programs, "they were very sympathetic, but they said,
'You know, we've mentioned that many times to the higher echelons, and it's not
sexy.' Someone would rather give money to build a school in Israel than build a
school . . . that would help the Jews in America. So we're going to shoot ourselves in the foot. We're going to be sending all our money out to Israel to help
other Jews, but we're not going to help ourselves."

Not until major Jewish donors see programs that support American Jewish
continuity as causes worth giving to, until supporting Jewish life here at home

becomes what Steven Bayme calls the "philanthropic norm," will sufficient cash begin to flow to those programs. "The real challenge to American Jewry is to do for our people precisely what Zionist PR people have so successfully done for Israel," an Ohio rabbi wrote to *Moment*. "[W]e need to show that Judaism here in this country can be a thrilling and exciting . . . part of our lives."[42]

And it can be—but it has to be part of your life before it can be a thrilling and exciting part of your life.

Because my mother had never lighted Shabbat candles, I had never lighted Shabbat candles. After I remarried, I wanted to start, but it felt weird, and the timing was off; I didn't want to light them alone, and my husband almost never got home from work until after I left for shul, let alone sundown. Luckily, I mentioned this to one of my first interview subjects, a rabbi I'd known for years. Don't worry about sundown, he said. If your husband doesn't get home till late, light the candles when you get home from temple. The important thing is to do it.

So we did it, around 10:30 PM, maybe every couple of weeks at first, then pretty much every week. Then after a couple of years, during some months when I was going out of town a lot, my husband started lighting the candles and saying the blessing himself when I wasn't home. Now he's beginning to persuade his employer that he needs to be home early on Friday evening and he's not available to work on Saturdays, and I no longer grade papers or run errands on Saturday. Now we often manage to cook a real dinner and sit down together and say a *kiddush* and a *motzi* before we eat. We will never be completely *shomer Shabbat*, but Shabbat is finally part of our lives.

"Just do it," thanks to Nike's ad agency, has become one of the great premillennial clichés, but it is completely appropriate to any discussion of how to head off marriages that won't serve the cause of Jewish continuity. In his excellent, practical book, *40 Things You Can Do to Save the Jewish People*, Joel Grishaver says really strong Jewish identity comes when you "tag all four bases": national Judaism, which is ethnic and political but at bottom is simply a sense of connection with other Jews; communal Judaism, finding an extended family within Jewish institutions; familial Judaism, bringing Jewish practices into the home; and personal Judaism, how being Jewish makes us feel inside.[43] It's not that hard to tag all four bases. It isn't even that expensive.

Home observance doesn't have to be white-tablecloth-matzo-balls-good-china. Traditionalists may shudder, but a lot of liberal educators have told harried parents that if saying *kiddush* over 7-Up and *motzi* over pizza is the best you can manage on a Friday night, then go for it; the important thing is to be together and share Shabbat together. One educator told me that when her kids were teenagers and wanted to go to high school football and basketball games instead of temple, she and some other Jewish parents would make tailgate Shabbats in the school parking lot; the kids would run out and light the candles with their folks, then run back in. This same woman and her family brought their *havdalah* ceremony to the Hollywood Bowl, and Jews came from all around the amphitheater to participate.

There are lots of children's books on Jewish subjects. Take a break from Dr. Seuss and read them to and with your kids. Make challah. Put up a mezuzah. If you don't have family, recruit some. Don't worry if you do something the wrong way. One of the nice things about Judaism is that you get to do things over and over, and there are lots of books and other materials to help you get it right.

Communal involvement is more problematic. If you live in or near a big city, it takes time and energy to find the right institution; if you're not in a metropolitan center, your options may be limited. You may be embarrassed by a lack of money or lack of Hebrew. You may be carrying all sorts of emotional baggage. I don't know how many people I've talked to over the years who seem convinced that if they step into any synagogue in America they will have exactly the same experience they had at age 12, no matter how much you tell them that the rabbi, the liturgy, the atmosphere, and the architecture are different.

This mind set, I'm convinced, is responsible for a lot of people who say, "I can be Jewish by myself." But that's just the problem: you *can't* be Jewish by yourself. Judaism requires community; it's set up to bring people together in a common space with common goals. Maybe your workplace, the local sports bar, or the other parents at Gymboree are enough community for you. If so, *mazel tov.* But if you are a disaffiliated Jew searching for spiritual fulfillment, it's time for you to reexplore your Jewish options.

And it's time to stop making excuses. *My parents never went to temple* is not a reason. *I hated Hebrew school* is not a reason. It's been twenty-five years since that conceited, bullying shmuck of a cantor at your parents' temple called you stupid when he was teaching you your Torah portion. He's retired, he's *dead*—get over it. If you don't know where to start looking for a congregation, call the Federation or a major movement's headquarters, or open the local Jewish newspaper.[44] Be prepared to compromise (or create your own minyan), because no synagogue is perfect, and don't let a temple be anything but welcoming. Speak up! If your Jewish knowledge isn't where you want it to be, take a class, read a book, order a CD for your computer. You felt stupid and gross when you joined the health club, didn't you? But if you stuck with it, after a while the muscles appeared and the workouts got much easier. Same thing.

As for the costs . . . Let's start by getting rid of the "pay to pray" hangup. Synagogues have expenses: mortgage, salaries, utilities, office supplies. They don't pass a collection plate every week; their income is dues and donations. Nevertheless, *no major-movement synagogue charges admission for worship* except for High Holiday services held in halls away from the temple. Most of the money raised from High Holiday tickets sold to nonmembers goes to cover the extra costs to the temple, such as renting the ballroom or theater. If a synagogue offers holiday tickets to the public, it will generally reduce or waive the fee for people who can't afford them.

If you want formal affiliation or you have kids you want in religious school, then spending the money has to be a priority. Is it worth as much to your family as the health club or that second weekend ski trip? Is there something you're spending 40 bucks a week on that you don't really have to have? Starting a Jewish life fund early on—when you get married, when the first baby is born—can make a huge difference. (Hint to parents of adult children: how about sending your newlyweds to Maui for one week instead of two and starting the fund with the difference?) If money is really a problem at the temple you want to join, be candid about needing a break in fees and why you need it. And again, stand up to anyone who gives you a hard time. Ask that person, is this synagogue interested in Jews living Jewishly and raising Jewish children or isn't it?

I won't tell you to take food out of your children's mouths or even to cancel your cable subscription in order to join a temple. I can tell you only that when you find a congregation that's a good spiritual and social fit, it's worth every nickel. And the options really are exciting. After years of ossification, some synagogues—and their congregants—are finally starting to evolve.

Just do it—then get someone else to do it.

Bringing Jewish Women and Men Together

Even if American Judaism does experience a spiritual revival, there's still the problem of how Jewish men and women perceive each other as romantic partners. Are there any signs that young Jewish adults are willing to break through their stereotypes and make "marrying Jewish" a goal rather than a chance occurrence?

In terms of teaching adolescents about the importance of endogamous relationships, the programs are out there, although how widely they're being used is open to question. Materials published by the UAHC's Commission on Reform Jewish Outreach, United Synagogue's Commission on the Prevention of Inter-marriage, and independent publishers concerning issues of interdating and stereotyping are available for use in Jewish classrooms, youth groups, and summer camps. In addition, Jewish educational organizations maintain program banks of materials and curricular ideas sent in by individual educators, and the major Jewish movements routinely conduct workshops on the subject of interdating at regional and national conventions.[45] All the programs focus on the building of personal Jewish identity as the cornerstone of the formation of endogamous relationships and the establishment of Jewish homes as adults. Not surprisingly, the Conservative materials stress inmarriage as the only way a Jewish family can be formed; the Reform materials, while expressing the hope that Jews will marry Jews, also recognize that youngsters may wind up asserting their Jewishness with a non-Jewish partner. Printed materials from both movements note the necessity of being sensitive to students who are the offspring of mixed couples.[46]

In the fight against labeling Jewish girls and boys as JAPs and nerds, again, the program ideas and the desire to use them certainly exist. Allen Maller would like to see the topic introduced at age 13 or 14, when kids are starting to date in groups. "Show a dozen photographs of different women and ask which ones they think are the most attractive," he suggested. "Why did you pick that one? What did you like about that one? Then ask them if they can pick out the ones who are Jewish. Why did you think that one was Jewish? Why didn't you think that one was Jewish? It would be interesting."[47] Harold Schulweis suggests fighting the stereotypes by training kids not to become princes and princesses, by teaching modesty, humility, and respect for money as Jewish values.

On the young adult level, there's certainly no dearth of programming for singles; open any local Jewish weekly and the listings will be there. But program designers are still trying to figure out what simply throws Jews in a room together and what establishes a basis for relationship. Most maligned are the Jewish equivalents of singles bars, the dances and parties labeled "meat markets" and "watering holes for losers" by many of their critics. Although Jewish couples certainly have met through such events, they seem by their very nature to encourage the kinds of superficial judgments based on physical appearance and first impressions that have harmed the cause of endogamy for the past generation. Some singles complain that social events sponsored by a particular synagogue or organization "have the same faces over and over again."[48]

More engaging for many singles are institution-based programs that bring young adults together for worship, study, or community projects. Synagogues across the country have drawn in the 22–40 crowd with strategies including holiday celebrations, Torah study circles, potluck meals in people's homes, low-cost memberships and High Holiday tickets, and young adult "temples-within-the-temple."[49] Some single adults are more comfortable in a worship setting that doesn't label them by marital status but simply includes them as equals. One woman praised a Los Angeles synagogue's large, eclectic Saturday morning minyan for being "multi-everything" and not pigeonholing her as a single. "It's one of the few places where I have felt very comfortable being a single, and yet I'm in a Jewish community. . . . There are tons of other single people here, but we're not being pulled in with, 'This is a singles [event].'" Her ambivalence is common among single adults who want to meet other Jews but who attend Jewish programs to be involved in Jewish life, not to get a date.

One tip the liberal Jewish community has picked up from the Orthodox world is the use of the *shadchan*. Non-Orthodox professional matchmakers, some of whom went into business in direct response to the rise in intermarriage, have set up shop across the country. "I believe Jewish people should marry in their own faith," said Gene Sadoff, a former magazine editor and computer maven who opened BayDates in San Jose, California, a few years ago. "There simply wasn't anyone out there who was really bringing Jewish singles together."[50] Matchmakers' fees vary widely, and so do client lists, both in length and breadth, so if you decide to go that route, shop around. In some cities, JCCs run matchmaking programs, and in 1991, Temple Emanuel of Denver became the first synagogue in the United States to open a dating service, the Colorado Jewish Social Network, which also sponsors interest groups, social events, and singles weekends.[51]

Again, we live in a consumer culture, and a lot of people, especially people who grew up, as many Jews have, with a strong sense of entitlement, have bought the idea that whatever they want in a partner, they can have. "You want to buy a VCR, there's a zillion different kinds. Cars come with different features; you can pretty much look for and buy what you want," says Rabbi Robert Rubin, who works with singles from his New Jersey congregation. "In the singles matching world, you end up sometimes getting into this mode where, especially with the matching services, the underlying assumption is you can come in, describe who you want, and that person somehow appears. Well, people don't come that way."

So a lot of Jews need to be reeducated, taught that the perfect mate is not necessarily blond, rich, tall, dangerous, terminally hip, pencil-thin, or twenty years younger; in fact, they need to figure out that there's no such thing as a perfect mate. They need to unlearn the stereotypes they've assimilated over the years and come to terms with their own ambivalence about being Jewish so they'll quit saying that they really want to marry Jews but all the Jews they meet are just awful.[52] Here, too, the liberal movements can learn from the Orthodox; the *baalei tshuvah* who run Aish HaTorah pack their halls with programs on sex and dating, attracting hundreds of secular Jews who don't particularly cotton to Aish's Orthodox party line but who want to meet Jews, learn something about Judaism, and discuss something sexy, all at the same time.[53]

Sylvia Barack Fishman predicts that as long as Jewish women keep postponing marriage until after their careers are on track, they're going to keep finding the Great Jewish Guys all taken by the time they're ready to settle down, and she has a suggestion she admits is somewhat retrograde: marry younger. "I think if women do want to marry Jewish men, if that is a priority, then they need to think about taking these guys seriously when they're young . . . guys who aren't neurotic and who just tend to fall in love when they meet a girl they like and don't have a list of 97 qualities that a woman has to pass in order to get to a first date," Fishman said. "They're not as attractive when they're young. . . . [but] if they meet somebody, they just fall in love and get married, because they don't have a lot of neurotic reasons for not getting married. And that's one of the reasons why a lot of the good Jewish men are taken when they're very young . . . [and why] a lot of wonderful Jewish women end up marrying wonderful non-Jewish men."

There are faint signs that younger Jews may be a little less quick to apply stereotypes, if only because they know they're not supposed to. When I spent an hour chatting with some Zeta Beta Tau fraternity members at Tufts, they all allowed that they knew some women who fit the JAP stereotype, but they were reluctant to use the "J-word," and a couple of them took pains to assure me that they had met Jewish women at college who proved that the stereotype was exactly that. A Hillel rabbi at a New York campus said he believes the virulence of the JAP label has turned the corner and is used only by people trying to bolster their own fragile egos. Besides, he said, "people know better than to talk about it now"; in New York, people will jump all over anyone who cracks a JAP joke. In addition, some rabbis and teenagers suggested to me that when kids are involved in Jewish life, they may view the Jews of the opposite sex in their own high schools and youth groups as too familiar to be desirable, but they have no trouble with their counterparts at regional events, other high schools, or in college.

As some young Jews realize that where they live may well help determine whom they marry—the intermarriage rate in New York, for example, is much lower than in the rest of the United States[54]—they are making life decisions to influence the odds. "The attitude at school amongst my friends was, yeah, they would prefer to meet someone Jewish, [but] if they didn't, it wouldn't be so horrible," a recent Brandeis alumna told me. "I think that's changing now, though. Now my friends more and more are talking about where can they go, where can they live, where can they go to grad school, where can they find a job where they will be around Jewish people? It's a big concern."

No Guarantees

A Jewish girl grows up in the Midwest: mother and father both active in the Conservative synagogue, Shabbat dinner every week, day school through sixth grade, bat mitzvah, Hebrew High, USY, president of B'nai B'rith Youth, Jewish sorority, Shabbat observance in her own apartment. In her early twenties, she moves to Atlanta, meets a Methodist, marries him in church, and converts to his faith.[55]

I interview a young stand-up comic who tells me about his semi-observant upbringing and his dating history, including his one long-term relationship with a non-Jewish woman, his desire to raise Jewish kids and his preference to meet and marry a Jewish woman. And he tells me about his two brothers, one of whom married a Gentile and is now completely nonreligious, one of whom became a Lubavitcher.

There are no guarantees.

A Jewish mother in Massachusetts, a woman who has kept a kosher home all her life, is frantic that her two college-age sons are involved with Gentile girls. " 'Do you honestly think you could someday marry a girl who isn't Jewish?' I ask, and mostly they just stare at me. . . . 'Well, it will break my heart if you do,' I answer their shrugs. Sometimes I launch into a monologue about the importance of Judaism to their father and me; other times, I just leave the room, hoping that my look of misery when I even mention the word 'intermarriage' will frighten them away from such an act."[56] Unfortunately for this mother, the combination of *kashrut* and guilt as a deterrent to intermarriage quit working sometime between Woodstock and Nixon's resignation.

Then you have the adult children of my parents' friends whom I interviewed, a small battalion of *b'nai* and *b'not mitzvah*, all raised in loving, intact, endogamous Jewish homes, all raised with pride in their Jewishness, all intermarried or interdating.

Nothing can guarantee that any young Jew who lives in contemporary American society will find and marry a Jewish partner. No parent, no school, no synagogue, no summer camp, no youth group, no circle of friends, no singles group or combination thereof can prevent a Jew from meeting and falling in love with a Gentile if the right person comes along.

However, parents who infuse their homes with the joy of Jewish living, synagogues that offer profound, meaningful worship, Jewish education that excites children's imagination and intellect, youth experiences that fill adolescents with pride in themselves and their Jewishness, and barrier-free opportunities for institutional involvement as young adults can guarantee plenty. They can guarantee marriageable adults for whom Judaism is as much a part of their lives as their height. They can guarantee Jews who will actively seek out Jewish partners. They can guarantee Jews who screen out, however reluctantly, religiously committed non-Jews as possible spouses. They can guarantee Jews for whom Jewish involvement, a Jewish home, and the raising of Jewish children are nonnegotiable. They can guarantee Jews who not only have "Jewish radar" but *new and improved* Jewish radar, the kind that connects not only to other Jews but to potential Jews. They can guarantee Jews who, if they happen to marry non-Jews, will make their *Yiddishkeit* an irresistible magnet to the people who love them. They can guarantee many more generations of Jews—if the doors of Jewish institutions are kept open.

9

A Time to Embrace

There are lots of people ... who say, "Anybody who wants to come to the Jewish community, all they have to do is knock on the door and we'll open the door." My sense is you don't wait for them to knock on the door, you open the door. Then you go out and ask them to come in. [We] don't have the luxury of waiting around for somebody to knock on the door.

—Rabbi Lavey Derby, Tiburon, California

Shammai's ill temper almost drove us from the world; Hillel's gentleness brought us under the wings of the Divine Presence.

—Three converts relating their experiences in the Talmud (*Shabbat* 31a)

Ten years after the Reform synagogue in which she had grown up told her to marry her non-Jewish fiancé somewhere else, Carla got a call from the temple's rabbi, who congratulated her on having had a baby. (Her son was three years old at the time, Carla says, something the rabbi must have known, since her parents were still members.) "He said, 'I just wanted to say that I hope you've given some thought to his Jewish education, and have you thought about joining [our] temple?'" Bemused by the rabbi's newly welcoming attitude, Carla mentioned the phone call to a friend who belonged to the temple. "Oh, haven't you heard?" the friend said. "We have outreach now."

Patrilineal Descent

The era of contemporary Jewish outreach—programming and policies within the major Jewish movements in response to the needs of intermarried couples, children of the intermarried, converts to Judaism, and potential converts to Judaism—began in December 1978, when UAHC president Rabbi Alexander Schindler called for the Reform movement to establish a comprehensive program that would welcome and serve these constituencies. The UAHC and the Central Conference of American Rabbis (CCAR), the Reform movement's rabbinic arm, created a joint task force on outreach that was elevated to commission status in 1983 and given a mandate (and a budget) to develop programming for the target populations.[1] During the 1980s, the UAHC placed outreach coordinators in its regional offices and began to disseminate programs to synagogues.

That same year, 1983, the CCAR voted to affirm that any child with one Jewish parent, mother or father, would be acknowledged as Jewish by Reform rabbis and institutions if the child's parents established an exclusive Jewish identity for the child through appropriate "public and formal acts of identification with the Jewish faith and people," such as *brit milah*, formal Jewish education, bar or bat mitzvah, and confirmation.[2] This flew in the face of established Jewish law, which for more than two thousand years had insisted that Jewish lineage could be determined only by the mother. To be acknowledged as a Jew by most Jewish institutions, a "patrilineal Jew" would have to make a formal conversion.

The Reform rabbis' position was nothing new; the CCAR had adopted a similar resolution in 1947 and reaffirmed it in the 1961 edition of the movement's *Rabbi's Manual*.[3] But the 1983 resolution caused a furor, probably because it was the first time a major movement had addressed the question of personal Jewish status since intermarriage rates had shot up. It was one thing to declare that the children of Jewish fathers and non-Jewish mothers were Jews when there were relatively few children in that situation; it was another when synagogues and Judaism as a whole could conceivably be asked to deal with tens of thousands of patrilineal Jews.

It didn't matter to more traditional Jews that the matrilineal principle itself had been a change from the way Jewish status was conferred in the Torah; in biblical times, the few women who married out of their tribes went with their husbands and became part of their people, so a non-Israelite woman who married an Israelite became a de facto Israelite through marriage. After the Babylonian exile, however, the Jews were surrounded by so many people of other ethnic groups that intermarriage became much more common, and the prophets Ezra and Nehemiah, in the fifth century B.C.E., met this challenge by declaring all intermarriages illicit. Patrilineality was still the rule; Ezra's wrinkle was that Jewish status was conferred *by* the father but could be conferred only *through* a Jewish mother, not a non-Jewish woman. By the time the Talmud was compiled early in the third century C.E., the rabbis had adopted the matrilineal rule, in accordance with the custom that the wife in an illicit marriage would return to her own people with her children, and also recognizing that it is easier to prove maternity than paternity.[4]

Non-Orthodox Jewish leaders who oppose opening Jewish status to patrilineals advance three basic arguments: it separates the most liberal movements from the rest of American Jewry; it reduces the standard for Jewish status to a lowest common denominator and cements Reform's image as a movement that promotes minimal observance and allegiance to Jewish law; and it puts most of the responsibility for Jewish child rearing in such families in the hands of non-Jewish women who are ill equipped to do a good job or who are bringing their own religious agendas to the task.[5]

"The argument I've heard that's most appealing for changing it is that we should treat men and women equally," Rabbi Bradley Shavit Artson, a Conservative rabbi in Southern California, said in an interview. "[But] I think *halacha* should reflect sociology, and the reality of the world is that the vast preponderance of children are raised by mothers, not by fathers," adding that the children of non-Jewish women and Jewish men can undergo ritual conversion when they're babies, a much simpler process than adult conversion, and be acknowledged as Jews. Artson, among others, also claims that the Reform movement is unlikely to hold any children of intermarriage to its stated standard of Jewish study and participation in childhood life cycle events, asserting that Reform rabbis will wind up according Jewish status to anyone who claims a Jewish parent of either sex, whether or not he or she has met the standards of Jewish identity.

Proponents of a "nonlineal" approach argue that matrilineal descent was just as expedient to the rabbis of the first couple of centuries C.E. as traditional rabbis claim acceptance of patrilineal descent is now. The rabbis had no trouble changing Jewish law to suit their purposes, despite dozens of biblical precedents for patrilineality, so why is it wrong now to adapt *halacha* to a changing world? At a time when there are no guarantees that committed Jewish fathers and Gentile mothers *won't* take responsibility for their children's Jewish lives or that disaffected Jewish women *will* make sure their children are raised as Jews, it makes sense to view either Jewish parent as a transmitter of Jewish identity and to require that all children of intermarriage become educated, visible participants in Jewish life in order to be recognized as Jews.[6]

Harold Schulweis, a Conservative rabbi who supports patrilineality, says the principle's biggest problem is its source: "First of all, if it comes from Reform, it's *treif* [non-kosher]. . . . Believe me, if somebody from the yeshiva said patrilineal ought to be looked at, they would treat it differently." It's rapidly becoming a nonissue among Conservative laity, the majority of whom are ready to accept patrilineal Jews as Jewish when those Jews are their sons- and daughters-in-law or their grandchildren.[7]

Although it remains to be seen whether the Reform movement's position on patrilineality will in fact produce a greater number of strongly identified Jews from mixed households, its attitude of inclusion has to be more conducive to Jewish continuity than the terrible public relations that occur when, for example, an Israeli soldier killed by terrorists is denied burial with others who served their country because his mother wasn't Jewish.[8] The daughter of Theodore Herzl, founder of modern Zionism, who was born to a non-Jewish mother, died at Theresienstadt concentration camp; traditional Jewish leaders surely need no reminder that which parent was Jewish mattered little to the Nazis.

Rabbinic Officiation at Intermarriages

Many mixed couples have their first outreach experiences on their way to the altar as they look for rabbis to perform their wedding ceremonies. Rabbis at Conservative and Orthodox synagogues are not allowed to officiate at weddings uniting Jews and non-Jews under any circumstances; Reform rabbis are discouraged from officiating but not prohibited.[9] Studies of members of the CCAR and the Reconstructionist Rabbinical Association indicate that 40–50 percent of Reform rabbis and about a third of Reconstructionist rabbis are willing to officiate at mixed weddings under various conditions, with most of those who don't officiate willing to refer couples to rabbis who do. Most rabbis who perform intermarriages do so under the condition that the partners commit to making a Jewish home and raising their children as Jews, and most also require that the rabbi be the only officiant—no clergy of another faith. Some require the non-Jewish partner to take a basic Judaism class or commit to a less formal course of study before the wedding. A small number of rabbis will co-officiate at interfaith weddings under almost any circumstances, including as co-officiants at weddings in church settings with Christian liturgy.[10]

Reform rabbis who don't officiate at intermarriages say they refuse because they don't consider a mixed marriage to be a Jewish marriage; because the language of the ceremony—"Be thou consecrated unto me according to the faith of Moses and Israel"—precludes performing a ceremony for a couple that includes a partner who isn't Jewish; because they think it gives rabbinic approval to intermarriage; and because it's unfair to people who have taken the trouble to convert to Judaism before their weddings. They also deny that rabbinic officiation makes an intermarried couple more likely to join a synagogue or raise their children unambiguously Jewish, as many proponents of officiation claim.[11]

These rabbis are liable to take a lot of heat from their congregants, many of whom expect their rabbis to perform their children's wedding ceremonies as a privilege of temple membership; young people who grew up in temple and enjoyed warm relationships with their rabbis are often shocked when those rabbis won't marry them. There's a deep split between the attitude toward officiation in the rabbinate and among the laity: overwhelming majorities of Reform and Conservative Jews think their rabbis should marry mixed couples who commit to raising Jewish children.[12] Many Reform congregations won't interview candidates for their pulpits who don't perform intermarriages, much to the dismay of the CCAR. Perhaps because of pressure from colleagues, some Reform rabbis keep their willingness to officiate off the record, and some say they don't when in fact they do.[13]

For many intermarrying couples planning to form Jewish families, it's frustrating to be denied rabbinic officiation when they know that any rabbi will marry a completely nonobservant endogamous Jewish couple. The rather lame reason rabbis give for marrying apathetic Jews when they won't marry a mixed couple committed to Jewish life is that the endogamous couple may develop a feeling for Judaism at some point, at which time they'd be better equipped to maintain a Jewish home than an intermarried couple. (One rabbi did say that he'd turned away Jewish couples who were "obtuse about spirituality and the spiritual dimensions of marriage.")

Nonofficiating rabbis are also taken to task for refusing to marry mixed couples but inviting them to join their temples after the weddings, which is often read as "I won't marry you, but my temple will be happy to take your money once somebody else does." The standard reply to that criticism is that Jewish law often differs on the response to an act before it happens and after the fact; the welcome intermarried couples receive in Reform synagogues is independent of the rabbi's stance on intermarriage. To try to defuse the anger and rejection that often arise around the issue of nonofficiation, many rabbis spend time with mixed couples, explaining their position and encouraging the pair's continued participation in Jewish life. "If it was the relationship that was the problem, we would not offer outreach programming for interfaith couples, period," one Reform rabbi said at a UAHC convention. "It's not so much the marriage that's the problem but . . . how they wish to officially vow love to one another and to a people."

"You can't make communal policy based on the great exceptions . . . [but] that doesn't mean you treat 'em all the same," says Mark Winer, explaining why he doesn't officiate. Faced with a committed Jew and a supportive non-Jewish partner, "I'd say, Look, you're not gonna convert, that's not important. Let me be your friend, let me be your rabbi. Let's study Judaism together. . . . They almost always end up studying Judaism with me, and they almost always end up converting to Judaism, because the more they learn, the more comfortable they feel, and the more they say, 'You know, I think I always was Jewish, I just didn't know it.' "

Rabbis who do officiate at mixed weddings, especially those who require a commitment from couples to maintain Jewish homes, insist that their approach not only leads to the creation of Jewish households raising Jewish kids, but a good number of formal conversions down the road. "When a couple calls me and says they want me to do their wedding . . . they come in and we sit and talk, and I ask them about kids, and they have already decided they're going to raise them as Jews," says David Fass. "They have a lot of evidence to confirm that they'll really do that. Why bother telling me that if it's not true? There's no percentage in it any more. Someone will marry them. So unless they're telling me the truth, there's no reason to say it. . . . Many of them send me pictures of the kids as they're born, and they tell me about brises and bar mitzvahs. These people, as far as I can tell, are raising Jewish kids."

Fass, who has been officiating at intermarriages for more than twenty years, claims that 75–80 percent of the non-Jews he has married to Jews have converted to Judaism, either before the wedding or, in most cases, later on, "usually precipitated by the birth of children."[14]

Officiating rabbis also express impatience with what they see as hypocrisy among colleagues who are perfectly willing to refer mixed couples to them. "My colleagues who are so interested in saying mixed marriages are verboten, you can't even get involved with them, you don't want to talk to these people . . . the minute they get married, the rabbi turns around and says, 'Why don't you join a synagogue?' " says New Jersey rabbi Harvey Goldman. Rabbi Lawrence Forman of Norfolk, Virginia, says he requires the couples he marries, including the mixed couples, to join his synagogue. "The ones who don't stay are the ones who come from the Conservative shul," Forman says. "They join for a year and stay for a quarter, and then they go back, because the hypocrisy of the Conservative movement is, 'Well, we'll let Forman do our dirty work, and then we'll take you back.'"

Among rabbis who are willing to co-officiate with non-Jewish clergy or place even fewer conditions on an intermarriage, some are in it at least partly for the money. "Rent-a-rabbis," especially those who operate in areas where congregational rabbis willing to officiate at mixed weddings are scarce, can command high fees—and have been known to charge more to interfaith couples than to unaffiliated Jewish couples. However, a number of rabbis, including some who have chosen to devote much of their ministry to intermarried couples, come to wide officiation out of a sincere desire to be there for the Jews who need them.[15]

Officiation at intermarriages is an emotional topic for rabbis and a highly charged issue for intermarrying couples, for whom it is often their first contact with institutional Judaism as adults. Nonofficiating rabbis are fond of saying that there is no statistical support for the idea that rabbinic officiation at a mixed wedding helps bring the non-Jewish partner into Jewish life, but there is strong anecdotal evidence that officiation, when it is offered in a caring spirit and in conjunction with premarital interviews and/or a requirement for study, can encourage participation in Jewish life. Moreover, even stronger evidence suggests that an arbitrary refusal to officiate, especially when a couple wants to create a Jewish home, is extremely alienating and has the power to turn off Jews and non-Jews to Jewish life.[16]

"It is impossible to stress too strongly how bitter the Jew feels when the rabbi refuses to marry him," one lay leader from Montreal commented. "He feels he is being rejected by the Jewish people, leaving a scar from which he rarely recovers. If a religious marriage is refused, it does not stop the couple from getting married—it only turns them away from the synagogue."[17] Such feelings may be immature or even unfounded—but they're real, and they have an impact on Jewish continuity. Harvey Goldman puts it most succinctly: "I don't understand my colleagues who think that they're going to preserve Judaism by turning people away."

In the interest of common sense, I offer some advice to mixed couples who may be planning a wedding at some point in the future:

- The religious content of your wedding should reflect the kind of household you're going to have. Unless you are planning a dual-identity family in which both of your religions will be practiced and taught conscientiously, having clergy from both faiths officiate doesn't make sense. If religion isn't that important to you, you should have a civil ceremony. People who sit in a rabbi's study and tell the rabbi that they don't really care about having a religious ceremony but their parents are insisting on one may not be ready to get married.

- If you've settled, out of conviction, on a Jewish ceremony and you're not connected in the Jewish community where you're getting married, be prepared for some frustration. If the rabbis at the temples you call don't perform mixed weddings, ask them to refer. Take no for an answer; most rabbis have made up their minds on officiation and will not make an exception for you. If you are lectured at, talked down to, or brushed off, don't take it personally; rabbis are busy human beings, and a lot of busy human beings are jerks. Even if you feel bullied or put down, thank the rabbi (or the rabbi's secretary) for his or her time and move on, keeping in mind that a single unsympathetic rabbi does not represent all of Judaism.

- Stay away from rent-a-rabbis or any rabbi who won't spend time with you before the wedding. A conscientious officiant will want to talk with both of you face to face at least a couple of times; any rabbi who just plans to show up for the ceremony is not a rabbi who will give your wedding the warmth and spirituality you want it to have. If you like the rabbi who agrees to marry you and he or she has a congregation, join it. Affiliation is a sign of good faith, and besides, once you've joined the temple, officiating at your wedding is no longer a favor the rabbi is doing for you; it's simply part of his or her job. The idea that the rabbi marrying you is "your rabbi" will make your wedding a little more special.

- Give yourselves lots of lead time before the wedding date. It may take you a while to find the right rabbi; good ones get booked way in advance. More importantly, you'll need time to fulfill whatever requirements the rabbi sets, which could mean several months if you're asked to take a full basic Judaism course. Make the time to do whatever the rabbi asks of you. It will make your wedding and your Jewish life together more meaningful.

- If you come up empty, you can still have a Jewish wedding without a rabbi. The rabbi is only a functionary of the state; the liturgy and customs of the traditional Jewish wedding don't require a rabbi to officiate or even be present. In fact, neither does Jewish law. There are publications that can help you plan a wedding with a civil officiant that has plenty of *Yiddishkeit.*[18]

• If you and your partner have any religious conflicts at all, get them straightened out *before the wedding*. Look ahead to what you want in terms of spiritual life for yourselves and your future children. Don't even begin to think, "Oh, these things work themselves out," because they only get worse. Many Jewish organizations offer workshops and programs for interfaith couples to make their way through issues that can bring tensions to their relationships. Use them.

Outreach Programs

Although the need has existed since at least the mid-1960s, it's only been during the past decade that a wide range of Jewish institutions have offered systematic programming designed to bring intermarried Jews, their partners, and their children into Jewish life. Following the lead of the UAHC, the Conservative movement, some local Federations, Jewish community centers, and numerous congregations have begun to institute programs that, a few individuals and families at a time, are proving to be effective in helping families make Jewish choices.

Some programs under the outreach umbrella, as mentioned above, are designed to encourage unaffiliated interfaith couples to examine, in a Jewish context, the differences in their religious backgrounds and what those differences mean for their relationships. Perhaps the most widespread of these programs is the Reform movement's workshop Times and Seasons: A Jewish Perspective for Intermarried Couples, which brings small groups of mixed couples together to discuss their religious backgrounds, articulate doctrinal differences between Judaism and Christianity, deal with the religious-cultural dichotomy, and work through issues surrounding extended family, holidays, and child raising. The aim is not to convert the non-Jewish partner but to open the lines of communication between partners and allow them to make decisions on a more informed basis. They can be found nationwide in a variety of venues, a first step for couples who want to explore what it means to be Jewish in a nonjudgmental, nonproselytizing setting.[19]

Another level of programming seeks to bring mixed couples into synagogue life or encourage already affiliated intermarried couples to be more active participants in their temples. Such programs are what the Conservative movement calls *keruv*, or in-gathering, and can include temple-based *chavurot* for interfaith couples where members can share their experiences in a safe environment as well as learn and socialize together, along with ongoing activities of interest to the wider synagogue membership, such as learners' minyans, holiday workshops, services for families with small children, and adult education classes in areas such as Hebrew, Jewish history, and Jewish literacy. On the community level, one-day events, festivals, and classes can attract unaffiliated Jews along with intermarried couples and non-Jews.[20]

Programs that reach out to unaffiliated interfaith families with opportunities to build Jewish identity in their children can be very effective. The most successful of these during the past decade has been Stepping Stones to a Jewish Me, which offers two years of Jewish education *free of charge* to the children of intermarried couples. Developed in 1985 at Temple Emanuel in Denver and now offered at a number of Reform synagogues, the program is designed for unaffiliated families in which the parents have not necessarily committed to raising their children as Jews but are interested in Judaism and are not already taking the kids to church. The classes cover the Jewish holidays and acquaint the children with the synagogue service and Jewish culture, and because everyone's parents are intermarried, the children can share their feelings and questions in a comfortable environment. It also includes a parallel parents' program, which offers instruction in basic Judaism and support groups in which participants can explore their own religious identities. In Denver, more than half the families who "graduate" from the program join temples; it has also led to a number of conversions.[21]

Possibly the most prevalent programs are the series of classes called Basic Judaism or Introduction to Judaism that have sprung up across the country to serve the needs of people with a serious thirst to learn about Judaism and, usually, a desire to become part of the Jewish community. They aren't necessarily conversion classes, often including children of intermarried parents or two Jewish parents who have not yet defined their own religious identities or know little about Judaism, along with single non-Jews. However, the primary consumers of such programs tend to be intermarried couples in which the non-Jewish partner is at least exploring the idea of conversion. The courses typically include academic study and experiential activities that allow students not only to gain knowledge about Judaism but also to behave as Jews in their homes and in the synagogue.[22]

Add programs for parents of intermarried Jews, and it's clear that the methodology and expertise exist to bring thousands of intermarried couples and their families into Jewish life. However, the outreach effort has reached only a fraction of the people whom it could and should be serving, because a key component is missing: ungrudging, unambiguous commitment and support from the Jewish establishment. So many non-Orthodox rabbis, communal workers, educators, and lay leaders are afraid of being perceived as giving aid and comfort to "bad Jews" when there aren't enough resources to serve all the "good Jews" that the "bad Jews" never discover how they can get to be "good Jews."

The synagogue, for example, is the gateway through which most adults enter or reenter Jewish life, and the party line in the Reform movement is that every congregation should be actively involved in outreach.[23] Yet the attitude of many Reform congregations and their rabbis toward intermarried families and converts to Judaism is, at best, benign neglect—and sometimes the neglect is not so benign. "I think that there is still, on the part of some rabbis, maybe a lot of rabbis, an ambivalence about bringing both Jews by choice and mixed-married couples into their congregations," says UAHC regional director Alan Bregman. "The question arises, do you welcome this and sort of be an enabler of intermarriage by welcoming all of this? Or do you resist it? And I think that's a question that is still staring rabbis in the face." Reform leaders are very much aware that outreach programs are implemented in a scattershot manner, and they also know that plenty of rabbis and synagogue trustees don't want outreach issues to see the light of day.[24]

The Conservative movement didn't develop an institutional response to intermarriage until 1985, and its congregational arm, the United Synagogue of Conservative Judaism, officially still doesn't deal with intermarried families; its only counterpart to the Commission on Reform Jewish Outreach is the quaintly titled Commission on the Prevention of Intermarriage. The movement's rabbinic arm, the Rabbinical Assembly, however, established an *ad hoc* Committee on Keruv and Giyur (conversion) to respond to issues of intermarriage several years ago, which included representatives from different United Synagogue programs. "The rabbis are caught between what is up here in theory, in our perfect world, and what's really happening in their congregations, and some place they have to meet in the middle," said Iris Henley, a synagogue administrator who represented her colleagues on the committee.

Outreach programming is tricky in Conservative synagogues, which do not admit non-Jews as members and do not, as a rule, recognize unconverted children of non-Jewish mothers and Jewish fathers as Jews. Non-Jewish partners in intermarried couples can attend services, take classes, and participate in social events but are barred from many synagogue activities and organizations, including, in most cases, Sisterhood and Men's Club.[25] That doesn't mean Conservative synagogues haven't implemented *keruv* programs; some are beginning to do so, and a few large synagogues, such as Adas Israel in Washington, D.C., offer a broad menu of services and classes designed to bring non-Jews, along with mar-ginal Jews, into Jewish life. It certainly doesn't mean that intermarried couples can't join Conservative synagogues, although only the Jewish partner is listed as a member. Asked at a rabbis' convention what synagogue policy is in regard to intake of intermarried couples, one Conservative rabbi replied, "They write the check and they're in."[26]

Institutional politics also kept the national Council of Jewish Federations, whose local members have to deal with synagogues, schools, and organizations across the Jewish ideological spectrum, from urging local Federations to get involved in outreach programming until 1994, although Federations in a few cities have sponsored and funded programs for intermarried families.[27] On the other hand, Jewish community centers and YM-YWHAs are often viewed as good venues for outreach programs, as they provide a more religiously neutral and less threatening setting to Jews and non-Jews who may not be ready to walk into a synagogue.[28]

Some observers warn that in their zeal to welcome the intermarried, some Jewish leaders are using scarce resources to try to attract disaffiliated Jews who don't want any part of Jewish life. Outreach works, Steven Bayme says, only when it reaches out to people who have already shown interest in Jewish conti-nuity. "Targeting outreach means avoiding chasing after people who have expressed no desire to be chased," he wrote.[29] Similarly, educator Jonathan Woocher acknowledges that Jewish institutions cannot ignore the intermarried and their children, but wonders,

> [C]an we justify expending precious resources on individuals and families who have often chosen to maintain a marginal relationship to the Jewish community? Here we must adopt a tough-minded approach. . . . First priority goes to those who evince a serious interest in cultivating and deepening their Jewishness. At least for the present, we should de-emphasize work with the uncertain or ambiva-lent, while placing greater emphasis on working with those who have already shown an interest in meeting the community at least halfway.[30]

In other words, Bayme and Woocher say, Jewish institutions should open the door only for those who knock.

But such a position overlooks the fact that some people are too shy to knock, to say nothing of those who don't know where to find the door. It also assumes that the people who knock will in fact be taken in, but that welcome is hardly a given. "The importance to Judaism of Jewish outreach to interfaith families cannot be underestimated," say Leslie Goodman-Malamuth and Robin Margolis, co-founders of an organization for children of interfaith parents. "Scores of children and grandchildren of intermarriage . . . have told us that they were made to feel distinctly unwelcome by the Jewish establishment. Some weathered the disapproval and became active, committed Jews, while others slunk away, wistful, disappointed, and even bitter."[31] It would also be helpful if Jewish leaders employed less condescension and more empathy, says Irwin Fishbein, a rabbi who has counseled and married many mixed couples through his Rabbinic Center for Research and Counseling in Westfield, New Jersey. "To work effectively with intermarried couples, we have to stop looking upon them as a catastrophe," Fishbein told a Reconstructionist convention. "We also have to stop approaching these couples with the parental attitude that we know what is best for them. Often, in truth, we do not know what is best for them."[32]

All the good will in the world, however, won't make a dent unless the Jewish establishment backs up a commitment to outreach with hard cash. The successful outreach programs are well publicized and have sufficient well-trained staff to run them efficiently, and that costs money. David Belin, past president of the Jewish Outreach Institute, has noted that while the Jewish community over the years has raised more than $100 million to memorialize the Jews who died during the Holocaust, the Reform movement's national annual budget for outreach efforts amounts to a few hundred thousand dollars, with the Conservative movement spending less than $50,000. "From a humanistic perspective, to place such a low funding priority on outreach is shameful. From a demographic perspective, it defies common sense," Belin asserts. "I would respectfully suggest that if we want to complete our goal of memorializing and honoring those Jews who perished in the Holocaust, the best way to do this would be to raise $6 million each year for programs of outreach to intermarried families so that Judaism will continue to flourish and survive."[33]

It will be years before we know whether outreach makes a difference, because it works on a few people at a time, on classes of twenty and support groups of ten, on every intermarried couple who gets a warm welcome in a strange synagogue. But it does work. You can see it work with every Stepping Stones family that joins a temple and every Stepping Stones parent who decides to convert to Judaism; with the Christian partners who come out of Times and Seasons understanding that they don't have to lose themselves in order to raise Jewish kids; with every rabbi who persuades the temple president to stop calling his daughter-in-law a *shikse*. This is a ball game that's going into a lot of extra innings.

Conversion to Judaism

Formal conversion to Judaism, of course, is the most desirable outcome of Jewish outreach. Data show clearly that conversionary families are more likely than intermarried families to join synagogues, attend services, observe Jewish holidays, and raise Jewishly identified children.[34] At present there are some 200,000 "Jews-by-choice" in the United States—about 1 out of about every 30 American Jews. Recent estimates of how many people convert to Judaism each year in this country run between 3,000 and 5,000, enough to fill five to eight good-sized congregations and several times the annual rate of thirty years ago, when fewer than 1,000 people a year were thought to have converted.[35]

However, the rate of conversion relative to the incidence of marriage between born Jews and people not born Jewish has declined since the early 1980s, up to which time about a third of the Gentile partners in relationships with Jews converted to Judaism, typically before the wedding or before the birth of the first child.[36] By the early 1990s, the cumulative conversion rate had slipped, depending on whose figures you used, to 25 percent or less.[37] Many Jewish leaders place the blame for the decline squarely on the CCAR's 1983 resolution affirming the Reform movement's acceptance of patrilineal descent. By proclaiming that you don't have to have a Jewish mother in order to be born Jewish, critics say, the CCAR eliminated an important motivation for Gentile women marrying Jewish men to become Jewish.

But there are many other possible reasons that the conversion rate slipped when it did. Rabbinic officiation at intermarriages may have been at its peak during the 1980s, reducing one impetus toward premarital conversion. Parental opposition to intermarriage had declined greatly, lowering in-law pressure on non-Jewish partners to convert. Conversely, the rising divorce rate and consequent higher incidence of remarriage for Jews, along with steadily rising ages among people contracting their first marriages, meant that intermarrying Jews and their partners were older and more resistant to parental pressure when it did occur. Also, by the early 1980s, most American Jews had become resigned to and even tolerant of a significant level of intermarriage. Marginal Jews who twenty years earlier might have asked a Gentile partner to convert to appease a stigmatizing community may no longer have felt or cared about the stigma.[38]

Keep in mind, also, that right around the time of the resolution on patrilineal descent was when intermarrying Jewish women began to catch up numerically with Jewish men. Males have never made up more than 20 percent of converts to Judaism, and an influx of nonconverting Gentile men probably helped inflate the mixed-marriage figures on the 1990 survey. The conventional wisdom is that men have more autonomy issues than women do, so that many view conversion as a relinquishing of their identities. The idea of circumcision, even the symbolic ritual called *hatafat dam brit*, which involves the taking of a drop of blood from the head of the penis, is a deterrent to some men. And because Jewish law will acknowledge the children of Jewish women and non-Jewish men as Jews, Gentile men married to Jewish women have experienced little pressure to convert.[39]

But just because a man hasn't converted to Judaism doesn't mean he never will. The people I talked with who teach Intro classes or otherwise work with potential converts have seen a slow but steady increase in the number of men making formal conversions. Stephen C. Lerner, a Conservative rabbi who runs the Center for Conversion to Judaism in Teaneck, New Jersey, gives feminism full marks for the increase: "It's a question of more assertive and self-confident Jewish women within the last ten or twenty years who are willing to say, 'I care, and I'd like you to look into it.' A woman forty years ago wouldn't have done that." Circumcision of newborn males, regardless of religion, became routine in American hospitals after World War II, so the specter of full adult circumcision, admittedly an unpleasant prospect, is greatly reduced for the non-Jewish men under age 50 whom contemporary Jewish women are likely to meet and marry.[40] As for the autonomy issue, we can but hope that contemporary society is beginning to produce young men who don't see the embrace of a loved one's religion as a surrender of personhood.

It may be that the decline in the conversion rate may not be inexorable, that the *timing* of conversion has changed, so that conversion relative to intermarriage, currently at a low, may be poised to rise *if* the Jewish community supports conversion as a principle and the programming to make it happen. When Elihu Bergman predicted the demographic near-death of American Jewry in 1977, it didn't occur to him that the precipitous drop in the Jewish birth rate during the 1970s, which was part of his calculations, was temporary; it happened because so many Jews in the first wave of the baby boom had postponed having babies until their careers were on track. Likewise, although many Gentile women and men who have been drawn into Jewish life are converting before they get married or have their first babies, many others are taking their time.

Without as much pressure as there used to be to convert in order to have a rabbi do the wedding or to establish a child as Jewish, we start to hear a lot of stories about women who decide to convert around the time their children start religious school—or who don't convert until eight years into the marriage because that's when they first get pregnant. A lot of the men don't even seem to think about it until their kids have been in Hebrew school for a while; around the time of their eldest child's bar or bat mitzvah it occurs to them that they may as well formalize what they've been living for fifteen years. It's only *been* fifteen years since really large numbers of Jewish women have started marrying these men.

Some of the factors contributing to the drop in the conversion rate, especially patrilineal descent and the greater presence of women among Jewish intermarriers, may in fact be partially responsible for a *delay* in conversion gains that in the long run will produce not only more converts to Judaism but converts who are more knowledgeable and more committed to Jewish life because they are married to committed Jews and perceive conversion for what it should be: not a sudden change of status for the sake of one's family and one's partner's tribe but a long evolutionary process undertaken to fulfill one's own spiritual potential.[41]

Traditionally, there was only one acceptable reason for a Gentile to become a Jew: sincere religious conviction, accompanied by a willingness to live according to *halacha*. Rabbis were required to discourage would-be converts, reminding them of the persecution Jews have suffered through the centuries and the "yoke of Torah" Jews must bear. Any hint of a Jewish partner was deemed evidence of an "ulterior motive" and resulted in rejection of the Gentile's request for conversion; the desire to marry or remain with a Jew compromised whatever religious feeling the Gentile had for Judaism and called into question his or her sincerity.[42]

In this century, even the Orthodox know better than to operate that way.

To be sure, Orthodox rabbis (along with rabbis of the other denominations) continue to frown on conversion solely for the sake of marriage. But rabbis going back to the Talmudic period, on the theory that an imperfectly motivated conversion is better than an intermarriage, have found ways to justify conversion when marriage is on the agenda, even when there's little assurance that the family will adhere to all the commandments.[43] Today, it is well understood across the ideological spectrum that most conversions are catalyzed by relationships with Jews, and among non-Orthodox rabbis a desire to create a Jewish home and family with a Jewish partner is considered a laudable starting point for one's own spiritual commitment. However, most converts who come to Judaism through a Jewish partner cite their personal sense of connection to Judaism, whether it developed sooner or later, as the factor that caused them to formalize the conversion.[44]

Considering the benefits of conversion to the Jewish family and the community at large, it's amazing that more Jews don't invite the Gentiles they love to explore conversion—but they don't, some because of an unwillingness to be perceived as exerting pressure in what is seen today as a private area of life and others, probably, out of ambivalence about their own Jewishness. Accordingly, outreach workshops and literature try to raise consciousness on the issue and encourage Jews to broach the subject. "It's not something that you want to hold back on," Mark Winer says. "One of the things that we need to be able to do is ask our spouses to do the things which are most important to us. . . . It would be much more helpful if [people] would feel comfortable saying . . . 'I love you, I love so much about you, but Judaism is the center of my life; I want us to share it . . . it's very important to me that you become a Jew so that you can share it with me.'"[45]

An invitation to become Jewish, however, is no guarantee of a welcome into the Jewish community. Converts and prospective converts to Judaism probably face more rejection, suspicion, blind prejudice, and just plain bad attitude than any other spiritual seekers. Frustrating enough when it comes from rank-and-file Jews; tragic when it emanates from in-laws and even partners; inexcusable when the doors are slammed by rabbis.

Although the passages from the Bible and the Talmud dealing with conversion that instruct Jews to welcome and treasure sincere converts overwhelmingly outnumber the teachings that express mistrust and condescension,[46] there are entirely too many rabbis who turn away prospective converts, some for philosophical reasons, others because they can't justify spending the time it takes to guide people through the process. The reluctance of a contemporary rabbi, whose hours rival those of medical residents, to take on conversion training is understandable, although some could certainly handle the request for such study with more courtesy than they do.[47]

But the cold shoulder converts get from some rabbis is a soak in the Jacuzzi compared to what they experience from many fellow congregants, casual Jewish acquaintances, and even friends. An appalling number of Jews, many of them nonobservant, display profound ignorance and even self-hatred in their comments to converts, with the following at the top of the hit parade:

What are you, crazy? To some Jews, Judaism is everything they left behind at age 13. To others, Judaism is four thousand years of persecution culminating in the Holocaust. Oblivious to the beauty of their own tradition, all they can think is, why would anybody want to join a tribe whose history is filled with pain and whose rituals are irrelevant to life in the twentieth century? A woman in the motion picture industry, tired of explaining why she chose Judaism, finally came up with a stock answer: "I tell them that since my career wasn't going anywhere in the movie business I decided to become a Jew."[48]

You only do that (or know that) because you're a convert. The common perception among the congregants of your average non-Orthodox synagogue is that only converts keep kosher; only converts attend Friday night services every week; only converts are familiar with the practices and history of the full holiday cycle. The most widely quoted Talmudic passage that disparages converts—"Proselytes are as difficult for Israel as leprosy"—was not, in fact, a statement that converts should not be accepted, one scholar wrote, but "merely conveyed a concern that the exceptional piety of proselytes embarrasses born Jews, and therefore is troublesome."[49]

Once a goy, always a goy. You can *daven* till you're blue in the face, you can chant Torah better than the rabbi, you can bake better challah than Manischewitz's grandmother—but you'll never *really* be Jewish. Lena Romanoff, whose *Your People, My People* is an excellent, common-sensical guide to the joys and woes of conversion, describes what happened when her status was revealed at her Conservative synagogue, not long after she was elected sisterhood president:

[A] friend in whom I had confided . . . unwittingly passed the word on to others, including at least one member of the sisterhood who apparently did not approve. This woman . . . made it her business to annul the election and unseat me as president. It was the synagogue's non-Jewish secretary who delivered the crushing news. "You are no longer sisterhood president because one of the members does not think that a convert is a real Jew," she told me quite matter-of-factly.[50]

Nan Fink, cofounder of *Tikkun* magazine, told a conference audience, "Hardly a day goes by that someone, somehow or another, someone born Jewish, doesn't say something or do something that reveals that they think of me as different or not really a Jew. . . . I hear the same thing from every other convert who's out."[51]

Jews are born, not made. A variation on *Once a goy, always a goy,* this statement summarizes the tension in Judaism between religion and ethnicity. Converts don't have the ethnic memories born Jews have, and their embrace of Judaism tends to be based on faith rather than a sense of ethnic identification, at least in the beginning. They equate being a "good Jew" with religious observance and feel Jewish by engaging in Jewish rituals.[52] Born Jews, on the other hand, don't have to set foot in a synagogue to feel Jewish. They took in their *Yiddishkeit* with mother's milk, and as far as many are concerned, that's exactly how you get to be

Jewish—biologically.[53] Or they define Jewishness strictly in terms of how they live it and label any convert inauthentic who doesn't conform to their image of what a Jew is.

Neal Weinberg calls the disparagement of converts for their lack of Jewish ethnicity ignorant and racist. "I don't think there is such a thing as a Jewish culture, because we have many different ethnic cultures," he said. "My wife is a Persian Israeli. . . . She didn't grow up having gefilte fish and matzo ball soup. So it's possible to be a Jew and be with another Jewish family and be in totally a different culture and ethnic group. If being Jewish means lox, cream cheese, and bagels . . . there's not much substance to that."

Statistically, converts and conversionary households generally score lower on measurements of ethnicity and Jewish peoplehood than born Jews and endogamous Jewish families. Conversionary families are more likely to keep putting up Christmas trees, and, most frighteningly in the eyes of many rabbis and demographers, they are much too sanguine about the possibility of their own children marrying non-Jews. Because of these numbers, some rabbis and demographers worry that conversion "does not always work"—that it produces a single generation of Jews who are incapable of passing down their identity to their children and that the presence of too many converts in our synagogues will eventually dilute the ethnic character of American Judaism.[54]

"How many can we really take in?" one Reform rabbi said to me.

[If] you have a huge influx, even though they may commit themselves outwardly to what you're doing, they still come from where they come. They are not that radically different than what they were, and if there's a sizable proportion of converts in a congregation, forget about non-Jews, you can have wonderful service attendance, people who are really going to be into Jewish observance . . . But the sense of Jewish communalism is weaker. What is the threshhold number that you can have before it starts to impact the society?

That's not a problem to Stephen Lerner, who welcomes the greater religiosity of converts:

I would like to think that the growing number of converts in Jewish life whose major concern is religion . . . may strengthen and help people rethink in a positive way the necessity for the centrality of religious faith and commitment in Jewish life. . . . I recognize that there's a serious problem with ethnicity, and I spend at least a half a session on ways to develop an ethnic sense. I take people on

Lower East Side tours, I give them all kinds of food. . . . But on the other hand, it's important to restore religious life to the center of Jewish life. And I think good converts can do that.

Moreover, Lydia Kukoff, an early leader of Reform Outreach, says that with today's Jewish kids three and four generations removed from their immigrant ancestors, there'd be no guarantee of ethnic identity being handed down even if born Jews married only each other. "Tomorrow's Jewish identity must . . . reflect that Jews are members of a post-post-immigrant, post-post-Holocaust genera-tion. We cannot transmit nostalgia; we can only transmit what we own and what lives in us." To say that *they* don't understand why the State of Israel is impor-tant, *they* don't support Jewish causes, and *they* want to shift the focus of Jewish identity from peoplehood to spirituality, Kukoff indicates, is to duck one's own responsibility for Jewish continuity.[55]

No wonder, then, that so many converts knock themselves out for their syn-agogues—and no wonder so many stay in the closet. Nan Fink said that when she asked a friend of hers, a teacher of Jewish meditation, if he were out as a convert, he said, "Forget it. I've done that in the past. When I've said I'm a con-vert, I could see the distrust that goes across the faces, the defenses going up, the receptivity going down . . . and that's really hard to live with."

Perhaps saddest of all are the converts whose partners and Jewish families can't relate to their new status: the Jewish husband who still refers to his wife as "my *shikse*" or sighs, "My God, I married my mother"; the spouse who won't go to Intro, won't go to temple, thinks lighting Shabbat candles is weird and keep-ing kosher completely unreasonable, and demands that the convert "feel Jewish" without doing Jewish things; the in-laws who turn their embarrassment over their own inadequate Jewish backgrounds into hostility toward the convert's "fanaticism"; the partners who are happy their spouses are Jewish—as long as they're not "too Jewish." Many people who work with converts have seen rela-tionships blow up because the new Jew's interest in spirituality and practice out-ran a born Jew's ability to change his or her attitude toward Judaism.[56]

Conversion and converts are not going away, and the Jewish establishment is simply going to have to get used to the fact that a growing proportion of the Jews in its institutions weren't raised Jewish. In their worry that converts will dilute the ethnic character of Judaism, Jewish leaders sound like impatient spouses: *Why can't they just feel Jewish now?* The answer, of course, is that it takes time. "The pain of anti-Semitism, the love of Israel, the affection for Jewish food, the history of Jewish family, all those are . . . much more difficult to absorb and acquire [than religiosity]," says Steven Cohen. "But they *are* acquirable. Speak to converts, and you find that they do it. Long-term converts are able to acquire the accoutrements of Jewish ethnicity, as far as I can tell. You become part of the culture; it's not that hard." Imagine how much easier it would be if synagogues and JCCs helped the process along with postconversion classes, support groups, and rabbinic follow-up; mentoring and adopt-a-family programs; and consciousness-raising efforts from the *bimah* and in temple bulletins, organizational publications, and local Jewish newspapers. No one, as one convert put it, should be "left dripping at the *mikvah*."[57]

Some totally subjective advice for people who want to become Jewish:

• Go for it. Don't let anything stand in your way. Don't wait for your mother to die. Don't wait for your partner to ask you. Don't let anyone tell you it's a bad idea. If it's really what you want to do, it's a *great* idea.

• Locate the study program that's right for you. The how-to books on conversion describe the different options in terms of time and structure. If you have a choice, choose the most rigorous course you can handle; you'll wind up knowing more. Do more than you're required to do; take responsibility for your own Jewish education. The more time and effort you put in, the more Jewish you'll feel. And if you have a Jewish partner, make sure that partner is with you every step of the way. Don't take no for an answer.[58]

• Don't stay in the closet. Think about having a conversion ceremony in your sponsoring temple after the *bet din* and *mikvah*; about one out of four converts affirm their membership in the Jewish people in a short ceremony during Friday night services. Your background won't make you any less Jewish, no matter what anybody else says, and only by confronting the ignorance and bigotry of the "goyim bashers" will converts make faster headway in gaining universal acceptance. By being "out," you're also telling born Jews that Judaism is worth choosing. So don't let yourself be labeled as anything other than a Jew, but don't hide where you came from. And memorize this line: *Really? What does Jewish look like?*[59]

Non-Jews in the Synagogue

In terms of membership and ritual participation, non-Jews are pretty much nonpersons in Conservative Judaism, and for all the Reform Outreach lip service on inclusion of non-Jewish partners in synagogue life, Reform leaders are deeply divided on the roles non-Jews may take on within the temple in terms of formal membership, governance, and ritual.[60]

The visibility of non-Jews in the synagogue has been a hot topic in Reform circles of late, and the rhetoric that surrounds it is reflective, once again, of the marauding-hordes, us-versus-them mentality that characterizes so much of the discussion around issues of intermarriage. "[We] cannot have a Gentile mouth what they clearly do not believe," former CCAR president Walter Jacob told the UAHC executive committee, assigning himself mind-reading capabilities that I respectfully submit he does not have.[61] The candle blessing 60 percent of Reform temples don't want a non-Jewish mother to recite in front of the congregation the night before her kid's bar or bat mitzvah is the same blessing the same woman might be reciting every Friday night at home—and the same blessing that professional choirs staffed with non-Jews used to sing from the lofts of classical Reform synagogues.[62] If Jewish prayer is changeable, Conservative historian Jack Wertheimer writes, what's to stop a non-Jewish temple member from introducing the Lord's Prayer into the service?[63] Such a question insults the non-Jews who spend time in synagogues, all of whom are well aware that Christian prayer is inappropriate in Jewish worship.

Reform congregations are pressured to keep track of who the non-Jews are in their congregations and to establish specific, all-purpose "boundaries" for membership, governance, and ritual—in effect, they're advised not to decide such matters on a case-by-case basis.[64] But that's exactly how many of them should be decided. There are many non-Jews who are so much a part of their synagogues that to deny them certain rights and honors is to treat them with contempt they don't deserve. An Episcopalian who drops off his kids at the temple for Sunday school on his way to church is different from a guy, long departed from the religion of his childhood, who's at temple almost every Friday night, takes an adult ed course every quarter, and handles minor legal matters for the temple without billing. The first man, obviously, is a poor candidate for temple leadership and *would* be uncomfortable in a prominent ritual role, but he also probably doesn't feel himself to be a part of the temple, and the subject is unlikely to come up. The second guy sounds like a dream candidate for the temple board of directors. He clearly feels himself to be part of the temple family, operating as what I have heard different rabbis describe as a de facto Jew, a behavioral Jew, a common-law Jew. Okay, maybe he shouldn't sit on the board, but what's inappropriate about his voting on the next temple budget, especially when his dues are part of that budget? Why shouldn't he hand the Torah to his son when nothing in Jewish law prohibits him from doing so?[65]

Centuries ago, the rabbis recognized a category of semi-proselytes known as *gerei toshav* (resident strangers) or *yirei adonai* (God fearers). These were people who had given up paganism and had agreed in the presence of three scholars to honor God and observe the principles of ethical monotheism and the Noachide laws, seven rules of moral conduct. In return, they were permitted to live in areas controlled by Jews and had rights equal to Jews in legal matters. They were not required to join in Jewish worship or to carry out religious commandments, although some did observe Jewish customs. With the rise of Christianity and Islam, contemporary rabbis say, these categories became meaningless, because any Christian or Muslim, whose religions are based on ethical monotheism and incorporate the Noachide laws, could be designated a *ger toshav* on the basis of his beliefs and conduct while pursuing a different faith. Because of that thinking, there is no official status in Judaism for an individual who lives among the Jewish people and abides by Jewish principles.[66]

If ever an ancient Jewish concept needed reviving, it's that of the *ger toshav*. Thousands of non-Jewish women and men live among us, have cast their lot with the Jewish people, and conduct their lives *and their relationship with God* according to Jewish principles. If they demonstrate that they are functional members of the Jewish community for some predetermined period and profess no allegiance to any other religion, why shouldn't they be able to go before a synagogue panel—the rabbi and two lay leaders, say—and explain why they're not ready to go to the *mikvah*, but they are ready to take an official role in Jewish life? If Jewish leaders were to take these particular people seriously, extend them membership in the synagogue, recognize our prayers as theirs, officiate at their weddings . . . they'd become *gerei tzedek*, formal converts, sooner than later.

In Norfolk, Lawrence Forman doesn't wait for *gerei toshav* to prove themselves; he signs them up right away. Forman developed a mechanism for people who want to learn about Judaism and be part of the Jewish community: the fellow traveler is given a "declaration of *teshuvah*" certifying that he or she, "having declared a desire to turn to Judaism, to study the beliefs and practices of the Jewish religion, and to learn to live in accordance with those beliefs and practices, has been duly welcomed and accepted into the household of Israel." In doing this, Forman asserts, he's operating along the lines of Hillel, who was noted for creating converts through his wisdom and tolerance. "Everybody else is like Shammai," Hillel's more tunnel-visioned colleague, Forman says. "Shammai said, 'You gotta study for a year, you gotta do this, that, and the other thing, then come back and see me later.' . . . I will give you this [status] in the beginning. You're in. You're a member of the temple. You're a part of us. . . . The rest is commentary; go and learn."

The Jewish community has become so obsessed with personal status that it runs the risk of alienating potential Jews at the very moment that a true act of *keruv* might spark their conversions. If liberal Jewish institutions treat the strangers who dwell among us as individuals and welcome them as individuals, more and more of them will decide that our temples are their temples, and our people will become their people. If, on the other hand, our "boundaries" become barriers, we may lose these potential Jews and the future generations of Jews they might have given us.

Proselytism

Should Jews encourage religiously nonpreferred Gentiles in the general community to embrace Judaism?

The idea that Jews have never been a proselytizing people is one of the Big Lies of Western civilization. The active encouragement of non-Jews to convert began in Jewish lore with Abraham and Sarah, and the Bible is studded with figures who adopted the Israelites as their people, most notably Ruth, ancestor of King David. When the Jews were exiled to Babylon after the First Temple was destroyed in 586 B.C.E., they realized that if God was everywhere, God could be worshiped anywhere, and if God could be worshiped anywhere, then anyone could hear's God's message and join the people who celebrated that message. Jews took seriously the biblical vision, "My house shall be a house of prayer for all peoples," and developed a religious mission that they carried throughout the Diaspora.

Many pagans in search of spiritual fulfillment were attracted to the concept of one God and the moral order inherent in Judaism, and by the beginning of the common era, conversion to Judaism was so widespread that some 10 percent of the Roman empire's population were either Jews (from birth or by choice) or *gerei toshav*. Jews were supposedly such eager proselytizers that one of the Christian gospels scolds the Pharisees for traveling sea and land for the sake of creating one convert (Matthew 23:15). The Jews even experienced being on the delivering end of an episode of forced conversion in the second century B.C.E., when the Hasmoneans (the Maccabees' tribe) forced the neighboring Idumeans to become Jewish—not our most shining hour as a people.

Jews began to pull back from missionary activity during the first and second centuries C.E., weakened by their unsuccessful revolts against Rome and the rising popularity of Christianity (which made fewer demands on its converts). Rabbinic language concerning conversion became more tentative, advising those approached by potential converts to warn them of the pitfalls of being Jewish, although the Jewish community continued to welcome proselytes. Only when Christianity became the state religion of the Roman empire and non-Christian proselytizing became a capital offense did Jews cease active missionary efforts. But rabbinic teachings continued to praise and welcome converts, and a thin but steady stream flowed into Judaism well into the Middle Ages. As the Crusades ended, however, and the Christian hierarchy began the systematic persecution of Jews, the Jewish community turned inward, substituting instructions to turn away prospective converts for the earlier teachings that welcomed them. In a hostile world, the Jews of Europe reasoned, you can trust only your own blood.[67]

But that was then, and this is now.

The landmark address in December 1978 by Alexander Schindler that launched Reform Outreach included a call to offer Judaism not only to non-Jewish partners of Jews but to Americans in general who are searching for a religious path. "I do not have in mind some kind of traveling religious circus," he told the UAHC board of directors.

> Let us establish information centers in many places, well-publicized courses in our synagogues, and the development of suitable publications to serve these facilities and purposes. In short, I propose that we respond openly and positively to those God-seekers whose search leads them to our door, who voluntarily ask for our knowledge. . . . No repressive laws restrain us. The fear of persecution no longer inhibits us. There is no earthly—and surely no heavenly—reason why we cannot reassume our ancient vocation and open our arms to all newcomers.[68]

Schindler's proposal received national publicity and a flurry of commentary, both critical and supportive, from other rabbis and Jewish leaders at the time he first made it and fifteen years later, when he again proposed low-key missionary efforts at the 1993 biennial convention of the UAHC.[69] But neither Reform Jewish Outreach nor the Conservative movement's programs have reached beyond non-Jewish partners of Jews, although they certainly welcome Gentiles without Jewish partners. Why haven't the major Jewish movements begun to reach out to the general public?

Some leaders use the old "don't rile the *goyim*" argument, or suggest that it's unseemly to borrow strategies from Christians. "Bold pronouncements about missionizing are like a red flag waved in front of a charging bull," Jack Wertheimer, worried that outreach to uncommitted Gentiles would give permission to church groups to proselytize among "unsynagogued" Jews, said in response to Schindler's 1993 address. "Let us not 'Protestantize' and 'evangelize' our precious heritage," a Reform rabbi commented. "Let us not become just another American religious sect."[70] These arguments border on paranoia; few Christian leaders are terribly worried about losing their faithful to Judaism, and no Jewish leader at any time has recommended that Jews engage in any aggressive proselytizing activity.[71]

Others insist that Jews have no business seeking converts in the wider community until everything possible has been done to bring Jews back into Jewish life. "I have no philosophical objection with the notion of 'If we have treasures, let us share them with others,'" Steven Bayme said. "What I do have objection to is the practical priorities of doing so. . . . To focus energies on all these people out there . . . in its most cynical form is like saying, 'We're gonna lose our people today, so let's bring in a new crew.'" A grandparent suggested that a better use of resources would be to help people like his son, who can't afford to join a temple and educate his children. "Can't we first take care of our own problems, then seek converts?" he wrote. At a time when Jewish donors are unwilling to put money into the most basic programs that serve Jewish continuity in America, his point is well taken.[72]

It's easy to be cynical about proselytism, to say that it can't possibly work because it admits defeat among our own people. But there were Jewish leaders who supported outreach to religiously nonpreferenced Americans long before Rabbi Schindler spoke in Houston; it's just never been attempted and supported on a large scale.[73] Properly funded and sensitively staffed, low-key, widespread Jewish outreach to the general public has the potential not just to add bodies to the census but to bring about a Jewish revival that affects not only former Gentiles but born Jews, that can provide a liberal alternative to the projects Orthodox groups are using to attract marginal Jews. Proselytism can be, to quote President Kennedy, the rising tide that lifts all boats.

This can happen because the missionary approach, by definition, is a positive presentation. The volunteer in the reading room and the staffer who returns calls to the hotline will be doing what they do, as the teachers of conversion classes already do, for one reason: to provide information that communicates the beauty and spiritual purposefulness of Judaism. A few years ago, Egon Mayer commented that Jewish efforts toward conversion were driven so completely by concerns about Jewish continuity that they were devoid of religious zeal.[74] That may be true of the way Jewish outreach programs have *invited* Gentiles—almost all of them partners of born Jews—to become Jewish up to now, but it is not true of the way competently taught conversion programs *indoctrinate* potential and prospective Jews.

If missionary activity to spiritual seekers is pursued properly, liberal Judaism's message will go out not only to Gentiles but to marginal and disaffiliated Jews. It will make effective use of an old marketing ploy: advertising that convinces established customers that they made the right choice as it attracts new customers. It will dispel the image of Judaism as a closed, impenetrable society and reduce anti-Semitism by giving more Gentiles Jewish children, grandchildren, siblings, nieces, and nephews. It will make "cultural Jews" wonder what they've been missing all these years and challenge Jews to learn about their own tradition.

"Something happens to the student who is called upon to teach," Harold Schulweis wrote in response to Schindler's 1978 address. "Something happens to the Jew who is asked to explain the character of his tradition to one outside the inborn circle. . . . Called upon to interpret the spiritual conscience of Judaism and its world wide vision to others, the Jew may gain for himself a new self-awareness, self-esteem and articulateness."[75]

We are such a contradictory people, we Jews: at once generous and begrudging, nomadic and xenophobic, learned and ignorant, progressive and reactionary, open-minded and mulish. There have been times in our history when the dominance of the less attractive of these qualities probably served us well. This is not one of those periods. If we are to flourish and grow as a people in this society, we must teach the secret handshake, write down the password. We must embrace the strangers among us, but not for a one-night stand—for the long haul. We can all fit under the sheltering wings of the Divine Presence.

Epilogue

On June 14, 1995, his forty-first birthday, my husband, Spencer G. Gill III, went before a cross-denominational *bet din* at the University of Judaism, immersed himself in the UJ *mikvah*, and became a Jew in the eyes of the non-Orthodox world. Two days later, he stood before our congregation at Friday night services and affirmed his allegiance to the Jewish people.

"I could have gone along for years without a formal conversion, but the more I participated and the more comfortable I began to feel, the more I felt that just going along wasn't enough," Spencer told the congregation. "Embracing Judaism really does involve becoming a member of a tribe, in this case a tribe whose ethics and beliefs I respect . . . a tribe I wanted to join. I wanted to be more than a fellow traveler." He credited the openhearted acceptance offered by our synagogue, Beth Chayim Chadashim, with making conversion a natural step.

Needless to say, I am thrilled beyond measure that my husband thought so highly of Jewish doctrine, ritual, and tradition that he wanted to adopt them as his own. But tucked away in a corner of my mind are some mixed feelings—not about Spencer becoming Jewish, but about the shift in the way he and I are now viewed by the Jewish community. Spencer decided, rather suddenly, to pursue conversion around the time I was completing the research on this book, and a lot of rabbis and demographers who railed about mixed marriage when I interviewed them—including a few who indicated that my home and marriage were less than Jewish—have been one happy *mazel tov!* after another when I've mentioned Spencer's plans in the course of follow-up calls. Before his conversion, Spencer was an interloper, a defiler, a *goy*, and I was pounding nails into the coffin of American Jewry. With the stroke of a pen and a dunk in the *mikvah*, the conversion has erased all that. Now Spencer's a great guy, and I'm the woman of valor who set him on the right path. Our marriage is no longer a stab in the back to *klal Yisrael*, and our home is now a Jewish home. All is forgiven.

But little, really, has changed in our lives. Spencer's conversion did not magically turn all his friends into Jews. He is still bothered, as I am, by much that goes on in the State of Israel. He did not run out and buy two sets of dishes, nor has he announced his candidacy for the temple board. The conversion didn't make our home a Jewish household. It was a Jewish household when Spencer moved into it in 1988; it continued to be a Jewish household for the next seven years, and it is a Jewish household now.

As it has been for us, so it is for thousands of intermarried families. I wish all mixed couples the same rich Jewish life together that we shared for those seven years, and I wish all *gerei tzedek* and their partners an experience as exciting and fulfilling as ours was and continues to be.

Directory

National and regional offices of the major Jewish movements can direct you to the congregation(s) in that denomination nearest to your home.

Reform

Union of American Hebrew Congregations
838 Fifth Avenue
New York, NY 10021
(212) 249-0100

The New York office houses the National Commission of Reform Jewish Outreach and the Outreach office for New York City, Westchester, and Long Island. In addition, the UAHC has Outreach coordinators in its regional offices:

Boston: (617) 449-0404
New Jersey/Hudson Valley: (201) 599-0080
Philadelphia: (215) 563-8183
Washington, D.C.: (202) 232-4242
Miami: (305) 592-4792
Cleveland: (216) 831-6722
Chicago: (312) 782-1477
St. Louis: (314) 997-7566
Dallas: (214) 960-6641
San Francisco: (415) 392-7080
Los Angeles: (213) 653-9962
Toronto: (905) 709-2275

Conservative

United Synagogue of Conservative Judaism
155 Fifth Avenue
New York, NY 10010
(212) 533-7800

For locations of synagogues and programs outside metropolitan New York, call one of United Synagogue's regional offices:

Boston: (617) 964-8210
Connecticut: (203) 563-5531
Albany, N.Y.: (518) 438-2052
New Jersey: (908) 925-3114
Philadelphia: (215) 563-8809
Washington, D.C. area: (301) 230-0801
Miami: (305) 474-4606
Cleveland: (216) 751-0606
Detroit: (810) 642-4890
Chicago: (312) 726-1802
Minneapolis: (612) 920-7068
Dallas: (214) 239-1951
Seattle: (206) 728-4849
San Francisco: (415) 377-0380
Los Angeles: (310) 472-1521
Montreal: (514) 484-4415
Toronto: (905) 738-1717

In addition, the Rabbinical Assembly recently established a toll-free number, which people can call for information about programs such as Introduction to Judaism classes: (800) ASK-N-LEA(RN) (275-6532).

Reconstructionist

To locate a Reconstructionist congregation in your area, contact the movement's national office:

Federation of Reconstructionist Congregations and Havurot (FRCH)
Church Road and Greenwood Avenue
Wyncote, PA 19095
(215) 887-1988

Jewish Renewal

To find a member *chavurah* of the Network of Jewish Renewal Communities, contact its parent organization:

ALEPH: Alliance for Jewish Renewal
7318 Germantown Avenue
Philadelphia, PA 19119-1793
(215) 242-4074, 247-9700

Introduction to Judaism Programs

Two of the largest programs are located in New York and Los Angeles:

Derekh Torah
92nd Street YM-YWHA
1395 Lexington Avenue
New York, NY 10028
(212) 427-6000

Miller Introduction to Judaism Program
University of Judaism
15600 Mulholland Drive
Los Angeles, CA 90077
(310) 476-9777

The synagogues and the Jewish Federation in your area may also be helpful in locating a basic Judaism class or interfaith workshop.

Support Groups

Lena Romanoff, author of *Your People, My People*, runs a support organization for converts to Judaism:

Jewish Converts Network
1112 Hagys Ford Road
Narberth, PA 19072
(610) 664-8112

Romanoff also provides counseling and workshops for interfaith couples and families. Your local Federation or the nearest regional office of the UAHC may be able to direct you to a support group for converts and potential converts. If there isn't one near you, create one!

Notes

Introduction

1. Although not everything I read is cited in the notes to this book, I read just about everything listed in the *Index to Jewish Periodicals* that was relevant to the various topics discussed, going back to about 1968, and most of the books published during the past 10–12 years on intermarriage, Jewish demographics, and the current condition of American Judaism. The Jewish periodicals I found most useful in my research (among dozens cited) were *Moment*, the *Journal of Jewish Communal Service*, the *Journal of Reform Judaism/CCAR Journal*, *Reform Judaism*, *Lilith*, and my local Jewish newspaper, the *Jewish Journal of Greater Los Angeles*, although I have gleanings from many local Jewish newspapers, especially the *Baltimore Jewish Times*. I also amassed a stack of publications produced by the Reform and Conservative movements and a number of demographic surveys. Many thanks to the academics and rabbis who not only sat for interviews but sent me print materials.

2. I taped formal interviews, either in person or over the phone, with 30 congregational rabbis across the United States; 15 rabbis who work for Jewish organizations (such as the UAHC or the 92nd Street Y); 14 sociologists and other academics; 9 communal workers, mostly in the field of outreach; 6 Jewish educators; 6 Hillel directors; 7 psychologists; 6 matchmakers; 12 professionals in the entertainment industry; and 5 prominent, long-time Jewish journalists. Besides the people I interviewed directly, I taped about 30 other rabbis, educators, communal workers, psychologists, and journalists during public lectures, panels,

conferences, and convention workshops. About 120 "case study" informants told me their stories directly, usually in taped interviews, although a few wrote letters that I did not follow up with interviews, and I have both letters from and interviews with some people. This group in no way comprises a scientific sampling of any population, nor is it offered as an accurate representation of intermarried Jews, interdating Jews, or people not born Jewish married to Jews. I reached about 40 of the informants through reader's queries in the *Los Angeles Times* and the *Boston Globe*, and 13 are children of my parents' friends, ages 27–37 at the time of interview. Other case study informants put on tape include fellow Brandeis alumni, relatives of friends and people referred to me by those relatives, and people I met at lectures, UAHC events, and social gatherings.

Case study informants are identified, if at all, by fictitious first names. Quotes are verbatim. No composites were used in the writing of this book.

I: Painting by Numbers

1. Susan Weidman Schneider, *Intermarriage: The Challenge of Living with Differences between Christians and Jews* (New York: Free Press, 1989), pp. 12–13; Anne Roiphe, *Generation without Memory* (New York: Summit, 1981), pp. 72–73; Benjamin Schlesinger, "Intermarriage: An Old Problem and a Modern Dilemma," *Journal of Jewish Communal Service* (Summer 1971): 323. Roiphe mentions that at one point during the Hellenistic period, a band of Jewish zealots would hunt down intermarriers on their wedding night and decapitate both partners.

2. David Biale, "Jewish Identity in the 1990s," *Tikkun* (November/December 1991): 61; Schneider, *Intermarriage*, p. 13; Roiphe, *Generation without Memory*, p. 73.

3. Alan Levenson, "Reform Attitudes, in the Past, Toward Intermarriage," *Judaism* (Summer 1989): 321–25; Schneider, *Intermarriage*, pp. 13–14.

4. Jacob Rader Marcus, *The American Jewish Woman, 1654–1980* (New York: KTAV, 1981), pp. 16, 20–23, 53–54.

5. Moshe Davis, "Mixed Marriage in Western Jewry: Historical Background to the Jewish Response," *CCAR Journal* (April 1972): 5.

6. Davis, "Mixed Marriage in Western Jewry," pp. 5–7; Levenson, "Reform Attitudes, in the Past, Toward Intermarriage," pp. 325–32. American Jewish leaders, including Reform leaders, were more vocal in their opposition to intermarriage than their German counterparts because American Jews had fewer barriers to social contact with Gentiles than did European Jews, and American society had more tolerance for Jews' efforts to maintain themselves as a distinct religious group.

7. Marshall Sklare, "Intermarriage and the Jewish Future," *Commentary* (April 1964): 46. Sklare took the figure from a 1920 study of intermarriage, Julius Drachsler's *Democracy and Assimilation* (New York: Macmillan, 1920).

8. Charles Silberman, *A Certain People: American Jews and Their Lives Today* (New York: Summit, 1985), p. 275; Davis, "Mixed Marriage in Western Jewry," p. 8. The quotation is taken from Kaplan's *Judaism as a Civilization* (New York: Macmillan, 1934).

9. Sidney Goldstein, "American Jewry, 1970: A Demographic Profile," and Arnold Schwartz, "Intermarriage in the United States," both in *The Jew in American Society*, edited by Marshall Sklare (New York: Behrman House, 1974), pp. 101, 313–16. Other books and monographs during the 1960s that reported intermarriage rates and related statistics were Werner J. Cahnman, ed., *Intermarriage and Jewish Life: A Symposium* (New York: Herzl Press, 1963); Erich Rosenthal, "Studies of Jewish Intermarriage in the United States," *American Jewish Year Book 1963* (New York: American Jewish Committee and Philadelphia: Jewish Publication Society, 1963), pp. 3–53; and Louis A. Berman, *Jews and Intermarriage: A Study in Personality and Culture* (South Brunswick, N.J.: Thomas Yoseloff, 1968). In addition, the U.S. Bureau of the Census produced a sample census, "Religion Reported by the Civilian Population of the United States: March 1957," *Current Population Reports*, Series P-200, No. 29, February 2, 1958. The sample census reported that of all married couples with at least one Jewish partner, 7.2 percent included a non-Jewish spouse. This was the statistic *du jour* through the early 1960s, and it made most Jewish demographers and leaders feel pretty good, since it came in under the figure for Roman Catholics (8.6 percent) and was one-third of the rate for Protestants (21.6 percent). In "Intermarriage and the Jewish Future," Marshall Sklare wrote that Jewish Federation demographer Alvin Chenkin referred to the 7.2 percent figure as a "nominal" rate of intermarriage in the 1959 *American Jewish Year Book*, but Sklare reminded his readers that this was a cumulative rate, part of a pool of marriages including many older Jews among whom outmarriage was unheard of, and the current rate for younger Jews was undoubtedly much higher.

   Rosenthal startled the Jewish community with two studies in largely nonurban states, reporting that of the marriages involving Jews contracted in Iowa between 1953 and 1959, 42.2 percent were intermarriages, and among marriages involving Jews between 1960 and 1963 in Indiana, 48.8 percent included a non-Jewish spouse (see "Jewish Intermarriage in Indiana," *American Jewish Year Book 1967*, for details of the second study). Rosenthal was also one of the first demographers to break down an intermarriage rate by generation. A 1956 survey of Jews in Washington, D.C., reported a higher-than-average 13.1 percent cumulative intermarriage rate. Rosenthal tabulated the outmarriages at 1.4 percent for Jews of the first generation, 10.2 percent for the second generation, and 17.9 percent for the third. See Sklare, "Intermarriage and the Jewish Future," for details and interpretation. Also widely cited during the 1960s and considered valuable as a broad-based survey that focused entirely on young people was a study of recent college graduates conducted by the National Opinion Research Center (NORC) in 1961, as they were graduating from college, and 1964. Fifty-seven percent of the Jewish students had married by 1964, about 12 percent to persons not born Jewish. However, Arnold Schwartz warned in "Intermarriage in the United States," that rate was bound to go up, since evidence showed that intermarriers married later than those who married endogamously.

10. Fred Massarik and Alvin Chenkin, "United States National Jewish Population Study: A First Report," *American Jewish Year Book 1973*, pp. 292–97. More than a fourth of those marriages, however, were not really intermarriages, because the non-Jewish partner had made a

formal conversion to Judaism, and in almost half the spouse not born Jewish was described as Jewish, either through conversion or on a de facto basis.

11. Elihu Bergman, "The American Jewish Population Erosion," *Midstream* (October 1977): 9–19, cited by almost everybody who has written about Jewish demographics since 1977. Bergman's projection was countered by Samuel S. Lieberman (a colleague whose numbers Bergman had used in his projection) and Morton Weinfeld in "Demographic Trends and Jewish Survival," *Midstream* (November 1978): 9–19. Lieberman and Weinfeld said that if the American Jewish population was decreasing, it specifically *wasn't* because of intermarriage.

12. Mark Winer, "Sociological Research on Jewish Intermarriage," *Journal of Reform Judaism* (Summer 1985): 41. For example, while metropolitan New York was reporting a cumulative intermarriage rate of 10 percent in the early 1980s, that rate had reached 28 percent in Seattle and 37 percent in Denver, with much higher rates of outmarriage among younger Jews.

13. Two of the better-known "warning" studies were conducted by Egon Mayer and published by the American Jewish Committee: *Intermarriage and the Jewish Future: A National Study in Summary* (written with Carl Sheingold) in 1979, and *Children of Intermarriage* (1983).

14. Silberman, *A Certain People*, pp. 295–97.

15. Barry A. Kosmin, Sidney Goldstein, Joseph Waksberg, Nava Lerer, Ariella Keysar, and Jeffrey Scheckner, *Highlights of the CJF 1990 National Jewish Population Survey* (New York: Council of Jewish Federations, 1991), pp. 4, 13, 14, 16.

16. Ephraim Z. Buchwald, "Stop the Silent Holocaust," letter, *Moment* (December 1992): 4.

17. Mark L. Winer and Aryeh Meir, *Questions Jewish Parents Ask about Intermarriage* (New York: American Jewish Committee, 1992), p. 6.

18. Jonathan Sarna, "The Secret of Jewish Continuity," *Commentary* (October 1994): 55.

19. Bernard Reisman, "Reflections on the 1990 National Jewish Population Survey," *Contemporary Jewry* (1993): 167.

20. Silberman, *A Certain People*, p. 169.

21. Lloyd P. Gartner, "Immigration and the Formation of American Jewry, 1840–1925," in *The Jew in American Society*, p. 42. Gartner points out that Galicia, where Jews were emancipated in 1867 and did not suffer pogroms during the period of mass immigration, had one of the highest rates of Jewish emigration at the time.

22. Stuart E. Rosenberg, *The New Jewish Identity in America* (New York: Hippocrene, 1985), p. 76; Silberman, *A Certain People*, p. 132.

23. C. Bezalel Sherman, "Immigration and Emigration: The Jewish Case," in *The Jew in American Society*, pp. 53–55; Silberman, *A Certain People*, p. 131. More than a third of American immigrants returned to their native lands between 1908 and 1937, but only 1 in 20 immigrant Jews returned.

24. Ben Halpern, "America Is Different," in *The Jew in American Society*, pp. 77–79; Leonard Fein, *Where Are We? The Inner Life of America's Jews* (New York: Harper and Row, 1988), p. 4.

25. Rosenberg, *The New Jewish Identity in America*, pp. 18, 126–27; Will Herberg, *Protestant-Catholic-Jew* (New York: Doubleday, 1956), pp. 198, 202.

26. Silberman, *A Certain People*, pp. 120–23, 225; Herberg, *Protestant-Catholic-Jew*, pp. 201, 203.

27. Rosenberg, *The New Jewish Identity in America*, pp. 25, 28–29; Silberman, *A Certain People*, pp. 177–79; Berman, *Jews and Intermarriage*, pp. 297–300.

28. Goldstein, "A Demographic Profile," pp. 135–39.

29. Barry A. Kosmin and Seymour Lachman, *One Nation under God* (New York: Simon and Schuster, 1993), pp. 65–67; Rosenberg, *The New Jewish Identity in America*, pp. 82–83; Goldstein, "A Demographic Profile," pp. 125–27.

30. Tom Tugend, "The Frozen Chosen," *Jewish Journal*, November 4–10, 1994, p. 17.

31. Barry A. Kosmin, "The Permeable Boundaries of Being Jewish in America," *Moment* (August 1992): 31; Goldstein, "A Demographic Profile," pp. 144–47; Steven Cohen, "Education and Intermarriage," *Moment* (November 1986): 18.

32. Sklare, "Intermarriage and the Jewish Future," p. 49; Leonard Fein, "Dilemmas of Jewish Identity on the College Campus," *Judaism* (Winter 1968): 11–12.

33. Yosef I. Abramowitz, "The De-Nerdification of Hillel," *Moment* (February 1995): 37ff; Fein, "Dilemmas of Jewish Identity on the College Campus," pp. 12–13; Trude Weiss-Rosmarin, "Non-Jewish Jews," *Jewish Spectator* (Fall 1969): 4.

34. Fein, "Dilemmas of Jewish Identity on the College Campus," p. 12; Marshall Sklare, "The Jewish Family and Jewish Identity," *Jewish Heritage* (Summer 1972): 29; Norman Mirsky, "Intermarriage: dilemmas," *Keeping Posted*, February 1974, p. P18.

35. Marshall Sklare and Joseph Greenbaum, *Jewish Identity on the Suburban Frontier: A Study of Group Survival in the Open Society*, 2d ed. (Chicago: University of Chicago Press, 1979), p. 317; Fein, *Where Are We?* pp. 163–64. Fein quoted a 1986 survey in which 96 percent of the American Jews polled agreed with the statement, "As Jews we should be concerned about all people, not just Jews," and 89 percent said, "I get just as upset by terrorist attacks on non-Jews as I do when terrorists attack Jews."

36. Sarna, "The Secret of Jewish Continuity," p. 56.

37. Silberman, *A Certain People*, p. 287.

38. Schwartz, "Intermarriage in the United States," p. 307.

39. Silberman, *A Certain People*, pp. 165–66; John Slawson, "Jewish Identity in the United States," *Journal of Jewish Communal Service* (Fall 1971): 42; Yehuda Rosenman, introduction to Egon Mayer and Carl Sheingold, *Intermarriage and the Jewish Future: A National Study in Summary* (New York: American Jewish Committee, 1979), p. 2.

40. Deborah Lipstadt, "Tomer Devorah," *Jewish Spectator* (Fall 1991): 63. Lipstadt cites a *Wall Street Journal* interview with Conservative rabbi Jack Moline, whom she calls "very brave" for listing the 10 things Jewish parents should say to their children and don't: "Number one on his list was: *I expect you to marry Jews.*" Moline's list (in which "I expect you to marry a Jew" is third) can be found in Program Department, United Synagogue of Conservative Judaism, *Intermarriage: What Can We Do? What Should We Do?* (New York: United Synagogue of Conservative Judaism, n.d.). See also Sklare and Greenblum, *Jewish Identity on the Suburban Frontier*, pp. 307–17; Sklare, "Intermarriage and Jewish Survival," *Commentary* (March 1970): 52–53; Schwartz, "Intermarriage in the United States," pp. 327–28; Mordechai Rimor, "Feelings and Reactions to Intermarriage," one in a series of CMJS Research Notes

published by the Maurice and Marilyn Cohen Center for Modern Jewish Studies, Brandeis University, December 1989; Calvin Goldscheider, *Jewish Continuity and Change: Emerging Patterns in America* (Bloomington: Indiana University Press, 1986), pp. 13–16; Kosmin et al., *Highlights,* p. 29. In Marshall Sklare's studies of a Chicago suburb during the late 1950s, a minority of his survey respondents were confident that their children would marry Jews, and only 29 percent said they would be "very unhappy" if a child of theirs were to intermarry. An overwhelming majority said they would rather have a child marry a non-Jew whom he or she loved than enter a loveless marriage with another Jew. In a series of population surveys taken in Boston, 70 percent of respondents in 1965 said they would oppose or discourage a child's potential intermarriage, but in 1975 and 1985 surveys the figure dropped to one in three. The 1990 National Jewish Population Survey reported that 22 percent of the respondents who identified themselves as "Jewish by religion" would oppose a child's marriage to a non-Jew; 46 percent said they would accept such a marriage; and one out of three said they would support it. See also Brenda Forster and Joseph Tabachnik, *Jews by Choice: A Study of Converts to Reform and Conservative Judaism* (Hoboken, N.J.: KTAV, 1991), p. 118. In a survey of converts and their partners who had been through the Introduction to Judaism program operated jointly by the Reform and Conservative movements in Chicago between 1973 and 1987, the investigators found that societal factors seemed to outweigh psychological factors in the choice of these Jews of a partner not born Jewish. Their parents had non-Jewish friends; they had gone to public school and college with non-Jews; they found themselves accepted by Gentiles; and they felt little opposition to their dating or even marrying non-Jews.

41. Mark L. Winer, Sanford Seltzer, Steven J. Schwager, *Leaders of Reform Judaism: A Study of Jewish Identity, Religious Practices and Beliefs, and Marriage Patterns* (New York: Union of American Hebrew Congregations, 1987), pp. 28, 30, 68–71, 73.

42. Irving Jacks, "How Teenagers See Interfaith Dating," *Jewish Digest,* March 1969, p. 55. In a 1965 sample of 225 Jewish, denominationally affiliated teenagers in a middle-sized Pennsylvania city, 83 percent of the kids disagreed with the statement, "Jewish teenagers should never date non-Jewish teenagers," including 70 percent of the Orthodox teens, and 61 percent reported that they had in fact dated a non-Jew, including almost half the kids who identified as Orthodox. In an early 1980s study by Gratz College sociologist Rela Geffen Monson, *Jewish Campus Life* (New York: American Jewish Committee, 1984), only 15 percent of her 1,300 respondents (Jewish college students from across the United States) said they don't date and would never date non-Jews; 70 percent of the students who identified themselves as coming from "highly religious" homes said they do or would interdate (pp. 32–35).

43. Linda R. Benson, "From Outrage to Outreach," *Baltimore Jewish Times,* January 7, 1992, p. 69; Egon Mayer, "The Impact of Intermarriage," *Reform Judaism* (Spring 1991): 30–31. In a survey taken among members of B'nai B'rith Women, 80 percent of more than 1,300 respondents said they would rather a 35-year-old daughter marry a non-Jew than stay single; in a similar poll conducted by the Jewish Outreach Institute, an interdenominational

agency, three-fourths of more than 2,000 respondents said they would not advise a Jewish man or woman older than 30 to break off a relationship with a non-Jew just to avoid intermarriage. Mayer expanded on the JOI survey, in which those polled were presented with a detailed scenario that featured a Jewish woman or man years past 30 who was not in a position to meet eligible Jews of the opposite sex, wanted badly to marry and start a family, and had fallen in love, despite initial resistance, with a compatible non-Jew who was comfortable with Jewish ritual and practice but did not want to convert to Judaism. An overwhelming majority of laypeople, both Reform and Conservative, wanted to see this person intermarry if the alternative was no marriage at all, and a large plurality, Mayer said, wanted the Jewish woman to marry even if the husband didn't commit to raising Jewish children. Moreover, more than three-fifths of the Reform rabbis in the survey said they would encourage the Jewish woman to intermarry, and almost half would advise the Jewish man to intermarry if the non-Jewish partner agreed in advance to raise the children as Jews.

44. Barry A. Kosmin, "A New Angle on the Intermarriage Rate," *Jewish Week*, August 12–18, 1994, p. 6.

45. Peter Y. Medding, Gary A. Tobin, Sylvia Barack Fishman, and Mordechai Rimor, *Jewish Identity in Conversionary and Mixed Marriages* (New York: American Jewish Committee/Jewish Publication Society, 1992), pp. 12–13; Steven Cohen, *American Assimilation or Jewish Revival?* (Bloomington: Indiana University Press, 1988), pp. 30–33; Egon Mayer, *Love and Tradition* (New York: Plenum Press, 1985), p. 104; Mayer and Sheingold, *Intermarriage and the Jewish Future*, pp. 10–11.

46. Kenneth L. Woodward, "The Intermarrying Kind," *Newsweek*, July 22, 1991, pp. 48–49.

47. The 1990 NJPS was the first nationwide survey of American Jews in almost 20 years. In the wake of the 1971 findings, the Central Conference of American Rabbis had a hot debate over rabbinic officiation, duly reported in the spring 1973 issue of the *CCAR Journal*, and *Keeping Posted*, the educational companion to *Reform Judaism* magazine, made intermarriage the focus of its February 1974 issue. In addition, in October 1976, *Congress Monthly* published a short piece, "Intermarriage and Jewish Continuity," by Allen S. Maller. As far as I know, no one published a book during the mid-1970s that dealt specifically with intermarriage, Jewish continuity, or the changing American Jewish community except for *The Jew in American Society*, the essays in which were written too early to incorporate or react to data from the 1971 NJPS.

48. Fred Massarik, "Rethinking the Intermarriage Crisis," *Moment* (June 1978): 29–33; Mayer, "A Cure for Intermarriage?" *Moment* (June 1979): 64; Steven M. Cohen and Calvin Goldscheider, "Jews, More or Less," *Moment* (September 1984): 43; Lieberman and Weinfeld, "Demographic Trends and Jewish Survival," pp. 12–13; Silberman, *A Certain People*, p. 303. The group of demographers who came out with optimistic forecasts for Jewish population during the 1970s and 1980s overlapped with the sociologists who developed a theory that American Jews, rather than succumbing to assimilation, were simply changing the ways in which they expressed their Jewishness. They may not perform the religious rituals their grandparents did, but these "transformationists" claimed they have found other ways to be

Jewish, such as traveling to Israel, becoming politically active, or playing basketball at the JCC, while continuing to observe Passover, Chanukah, and the High Holidays, to identify with major Jewish movements, and to maintain Jewish friendships. For detailed discussion of the transformationist concept, see Calvin Goldscheider and Alan Zuckerman, *The Transformation of the Jews* (Chicago: University of Chicago Press, 1984); Goldscheider, *Jewish Continuity and Change*, pp. 152–53, 165–68; Cohen, *American Assimilation or Jewish Revival?* pp. 10–18, 113–17, 123–25. Goldscheider especially has kept faith with the transformationist approach since the 1990 NJPS came out. In 1992, he told an audience in Baltimore that a new definition of Jewish community was needed. "Playing golf in a Jewish country club, swimming at a Jewish community center, or using day care facilities in a Jewish institutional setting do not seem on the surface to be very Jewish, but they are," he said. Such activities "enhance the values of Jewish life, intensify shared secular-religious commitments, increase the social, family and economic networks that sustain the continuity of the Jewish community" (Daniel Schifrin, "No Prophet of Doom," *Baltimore Jewish Times*, September 18, 1992, p. 38). The quote from Goldscheider at the head of this chapter is from "Jews, More or Less" (p. 44).

49. Mayer and Sheingold, *Intermarriage and the Jewish Future*, pp. 16–20; Mayer, *Love and Tradition*, pp. 108–9; Mayer, *Children of Intermarriage*, p. 7; Samuel Spiegler, "Fact and Opinion," *Journal of Jewish Communal Service* (Spring 1984): 263; Mordechai Rimor, "Some Basic Trends in Intermarriage: The Case from the Boston Data," *Journal of Jewish Communal Service* (Fall 1989): 38–39. The figures for Jewish identity among children of mixed couples that Mayer comes up with in his *Children of Intermarriage* study are strikingly similar to those in the 1990 NJPS: 24 percent called themselves Jewish, 34 percent claimed no religion, and 42 percent said they had a religion other than Jewish.

50. Medding et al., *Jewish Identity in Conversionary and Mixed Marriages*.

51. Sylvia Barack Fishman, Mordechai Rimor, Gary A. Tobin, and Peter Medding, *Intermarriage and American Jews Today: New Findings and Policy Implications* (Waltham, Mass.: Cohen Center for Modern Jewish Studies, October 1990), p. 27; Medding et al., *Jewish Identity in Conversionary and Mixed Marriages*, p. 37.

52. Barry Shrage, "A Communal Response to the Challenges of the 1990 CJF National Jewish Population Survey: Toward a Jewish Life Worth Living," *Journal of Jewish Communal Service* (Summer 1992): 322; Medding et al., *Jewish Identity in Conversionary and Mixed Marriages*, p. 35.

53. Fishman et al., *Intermarriage and American Jews Today*, p. 4; Medding et al., *Jewish Identity in Conversionary and Mixed Marriages*, p. 6; Mayer, "A Cure for Intermarriage?" p. 62; Silberman, *A Certain People*, p. 297; Massarik and Chenkin, "United States National Jewish Population Study: A First Report," pp. 292, 296–97; Mayer, *Intermarriage and the Jewish Future*, pp. 21–22.

54. Medding et al., *Jewish Identity in Conversionary and Mixed Marriages*, p. 8. The 1990 NJPS shows a cumulative conversion rate of about 13 percent, one of every eight marriages between a Jew and someone not born Jewish (*Highlights*, p. 13).

55. Medding et al., *Jewish Identity in Conversionary and Mixed Marriages*, pp. 21–33, 36–37; Mayer,

Intermarriage and the Jewish Future, pp. 23–25; Massarik, "Rethinking the Intermarriage Crisis," p. 33; Winer, "Sociological Research on Jewish Intermarriage," pp. 38, 45–46; Spiegler, "Fact and Opinion," p. 264; Allen S. Maller, "New Facts about Mixed Marriage," *Reconstructionist*, March 21, 1969, pp. 28–29.

56. Cohen, "Education and Intermarriage," p. 20; Medding et al., *Jewish Identity in Conversionary and Mixed Marriages*, pp. 10–11.

57. Steven Bayme, "Changing Perceptions of Divorce," *Journal of Jewish Communal Service* (Winter/Spring 1994): 122; Mayer, *Love and Tradition*, pp. 90–91; Medding et al., *Jewish Identity in Conversionary and Mixed Marriages*, p. 9; Rachel Cowan and Esther Perel, "A More Perfect Union: Intermarriage and the Jewish World," *Tikkun* (May/June 1992): 62; Winer, "Sociological Research on Jewish Intermarriage," pp. 42–43, and "Jewish Demography and the Challenges to Reform Jewry," *Journal of Reform Judaism* (Winter 1984): 23. The estimates range from Mayer's citation of Erich Rosenthal's 1963 figure of second marriages as 50 percent more likely to be intermarriages than first marriages and Perel's statement that intermarriage is almost twice as frequent in second marriages to Winer's belief that intermarriage is 4–10 times as prevalent among second marriages.

58. Kosmin et al., *Highlights*, p. 9. In their 1990 report (*Intermarriage and American Jews Today*, pp. 10–11), the Cohen Center researchers note that Jewish women are marrying non-Jewish spouses in increasing numbers, while adding that in most of the cities they studied, male intermarriage still outstrips female intermarriage. According to their graph, this is true for the 1980s, but during the 1970s female intermarriage seems to have been about even in three of the cities charted and well ahead in another, and during the 1960s female intermarriage was greater than men's in two cities. Hebrew Union College sociologist Bruce Phillips reports mid-1980s figures for Los Angeles showing that among Jews under 30, more women were intermarrying than men ("Los Angeles Jewry: A Demographic Portrait," *American Jewish Year Book 1986*, pp. 145–47, 153, 177–78). In personal interviews conducted in the spring of 1992, before the large increase in Jewish women intermarrying was widely acknowledged, both Egon Mayer and Steven Cohen said that Jewish women had just about caught up with Jewish men and were marrying non-Jews at about the same rate. Mayer, in fact, saw evidence that the rate of intermarriage for Jewish women was rising back in the 1970s and said so in *Intermarriage and the Jewish Future* (p. 31).

59. For example, Massarik and Chenkin, "United States National Jewish Population Study: A First Report," pp. 295–96; Winer, "Sociological Research on Jewish Intermarriage," p. 42; Mirsky, "Intermarriage: dilemmas," p. P19; Maller, "New Facts about Mixed Marriage," p. 28.

60. Rabbi Irwin Fishbein, who over the years has made a point of officiating at weddings between Jews and non-Jews, said in an interview that among the 200 or more mixed couples he married during the early 1970s, Jewish women outnumbered Jewish men, and Jewish women were close to parity with Jewish men before and after. In an article for *CCAR Journal* ("Marrying 'in,' Not 'Out'," Spring 1973) Fishbein analyzed a survey of some 400 mixed marriages and found that for those contracted during the years 1962–66, Jewish

men outnumbered Jewish women three to one, but from 1967 to 1969 they outnumbered women nine to eight, and in the period 1970–71 Jewish women in the survey outnumbered Jewish men by a three-to-two margin (p. 34). Another rabbi who surveyed the mixed couples at whose weddings he had officiated between 1965 and 1970 noted that more than half the couples included Jewish-born wives (Henry Cohen, "Mixed Marriage and Jewish Continuity," *CCAR Journal* [April 1972]: 48). Rabbi Allen Maller noted a rise in Jewish women marrying Gentile men in a small survey he conducted in Los Angeles in 1973 and also cited a report by Rabbi David Max Eichhorn in which he counted a slight majority of Jewish women among the more than 500 intermarriages he performed between 1966 and 1972 ("Mixed Marriage and Reform Rabbis," *Judaism* [Winter 1975]: 44–45; "Jewish-Gentile Marriage: Another Look at the Problem," *CCAR Journal* [Winter 1976]: 71).

61. Mirsky, "Intermarriage: dilemmas," p. P19.

62. Susan Weidman Schneider, *Jewish and Female: Choices and Changes in Our Lives Today* (New York: Simon and Schuster, 1984), p. 336; the delineation between Jewish parents' expectations for sons and daughters comes from an essay by Rela Geffen Monson, "The Case of the Reluctant Exogamists."

63. Sylvia Barack Fishman, *A Breath of Life: Feminism in the American Jewish Community* (New York: Free Press, 1993), pp. 24–25; Schneider, *Jewish and Female*, pp. 300–302. See also Kosmin and Lachman, *One Nation under God*, p. 222: in their survey, only 18 percent of Jewish women under 25 were married.

64. William Novak, "Are Good Jewish Men a Vanishing Breed?" *Moment* (January/February 1980): 18; Fishman, *A Breath of Life*, p. 25.

65. Novak, "Are Good Jewish Men a Vanishing Breed?" p. 16; Monson's essay in *Jewish and Female* also refers to an imbalance in the sex ratio (p. 335).

66. Schneider, *Jewish and Female*, p. 335; also Fishman, *A Breath of Life*, pp. 27–28. Fishman, using data from Medding et al., *Jewish Identity in Conversionary and Mixed Marriages*, notes that the average age of Jewish women who marry Jews is 23.2 years, while the average age of inter-marrying Jewish women is 26 years.

2: I'm Not OK, Mom's Not OK, You're Not OK

1. Judith Weinstein Klein, *Jewish Identity and Self-Esteem: Healing Wounds through Ethnotherapy* (New York: American Jewish Committee, 1989), pp. 17–25; also, remarks made by Klein at a Jewish Federation-Council Young Leadership program in Orange County, California, January 5, 1992. The opening statement is from the program; the description of the different identifiers from the monograph and program remarks.

2. Klein, *Jewish Identity and Self-Esteem*, p. 16. Klein associates the ambivalent identifier with the "marginal man" described by sociologist Kurt Lewin in his 1948 work *Resolving Social Conflict* (Souvenir Press) who accepts the values of the dominant group in a given society at the expense of the natural tendency to favor his or her own group, expressing hostility toward members of his or her group rather than the more powerful dominant group and assimi-

lating the negative stereotypes the majority culture spreads about minority group members. Egon Mayer cites sociologist Charles Liebman, who asserts in *The Ambivalent American Jew* that *all* American Jews are ambivalent identifiers (Mayer, *Love and Tradition* [New York: Plenum Press, 1985], p. 107).

3. Klein, *Jewish Identity and Self-Esteem*, pp. 17–24.

4. Estelle Frankel, "The Promises and Pitfalls of Jewish Relationships," *Tikkun* (September/October 1990): 19–20.

5. Louis A. Berman, *Jews and Intermarriage: A Study in Personality and Culture* (South Brunswick, N.J.: Thomas Yoseloff, 1968), pp. 55–56.

6. Seidler-Feller made these comments during a lecture on Jewish identity at Congregation Kehillat Ma'arav in Santa Monica, California, March 19, 1992.

7. Sanford Seltzer, "The Psychological Implications of Mixed Marriage," *Journal of Reform Judaism* (Summer 1985): 32–34.

8. Diana Bletter and Lori Grinker, *The Invisible Thread: A Portrait of Jewish American Women* (Philadelphia: Jewish Publication Society, 1989), p. 160.

9. Frankel, "The Promises and Pitfalls of Jewish Relationships," p. 21.

10. Seidler-Feller made these remarks at a symposium entitled "Jewish Men and Women: Love or War?" sponsored by UCLA Hillel on April 27, 1994. Klein also mentioned, in her January 1992 presentation, that Jewish culture, unlike American culture, historically has not placed a high value on athleticism, military prowess, or physical strength. Sociologist Michael Kimmel writes of the Jewish penchant for education, "In a culture characterized by love of learning, literacy may be a mark of dignity. But in the United States . . . literacy is a cultural liability. Americans contrast egghead intellectuals, divorced from the real world, with men of action—instinctual, passionate, fierce, and masculine" (Michael S. Kimmel, "Judaism, Masculinity and Feminism," in *A Mensch Among Men: Explorations in Jewish Masculinity*, edited by Harry Brod [Freedom, Ca.: Crossing Press, 1988], p. 154). See also Bob Lamm, "American Jewish Men: Fear of Feminism," *Lilith* (Fall 1976): 23–24, 44.

11. See Louis A. Berman, *Jews and Intermarriage: A Study in Personality and Culture* (South Brunswick, N.J.: Thomas Yoseloff, 1968), p. 348.

12. Ibid., pp. 120–21. See also Marlene Adler Marks, "The Problem with Jewish Men," *Jewish Journal*, April 15–21, 1988, p. 12.

13. Philip Roth, *Portnoy's Complaint* (New York: Random House, 1969), p. 235. In Paul and Rachel Cowan's much-read book on intermarriage, *Mixed Blessings*, journalist and professor Max Lerner describes how he went to Yale in 1919, 12 years after arriving in the United States, completely captivated by America—and non-Jewish girls. "They were the daughters of the conquerers," he said. "They represented all the values attached to the promised land. I wanted to shine in the context of this country. I was a very literary young man. I had read all the novels and all the romantic poetry. Except for Rebecca in *Ivanhoe*, the heroines were always what I call the possessors. . . . I suppose that if I could conquer the possessor, I validated myself" (Paul Cowan with Rachel Cowan, *Mixed Blessings: Marriage between Jews and Christians* [New York: Doubleday, 1987], p. 98).

14. Daphne Merkin, "Dreaming of Hitler: A Memoir of Self-Hatred," *Testimony: Contemporary Writers Make the Holocaust Personal*, edited by David Rosenberg (New York: Times Books, 1989), p. 18.

15. Anne Roiphe, *Generation without Memory* (New York: Summit, 1981), p. 28.

16. Susan Miron, "Jewish Anatomy: Is It Destiny?" *Congress Monthly*, November/December 1992, pp. 18–19.

17. Klein, *Jewish Identity and Self-Esteem*, pp. 17, 20; also comments in her January 1992 presentation.

18. See also Paul Cowan's description of his self-image in comparison to his classmates at Choate and how that affected his taste in girls (*Mixed Blessings*, pp. 10, 12).

19. Lena Williams, "Girl's Self-Image Is Mother of the Woman," *New York Times*, February 6, 1992, pp. A1, A12; Janet Mesrobian, " 'Ideal' Fashion-Model Body Not So Ideal," *Brandeis Reporter*, January 24, 1992, p. 7; Mary Tannen, "That Scitex Glow," *New York Times Magazine*, July 10, 1994, pp. 44–45; Susan Dworsky, letter to the editor, *Tikkun* (November/December 1991): 3–4. See also Naomi Wolf's *The Beauty Myth* (New York: William Morrow, 1991), and Susan Weidman Schneider's *Jewish and Female: Choices and Changes in Our Lives Today* (New York: Simon and Schuster, 1984), pp. 242–44. A study done at Brandeis University in 1991 found that the average female fashion model was 5 feet 9½ inches tall and weighed 122.8 pounds, whereas the average female Brandeis student was 5 feet 4 inches and weighed 126.2 pounds. The models, dancers, and actresses who are displayed as the "normal" and desirable size and shape for American women are thinner than 95 percent of American women. Also, computer technology allows images of models in print ads and on commercials to be retouched or morphed so that skin, facial features, and body contours can be perfected to exceed reality.

20. Susan Weidman Schneider, *Jewish and Female: Choices and Changes in Our Lives Today* (New York: Simon and Schuster, 1984), p. 246; Sylvia Barack Fishman, *A Breath of Life: Feminism in the American Jewish Community* (New York: Free Press, 1993), p. 97.

21. Merkin, "Dreaming of Hitler," pp. 16, 27.

22. Wolpe was speaking at the Mountaintop Minyan, Stephen S. Wise Temple, Los Angeles, February 8, 1992.

23. R. J. Kamatovic, Drew Seibert, and Shannon Holmes, "The Brandeis Avenger," *The Justice*, October 18, 1994, p. 20.

24. Dorfman included the comment in a speech to the ADL Leadership Forum at Camp Ramah, Ojai, California, May 10, 1982. He later incorporated much of the speech in an article, "Jewish Singles and Their Stereotypes," *Sh'ma*, January 21, 1983, pp. 41–43.

25. Susan Weidman Schneider, "Detoxifying Our Relationships: Interview with Esther Perel," *Lilith* (Fall 1987): 16.

26. David Biale, *Eros and the Jews: From Biblical Israel to Contemporary America* (New York: Basic Books, 1992), p. 54; Susan Weidman Schneider, " 'In a Coma! I Thought She Was Jewish!' " *Lilith* (Spring/Summer 1977): 7; Fishman, *A Breath of Life*, p. 99.

27. Biale, *Eros and the Jews*, pp. 5, 35, 37, 44, 133, 176ff.

28. Schneider, " 'In a Coma! I Thought She Was Jewish!' " p. 8.

29. Schneider, "Detoxifying Our Relationships," p. 16.

30. Berman, *Jews and Intermarriage*, p. 392.

31. Lori Lefkovitz, "Coats and Tales: Joseph Stories and Myths of Jewish Masculinity," in *A Mensch Among Men*, pp. 25, 28; Andrea Dworkin, "The Sexual Mythology of Anti-Semitism," in *A Mensch Among Men*, p. 120; Biale, *Eros and the Jews*, p. 76; Livia Bitton-Jackson, *Madonna or Courtesan? The Jewish Woman in Christian Literature* (New York: Seabury Press, 1982), pp. 19, 20, 23, 46–53, 54–62, 67, 68–72, 79, 102, 108–9, 117–21; Schneider, *Jewish and Female*, pp. 297–98; Berman, *Jews and Intermarriage*, pp. 439–45. Bitton-Jackson notes that Rebecca of York in Sir Walter Scott's *Ivanhoe* was written after Rebecca Gratz, a leader of early nineteenth-century Jewish society in Philadelphia who remained unmarried after falling in love with the son of a minister.

32. Charlotte Baum, Paula Hyman, and Sonya Michel, *The Jewish Woman in America* (New York: New American Library, 1975), pp. 98–99. See also Judy Timberg, "Are Jewish Women Oppressed?" in *Jewish Radicalism: A Selected Anthology*, edited by Jack Nusan Porter and Peter Dreier (New York: Grove Press, 1973).

33. Anne Roiphe, "The Jewish Family: A Feminist Perspective," *Tikkun* (March/April 1986): 70.

34. Schneider's address, "*Lilith* Speaks: Unmasking Stereotypes, Creating New Images," was presented at Developing Images: Representations of Jewish Women in American Culture, a conference at Brandeis University, Waltham, Massachusetts, March 15, 1993. Anne Roiphe's article, "The Jewish Family: A Feminist Perspective," also provides an excellent analysis of how the perceived role of the Jewish mother has affected relations between Jewish men and women. In the late 1960s, psychiatrist Alexander Grinstein published an essay, "Portrait of a Doll," about second-generation Jewish women, that described them in the most scathing terms: crude, loud, badly dressed, self-absorbed, and resistant to change—somewhat more affluent throwbacks to their own "primitive" mothers. His assumption that these women represented a cultural type, inferior to "normal" American women, without bothering to examine why they exhibited those characteristics set the tone for many others who were quick to type Jewish women on the basis of superficial behavior and appearance without inquiring into the social forces that created them (Baum, Hyman, and Michel, *The Jewish Woman in America*, pp. 240–41; Sonya Michel, "Mothers and Daughters in American Jewish Literature: The Rotted Cord," in *The Jewish Woman: New Perspectives*, edited by Elizabeth Koltun [New York: Schocken, 1976], pp. 278–79).

35. Nancy Chodorow, *The Reproduction of Mothering* (Berkeley: University of California Press, 1978), pp. 181–83.

36. Ibid., pp. 184–85.

37. Frankel, "The Promises and Pitfalls of Jewish Relationships," p. 96.

38. Berman, *Jews and Intermarriage*, p. 130.

39. Barbara Wyden and Gwen Gibson Schwartz, *The Jewish Wife* (New York: P. H. Wyden, 1969), p. 7; Baum, Hyman, and Michel, *The Jewish Woman in America*, p. 243. Both works cite Zena Smith Blau, "In Defense of the Jewish Mother," *Midstream* (February 1967): 42–49.

40. Timberg, "Are Jewish Women Oppressed?" p. 249. Wyden and Schwartz, in *The Jewish Wife*,

cite a study from the 1960s of 5,000 high school students that showed Jewish teenagers outranking youngsters in all other religious groups in self-esteem (p. 169).

41. Chaim I. Waxman, "The Jewish Father: Past and Present," in *A Mensch Among Men*, pp. 64–65.

42. Chodorow, *The Reproduction of Mothering*, pp. 175–77. See also Barbara Breitman, "Lifting Up the Shadow of Anti-Semitism: Jewish Masculinity in a New Light," in *A Mensch Among Men*, pp. 105–12.

43. Robert Eshman, "Hail the New Jewish Man!" *Jewish Journal*, February 25–March 3, 1994, p. 8.

44. Fredda M. Herz and Elliott J. Rosen, "Jewish Families," in *Ethnicity and Family Therapy*, edited by Monica McGoldrick, John K. Pearce, and Joseph Giordano (New York: Guilford Press, 1982), pp. 377, 380.

45. Berman, *Jews and Intermarriage*, pp. 112–13; Susan Weidman Schneider, *Intermarriage: The Challenge of Living with Differences between Christians and Jews* (New York: Free Press, 1989), pp. 18–19.

46. Sometimes the most frustrating aspect of Jewish parents' expectations is that they are not specific enough. "The pressure that family members feel is often exacerbated by expectations that are implicit and unspoken and therefore can never really be met," Herz and Rosen write, giving the example of a respected (but unmarried) young university professor who took endless grief from his parents and his older brother because the brother, a manufacturer, was earning big money and providing the parents with grandchildren. The professor couldn't understand why his accomplishments didn't get equal respect (*Ethnicity and Family Therapy*, p. 370).

47. Susan Schnur, "Blazes of Truth," *Lilith* (Fall 1987): 11.

48. Schneider, *Intermarriage*, p. 24; Berman, *Jews and Intermarriage*, p. 266.

49. Richard L. Rubenstein, "Intermarriage and Conversion on the American College Campus," *Intermarriage and Jewish Life*, pp. 137–38. Writing at a time when most known Jewish intermarriers were men, Louis Berman said, "It is in the nature of the incest taboo that a Jewish male's sexual inhibitions should be more readily elicited by a *Jewish* girl [author's italics]—and the Jewish male would be no more than human to place some of the blame on the girl, for his relative lack of sexual arousal. If a Jewish girl arouses his ambivalence toward intimacy, he may in turn arouse her anxiety and thereby set in motion a vicious cycle which inhibits sexual adventure" (*Jews and Intermarriage*, p. 386).

50. Merkin, "Dreaming of Hitler," pp. 27–28.

51. Anonymous respondent, "We Are Many," *Moment* (April 1977): 37.

52. Schneider, *Jewish and Female*, p. 153.

53. Schnur, "Blazes of Truth," p. 11. See also Lamm, "American Jewish Men," pp. 23–24.

54. Marks, "The Problem with Jewish Men," p. 12.

55. David Margolis, "Dating Jewish Women," *Jewish Journal*, November 17–23, 1989, p. 6.

56. Lawrence Bush, "Jewish Men Play It Safe," *Reform Judaism* (Spring 1993): 28.

57. Jeffrey Salkin, "Shylock in Drag?" *Moment* (March 1983): 38.

3: Rush to Judgment

1. Jacob Rader Marcus, *The American Jewish Woman, 1654–1980* (New York: KTAV, 1981), p. 60; Riv-Ellen Prell, "The Begetting of America's Jews: Seeds of American Jewish Identity in the Representations of American Jewish Women," *Journal of Jewish Communal Service* (Winter/Spring 1993): 8–12, 18; Sherry Chayat, "JAP-Baiting on the College Scene," *Lilith* (Fall 1987): 6; Susan Weidman Schneider, *Jewish and Female: Choices and Changes in Our Lives Today* (New York: Simon and Schuster, 1984), pp. 283–84; Sylvia Barack Fishman, *A Breath of Life: Feminism in the American Jewish Community* (New York: Free Press, 1993), p. 22; Jeffrey Salkin, "Shylock in Drag?" *Moment* (March 1983): 37; Louis A. Berman, *Jews and Intermarriage: A Study in Personality and Culture* (South Brunswick, N.J.: Thomas Yoseloff, 1968), pp. 343–44. Berman cites a Belgian educator who in 1877 warned that Jewish girls had become so pampered and well educated that their expectations of potential husbands were impelling many young Jewish men to choose Gentile women as wives, as well as a sociologist who warned Jewish parents in 1963 that their financial expectations of sons-in-law were so oppressive that the young men would be driven away from Jewish girls entirely. "Jewish mothers sensitize their daughters more to their rights than to their obligations, so that they insist that their future husbands be conveniently docile in the home, inordinately 'ambitious' in the marketplace, and capable of satisfying the highest material expressions of 'happiness.'"

   In her *Lilith* article, "Blazes of Truth," Rabbi Susan Schnur describes a course she taught at Colgate University in which the JAP issue came up again and again. In a class journal, one student wrote, "When my best girlfriend from childhood was bat mitzvahed, her grandmother gave her a 'JAP-training' diamond-chip necklace. It's like the grandmother was saying, 'When I was your age, I had to sew plackets in a Lower East Side sweatshop. So you girls be JAPs. Take whatever you can and be proud of it.'" In *Jewish and Female*, Schneider describes the father's indulgence of his daughter's materialism as a symbol of his professional or business success. See also Marlene Adler Marks, "The Problem with Jewish Men," *Jewish Journal*, April 15–21, 1988, p. 12.

2. Prell, "The Begetting of America's Jews," pp. 19–20. The same material appears in Prell's essay, "Why Jewish Princesses Don't Sweat: Desire and Consumption in Postwar American Jewish Culture," in *People of the Body: Jews and Judaism from an Embodied Perspective*, edited by Howard Eilberg-Schwartz (Albany: State University of New York Press, 1992), pp. 329–55.

3. Letty Cottin Pogrebin, *Deborah, Golda, and Me* (New York: Crown, 1989), p. 217. The stereotype and its acronym may have received its first big push into American culture and vernacular with an article by Julie Baumgold, "The Persistence of the Jewish American Princess," in *New York*, March 22, 1971, cited in Charlotte Baum, Paula Hyman, and Sonya Michel, *The Jewish Woman in America* (New York: New American Library, 1975), p. 254.

4. Aviva Cantor Zuckoff, "An Exclusive Interview with Dr. Phyllis Chesler," *Lilith* (Winter 1976/77): 26–27.

5. Elisa New, "Killing the Princess: The Offense of a Bad Defense," *Tikkun* (March/April 1989): 17. New's article discusses Shirley Frondorf's book on the Steinberg case, *The Death of a "Jewish American Princess": The True Story of a Victim on Trial* (New York: Villard, 1988). See also Janice Booker, *The Jewish American Princess and Other Myths: The Many Faces of Self-Hatred* (New York: Shapolsky, 1991), p. 59.

6. Salkin, "Shylock in Drag?" p. 37.

7. Anna Sequoia, *The Official J.A.P. Handbook* (New York: New American Library, 1982), p. 8. An interesting 1970s artifact is a book written by Leslie Tonner, *Nothing but the Best: The Luck of the Jewish Princess* (New York: Coward, McCann & Geoghegan, 1975). Writing perhaps in reaction to the Jewish princess's early notoriety, Tonner takes the position that not only is a Jewish princess a wonderful thing to be but that every contemporary American Jewish woman is a princess in some way or another because of her relative affluence; she simply may not dress or act the part. The Jewish princess's materialism, according to Tonner, is just a means to the end of making herself and her home beautiful; the Jewish prince, her natural consort, appreciates this and loves her for it. (She provides a long description of Jewish parents' relentless judgment of their daughter's dates by their earning potential without a thought to how this might affect the young men involved.) In a chapter on sex, Tonner swallows whole the stereotype of the sexually cold Jewish woman; only now, in the liberated 1970s, will a Jewish princess have premarital sex, Tonner says, and only because she now has to compete with non-Jewish women to land a Jewish man for a husband. The contemporary Jewish princess's sense of privilege, her superior education, and her parents' message that there's nothing she can't do or have not only equip her well for making a beautiful home but give her the confidence to succeed in the professional world as well, Tonner asserts. "Isn't it about time that we got it into our heads that being a Jewish Princess is something she, and we, can be proud of?" Tonner concludes. "She represents generations of achievement, years of industry, and training, a lifetime of indulgence and hard work. It is not easy to be a Jewish Princess" (p. 190).

8. *Lilith* (Fall 1976): 35. The "Oy Vey!" feature in *Lilith*, analogous to the "No Comment" page in *Ms.*, presented clips from Jewish publications that the editors considered blatantly sexist.

9. Gary Spencer, "An Analysis of JAP-baiting Humor on the College Campus," *Humor: International Journal of Humor Research*, Vol. 2, No. 4, 1989, pp. 335–44. Similarly reported by Judith Allen Rubenstein, "The Graffiti Wars," *Lilith* (Fall 1987): 8–9; Ruth Atkin and Adrienne Rich, "'J.A.P.'-Slapping: The Politics of Scapegoating," *Agenda* (Spring 1988): 4; Evelyn Torton Beck, "Therapy's Double Dilemma: Anti-Semitism and Misogyny," in *Jewish Women in Therapy: Seen But Not Heard*, edited by Rachel Josefowitz Siegel and Ellen Cole (New York: Harrington Park Press, 1991), pp. 23–25; Laura Shapiro, "When Is a Joke Not a Joke?" *Newsweek*, May 23, 1988, p. 79; Pogrebin, *Deborah, Golda, and Me*, pp. 231–32.

10. Beck, "Therapy's Double Dilemma," p. 25.

11. Developing Images conference, Brandeis University, March 15, 1993.

12. Estelle Frankel, "The Promises and Pitfalls of Jewish Relationships," *Tikkun* (Septem-

ber/October 1990): 19–20. In discussing the JAP dynamic, Frankel asserts, "Those Jewish women who actually do fit the description of the JAP often use the characteristic attitude of entitlement as a defense against deep feelings of emptiness and unworthiness. They turn to an indulgent consumerism hoping to cover up these painful feelings" (p. 22).

13. Letter, "SJM Seeks . . ." in the "Dear Deborah" column, *Jewish Journal*, October 7–13, 1994, p. 25. See also Marlene Adler Marks, "The Problem with Jewish Men," *Jewish Journal*, April 15–21, 1988, p. 12.

14. Susan Weidman Schneider, "Detoxifying Our Relationships: Interview with Esther Perel," *Lilith* (Fall 1987): 18.

15. Barbara Wyden and Gwen Gibson Schwartz, *The Jewish Wife* (New York: P. H. Wyden, 1969), pp. 26–28, 224–25.

16. Schneider, *Jewish and Female*, p. 293; Marks, "The Problem with Jewish Men," p. 12. In *Eros and the Jews* (p. 208), David Biale cites Rabbi David Kirschenbaum's 1958 book, *Mixed Marriage and the Jewish Future* (New York: Bloch, 1958). In *Jews and Intermarriage*, Louis Berman quotes Kirschenbaum's fulminations about the expensive tastes and material expectations of young Jewish women at length. "Their behavior is that of a child-aristocrat. Their greatest ideal is fine clothes, expensive jewelry, and an elaborately furnished home, and they do not hesitate to let this be known to the young men who court them" (pp. 342–43).

17. Schneider, "Detoxifying Our Relationships," p. 18.

18. Shapiro, "When Is a Joke Not a Joke?" p. 79. Even more deluded was the young woman participating in a 1991 discussion during a Judaic studies class at Brown University who commented, "I come from the Five Towns [Long Island], and where I come from calling someone a JAP is a compliment. Being a JAP means that you've made it. Being a JAP means you have money and prestige, and you know how to use both. A JAP knows and wears what is stylish—she knows exactly where to buy it and how to put things together. And a JAP knows how to get other people to do things for her. Isn't that power? What's more American than power? Being a JAP is being a powerful woman." (Sylvia Barack Fishman, *Follow My Footprints: Changing Images of Women in American Jewish Fiction* [Hanover, N.H.: University Press of New England and Brandeis University Press, 1992], p. 32.)

19. Chayat, "JAP-Baiting on the College Scene," p. 7.

20. Schnur, "Blazes of Truth," p. 11.

21. Spencer, "An Analysis of JAP-baiting Humor on the College Campus," p. 334. In Judith Allen Rubenstein's article for *Lilith*, "The Graffiti Wars," the dean of the School of Social Work at Syracuse is quoted as saying he didn't know the graffiti was on campus, adding, "When the issue gets raised in discussion, one will frequently be told that very often it's the Jewish kids themselves who use the phrase or laugh at the joke." Rubenstein reported that every Syracuse student asked about use of the term *JAP* denied that it was meant as an ethnic pejorative.

22. Beck, "Therapy's Double Dilemma," p. 26.

23. Rubenstein, "The Graffiti Wars," p. 9.

24. It also took until 1987 for the American Jewish Committee to organize the first national

conference on the JAP stereotype and for the Reform National Federation of Temple Sister-hoods to adopt a resolution condemning JAP jokes and images and calling on synagogues to stop selling items with "JAP" logos in their gift shops.

25. Anne Roiphe, "The Jewish Family: A Feminist Perspective," *Jewish Heritage* (Summer 1972): 73. Roiphe provides a detailed analysis of the Jewish American princess stereotype, its inherent misogyny and anti-Semitism, and how the hostility engendered by stereotyping damages relationships among Jews and feeds intermarriage.

26. Diana Bletter and Lori Grinker, *The Invisible Thread: A Portrait of Jewish American Women* (Philadelphia: Jewish Publication Society, 1989), p. 30. See also Marks, "The Problem with Jewish Men," p. 15.

27. Marlene Marks, "Heart of the Matter," *Jewish Journal*, May 6–12, 1994, p. 7. See also Lamm, who was well ahead of the curve in "American Jewish Men: Fear of Feminism," *Lilith* (Fall 1976): 24.

28. New, "Killing the Princess," p. 114.

29. Steve Emmons, "Singles Happy but Looking for True Love," *Los Angeles Times*, September 14, 1994, p. A15.

30. Wyden and Schwartz, *The Jewish Wife*, pp. 28–30, 229.

31. Beck, "Therapy's Double Dilemma," p. 27.

32. Schneider, *Jewish and Female*, p. 286.

33. Nora Ephron, *Heartburn* (New York: Knopf, 1983), pp. 20–21. The Jewish prince, by the way, has his handbook, too: four years after publishing *The Jewish American Princess Handbook* (Chicago: Turnbull & Willoughby, 1982), Sandy Toback and Debbie Haback produced *The Jewish American Prince Handbook* (Chicago: Turnbull & Willoughby, 1986).

34. Roiphe, "The Jewish Family: A Feminist Perspective," p. 73; see also Schneider, *Jewish and Female*, p. 285.

35. Mopsie Strange Kennedy, "The Jewish American Prince," *Moment* (May/June 1976): 12. This is probably the first and possibly the only essay in a national Jewish publication that focuses entirely on the persona of the Jewish prince. Kennedy, whose article quotes some very annoyed women on the favoritism shown their brothers, asserts that the Jewish prince is unlike his counterparts in other ethnic groups because he is running away from women of his own group. At the end of the piece, she runs a disclaimer, conceding that no one could conform to every detail of such a monstrous stereotype; "the character of the Jewish prince, while it has some basis in reality, is more than anything a projection of the frustrations and anger of Jewish women."

36. Michele Bograd, "Countertransference," *Lilith* (Fall 1989): 24.

37. Dan Dorfman, "Jewish Singles and Their Stereotypes," *Sh'ma*, January 21, 1983, p. 42.

38. Fishman, *A Breath of Life*, pp. 28–29.

39. Similarly, Boston-area matchmaker Linda Novak reported, "Many men . . . want women who are independent, who have careers, who are terrific and assertive. At the same time, they also want homebodies and nurturers. . . . The men complain that the women they're meeting aren't both assertive and motherly at the same time" ("Make Me a Match, 1985: A *Moment* Interview with Linda Novak," *Moment* [October 1985]: 48).

40. See William Novak, "Are Good Jewish Men a Vanishing Breed?" This essay does a superb job of capturing the frustration felt by thousands of Jewish women born during the first wave of the baby boom who waited until they established careers or completed graduate degrees to start looking seriously for a partner. The women Novak writes about want to marry Jewish men, but they describe all the Jewish men they meet as immature or egotistical—without rancor, Novak says; these women are sure Great Jewish Guys are out there. "Some of the best young people that the Jewish community has produced are not getting married—although they very much want to," Novak wrote in closing. "They feel strong pressures against intermarriage, but they also don't want to end up alone. . . . What happens to these women—or what fails to happen—will matter significantly not only to their own lives, but to the future of American Judaism."

41. If you're still not convinced that Jewish stereotypes are self-perpetuating and the result of poor self-image, consider *JP: The Magazine of the Jewish Professional*, published by the Society of Young Jewish Professionals. The magazine promoted the SYJP with two ads. One shows two GQ types, one saying to the other, "She's a great tennis player, doesn't paint her nails red. *And* that's the nose she was born with." The subtext? The Jewish woman he's met through the SYJP doesn't look Jewish or act Jewish—good! The other ad shows Jewish women in conversation. The text reads, "He's a lawyer, never wears gold chains. *And* he doesn't like to talk about his mother." Subtext: What a catch! He's what a Jewish guy is "supposed" to be—educated and affluent—but not what most Jewish guys are: sleazy, desperate, and mother-ridden. "The ads seem to target assimilated, unaffiliated Jews who wouldn't think twice about intermarriage, and I applaud SYJP for reaching out to that group," a reporter writes. "But they attempt to entice these Jews to join the SYJP by sending the message that SYJP members don't have all those negative traits ascribed to Jews. . . . The ads idealize non-Jewishness because Jewishness has been reduced to trite, shallow stereotypes of people's appearance and behavior." (Susan Josephs, "Reading Between the Lines," *Jewish Journal*, December 17–23, 1993, p. 33; reprinted from New York's *Jewish Week*.)

4: That's Entertainment

1. See Ben Hecht's *A Jew in Love* (New York: Covici, Friede, 1931) for an example of the self-hating Jewish protagonist described in very unflattering terms.

2. Bernard Cohen, *Sociocultural Changes in American Jewish Life as Reflected in Selected Jewish Literature* (Rutherford, N.J.: Fairleigh Dickinson University Press, 1972), pp. 129–33; Fiedler, *The Jew in the American Novel* (New York: Herzl Press, 1959), pp. 22–24.

3. Irving Howe, ed., *Jewish-American Stories* (New York: New American Library, 1977), pp. 6–7.

4. The introductory essay to Sylvia Barack Fishman's anthology of fiction by and about Jewish women, *Follow My Footprints: Changing Images of Women in American Jewish Fiction* (Hanover, N.H.: University Press of New England and Brandeis University Press, 1992), contains an excellent discussion of the "woman of valor" in Yiddish and immigrant fiction (pp. 14–22); see also Harold Fisch, "Fathers, Mother, Sons and Lovers: Jewish and Gentile Patterns in Literature," *Midstream* (March 1972): 37–38, 40–41.

5. Sonya Michel, "Mothers and Daughters in American Jewish Literature: The Rotted Cord," pp. 273–76; Fishman, *Follow My Footprints*, pp. 25–28.

6. Fishman, *Follow My Footprints*, pp. 30, 35–36; Michel, "Mothers and Daughters," p. 279; Marc Lee Raphael, "Female Humanity: American Jewish Women Writers Speak Out," *Judaism* (Spring 1981): 218–19.

7. Besides *Portnoy's Complaint* (New York: Random House, 1969), classically overbearing Jewish mothers can be found in Herbert Gold's *Fathers* (New York: Random House, 1966), Lois Gould's *Such Good Friends* (New York: Random House, 1970), and Bruce Jay Friedman's *A Mother's Kisses* (New York: Simon and Schuster, 1964). In *The Kingdom of Brooklyn* (Atlanta: Longstreet Press, 1992), Merrill Lynn Gerber one-ups Roth in the food-fixation department. Melvin J. Friedman presents a good rundown of Jewish mothers in books of the 1960s, including Dan Greenburg's seminal "handbook," *How to Be a Jewish Mother* (Los Angeles: Price/Stern/Sloan, 1964), in his essay "Jewish Mothers and Sons: The Expense of *Chutzpah*," in *Contemporary American-Jewish Literature: Critical Essays*, edited by Irving Malin (Bloomington: Indiana University Press, 1973), pp. 156–70; also see Theodore Solotaroff, "Remember Those Tissues They Wrapped the Fruit In—?" in *The Red Hot Vacuum and Other Pieces on the Writing of the 1960s* (New York: Atheneum, 1970), pp. 238–39. Fisch, in "Fathers, Mothers, Sons and Lovers," and Robert Alter, in "Defaming the Jews," *Commentary* (January 1973): 78–79, among others, remind us that not all manipulative, overbearing mothers in literature are Jewish.

   The incidence of novels in which Jewish sons fulminate about their obnoxious mothers has dropped off since *Portnoy's Complaint* (daughters have done most of the bitching for the past generation), but a recent volume that can be found in the "humor" section of your local bookstore, Sam Bobrick and Jule Stein's *Sheldon and Mrs. Levine* (Los Angeles: Price/Stern/Sloan, 1993), presents a series of letters between an angry, guilt-ridden Jewish son and a guilt-inflicting Jewish mother from hell.

8. Ruth Wisse, *The Schlemiel as Modern Hero* (Chicago: University of Chicago Press, 1971), p. 95.

9. Among first-generation writers, Anzia Yezierska cops the prize for Dad from Hell in *Bread-Givers* (New York: Doubleday, 1925); Henry Roth gets the Generation II Bad Father award for Albert Schearl in *Call It Sleep* (New York: Robert Ballou, 1934; Avon, 1964); and Joseph Heller presents a particularly toxic Jewish father in *Good as Gold* (New York: Simon and Schuster, 1979) (see Sanford Pinsker, "Bashing the Jewish-American Suburbs," *Jewish-American Fiction, 1917–1987* [New York: Twayne, 1992], p. 101). In Saul Bellow's novel *Herzog* (New York: Viking, 1964), the title character remembers his father as a *schlemiel*, failing at one business after another (Wisse, *The Schlemiel as Modern Hero*, p. 93). The only time Alex Portnoy thinks of his dad as manly is at the steam bath, where little Alex was brought face to face, so to speak, with his father's genitals (*Portnoy's Complaint*, p. 50).

10. Fishman, *Follow My Footprints*, pp. 22, 47–48; Evelyn Torton Beck, "I. B. Singer's Misogyny," *Lilith* (1979): 34–36; Nikki Stiller, "The Shiksa Question," *Moment* (July/August 1980): 22–25; Mark F. Goldberg, "The Jew as Lover," *National Jewish Monthly* (November 1969): 66–67; Chaim Potok, "Bellow and the Love Scene," *Tikkun* (July/August 1987): 77.

11. Herman Wouk is often cited as the creator of the contemporary JAP in his novel *Marjorie Morningstar* (New York: Doubleday, 1955), but that book is set almost entirely in the 1930s, when the parameters of what constituted a Jewish princess were much more specific than those of the suburban model that appeared in the 1950s. (See Leslie Tonner's description of the 1930s West End Avenue princess in *Nothing but the Best: The Luck of the Jewish Princess* [New York: Coward, McCann & Geoghegan, 1975], pp. 65–68.) Marjorie, shown in action from ages 17 to 24, doesn't conform to the modern JAP stereotype in many ways: when her father is rich, she continues attending lowly Hunter College, and when Dad suffers business reverses, she is supportive and gracious; in fact, she works for pay—and works hard—through much of the novel. Her dream of becoming an actress is unrealistic, but she exerts a great deal of effort, even humiliates herself, to achieve her goal (rather than waiting for success to come to her, as a true princess would), and she surrenders gracefully when she finally realizes the dream is beyond her grasp. As for her relationship with Noel Airman, the talented *luftmensch* who represents everything the other Jewish men in her life are not, yes, she wants to bring him down to earth and live with him in middle-class comfort, but that's partly because she knows that the work he does best is the kind that brings in a steady paycheck. She sleeps with him not to rope him into marriage but because she loves him, and her inability to enjoy the sex fully is not a princess's withholding but a result of the sexual repression felt by thousands of young women in her day. (One essayist insisted that the novel would have had a very different outcome if Wouk had let Marjorie have an orgasm.) In the novel's epilogue, Marjorie is living the married, middle-class life one could have predicted for her, but she is also unpretentious, gray-haired (as no real Jewish princess would allow herself to be at 40), and contented with her life. Her ex-bohemian friend Marsha is the princess: nervous, garishly dressed, borderline anorexic, with nothing to do but drive her Cadillac around Westchester County and spend her husband's money.

    For discussion of *Marjorie Morningstar*, see Elenore Lester, "Marjorie Morningstar Revisited," *Lilith* (Fall 1976): 13–15, 42; David Margolis, "Marjorie's Message," *Jewish Journal*, July 1–7, 1994, p. 35; and Fishman, *Follow My Footprints*, pp. 33–34. Another interesting glimpse of the 1930s Jewish princess can be found in Noah Gordon's popular novel *The Rabbi* (New York: McGraw-Hill, 1965).

12. Prell, "Why Jewish Princesses Don't Sweat," pp. 348–54; Pinsker, *Jewish-American Fiction*, pp. 81–86; Fishman, *Follow My Footprints*, pp. 34–35; Michel, "Mothers and Daughters," p. 279. The excerpt from *Goodbye, Columbus* (Boston: Houghton Mifflin, 1959; New York: Bantam, 1976) is taken from p. 46 of the Bantam edition. The really scary Jewish princess in *Goodbye, Columbus* is Brenda's 10-year-old sister, Julie, who has an even greater sense of entitlement than Brenda has. With the exception of Lois Gould's *Necessary Objects* (New York: Random House, 1972), which is centered on four very spoiled sisters, relatively few Jewish princesses appear in American Jewish fiction, turning up mostly as minor characters in popular novels. They include the protagonist's dead wife in Glenn Savan's *White Palace* (New York: Bantam, 1987), a wildly caricatured mother and teenaged daughter in Rhoda Lerman's *The Girl That He Marries* (New York: Holt, Rinehart and Winston, 1976), the

protagonist's sister in Judy Blume's *Wifey* (New York: Putnam, 1978), and several Long Island matrons in Susan Isaacs' *Compromising Positions* (New York: Times Books, 1978). Female characters in American Jewish fiction are often misidentified as princesses when they have protective parents or are pretty and pay attention to their looks, even if they are rebellious, intellectual, nurturant, and/or self-supporting (Raphael, "Female Humanity," pp. 217–18). In Rebecca Goldstein's novel *The Dark Sister* (New York: Viking, 1991), the dour protagonist, Hedda, a writer of novels with angry, militant female heroines, is horrified when she hears that her flighty sister is planning to write a series of mystery novels about a JAP who solves crimes without so much as getting up from her leather couch. Later, she conjures up an image of this JAP, an overdecorated but pretty woman with a thick Long Island accent who tells Hedda some home truths about her family and her life—Goldstein's reminder to the reader that whatever her faults, the Jewish princess is no airhead (pp. 192–95).

13. Gail Parent, *David Meyer Is a Mother* (New York: G. P. Putnam's Sons, 1975), pp. 3, 5, 6.

14. Other Jewish princes in popular fiction include Richard Slentz, the Gentile protagonist's boyfriend in *The Girl That He Marries*; Norman Pressman, the protagonist's husband in *Wifey*; Michael Rappaport, a failed fiancé in Iris Rainer Dart's *'Til the Real Thing Comes Along* (New York: Bantam, 1987); and the protagonists' husbands in both of Susan Isaacs's Long Island–based murder mysteries, *Compromising Positions* and *After All These Years* (New York: HarperCollins, 1993). A couple of Isadora Wing's husbands are Jewish princes, as is the conductor she spends an interlude with in *Fear of Flying* (New York: Holt, Rinehart and Winston, 1973), explicitly labeled as such; also wearing the crown is the unfaithful Mark Feldman in Nora Ephron's *Heartburn* (New York: Knopf, 1983). Lois Gould and Sue Kaufman wrote a number of unappealing Jewish proto-yuppies into their novels during the 1970s, and Gail Parent created a hybrid Sheldon-prince in *A Sign of the Eighties* (New York: Putnam, 1987).

15. For a detailed discussion of "Rambowitz" fiction, see Paul Breines, *Tough Jews* (New York: Basic Books, 1990).

16. An example of a tough guy whose Jewishness *is* more than incidental is Peter Decker, protagonist of Faye Kellerman's series of detective novels.

17. Philip Roth has come in for most of this criticism since he began his career. See Theodore Solotaroff, "Philip Roth and the Jewish Moralists," in *Contemporary American Jewish Literature*, pp. 15–16, and *The Red Hot Vacuum*, p. 311; Irving Howe, "Philip Roth Reconsidered," *Commentary* (December 1972): 76; Philip Roth, *Reading Myself and Others* (New York: Farrar, Straus and Giroux, 1975), pp. 9–10; and Roth's *The Ghost Writer* (New York: Farrar, Straus and Giroux, 1979), in which he lampoons his own early critics. All things considered, Roth has been unjustly maligned as the writer who is singlehandedly responsible for the rising tide of marriage between Jews and non-Jews. He has never portrayed young Jewish women as unattractive; they may have been princesses or, in the case of the Israeli woman Alex Portnoy tries to sleep with at the end of *Portnoy's Complaint*, aggressive and contemptuous, but they were also good-looking and sexy, and usually smart. Most of the non-Jewish

female characters he has drawn until recently are beautiful but dysfunctional—Gentile women are rarely presented as successful partners or good potential spouses in his work. Roth wrote a couple of bitchy Jewish mothers into his early work, including Brenda Patimkin's, but Sophie Portnoy was his only over-the-top portrayal of the stereotype. The mothers of his protagonists since *Portnoy's Complaint* have been soft-spoken and self-effacing, much the way Roth portrays his own mother in his memoir *The Facts* (New York: Farrar, Straus and Giroux, 1987). It really isn't Roth's fault that *Portnoy's Complaint* and *Goodbye, Columbus* (which became more widely read after *Portnoy* was published) captured the imagination of a large population of adolescent and aging-adolescent Jewish men at the precise moment they were hacking through their sexual repressions and looking for someone to blame for them. As for charges of being a self-hating Jew, Solotaroff and Roth himself point out that if Roth did not care about his own Jewishness, he wouldn't incorporate it into his fiction.

18. Raphael, "Female Humanity," pp. 217–18.

19. Parent, *A Sign of the Eighties*, p. 103.

20. In at least half a dozen novels I read in preparing to write this book, a young Jewish woman has had a nose job or has thought about it, including *Sheila Levine Is Dead and Living in New York* (New York: Putnam, 1972), *A Sign of the Eighties*, *Necessary Objects*, and Louise Blecher Rose's *The Launching of Barbara Fabrikant* (New York: David McKay, 1974). Weight looms large as a source of low self-esteem in *Sheila Levine*, *Barbara Fabrikant*, and a few other protagonists of "ugly duckling" novels of the early 1970s. Some female writers of "literary" Jewish fiction have dealt with issues of physical self-image by creating female protagonists who live almost entirely in their minds, such as Cynthia Ozick's Puttermesser in *Levitation: Five Fictions* (New York: Dutton, 1983) and Hedda in Rebecca Goldstein's *The Dark Sister*.

21. Roth, *Portnoy's Complaint*, pp. 149–50.

22. Roth's phrase, not mine: *Portnoy's Complaint*, p. 124.

23. In Erica Jong's three novels about Isadora Wing, two of Isadora's three husbands are Jewish, along with a couple of lovers, although one of the Jewish husbands is schizophrenic and the other is a spoiled brat. The only man (of many) who gives Sheila Levine an orgasm is one Harold Feinberg. In *Wifey*, Sandy has an extracurricular affair with a Jewish boyfriend from high school; he betrays her, but while it lasts, the sex is a lot better than the dull routine she carries out with her husband.

24. Roth, *Portnoy's Complaint*, pp. 151–53; see also Mordecai Richler, *Joshua Then and Now* (New York: Knopf, 1980), p. 178.

25. Roth, *Reading Myself and Others*, pp. 142–43; see also Joel Grossman, " 'Happy as Kings': Philip Roth's Men and Women," *Judaism* (Winter 1977): 9–10, 15–16; Bernard Sherman, "The Fictive Jew: Jewish-American Education Novels, 1916–1964," Ph.D. diss., Northwestern University, 1966; Solotaroff, *The Red Hot Vacuum*, pp. 327–28.

26. Erica Jong, *Any Woman's Blues* (New York: Harper and Row, 1990), p. 20. In *Fear of Flying*, Isadora's best friend, Pia Wittkin, has a succession of Gentile lovers. "They all seemed to have hollow cheekbones and lank blond hair. She was hung up on the midwestern *shagetz*

the way certain Jewish guys are hung up on *shikses*. It was as if they were all the same guy. Huck Finn without a raft. Blond hair, blue denim, and cowboy boots. And they always wound up walking all over her" (p. 99). Later, in *Parachutes and Kisses* (New York: New American Library, 1984), Isadora thinks up an idea for two TV game shows: " 'Shiksa-mania' was the first. . . . The show would have a split screen and on each side would sit *shiksa* and Jewish consort, the Jewish consorts both competing in describing their ladyloves' excellent *shiksa*-like qualities—ski-jump Draw-Me-girl noses, perfectly conical breasts, small waists, high, firm asses. The mirror image of this show would be called 'Shaygets-o-Rama,' in which two Jewish girls would appear with their *shkotzim*" (p. 302). Among earlier writers, Anzia Yezierska was especially interested in WASPy men, seeing them as representative of all that was intelligent and beautiful about America; during the 1920s, Yezierska had an affair with educator John Dewey. Many of Yezierska's stories featured a Jewish woman falling in love with a young WASP spending time in the ghetto. The protagonist of Susan Isaacs' novel *Close Relations* (New York: Lippincott and Crowell, 1981), who spends much of the story as the mistress of an Irish politico, winds up with the best of both worlds: a tall, wealthy, sexually gifted, very sweet man from a highly assimilated German-Jewish family. "One of your attractions for me is that you're so . . . un-Jewish. It's like marrying a Protestant without the guilt" (p. 255). Her fiancé, in turn, is enchanted by her ethnicity and street savvy. Again, that's why they call it fiction.

27. Patricia Erens, *The Jew in American Cinema* (Bloomington: Indiana University Press, 1984), pp. 38–39, 48–49, 91, 102–4, 106–7; Neil Gabler, *An Empire of Their Own: How the Jews Invented Hollywood* (New York: Crown, 1988), pp. 144–45.

28. Lester D. Friedman, *The Jewish Image in American Film* (Secaucus, N.J.: Citadel Press, 1987), pp. 34–35. Samuel Goldwyn at one point had been a glove salesman, Carl Laemmle and Adolph Zukor furriers, William Fox made dresses, and Harry Cohn had a stint as a song plugger. For detailed sketches of the lives of the movie moguls, see Gabler's *An Empire of Their Own*.

29. Erens, *The Jew in American Cinema*, pp. 138–39; Gabler, *An Empire of Their Own*, pp. 168, 284; Norman L. Friedman, "Hollywood, the Jewish Experience, and Popular Culture," *Judaism* (Fall 1970): 483–84; Friedman, *The Jewish Image in American Film*, p. 35. Moser's remarks are from a lecture to the Third Reconstructionist Institute: Jews, Media and Culture, held November 7, 1993, at the University of Judaism in Los Angeles.

30. Among actors who began their careers before or around World War II, Paul Muni (who came out of Yiddish theater), Edward G. Robinson, Sylvia Sidney, Melvyn Douglas, Lee J. Cobb, Paulette Goddard, John Garfield, Kirk Douglas, and Judy Holliday, along with less well-remembered leading players like Ricardo Cortez (born Jacob Krantz) and Carmel Myers, Anglicized their names and played non-Jewish roles. Charles "Buddy" Rogers, the very WASPy hero of *Wings*, played Abie in *Abie's Irish Rose*, and John Barrymore played the Jewish attorney married to a socialite in one of the few films of the 1930s to portray explicitly Jewish characters, *Counsellor-at-Law* (1933). In Bible epics, Ramon Navarro and Charlton Heston played the title character in different versions of *Ben-Hur* (1925 and

1959); Heston portrayed Moses in *The Ten Commandments* (1956); Victor Mature was the "Danite" Samson in *Samson and Delilah* (1949). Natalie Wood and a wildly miscast Gene Kelly (he was much too old) played the title role and the glamorous Noel Airman in *Marjorie Morningstar* (1958). The angelically blond Jill Haworth played the refugee Karen in *Exodus* (1960), while George Peppard led a task force of Palestinian Jews in *Tobruk* (1966). More recently, directors have been criticized for casting non-Jewish actresses like Ellen Burstyn, Olympia Dukakis, and Shirley MacLaine as Jewish mothers.

31. Pogrebin, *Deborah, Golda, and Me*, pp. 256–58.

32. Erens, *The Jew in American Cinema*, pp. 255–56; Friedman, *The Jewish Image in American Cinema*, pp. 61–66.

In recent years, however, the pendulum has swung away from overtly Jewish characters and situations in Hollywood films. Barry Levinson's 1990 film *Avalon*, cast almost completely with non-Jewish actors, was criticized for its lack of cultural markers, while the Jewish content was leached out of the 1995 film adaptation of Max Apple's memoir, *Roommates*, and the upcoming film based on Rosellen Brown's novel *Before and After* (the central family's name was changed from Reiser to Ryan after Meryl Streep and Liam Neeson were cast as the parents). See Rebecca Ascher-Walsh, "Does Hollywood Have a Jewish Problem?" *Entertainment Weekly*, August 18, 1995, pp. 28–31.

33. Erens, *The Jew in American Cinema*, pp. 256–57.

34. Ibid., pp. 258–64; Pogrebin, *Deborah, Golda, and Me*, pp. 259–60. In the overbearing but well-meaning category are the mothers in *Enter Laughing* (1967) and *Next Stop, Greenwich Village* (1973), both played by Shelley Winters; less sympathetic Jewish mothers were portrayed in *No Way to Treat a Lady* (1968), *I Love You, Alice B. Toklas* (1968), and the film version of *Goodbye, Columbus* (1969); and over-the-top mothers are found in *Where's Poppa?* (1970) and *Portnoy's Complaint* (1972). The mothers in *No Way to Treat a Lady* and *Where's Poppa?* are widows; the dads in most of the other films listed are firmly under mama's thumb. In a few films, such as *Move* (1970) and the 1980 remake of *The Jazz Singer*, Jewish men are shown as alienated not from their mothers but from wives who represent the same emotional and mental bondage.

35. Jewish princesses play supporting roles in *Such Good Friends* (1971), *White Palace* (1990), *I Don't Buy Kisses Any More* (1992), and as a fractious mother and daughter in *Shampoo* (1975).

36. Pogrebin (*Deborah, Golda, and Me*, pp. 265–67) provides a detailed discussion of *Private Benjamin*; she likes the movie but is bothered by the implication that for Judy to stop being a JAP she has to join the American mainstream (by succeeding in the Army) and essentially renounce her Jewishness. A recent film, *Clueless* (1995), has as its protagonist the not very Jewish but every inch a princess Cher Horowitz, who doesn't change that much in the course of the film but does learn a few life lessons, especially that all the charm in the world won't get you a driver's license.

37. Erens clearly posits that this group of "awkward, ill-mannered, oversexed females" in such films as *Me, Natalie* (1969), *Made for Each Other* (1971), and *Sheila Levine Is Dead and Living in New York* (1975) is part of the misogynist trend in Jewish literature and film of the period

and bolsters the appeal of the non-Jewish woman. (Erens, *The Jew in American Cinema*, pp. 310–11.)

38. Ibid., p. 226.

39. Annie Korzen, "Casting with More *Chutzpah* Might Help," *Los Angeles Times*, September 6, 1993, p. F3.

40. Pogrebin, *Deborah, Golda, and Me*, pp. 264–65; Erens, *The Jew in American Cinema*, pp. 312–13; Friedman, *The Jewish Image in American Cinema*, pp. 200–201. Erens and Pogrebin emphasize how unattractive the film makes Jewish girls seem, while Friedman seems to think the emptiness of Lenny's victory is more important. Among the reviews I read, only one critic (Pauline Kael in the *New Yorker*) described Lila in any but unflattering terms; reviewers for the *Wall Street Journal, Time, Newsweek,* and the *Los Angeles Herald-Examiner*, no matter how much they disliked Lenny for his weasely selfishness, didn't see anything in Lila that should have held him. The actress who played Lila, Jeannie Berlin, told the *New York Times*: "I was a little bit afraid of the role. You see, I didn't want to make that girl stupid" ("More Than Elaine May's Daughter," *New York Times*, January 7, 1973, p. 16). However, reviewers repeatedly described Lila as dumb. Screenwriter Neil Simon insisted that he never meant his script to be about a guy who dumps a homely girl for a beautiful one; he says he had wanted Diane Keaton, just beginning her career, to play the role ("Playgirl Interview: Neil Simon," *Playgirl*, February 1976). Erens picked up a similar comment from a book by John Brady, *The Craft of the Screenwriter* (New York: Simon and Schuster: 1981), pp. 330–31.

41. Diana Katcher Bletter, "Hollywood's Heartbreaks," *Keeping Posted*, February 1974, pp. P20–P21.

42. Bridget Byrne, " 'Nobody Ever Told Me I Looked Jewish Before,' " *Los Angeles Herald-Examiner*, January 14, 1973, p. D1; Charles Grodin, *It Would Be So Nice If You Weren't Here* (New York: William Morrow, 1989), pp. 193–94.

43. Robert F. Moss, " 'Blume' and 'Heartbreak Kid'—What Kind of Jews Are They?" *New York Times*, September 9, 1973, sec. 2, p. 1. Moss comments on the injustice of presenting Lila as "a cruel compendium of every unpleasant trait that has ever been associated with Jewish girls" while making Lenny not only better-looking but less Jewish-looking than Lila, which to him indicates that Simon and May "are obviously unable to find much to praise in Jewish culture." The film also veers widely from Bruce Jay Friedman's original short story, "A Change of Plan," in *Black Angels* (New York: Simon and Schuster, 1966). In the story, Cantrow and his bride have clearly slept together before the wedding and have married because their relationship reached one of those dead ends where you either get married or break up; the bride has a silly sense of humor and a loud voice but is not described physically except as weighing 104 pounds; it's the blond girl who has "a nice fleshiness." When Cantrow announces that he's leaving his bride, there are no hysterics, and the blond girl's father has none of the hard edge he has in the movie; no anti-Semitism, no bribe. When he sees Cantrow is serious, he drops his opposition and welcomes Cantrow as family.

44. Midler played a sexy Jewish entertainer in *Beaches* (1988); Grey (with her old nose) attracted

Patrick Swayze in *Dirty Dancing* (1987); Kavner wound up with Jewish men in *Oedipus Wrecks* and *This Is My Life* (1992); Amy Irving was a charming bookseller in *Crossing Delancey*; and Sarah Jessica Parker played a nice Jewish girl contemplating marriage with a hunk of a boyfriend in *Miami Rhapsody* (1995).

45. Naomi Pfefferman, "26 under 40," *Jewish Journal*, June 30–July 6, 1995, pp. 11–12. The article profiles screenwriter Andrea King, the model for her own protagonist.

46. Erens, *The Jew in American Cinema*, pp. 58–59. Beginning in the 1960s, the Jew as Man of Action did begin to appear from time to time, especially in films set in Israel, as in *Exodus*, *Tobruk*, and *Cast a Giant Shadow* (1966), although the last film is the only one in which the central character was played by a Jewish actor (Kirk Douglas).

47. Erens, *The Jew in American Cinema*, p. 272. Track Allen's films over the years: in *What's New, Pussycat?* (1965), he's sexually inexperienced and doesn't get laid; in *Bananas* (1971) he gets the girl but is lousy in bed; in *Play It Again, Sam* (1972), he's good in bed but doesn't get the girl; in *Annie Hall* (1977), he gets the girl until she outgrows him; and in *Manhattan* (1979), he has two golden goddesses vying for him, one of them 17 years old. David Biale discusses Woody Allen as a sexually insecure but sexually active schlemiel in *Eros and the Jews: From Biblical Israel to Contemporary America* (New York: Basic Books, 1991), pp. 205–7.

48. Michael Medved, "Hollywood's Mixed Message," *Reform Judaism* (Spring 1991): 21.

49. Erens, *The Jew in American Cinema*, p. 366.

50. Judi Greenwald, letter to *Tikkun* (May/June 1990): 4; see also a letter from Ellen Epstein and Jane Lewit to *Moment* (June 1993: 8–9) in which they complain about stereotyping of Jewish women and especially "the lighthearted images of intermarriage broadcast by leaders in the entertainment world."

51. In 1949, *The Goldbergs* premiered and ran for five seasons, the first TV show written about a Jewish family—and the last for almost 20 years. Probably the best-known Jewish character who appeared each week on a series was Buddy Sorrell, played by comedian Morey Amsterdam, on *The Dick Van Dyke Show* (1961–66); he celebrated his bar mitzvah (30 years late) on the show. "Jewish" scripts have regularly turned up on dramas with medical and courtroom settings and, interestingly, on westerns (typically the series lead or leads would help a Jewish individual or family combat anti-Semitism; such an episode aired as recently as the 1994–95 season on *Dr. Quinn, Medicine Woman*).

52. The only really egregious Jewish princess portrayed in a series was played by Fran Drescher in the 1991 sitcom *Princesses*, and she was no more shallow or materialistic than the WASP princess or the British royal who shared an apartment with her—just more nasal. Jewish ugly ducklings were never given the nasty treatment they were in feature films: Rhoda Morgenstern's chubby sister Brenda on *Rhoda* (1974–78) was generally portrayed as a girl who would be perfectly appealing if she developed a little self-esteem. Another plain, plump Jewish girl, Natalie on the 1980s sitcom *The Facts of Life*, overcame her looks with a sunny personality—and lost her virginity with a long-term boyfriend on the show. Former child actor Barry Gordon played a shleppy accountant on *Archie Bunker's Place* in the late 1970s. *Rhoda* also gave America what might have been television's first Jewish prince, the sisters'

neighbor Gary Levy, an underachiever set up in business by his parents whose usual tactic when facing opposition was either to flatter or to whine until he got his way.

Chicken Soup, a short-lived sitcom starring the comedian Jackie Mason, dealt heavily in cultural stereotypes, including a meddlesome Jewish mother and, of course, Mason himself. Other than that, the only recurring Jewish mothers of the loud, overbearing school portrayed on television of late have been those played by Renee Taylor on Dream On, Daddy Dearest, and The Nanny. Michael and Melissa Steadman's mothers, each portrayed on multiple episodes of thirtysomething, and Joel Fleischman's on Northern Exposure were gentle, softspoken women; Miles Silverberg's on Murphy Brown was a vibrant political activist; Jack Stein's on Love & War was somewhat braying and overprotective, but also hip enough to have had a fling with Jack's girlfriend's dashing artist father.

53. Robert Milch, "Why Bridget Loves Bernie," Jewish Spectator (December 1972): 25–26; Jonathan and Judith Pearl, "All in the (Jewish) Family: Understanding, Utilizing, and Enhancing Images of Intermarriage and Other Jewish Family Relationships on Popular Television," Journal of Jewish Communal Service (Winter/Spring 1993): pp. 27, 29; "As Others See Us: Jews on TV," Moment (October 1990): 43; and "Jews on Prime Time," Reform Judaism (Summer 1993): 34. In Chicken Soup, the mother of a 52-year-old man who is dating a non-Jewish woman was described as "Orthodox" by several reporters and reviewers when the show premiered in 1989, but when she has a strong reaction to her son's interdating, he replies, "I don't understand you; you're not even that religious." The mother then tells him that she assumed his Jewish identity was passed down genetically—another Jewish parent who thinks instilling Jewish identity requires no active effort on the parent's part (Pearl, "All in the [Jewish] Family," pp. 28–29).

54. A number of examples of Jewish self-assertion have turned up during the past 10 years. On L.A. Law, attorney Stuart Markowitz, faced with the genteel anti-Semitism of his fiancée's mother and her friends, reacted by pulling over a china cabinet. Later, the completely nonobservant Stuart could explain only that he suddenly felt "the weight of five thousand years." Tess Kaufman, a district attorney on Reasonable Doubts, entered a synagogue for the first time in a long time after prosecuting a troubling case involving neo-Nazis. Beverly Hills 90210 character Andrea Zuckerman-Vasquez, who wasn't even identified as Jewish the first couple of seasons, "came out" as a Jew during rush week of her freshman year of college and later led a protest against an anti-Semitic speaker; she was also at odds with her Latino husband over the religious identity of their baby daughter. Jessica Cohen, a college student on the short-lived dramatic series Class of '96, checked out Hillel after becoming the victim of JAP-baiting on her campus. On Murphy Brown, Miles Silverberg, armtwisted into preparing the decorations for the office Christmas party, went all-out with a Chanukah theme (Michele Willens, "Being Jewish in Prime Time," Los Angeles Times, September 10, 1989, p. 78; Pearl, "As Others See Us," pp. 39, 41, 42). Northern Exposure did several scripts in which Joel Fleischman pondered his identity as a Jew, including one in which he acquired, then rejected, a Christmas tree and a couple in which the rabbi of his temple showed up in dream sequences. Michael Steadman of thirtysomething pondered his

relationship to Judaism at several life-cycle moments, including his daughter's first Christmas, his father's *yahrzeit*, and his son's birth. Miniseries and specials that have explored or touched on issues of Jewish identity and faith include *Holocaust* (1978), *The Winds of War* (1983), *Skokie* (1981), and *Miss Rose White* (1992).

For more detailed discussion of *thirtysomething* and *Northern Exposure*, see Jay Rosen, "'thirtysomething,'" *Tikkun* (July/August 1989): 32; Michael Lerner, "'thirtysomething' and Judaism," *Tikkun* (November/December 1990): 6–8; Jonathan Pearl and Judith Pearl, "Television Grapples with Jewish Identity," *Moment* (October 1993): 41–42; Willens, "Being Jewish in Prime Time," pp. 78–79.

55. Willens, "Being Jewish in Prime Time," pp. 6, 78–79; see also Alan D. Abbey, "Jewish Characters on TV: Why So Few?" *Jewish Journal*, September 29–October 5, 1989, p. 36. The ambivalence is still widespread among executives responsible for feature films as well; see Ascher-Walsh, "Does Hollywood Have a Jewish Problem?" p. 31.

56. Harry F. Waters, "A Jesting Jackie in the Box," *Newsweek*, September 18, 1989, p. 70.

57. Naomi Pfefferman, "The Invisible Jewish Woman," *Jewish Journal*, October 21–27, 1994, p. 8.

58. Judith Peiss, "Why Won't TV Show Jewish Couples?" *Los Angeles Times*, May 2, 1994, p. F3. Scriptwriter David Isaacs angered women in the audience at a 1991 panel discussion on "The Image of Jews in Television" when he told them the reason Jewish men on television series don't have Jewish wives is "merely coincidence" and added, "When you create characters on television you look for the most conflict. If both the husband and wife are Jews, what conflict could there be?" (Marlene Adler Marks, "Where's Rhoda Now?" *Jewish Journal*, November 29–December 5, 1991, p. 33).

59. The descriptions are of characters featured on *L.A. Law*; *Anything but Love*, a sitcom starring Richard Lewis and Jamie Lee Curtis that ran for a couple of years *circa* 1990; HBO's raunchy sitcom *Dream On*; and a short-lived Fox comedy, *Flying Blind*. These characters are four of perhaps a dozen male Jewish characters on episodic dramas and situation comedies of the past decade who are married to or romantically involved with conventionally attractive non-Jewish women. Others include central characters on *Love & War*, *Northern Exposure*, *Chicken Soup*, *thirtysomething*, *Sisters*, and *Chicago Hope*. In addition, the characters played by Paul Reiser and Jerry Seinfeld on *Mad about You* and *Seinfeld*, respectively, are considered by most Jewish viewers to be Jewish, although their ethnicity is not explicitly indicated. The Sheldon-turned-sex-god syndrome appears to be returning to the big screen as well: in *Miami Rhapsody*, the protagonist's cute, oversexed kid sister, recently married to a conventionally handsome professional football player, sleeps with an old friend, a balding (but sexually supercharged) Jewish dentist, and eventually leaves her new husband for him, while the protagonist's brother, a short, standard-issue Jewish guy, is having an affair with a woman played by supermodel Naomi Campbell.

60. Marks, "Where's Rhoda Now?" p. 33.

61. Thirteen television series set against either a medical or legal background ran during the five TV seasons between fall 1990 and spring 1994. Among the law-office programs, only one, *Reasonable Doubts*, featured a female Jewish attorney, and not one of the medical

shows had a female Jewish physician as a regular character. (Nor did *St. Elsewhere*, a long-running series of the 1980s with a hospital setting, nor do the current *ER* and *Chicago Hope*.)

A female Jewish doctor was featured on the daytime soap opera *Days of Our Lives* in a storyline that ran for a year and a half in 1986 and 1987. Dr. Robin Jacobs, a surgeon and the daughter and niece of Holocaust survivors, fell in love, very much against her own convictions, with a non-Jewish colleague, Mike Horton. The writer, an observant Jewish woman from an Orthodox Jewish background, would not allow an intermarriage on the show and had Mike studying for conversion to Judaism (and Robin wondering how sincere his conversion would be) when the actress playing Robin decided to leave the show, ending the storyline before a wary network had to decide whether it would allow Mike to become Jewish. True to screen history, the actress playing Robin wasn't Jewish, and the actor who played Mike was. See Naomi Pfefferman, "Star-Crossed Romance, 1987, N.B.C.," *Lilith* (Winter 1987/88): 16–17; Mark C. Guncheon, "Between Commercials, the Jews," *Moment* (December 1986): 43–47.

62. Marks, "Where's Rhoda Now?" p. 34. "We're all but invisible," one female comedy writer told a reporter (Lois K. Solomon, "Farewell Fleischman," *Jewish Journal*, March 3–9, 1995, p. 30).

63. Other regular young-to-youngish Jewish female characters on recent series are Roxanne Melman, a legal secretary on *L.A. Law*; Alex Buchanan, one of *The Five Mrs. Buchanans*, a former New York political activist living in a small Indiana town; Cherlyn Markowitz, a college student in the sitcom *704 Hauser Street*; and Jessica Cohen, a wealthy college student trying to avoid being typed as a Jewish princess in *Class of '96*. Of these, Alex was married to a non-Jewish man, Roxanne was involved with two non-Jewish men and ended the series married to a man of unstated ethnicity; Cherlyn was in a steady interracial relationship; and Jessica was dating a non-Jewish classmate. Lilith Sternin Crane, married to Frasier Crane on *Cheers*, was Jewish because the actress who played her, Bebe Neuwirth, is Jewish; her ethnicity came into play only when she and Frasier had a baby son and arranged a *brit milah*. *Beverly Hills 90210*'s Andrea Zuckerman dated a Jewish guy briefly but married a Mexican-American law student after he got her pregnant. An interesting guest shot early in *Northern Exposure* was that of Joel Fleischman's attractive and warm-hearted Jewish fiancée, Elaine Shulman, who visited Joel in Alaska. During the episode, Joel has a dream in which he's married to series regular Maggie O'Connell and Elaine is his sister.

64. Louise Farr, "Melanie Mayron's Got Muscle—Just Ask Peter Horton," *TV Guide*, July 15, 1989, pp. 12–14; Hal Rubenstein, "Talking to . . . Melanie Mayron," *Vogue*, June 1988, pp. 138, 140; Marks, "Where's Rhoda Now?" p. 33; Pfefferman, "The Invisible Jewish Woman," p. 8.

65. Andy Meisler, "Mary Poppins She's Not," *New York Times*, December 18, 1994, pp. 35, 47; Layne Drebin Murphy, "Broadcast Snooze," *Jewish Journal*, January 7–13, 1994, p. 32; Peiss, "Why Won't TV Show Jewish Couples?" p. F3; Pfefferman, "The Invisible Jewish Woman," p. 8. The quote from Fran Drescher at the head of this chapter is from Lisa Schwarzbaum,

"A New York State of Mind," *Entertainment Weekly*, November 5, 1993, p. 56. To show how quick some people are to label any loud, New Yorky Jewish woman a princess, I have seen print references to Drescher's character and heard several people refer to her as "JAPpy," when in fact she is from a working-class background and is the last thing any real Jewish princess would be—a servant.

66. Fran Drescher, "'The Nanny' Is Jewish and Proud of It," *Los Angeles Times*, May 9, 1994, p. F3; Meisler, "Mary Poppins She's Not," p. 47.

67. Marks, "Where's Rhoda Now?" p. 33. See similar remarks in Pfefferman, "The Invisible Jewish Woman," pp. 8–9, 24.

68. Pfefferman, "The Invisible Jewish Woman," p. 8.

69. Pearl, "All in the (Jewish) Family," pp. 24–25.

70. Sherill Kushner, "Portrayal of Jewish Women by the Media: Engaging or Enraging?" *Lilith* (Winter 1994): 5.

71. Diana Bletter and Lori Grinker, *The Invisible Thread: A Portrait of Jewish American Women* (Philadelphia: Jewish Publication Society, 1989), p. 58.

72. Amy Nemko, "Television Shows Anything but Jewish Love," *Ha'am* (student newspaper of the UCLA Jewish community), March 1992.

5: Thirteen and Out

1. Jack Wertheimer, *A People Divided: Judaism in Contemporary America* (New York: Basic Books, 1993), pp. 46–49; Sara Bershtel and Allen Graubard, *Saving Remnants: Feeling Jewish in America* (New York: Free Press, 1992), pp. 99–100. During the early 1980s, 44 percent of Americans in general reported that they attended church services at least once a month, whereas 24 percent of Jews said they went to temple at least monthly, a figure shown by later population surveys to be inflated. Non-Jews may be exaggerating too. A 1992 Gallup poll reported that 45 percent of American Protestants and 51 percent of Roman Catholics attend services weekly, but the December 1993 issue of *American Sociological Review* published a study based on actual head counts that determined that only 20 percent of Protestants and 28 percent of Catholics show up in church every Sunday (Kenneth L. Woodward, "The Rites of Americans," *Newsweek*, November 29, 1993, p. 80). In most communities during the 1980s, between one-third and one-half of Jews said they never attended services or went only on the High Holidays. The 1990 National Jewish Population Survey reports that 41 percent of households containing all Jewish members belong to synagogues, with lower figures for intermarried households, representing a continuing downward drift since the national survey of 1970–71. The Cohen Center's 1992 study, *Jewish Identity in Conversionary and Mixed Marriages* (by Peter Y. Medding, Gary A. Tobin, Sylvia Barack Fishman, and Mordechai Rimor; New York: American Jewish Committee/Jewish Publication Society, 1992), reports an affiliation rate closer to 60 percent among all-Jewish households in the cities it examined.

2. Charles Silberman, *A Certain People: American Jews and Their Lives Today* (New York: Summit, 1985), p. 171.
3. Ibid., pp. 172, 173, 176. Only one family in four was affiliated with a synagogue in the late 1930s.
4. Ibid., p. 176; also Wertheimer, *A People Divided*, p. 4.
5. Lawrence Bush, "The Journey of a Wondering Jew," *Moment* (June 1987): 27; Michael Lerner, *Jewish Renewal: A Path to Healing and Transformation* (New York: Grosset/Putnam, 1994), p. 162.
6. Michael Walzer, "Toward a New Realization of Jewishness," *Congress Monthly*, June/July/August 1994, pp. 3–4; Lerner, *Jewish Renewal*, p. 163; Stuart E. Rosenberg, *The New Jewish Identity in America* (New York: Hippocrene, 1985), p. 137.
7. Wertheimer, *A People Divided*, pp. 4–6; Bershtel and Graubard, *Saving Remnants*, p. 12; Silberman, *A Certain People*, p. 177; Egon Mayer, "The Coming Reformation in American Jewish Identity," in *Imagining the Jewish Future: Essays and Responses*, edited by David Teutsch (Albany: State University of New York Press, 1992), pp. 188–89; Rosenberg, *The New Jewish Identity in America*, pp. 138, 146.

The Reform movement almost doubled its number of member congregations between 1948 and 1966 (from 334 to 664). The Conservative movement went from 350 congregations in 1945 to 800 in 1965, adding some 131 new congregations during a two-year period in the mid-1950s. Existing congregations became much larger: In 1937, only 6 Reform synagogues had more than 1,000 member households; by 1963, 20 temples had more than 1,400 member units, and a few had passed the 2,500-member mark. Wertheimer cites several Reform congregations that ranged between 100 and 350 member households in 1937 and had all exceeded 1,300 families by 1965. Enrollment in Jewish schools rose from 190,000 in 1940 to 231,028 in 1946, doubling to 488,432 by 1956, and peaking at about 590,000 in the early 1960s. That is, in 20 years the enrollment of children in Jewish education tripled. Some 90 percent of these children were in synagogue-based supplementary schools. See also Alvin I. Schiff, "On Responding to the Challenge of the Alienated and Indifferent Jew in America," *Journal of Jewish Communal Service* (Spring 1984): 198.

8. Bershtel and Graubard, *Saving Remnants*, pp. 53–54; see also p. 77 for testimony from a man who displays an intense ethnocentrism but an utter contempt for religiosity.
9. Hoffman made these comments during a lecture at the 1993 biennial convention of the Union of American Hebrew Congregations, San Francisco, October 21, 1993. See also Lawrence A. Hoffman, "From Common Cold to Uncommon Healing," *CCAR Journal* (Spring 1994): 10; Deborah E. Lipstadt, *Moment* (October 1994): 24; Bershtel and Graubard, *Saving Remnants*, pp. 142–43; Silberman, *A Certain People*, pp. 178–79; Wertheimer, *A People Divided*, pp. 4, 6; Rosenberg, *The New Jewish Identity in America*, pp. 152–53; Barbara Wyden and Gwen Gibson Schwartz, *The Jewish Wife* (New York: P. H. Wyden, 1969), pp. 278–81, 284–86.

Some of the comments in this last source are very telling; the women in Schwartz and Wyden's sample generally had rock-solid cultural identities but saw religious activities as strictly for kids; 57 percent said they never went to services, as opposed to 16 percent in the book's non-Jewish sample.

10. Hoffman, "From Common Cold to Uncommon Healing," pp. 5–6; Diane Winston, "Searching for Spirituality: Reform Judaism Responds," *Moment* (June 1992): 32–33; Daniel Gordis, "Where Has All the Passion Gone? American Jews and Their Jewish Estrangement," *Jewish Spectator* (Summer 1993): 9–10.

11. Wade Clark Roof, *A Generation of Seekers: The Spiritual Journeys of the Baby Boom Generation* (New York: HarperCollins, 1993), pp. 37–39, 52, 56.

12. Ibid., p. 41.

13. Ibid., pp. 51–52; also Hoffman, "From Common Cold to Uncommon Healing," p. 11.

14. Hoffman, "From Common Cold to Uncommon Healing," p. 14.

15. Tamar Frankiel, "Another Look at Intermarriage," *Jewish Spectator* (Spring 1993): 44.

16. Rodger Kamenetz, *The Jew in the Lotus* (New York: HarperCollins, 1994), pp. 151, 150; see also Michael Wyschogrod, column in *Moment* (December 1992): 18; Joshua Haberman, "The New Exodus Out of Judaism," *Moment* (August 1992): 34–37, 51–52; and Lerner, *Jewish Renewal*, pp. 5, 12–13, 200–201, 207, 212.

17. Lerner, *Jewish Renewal*, pp. 175; Wyschogrod in *Moment*, p. 18; Daniel Schifrin, "'A Theological Black Hole,'" *Baltimore Jewish Times*, December 20, 1992, p. 30.

18. Kamenetz, *The Jew in the Lotus*, p. 48; Lerner, *Jewish Renewal*, pp. 8, 10–11, 16, 171.

19. Lerner, *Jewish Renewal*, pp. 2–3, 166–67; Anne Roiphe, *Generation without Memory* (New York: Summit, 1981), pp. 23–25.

20. Lerner, *Jewish Renewal*, pp. 6–7, 156, 166–67; Bershtel and Graubard, *Saving Remnants*, pp. 118–20; Chaim Seidler-Feller, "Our Own Worst Enemy," *Jewish Journal*, June 12–18, 1994, p. 31; Ephraim Buchwald, "The Holocaust Is Killing America's Jews," *Los Angeles Times*, April 28, 1992, p. B7.

21. Sylvia Barack Fishman, *A Breath of Life: Feminism in the American Jewish Community* (New York: Free Press, 1993), pp. 139–41; Susan Weidman Schneider, *Jewish and Female: Choices and Changes in Our Lives Today* (New York: Simon and Schuster, 1984), pp. 33–35, 306; Letty Cottin Pogrebin, "Will Our Children Remain Jewish in America?" *Congress Monthly*, May 1981, pp. 12–13; Trude Weiss-Rosmarin, "The Unfreedom of Jewish Women," *Jewish Spectator* (October 1970): 4–6; Bershtel and Graubard, *Saving Remnants*, pp. 268–69; Roiphe, *Generation without Memory*, pp. 22, 199–200; Lerner, *Jewish Renewal*, p. 9; Bletter and Grinker, *The Invisible Thread*, pp. 22–23.

22. Ozick is quoted in Pogrebin, "Will Our Children Remain Jewish in America?" pp. 12–13, and in Roiphe, *Generation without Memory*, p. 202; see also Fishman, *A Breath of Life*, p. 204.

23. Fishman, *A Breath of Life*, pp. 7, 153, 181ff; Aviva Cantor Zuckoff, "An Exclusive Interview with Dr. Phyllis Chesler," *Lilith* (Winter 1976/77): 24, 29; Schneider, *Jewish and Female*, pp. 46–47, 80–81, 159, 163–66; Jacob Rader Marcus, *The American Jewish Woman, 1654–1980* (New York: KTAV, 1981), p. 157; Ari L. Goldman, "Religion Notes," *New York Times*, December 1, 1990, p. A14. In 1973, the Committee of Jewish Law and Standards of the Rabbinical Assembly ruled that Conservative congregations could open their minyans to

women and call them to the Torah. By 1987, 61 percent of Conservative synagogues counted women in the minyan and called women regularly to the Torah; these figures had improved to 68 and 66 percent, respectively, in 1990.

24. Berman spoke at a conference sponsored by *Tikkun* magazine, November 5, 1994, at Ansche Chesed synagogue, New York. See also Letty Cottin Pogrebin, *Deborah, Golda, and Me* (New York: Crown, 1989), pp. 246–47.

25. Gary A. Tobin, "What We Know about . . . Demography," in *What We Know about Jewish Education*, edited by Stuart L. Kelman (Los Angeles: Torah Aura Productions, 1992), pp. 72, 79; Leora W. Isaacs, "What We Know about . . . Enrollment," in *What We Know about Jewish Education*, pp. 62–66; Janet Marder, "The Trouble with . . . Jewish Education," *Reform Judaism* (Summer 1993): 19. Approximately 70–80 percent of American Jews receive some sort of Jewish education during their lifetimes, with higher rates in some Eastern and Midwestern cities and lower in some parts of the Southwest, but only 35–40 percent of Jewish children ages 5–18 are enrolled at any given time. The peak years are the three or four before bar and bat mitzvah, when 57 percent of Jewish kids are enrolled; attendance drops off sharply thereafter.

26. Norman Mirsky, "Intermarriage: dilemmas," *Keeping Posted*, February 1974, p. P18; Silberman, *A Certain People*, p. 180.

27. Jack Wertheimer, "Family Values and the Jews," *Commentary* (January 1994): 33; David Schoem, "What We Know about . . . the Jewish Supplementary School," in *What We Know about Jewish Education*, pp. 163–65; Seidler-Feller, "Our Own Worst Enemy," p. 31; Benjamin Kahn, "Profile of the Young American Jew: His Views and Needs as a Jew," *Jewish Digest*, October 1967, p. 25. Kahn's article was condensed from a speech he gave as national director of the B'nai B'rith Hillel Foundation in 1963, in which he noted that in a study of Jewish freshmen in three different colleges, only 17 percent of 400 students polled were able to relate the Maccabees to Chanukah, and only 14 percent could name three Hebrew prophets.

28. Nessa Rapoport, "The Jewish Teacher Demystified," *Reform Judaism* (Spring 1995): 52–54; Isa Aron, "What We Know about . . . Jewish Teachers," in *What We Know about Jewish Education*, pp. 37–38; Linda Sharlin Warren, "Hebrew Literacy," letter to *United Synagogue Review* (Spring 1994): 4–5; Randy Medoff, "The Jewish Identity Crisis," *New York Times*, July 2, 1978, sec. XXII, p. 12. Aron cites studies from the 1980s that, taken in the aggregate, suggest that about a third of Jewish religious school teachers have not taken college-level courses in Jewish studies or education. Jewish teachers are experienced, though; both Rapoport and Aron reported small percentages of rookie teachers, with the majority in the Jewish classroom five years or more.

29. Jonathan Woocher, "Jewish Education: Crisis and Vision," in *Imagining the Jewish Future: Essays and Responses*, edited by David Teutsch (Albany: State University of New York Press, 1992), pp. 66–67; Marder, "The Trouble with . . . Jewish Education," pp. 20–21; Schoem, "What We Know about . . . the Jewish Supplementary School," pp. 163–64; Arnold Dashefsky, "What We Know about . . . the Effects of Jewish Education on Jewish Identification," in

What We Know about Jewish Education, pp. 104–8; Alvin I. Schiff, "Trends and Challenges in Jewish Family Education," *Journal of Jewish Communal Service* (Summer 1991): 264–65; Steven M. Rosman, "Reclaiming the Bar/Bat Mitzvah," *Compass* (Fall 1993): 14–15; Steven Cohen, *American Assimilation or Jewish Revival?* (Bloomington: Indiana University Press, 1988), pp. 84–85, 88–89. Dashefsky cites studies that show even minimal Jewish education is effective in terms of building Jewish identification if parents are observant at home, and the effects of full-time Jewish education are most obvious in students with religious parents. The amount of time spent in the classroom is also a factor. Dashefsky and Cohen cite work by Himmelfarb, who reported in 1975 that it took a minimum of 3,000 hours of religious instruction before Jewish education has a lasting impact, rendering the Jewish schooling received by more than 80 percent of American Jews who go to religious school "a waste of time." Another academic, Bock, found that Jewish education begins to have an effect on Jewish identification at about 1,000 hours (which is about what a child gets in five years of six-hour-a-week supplementary school), with influence increasing the more hours a child accumulates.

30. Wyden and Schwartz, *The Jewish Wife,* pp. 299–301.
31. Schiff, "On Responding to the Challenge of the Alienated and Indifferent Jew in America," p. 198. Supplementary school enrollment dropped from its peak in 1962 of 540,000 to 220,000 in 1983; it drifted upward to 260,000 in 1990, fed by late-reproducing baby boomers' children. During the same period, Jewish day school enrollment doubled, from 60,000 to 117,000, between 1962 and 1983, and rose to 158,000 by 1990. By that time day schools across the denominational spectrum and Orthodox yeshivas accounted for 40 percent of the total enrollment in Jewish schools in North America.
32. Sanford Seltzer, "Assessing the Jewish Attitudes of Reform College Students," *Journal of Reform Judaism* (Winter 1983): 67–70, plus responses to Seltzer's article by Samuel Z. Fishman, pp. 72–75, and Joseph H. Levine, pp. 75–77; Marder, "The Trouble with . . . Jewish Education," pp. 20–21.
33. Edward Hoffman, "Jewish Spirituality," *Sh'ma,* January 25, 1991, p. 45; see also Hoffman, "From Common Cold to Uncommon Healing," p. 3ff.
34. Hoffman, "From Common Cold to Uncommon Healing," p. 22; see also Martin Berkowitz, "Homeless Judaism," *Conservative Judaism* (Winter 1993): 64–66. Berkowitz lists three problems with the contemporary non-Orthodox synagogue service: distraction, the externals of reading, reciting, and listening to instructions that take one's attention away from one's inner self; intrusion, the constant input of the service leader, creating passivity on the part of the worshiper; and dysfunction, the clumsiness of the prayerbook translation, which renders the literal Hebrew into English but fails to address the emotional needs of the worshiper.
35. Steven M. Cohen and Calvin Goldscheider, "Jews, More or Less," *Moment* (September 1984): 45–46.
36. Susan Weidman Schneider, *Intermarriage: The Challenge of Living with Differences between Christians and Jews* (New York: Free Press, 1989), p. 27.

37. Barry Kosmin, "How Affordable Is Jewish Living? Two Views," *Reform Judaism* (Spring 1994): 48.

38. Rela Geffen Monson and Ruth Pinkenson Feldman, "The Cost of Living Jewishly in Philadelphia," *Journal of Jewish Communal Service* (Winter 1991–92): 148.

39. Ibid., pp. 148–57; L. E. Scott, "The High Cost of Jewish Life," *Jewish Journal*, May 8–14, 1992, pp. 14, 19; Gerald B. Bubis, "Jewish Dollars Drying Up: Statistics Shatter the Illusion of Jewish Generosity," *Moment* (December 1992): 30; Rela Geffen, "How Affordable Is Jewish Living? Two Views," *Reform Judaism* (Spring 1994): 47, 50; Barry A. Kosmin, Sidney Goldstein, Joseph Waksberg, Nava Lerer, Ariella Keysar, and Jeffrey Scheckner, *Highlights of the CJF 1990 National Jewish Population Survey* (New York: Council of Jewish Federations, 1991), p. 19. The *Jewish Journal* article describes an American Jewish Committee study completed in 1990 that estimated that the cost of living a "fully involved Jewish life" for a family of five, including temple dues, day school, summer camp, JCC membership, and a donation to Federation, was between $18,000 and $25,000, necessitating a household income of $80,000 to $125,000 per year at a time when the median annual income for American Jewish families was $39,000 and fewer than 25 percent of American Jewish households took in more than $60,000 a year.

40. Kosmin, "How Affordable Is Jewish Living?" pp. 48, 50; Jeffrey K. Salkin, "The Jews We Don't See: What to Do about the Unaffiliated," *Reform Judaism* (Winter 1991): 5; "Dues and Don'ts," *Reform Judaism* (Spring 1994): 54–55, 89.

41. Gary A. Tobin, "Will the Synagogue Survive?" *Moment* (August 1990): 44–45; Gary A. Tobin, "The Synagogue's Evolving Mission," booklet created for the 62nd General Assembly of the UAHC, October 1993; Schiff, "On Responding to the Challenge of the Alienated and Indifferent Jew in America," p. 197; Roof, *A Generation of Seekers*, p. 42. In the *Moment* article, Tobin says the one-third figure on membership is probably inflated because many people say they're affiliated when they're not.

42. Roof, *A Generation of Seekers*, pp. 194–95, 200; Wertheimer, *A People Divided*, pp. 44, 191–92; Barry A. Kosmin and Seymour Lachman, *One Nation under God* (New York: Simon and Schuster, 1993), p. 233; Medding et al., *Jewish Identity in Conversionary and Mixed Marriages*, pp. 14–17. In *Jewish Identity*, the Cohen Center researchers discuss Jewish religious privatism at length, positing that group belongingness, once a matter out of one's control, is now a matter of personal choice, and introducing the idea that one can feel unambiguously Jewish but consider Jewishness to be just one segment of personal identity. Jews with segmented and unambiguous Jewish identities can enter into mixed marriages believing that, because Jewish identity is a personal issue, they can demonstrate strong expressions of Jewishness without impinging on a partner's identity.

43. Roof, *A Generation of Seekers*, pp. 70–71, 198–99.

44. Schneider, *Intermarriage*, pp. 50, 60–61, 63–65, 82; Silberman, *A Certain People*, pp. 72, 76–77; Rachel Cowan and Esther Perel, "A More Perfect Union: Intermarriage and the Jewish World," *Tikkun* (May/June 1992): 63; Sanford Seltzer, *Jews and Non-Jews: Falling in Love* (New York: Union of American Hebrew Congregations, 1976), pp. 24–25.

45. Wertheimer, *A People Divided*, pp. 63–65. Wertheimer cites a 1989 study by Steven Cohen in which almost 1 in 5 Jews expressed skepticism about the existence of God; more than 9 out of 10 people in the general American population affirmed a belief in God at that time. Cohen also found that about 30 percent of Jews did not view religion as very important in their lives, as opposed to 14 percent of the larger population. Kosmin and Lachman, in *One Nation under God*, cite a December 1991 Gallup poll in which only 34 percent of New York Jews polled said religion was very important to their lives, the lowest score among white Protestants (47 percent), white Catholics and Hispanics (57 percent), and blacks (74 percent) in the same city. Wertheimer estimates that religious ritual and worship play a minimal role in the lives of as many as half the Jews in America. See also Berman, *Jews and Intermarriage*, pp. 301–3.

46. Roof, *A Generation of Seekers*, pp. 70–72, 198–99, 201–2.

47. Arnold Eisen, "Theology and Community," in *Imagining the Jewish Future*, pp. 253–54; see also Kenneth L. Woodward, "The Intermarrying Kind," *Newsweek*, July 22, 1991, pp. 48–49.

48. Bershtel and Graubard, *Saving Remnants*, p. 15.

49. Roof, *A Generation of Seekers*, pp. 155–59; Kosmin and Lachman, *One Nation under God*, p. 231.

6: Don't Tell Us Who We Are

1. Nessa Rapoport, "Summoned to the Feast," *Writing Our Way Home: Contemporary Stories by American Jewish Writers*, edited by Ted Solotaroff and Nessa Rapoport (New York: Schocken, 1992), pp. xxvii–xxviii; Leonard Fein, *Where Are We? The Inner Life of America's Jews* (Harper and Row, 1988), pp. 139–40.

2. Barry Kosmin, Sidney Goldstein, Joseph Waksberg, Nava Lerer, Ariella Keysar, Jeffrey Scheckner, *Highlights of the CJF 1990 National Jewish Population Survey* (New York: Council of Jewish Federations, 1991), p. 2.

3. Sidney Goldstein, "Beyond the 1990 National Jewish Population Survey: A Research Agenda," *Contemporary Jewry* (1993): 150; Fred Massarik, "Knowledge about U.S. Jewish Populations: Retrospect and Prospect 1970–2001," *Journal of Jewish Communal Service* (Summer 1992): 302–4; Silberman, *A Certain People: American Jews and Their Lives Today* (New York: Summit, 1985), p. 295.

4. Silberman, *A Certain People*, p. 290. Silberman also notes that, among other problems, the 1971 NJPS researchers had to halve the number of remaining field interviews midway through the process because of budget overruns, creating a larger-than-normal margin of error.

5. Henrietta Wexler, "Intermarriage: What Future for Jews?" *Humanistic Judaism* (Winter 1990): 7–8.

6. Egon Mayer, "Will the Grandchildren of Intermarrieds Be Jews? The Chances Are Greater Than You Think," *Moment* (April 1994): 50–53. Full marks to Mayer for exposing this inflammatory misuse of data. In *Moment*'s August 1994 letters column, DellaPergola acknowledged that the sample was small but the "zero" statistic was telling, and besides,

the 1990 survey later showed that very few grandchildren of intermarrieds were being raised as Jews. Mayer replied that none of DellaPergola's arguments excused his making sweeping generalizations about a large class of people based on a handful of examples.

7. Steven M. Cohen and Gabriel Berger, "Understanding and Misunderstanding the 1990 National Jewish Population Survey," unpublished, October 1991, pp. 2, 4, 5; Steven M. Cohen, "Why Intermarriage May Not Threaten Jewish Continuity," *Moment* (December 1994): 89.

8. Cohen, "Why Intermarriage May Not Threaten Jewish Continuity," pp. 89, 95. Cohen gave a similar analysis during a personal interview on May 22, 1992. Jewish publications and Jewish leaders are beginning to cite the recent intermarriage rate as "between 40 and 52 percent."

9. Ibid., p. 57; Cohen and Berger, "Understanding and Misunderstanding the 1990 National Jewish Population Survey," pp. 15, 18–20, 24. The NJPS researchers had it out with Cohen in the April 1995 issue of *Moment*, standing by their methodology and results, claiming that there were as many "switchers" out of Judaism, although perhaps not through formal conversion, as there were Jews by choice, and defending other aspects of their operation. They also claimed that Cohen was the only scholar during the past four years who had serious problems with the NJPS data and noted that Cohen had been on the committee that planned and implemented the survey and kept telling the members that they had to put a positive spin on their analyses of the data to back up his previously published work (Sidney Goldstein et al., "Twelve Angry Men and Women," *Moment* [April 1995]: 66–67). In the same issue, Cohen defended his divergent analyses, gave specific examples of respondents misidentified by the researchers, listed other sociologists who back him up, and scolded the NJPS team for its ad hominem attack (Steven M. Cohen, "Cohen Defends His Views," *Moment* [April 1995]: 68–69).

10. Bernard Reisman, "The Leadership Implications of the National Jewish Population Survey," *Journal of Jewish Communal Service* (Summer 1992): 352; Bernard Reisman, "Reflections on the 1990 National Jewish Population Survey," *Contemporary Jewry* (1993): 166–67; Sylvia Barack Fishman, "Triple Play: Deconstructing Jewish Lives," *Contemporary Jewry* (1993): 30–32. Speaking at UCLA in 1994, Bruce Phillips, who worked on the NJPS, commented that it left out questions about intensive youth experiences such as summer camp and temple youth group.

11. Goldstein, "Beyond the 1990 National Jewish Population Survey," pp. 154–55; Massarik, "Knowledge about U.S. Jewish Populations," pp. 302–4; Reisman, "Reflections on the 1990 National Jewish Population Survey," p. 171.

12. Mayer, "Will the Grandchildren of Intermarrieds Be Jews?" p. 78.

13. Steven Cohen, "The Self-Defeating Surplus," *Moment* (June 1987): 31. See also Reisman, "The Leadership Implications of the National Jewish Population Survey," p. 354, in which Reisman scolds Jewish leaders for using 1990 NJPS data toward survivalist ends.

14. Suzanne F. Singer, "A 'Critical Mass' of Judaism May Prevent Intermarriage," *Moment* (October 1991): 4; Dennis Prager, "Prager's Thirteen Principles of Intermarriage," *Moment*

(February 1993): 18; Ruth Wisse, "My Jewish Son-in-Law," *Jewish Journal*, February 21–27, 1992, p. 31; Bradley Shavit Artson, "Facing Intermarriage," *Women's League Outlook* (Winter 1993): 8.

15. Naomi Ruth Goldenberg, "Current Debate/Intermarriage: A Response to Anne Roiphe on the Jewish Family: The Problem of Intermarriage," *Tikkun* (January/February 1987): 118–19; similar sentiments are expressed by Amy Sheldon, "A Feminist Perspective on Intermarriage," in *Jewish Women in Therapy: Seen But Not Heard*, edited by Rachel Josefowitz Siegel and Ellen Cole (New York: Harrington Park Press, 1991), pp. 82–85. See also Eric Cytryn, "Making All Jews Good Jews," *Sh'ma*, March 8, 1991; Edwin H. Friedman, "The Myth of the Shiksa," in *Ethnicity and Family Therapy*, edited by Monica McGoldrick, John K. Pearce, and Joseph Giordano (New York: Guilford Press, 1982), p. 500; Mayer, "Will the Grandchildren of Intermarrieds Be Jews?" p. 53; and Leslie Goodman-Malamuth and Robin Margolis, *Between Two Worlds: Choices for Grown Children of Jewish-Christian Parents* (New York: Pocket, 1992); in the last source, the authors attack the myth that only "bad Jews" intermarry, pointing out that 51 percent of the Jewish parents of the children of inter-marriage they interviewed grew up in Conservative or Orthodox homes (pp. 161–62).

16. Peter Y. Medding, Gary A. Tobin, Sylvia Barack Fishman, and Mordechai Rimor, *Jewish Identity in Conversionary and Mixed Marriages* (New York: American Jewish Committee/Jewish Publication Society, 1992), pp. 37–38; Susan Weidman Schneider, *Intermarriage: The Challenge of Living with Differences between Christians and Jews* (New York: Free Press, 1989), pp. 148–50; Wertheimer, *A People Divided: Judaism in Contemporary America* (New York: Basic Books, 1993), pp. 61–62, 176–77; Mark L. Winer and Aryeh Meir, *Questions Jewish Parents Ask about Intermarriage* (New York: American Jewish Committee, 1992), p. 24, and many other sources. One rabbi told me solemnly that a child of intermarriage who is the same sex as the Gentile partner will *inevitably* explore the Gentile parent's birth religion as an act of same-sex solidarity.

17. Phyllis Klasky Karas, "Mating Call," *Jewish Journal*, July 8–14, 1994, p. 25.

18. Michael D'Antonio, "Jewish Husbands, Christian Wives (and Vice Versa)," *Present Tense* (Autumn 1985): 8.

19. See Lena Romanoff with Lisa Hostein, *Your People, My People: Finding Acceptance and Fulfillment as a Jew by Choice* (Philadelphia: Jewish Publication Society, 1990), p. 64; David W. Major, "Keeping the Faith?" *Princeton Living*, June 1994, p. 19; Schneider, *Intermarriage*, pp. 50–52, 55–56, 90; Paul Cowan with Rachel Cowan, *Mixed Blessings: Marriage between Jews and Christians* (New York: Doubleday, 1987), pp. 47, 50–51, 128–31; Rachel Cowan and Esther Perel, "A More Perfect Union: Intermarriage and the Jewish World," *Tikkun* (May/June 1992): 59.

20. Steven Cohen, "What We Know about . . . the Marginally Affiliated," in *What We Know about Jewish Education*, edited by Stuart L. Kelman (Los Angeles: Torah Aura Productions, 1992), p. 123.

21. Kosmin et al., *Highlights*, p. 16. In *Love and Tradition* (New York: Plenum Press, 1985), Egon Mayer proposed four categories: Assimilationist, in which the Jewish partner converts to

the non-Jewish partner's faith; Rejectionist, in which both partners do without religious identity; Conversionist, where the non-Jewish partner converts to Judaism; and Integrationist, the dual-identity household. He calculated each type of household to account for 10, 17, 33, and 40 percent, respectively, of the intermarrying population (p. 282). See also Brenda Forster and Joseph Tabachnik, *Jews by Choice: A Study of Converts to Reform and Conservative Judaism* (Hoboken, N. J.: KTAV, 1991), pp. 8–9.

22. Bruce Phillips, a member of the National Technical Advisory Committee on Jewish Population Studies, which designed and implemented the 1990 NJPS, concurred with this analysis of the "41 percent" in a personal interview, October 6, 1994.

23. Michael D'Antonio, "Growing up without Religion," *Newsday*, September 20, 1985, pp. 2–3, Part II; Judy Petsonk, "Raising a Jewish Child in an Intermarried Family," *Jewish Currents*, January 1990, pp. 4–9, 36. Petsonk, who gives the issue a Jewish secularist spin, gives advice on how to develop a strong cultural Jewish identity. Secular solutions involving both parents' traditions are contained in the responses following Petsonk's article. A case study of a couple who chose Unitarianism can be found in Cowan, *Mixed Blessings* (pp. 232–36). See also Judy Petsonk and Jim Remsen, *The Intermarriage Handbook: A Guide for Jews and Christians* (New York: William Morrow, 1988), pp. 206, 225–26, 272–75, for discussion of Unitarianism and Ethical Culture as possible belief systems for interfaith families.

24. Kosmin et al., *Highlights*, pp. 16, 34. If you add up all the Jewish-only denominational preferences of mixed households in Table 26, you get 34.4 percent, mostly Reform and Conservative.

25. D'Antonio, "Growing up without Religion," p. 2. A Gallup poll reported that 6 percent of Americans were "nonreligious" in 1974, a figure that rose to 9 percent in 1984. Susan Weidman Schneider, in her book *Intermarriage*, presents the option as well, but warns that the secular route was easier to take a generation ago, when a couple could more readily find a political or countercultural substitute for religion.

26. Schneider, *Intermarriage*, pp. 162; Cowan, *Mixed Blessings*, pp. 201–15, 220–31; Petsonk and Remsen, *The Intermarriage Handbook*, pp. 206–7, 222; Andrew H. Malcolm, "Counseling Interfaith Couples to Bridge Gaps," *New York Times*, October 1, 1991, p. B2; Woodward, "The Intermarrying Kind," p. 48. Schneider takes the stance that one partner's heritage will always dominate; the Cowans present a case study of a family that even-handedly put the effort into a Jewish-Catholic household. The *Times* article is still being waved around by rabbis livid over the two couples profiled who say they're going to raise their sons Jewish and the daughters Christian. (Neither couple had children as yet.) Woodward's article, on the other hand, published in *Newsweek* the month after the NJPS findings were released, opens with a description of Shabbat dinner at the home of a Bay Area family in which the daughter is Catholic like Mom, the son is an observant Jew like Dad, and from all appearances it's working out fine. Other books on how to conduct a true dual-identity marriage include Roy A. Rosenberg, Peter Meehan, and John Wade Payne, *Happily Intermarried: Authoritative Advice for a Joyous Jewish-Christian Marriage* (New York: Macmillan, 1988); and Lee F.

Gruzen, *Raising Your Jewish/Christian Child: How Interfaith Parents Can Give Children the Best of Both Their Heritages* (New York: Newmarket Press, 1990).

27. In *Love and Tradition*, Egon Mayer reports that 10 percent of the Jews who intermarry become Christians, but that may be a cumulative rate through about 1980, including the conversions of a more assimilationist day; in his 1979 publication *Intermarriage and the Jewish Future: A National Study in Summary* (New York: American Jewish Committee; written with Carl Sheingold), Mayer notes that the number of intermarried couples in which the born-Jewish partner had converted to another faith was too small to analyze (p. 5). Forster and Tabachnik, in *Jews by Choice*, report that among the partners of converts and prospective converts in their survey, "most partners were not drawn to the gentile partners' religion: 59 percent disliked Christian services, one-third weren't much interested in learning about Christianity, and only a handful (6 percent) had ever considered converting themselves" (p. 117). During the first six years of Paul and Rachel Cowan's interfaith workshops, they saw couples make a wide variety of religious choices, and they saw couples break up over religion, but they didn't meet one Jew who decided to become a Christian (Cowan, *Mixed Blessings*, pp. 196–97).

   See also Ruth Mason, "When Jews Convert," *Reform Judaism* (Fall 1991): 4–6, 10; and Debra Nussbaum Cohen, "Jews in the Pews," *Jewish Journal*, December 31, 1993–January 6, 1994, p. 21. Although people raised as Jews who make a formal conversion to Christianity tend to come from nonobservant homes, are not always given Jewish educations (only 35 percent say they had some form of formal Jewish schooling), and comment that they found the spiritual sustenance in Christianity that they failed to find in Judaism, 90 percent of the converts who are married are married to non-Jews. Also, the majority of converts out of Judaism had a non-Jewish parent and therefore grew up with the ambivalence that marked the Jewish partners in most intermarriages of earlier generations.

28. Cowan, *Mixed Blessings*, p. 163; Silberman, *A Certain People*, p. 303; Petsonk and Remsen, *The Intermarriage Handbook*, pp. 162–64, 203–4; Cowan and Perel, "A More Perfect Union," p. 60; and many other sources.

29. Barry Shrage, "A Communal Response to the Challenges of the 1990 CJF National Jewish Population Survey: Toward a Jewish Life Worth Living," *Journal of Jewish Communal Service* (Summer 1992): 325.

30. Allen S. Maller, "Religious Identity of Children in Mixed Marriages," *Jewish Spectator* (Spring 1991): 12; Petsonk, "Raising a Jewish Child in an Intermarried Family," p. 6; Josie E. Martin, "Half Jewish," *Jewish Journal*, December 3–9, 1993, p. 9; John Dart, "Jews Gain Range of Options for Spiritual Expression," *Los Angeles Times*, August 5, 1989, Part II, p. 6; and many other columns and letters to the editor. Andrea King's *If I'm Jewish and You're Christian, What Are the Kids?* (New York: UAHC Press, 1993) contains a long, devastating portrait of a family in which the parents insist they have given their children the best of both cultures but never did much more than celebrate a few holidays. "What do we kids have? Nothing," their 16-year-old snaps. Steven Carr Reuben's how-to book, *But How Will You Raise Your Children? A Guide to Interfaith Marriage* (New York: Pocket, 1987), contains a discussion

of the pitfalls of dual-minimal child rearing (pp. 200–210). Lena Romanoff, author of *Your People, My People,* has produced a video, *Who Am I?* that underscores the advisability of adopting a unified approach to religion in child rearing.

31. Harold M. Schulweis, "The Hyphen between the Cross and the Star: Why Judaism and Christianity Don't Mix," in *In God's Mirror* (Hoboken, N.J.: KTAV, 1990), pp. 168–77; Alan Silverstein, *Dual Faith Parenting: Second Thoughts on a Popular Trend* (New York: Federation of Jewish Men's Clubs, 1993); Cowan, *Mixed Blessings,* pp. 32–34; Petsonk and Remsen, *The Intermarriage Handbook,* p. 200; Michael Wasserman, "Outreach to Interfaith Couples: Two Conceptual Models," *Conservative Judaism* (Fall 1988): 20–21; Major, "Keeping the Faith?" pp. 19, 37; Arlene S. Chernow, "Four Children," *Compass* (Spring/Summer 1991).

32. Charlotte Anker, "We Are the Children You Warned Our Parents About," *Moment* (February 1991): 37–38; Susan Greenberg, "Don't Raise Children 'Both Ways,'" *Reform Judaism* (Summer 1992): 56. The "time bomb" phrase in this context was coined by Paul Cowan and Rachel Cowan in *Mixed Blessings.*

33. Helen Sloss Luey, "Please Don't Blame Our Marriage," *Reform Judaism* (Spring 1986): 32–33.

34. This is not to say that the Jewish community is oblivious to or unconcerned with these issues as they involve endogamous Jewish families. Jewish leaders are well aware that even Jews with solidly religious upbringings can be vulnerable to appeals from alternative belief systems, and articles about the persuasive tactics of evangelical Christian denominations, so-called Messianic Jewish groups such as Jews for Jesus, and more bizarre personality-based cults abound in the Jewish press. In response to this problem, the UAHC has a Committee on Cults and Missionaries. The Reform movement is also aware that endogamous Jewish partners can have conflicting attitudes about religion; the summer 1995 issue of *Reform Judaism* magazine touched on the need for endogamous couples to accommodate each other's religious styles and negotiate the Jewish upbringing of their children in its "Focus on Marriage" section; see Susan Kleinman, "The Triviality Trap," *Reform Judaism* (Summer 1995): 44–46; and Richard Litvak and Beth M. Gilbert, "How Your Marriage Can Beat the Odds," *Reform Judaism* (Summer 1995): 47–48, 54–55.

35. "Christmas," *Microsoft Encarta: The Complete Multimedia Encyclopedia* (Redmond, Wash.: Microsoft, 1993). *Encarta* incorporates *Funk and Wagnall's New Encyclopedia.*

36. Cowan, *Mixed Blessings,* pp. 176–82; Schneider, *Intermarriage,* pp. 80, 85.

37. Medding et al., *Jewish Identity in Conversionary and Mixed Marriages,* pp. 31–34.

38. Cowan, *Mixed Blessings,* pp. 144–45, 182–85. The Cowans describe workshop discussions of the visceral reactions many Jews have to the cross and the crucifix.

39. Barbara Wyden and Gwen Gibson Schwartz, *The Jewish Wife* (New York: P. H. Wyden, 1969), pp. 286–88.

40. Sara Bershtel and Allen Graubard, *Saving Remnants: Feeling Jewish in America* (New York: Free Press, 1992), pp. 25–26. See also Anne Roiphe, "Christmas Comes to a Jewish Home," *New York Times,* December 21, 1978, p. CI, reprinted in *Moment* (January/February 1979): 18–19.

41. Jack Wertheimer, in *A People Divided*, cites Sidney Goldstein's "Profile of American Jewry" in the 1992 *American Jewish Year Book*, which shows 10 percent of inmarried Jews saying they put up Christmas trees (p. 51); Forster and Tabachnik in *Jews by Choice* found that 13 percent of a group of mostly affiliated endogamous Jews that they used as a comparison to the Jews married to Jews-by-choice in their study observed Christmas (p. 131); the 1990 National Jewish Population Survey listed 82 percent of "entirely Jewish" households reporting that they never have a tree, indicating that 18 percent do (*Highlights*, p. 36); in a personal interview on August 3, 1994, Barry Kosmin estimated that 14 percent of endogamous households put up trees.

42. "Raising Kids Jewish in a Mixed Marriage" (first-person accounts), *Lilith* (Fall/Winter 1983): 29. See also Josie Levy Martin, "Why Some Jews Celebrate Christmas," *Jewish Journal*, January 1–7, 1993, p. 9.

43. Judith Colp Rubin, "Social Investigator," *Jerusalem Post Magazine*, March 18, 1994, p. 6; Cohen, "Why Intermarriage May Not Threaten Jewish Continuity," p. 54; Kosmin, "The Permeable Boundaries of Being Jewish in America," *Moment* (August 1992): 33; Anthony Day, "Troubling Times for U.S. Jews," *Los Angeles Times*, January 23, 1992. In a presentation at UCLA on May 5, 1994, demographer Sergio DellaPergola described a trend toward a slightly smaller American Jewry in absolute numbers but one that, as a smaller proportion of the American population, might have less political and social influence.

44. Mayer, "Will the Grandchildren of Intermarrieds Be Jews?" p. 78; Bershtel and Graubard, *Saving Remnants*, pp. 59–60; Reisman, "The Leadership Implications of the National Jewish Population Survey," p. 355.

45. See also Rubin, "Social Investigator," p. 7. The reporter quotes scholar Charles Liebman, who sees a mass assimilation by American Jews in which they don't stop identifying as Jews but evolve "an identity and a sense of self that blurs their distinctiveness from other Americans while emphasizing their distinctiveness from traditional Judaism or from non-American Jews."

46. Allen S. Maller, "Intermarriage and Jewish Continuity," *Congress Monthly*, October 1976, p. 14; Allen S. Maller, "The Sexism of Intermarriage," *Sh'ma*, February 6, 1976, p. 54; Louis A. Berman, *Jews and Intermarriage: A Study in Personality and Culture* (South Brunswick, N. J.: Thomas Yoseloff, 1968), p. 154.

47. Silberman, *A Certain People*, p. 303; Allen S. Maller, "Recent Data on Religious Identity of College Freshmen: A Note," *Jewish Social Studies* (Summer/Fall 1987): 320; Allen S. Maller, "Religious Identity of Children in Jewish-Christian Marriages," *Journal of Reform Judaism* (Winter 1989): 26.

48. Marlene Adler Marks, "Freeze!" *Jewish Journal*, September 3–9, 1993, p. 8. See also Allen S. Maller, "Sexism, Drop-outs and Jewish Federations," *Jewish Frontier*, September 1973, p. 29; and Fishman, "Triple Play," p. 29, for other data correlating continued Jewish education for girls with lower intermarriage rates. The Jewish education factor can be applied to those women who convert out of Judaism as well. The 1990 NJPS shows 90 percent of converts out as having had one non-Jewish parent, more often the father than the mother,

which, Egon Mayer says in a *Reform Judaism* article, challenges the idea that Jewish women raise Jewish children (Mason, "When Jews Convert," p. 5). In fact, the article continues, two-thirds of the Jews who convert to another faith are women, which calls into question the idea that women are more loyal to Judaism than men. No one bothered to relate that figure to the almost two-thirds of Jewish apostates who didn't receive any formal Jewish education (p. 4). In addition, Steven Cohen found that among Jews with *no* religious education, women consistently scored higher on an index of Jewish identification measures (ritual observance, having Jewish friends, maintaining communal ties) than men did (Steven Cohen, *American Assimilation or Jewish Revival?* [Bloomington: Indiana University Press, 1989], p. 89).

49. Schneider, *Intermarriage*, pp. 146, 201.
50. Barry Kosmin, personal interview, August 3, 1994.
51. Friedman, "The Myth of the Shiksa," pp. 499, 503.
52. Diana Bletter and Lori Grinker, *The Invisible Thread: A Portrait of Jewish American Women* (Philadelphia: Jewish Publication Society, 1989), p. 162.

7: Who's Marrying In?

1. Martha Sawyer Allen, "Raised Baptist, He Wants Sons to Be Good Jewish Boys," *Minneapolis Star-Tribune*, September 5, 1994, p. B5.
2. Louis A. Berman, *Jews and Intermarriage: A Study in Personality and Culture* (South Brunswick, N.J.: Thomas Yoseloff, 1968), pp. 139–40.
3. Susan Weidman Schneider, *Intermarriage: The Challenge of Living with Differences between Christians and Jews* (New York: Free Press, 1989), p. 40; Paul Cowan with Rachel Cowan, *Mixed Blessings: Marriage between Jews and Christians* (New York: Doubleday, 1987), pp. 149, 159. The Cowans present two case studies involving Jewish men who had been avoiding Jewish women at the time they met their partners. One said, "I had so many stereotypes of controlling, obnoxious Jews that I couldn't imagine myself marrying one," and, as a graduate student, married the "undemanding" daughter of a professor. The other, who met his wife at a frat party, said of her, "I felt that she was out to please. To me, Jewish women were out to *be pleased.*"
4. Berman, *Jews and Intermarriage*, pp. 167–70.
5. Susan Weidman Schneider, *Jewish and Female: Choices and Changes in Our Lives Today* (New York: Simon and Schuster, 1984), p. 298.
6. Cowan, *Mixed Blessings*, pp. 144.
7. See Berman, *Jews and Intermarriage*, p. 76.
8. Similar comments appear in Cowan, *Mixed Blessings* (pp. 16, 172) and Berman, *Jews and Intermarriage* (p. 175).
9. Brenda Forster and Joseph Tabachnik, *Jews by Choice: A Study of Converts to Reform and Conservative Judaism* (Hoboken, N.J.: KTAV, 1991), p. 65; Barry A. Kosmin, "The Permeable Boundaries of Being Jewish in America," *Moment* (August 1992): 31; Berman, *Jews and Intermarriage*, p. 173; Egon Mayer, *Love and Tradition* (New York: Plenum Press, 1985), pp. 100–103.
10. Forster and Tabachnik, *Jews by Choice*, p. 69.
11. Mayer, *Love and Tradition*, p. 91; see also Forster and Tabachnik, *Jews by Choice*, p. 70.

12. Louis Berman, "Decorum, Prudery and Intermarriage," *Reconstructionist*, May 31, 1968, pp. 12–13; also, Berman, *Jews and Intermarriage*, p. 141; Schneider, *Intermarriage*, p. 19; Paul Cowan and Rachel Cowan, "Jews by Choice—and Acceptance," *Moment* (May 1983): 61; Antonia M. Bookbinder, "Coming Home," in *Lifecycles: Jewish Women on Life Passages and Personal Milestones*, edited by Debra Orenstein (Woodstock, Vt.: Jewish Lights, 1994), pp. 244–47.

13. Allen Maller spotted this phenomenon 20 years ago: "Intermarriage and Jewish Continuity," *Congress Monthly*, October 1976, p. 14; see also Schneider, *Jewish and Female*, pp. 296–97; Schneider, *Intermarriage*, p. 32.

14. See also Peter Y. Medding, Gary A. Tobin, Sylvia Barack Fishman, and Mordechai Rimor, *Jewish Identity in Conversionary and Mixed Marriages* (New York: American Jewish Committee/Jewish Publication Society, 1992), p. 18, in which the authors use language that assumes mixed marriage always involves competing religious heritages.

15. Woodward, "The Rites of Americans," p. 82; Albert S. Axelrad, *Meditations of a Maverick Rabbi* (Chappaqua, N.Y.: Rossel Books, 1985), pp. 67–68; Egon Mayer and Carl Sheingold, *Intermarriage and the Jewish Future: A National Study in Summary* (New York: American Jewish Committee, 1979), p. 16; Charles Silberman, *A Certain People: American Jews and Their Lives Today* (New York: Summit, 1985), pp. 307–10; Schneider, *Intermarriage*, p. 22; Michael D'Antonio, "Jewish Husbands, Christian Wives (and Vice Versa)," *Present Tense* (Autumn 1985): 7. In his analysis of the Gentile adults living with Jews in the 1990 NJPS, Bruce Phillips identified about 25 percent of them as nonreligious. By contrast, about 20 percent of the Jews in the 1990 survey described themselves as having no religion (Barry A. Kosmin, Sidney Goldstein, Joseph Waksberg, Nava Lerer, Ariella Keysar, and Jeffrey Scheckner, *Highlights of the CJF 1990 National Jewish Population Survey* [New York: Council of Jewish Federations, 1991], p. 4).

16. Religious News Service, "Fewer Than Half of Americans Stay in Parents' Denomination," *Los Angeles Times*, August 20, 1994, p. B5; David Briggs, "Study Finds Many Who Quit Religion Adopt No New Faith," *Daily News* (Los Angeles), January 8, 1994, p. 9; Schneider, *Intermarriage*, p. 146.

17. Josie Levy Martin, "Why Some Jews Celebrate Christmas," *Jewish Journal*, January 1–7, 1992, p. 9.

18. Cowan, *Mixed Blessings*, pp. 153–58, 173, 199–200; Schneider, *Intermarriage*, pp. 69, 139, 140–41.

19. "Jews by Choice: A Discussion with Converts," *Moment* (March 1979): 29–30; also, Evelyn Lauter, "Trend Toward Conversion TO Judaism, Not from It," *National Jewish Monthly* (July/August 1969): 9; Gina Centanni Weinberg, "A Jewish Life," *Reform Judaism* (Summer 1992): 10–11.

20. Mary Lynn Kotz, "Jewish Is Becoming," *Moment* (June 1981): 30.

21. Gloria Ulmer, "Congregationalist Came 'Home' to Judaism," *Jewish News* (Cleveland), December 31, 1993, p. 16.

22. Layne Murphy, "A Jew Named Murphy," *Jewish Journal*, October 1–7, 1993, p. 30.

23. Major, "Keeping the Faith?" pp. 37, 19; see also Steven Carr Reuben, *But How Will You Raise Your Children? A Guide to Interfaith Marriage* (New York: Pocket, 1987), pp. 123–24.

24. "Jews by Choice: A Discussion with Converts," p. 29; Kenneth L. Woodward, "Becoming a 'Jew-by-Choice,'" *Newsweek*, January 28, 1985, p. 73.

25. "Raising Kids Jewish in a Mixed Marriage," *Lilith* (Fall/Winter 1983): 29–30.

26. Ibid., pp. 27, 28.

27. Nancy Datan, "A Light unto the Nations," *Moment* (December 1980): 49–51.

28. Carol Hanson, "Hello Intermarrieds," *Jewish Journal*, July 29, 1994, p. 5. For similar testimony, see Amy Sheldon, "A Feminist Perspective on Intermarriage," in *Jewish Women in Therapy: Seen But Not Heard*, edited by Rachel Josefowitz Siegel and Ellen Cole (New York: Harrington Park Press, 1991), pp. 79–89; Rachel Altman, "Jews Who Choose Jews," *Lilith* (Summer 1994): 11; Diane Solomon, "Outreach, Inreach, and Overreach: How Should We Interact with the Intermarried?" *Moment* (February 1995): 57, 86; Woodward, "The Intermarrying Kind," p. 49; Na'ama Batya Lewin, "When Couples Intermarry," *Washington Jewish Week*, March 17, 1994, pp. 28, 50; E. M. Lowell, "Non-Jewish Spouses More Observant Than Jewish Couples" (letter to the editor), *Moment* (June 1993): 9–10; Susan Gordon Bilheimer, "A Bris among Non-Jews," *Sh'ma*, October 30, 1992, pp. 154–55; Reuben, *But How Will You Raise Your Children?*, pp. 120–21; Elizabeth Warner Frank, "On Being Intermarried," in *Lifecycles*, pp. 229–30.

29. Schneider, *Intermarriage*, pp. 141, 152–53.

30. Ira Rifkin, "Jews by Association," *Jewish Journal*, February 7–13, pp. 16, 21. See also Judy Petsonk and Jim Remsen, *The Intermarriage Handbook: A Guide for Jews and Christians* (New York: William Morrow, 1988), pp. 203–4, for a case study of a family in which the non-Jewish parent supports a Jewish lifestyle and Jewish child rearing while maintaining a personal affiliation as a Christian.

8: So You Want Your Kids to Marry Jews

1. Barry W. Holtz, "Schools That Succeed," *Reform Judaism* (Spring 1995): 55–57; Michael Shapiro, "Hebrew School Stories," and Naomi Pfefferman, "Mixed Reviews," both in *Jewish Journal*, June 26, 1992, pp. 8–9.

2. Joseph Reimer, "What We Know about . . . Jewish Family Education," in *What We Know about Jewish Education*, edited by Stuart L. Kelman (Los Angeles: Torah Aura Productions, 1992), pp. 179–81; Harlene W. Appelman, "Learning Together: Parents and Children Find Judaism Works," *Moment* (August 1993): 46–47; Gerald M. Kane, "Moving from Dropping off to Jumping In," *Compass* (Fall 1993): 9–10; Joseph Reimer, "Jewish Family Education: Evaluating Its Course, Looking to Its Future," *Journal of Jewish Communal Service* (Summer 1991): 271–77; Alvin I. Schiff, "Trends and Challenges in Jewish Family Education," *Journal of Jewish Communal Service* (Summer 1991): 265–68; Janet Marder, "The Trouble with . . . Jewish Education," *Reform Judaism* (Summer 1993): 22–23. See also the sidebar to Marder's article, "Exciting Educational Programs," which lists a number of activities that are working well in various Reform synagogues (p. 67).

3. Holtz, "Schools That Succeed," pp. 56–57; Seymour Rossel, "Reform Teacher Training

Opportunities," *Reform Judaism* (Spring 1995): 57; Pfefferman, "Mixed Reviews," p. 9; Michael Lerner, *Jewish Renewal: A Path to Healing and Transformation* (New York: Grosset/Putnam, 1994), pp. 303–4; Jonathan Woocher, "Jewish Education: Crisis and Vision," in *Imagining the Jewish Future: Essays and Responses*, edited by David Teutsch (Albany: State University of New York Press, 1992), p. 71; Marder, "The Trouble with Jewish Education," pp. 22–23.

4. Joel Lurie Grishaver, *40 Things You Can Do to Save the Jewish People* (Los Angeles: Alef Design Group, 1993), pp. 170–74; James Prosnit, "Reconfirm Confirmation," *Reform Judaism* (Spring 1994): 96. Michael Lerner in *Jewish Renewal*, on the other hand, urges Jewish parents not to force their children to be where they don't want to be and not to force bar or bat mitzvah until they're ready (pp. 305–6).

5. Shapiro, "Hebrew School Stories," p. 8.

6. Alvin I. Schiff, "What We Know about . . . the Jewish Day School," in *What We Know about Jewish Education*, pp. 156–60; Stewart Ain, "Stay in School," *Jewish Week*, October 28–November 3, 1994, p. 10; Stuart L. Kelman, "What We Know about . . . Parent Motivation," in *What We Know about Jewish Education*, pp. 189–90; Irwin N. Graulich, "Why Jewish Education?" *Moment* (February 1994): 41; Abraham P. Gannes, "Needed: More Serious Questions and Responses," *Jewish Education* (Fall 1991): 16; Nessa Rapoport, "The Jewish Teacher Demystified," *Reform Judaism* (Spring 1995): 52.

7. Barry Chazan, "What Is Informal Jewish Education?" *Journal of Jewish Communal Service* (Summer 1991): 302–3.

8. Barry Shrage, "A Communal Response to the Challenges of the 1990 CJF National Jewish Population Survey: Toward a Jewish Life Worth Living," *Journal of Jewish Communal Service* (Summer 1992): 328; Allan L. Smith, "The Challenge of Informal Education," *Compass* (Fall 1993): 7–8; Jerry Wische, "A Jewish Community Center Response," *Jewish Education* (Fall 1991): 33; Grishaver, *40 Things*, p. 7.

9. Hadar Dubowsky, "Identity Politics at Summer Camp," *Lilith* (Spring 1993): 20. See also Julie Gruenbaum Fax, "Jewish Summer Camps: Making Machers," *Moment* (February 1994): 50–52.

10. Yosef I. Abramowitz, "The De-Nerdification of Hillel," *Moment* (February 1995): 37–43, 81–82; James David Besser, "The 'New Hillel,'" *Jewish Journal*, September 3–9, 1993, pp. 28–29; Gary Rosenblatt, "Spinning Our Wheels," *Baltimore Jewish Times*, May 7, 1993, p. 9; Susan Josephs, "Judaism 101" (outreach to the unaffiliated at Columbia), *Jewish Week*, October 21–27, 1994, p. 25; Naomi Pfefferman, "A Generation at Risk" (budget problems at Los Angeles campus Hillels), *Jewish Journal*, June 11–17, 1993, pp. 8–9.

11. Richard S. Moline, "The College Campus: Is the Jewish Glass Half Empty or Half Full?" *United Synagogue Review* (Fall 1994): 28–29; sidebar to James S. Diamond, "Kosher on Campus," *United Synagogue Review* (Spring 1993): 19.

12. Stacey Elise Torman, "The Scoop on Campus Jewish Life," *Jewish Journal*, March 25–31, 1994, pp. 23–24; Richard M. Joel, "Advice for Parents of College-Bound Kids," *Baltimore Jewish Times*, September 4, 1992, pp. 13–14; Diamond, "Kosher on Campus," pp. 18–19,

33. Torman's article is about the *Hillel Guide to Jewish Life on Campus,* a book available through the B'nai B'rith Hillel Foundations in Washington.

13. Betsy Dolgin Katz, "What We Know about . . . Adult Education," in *What We Know about Jewish Education,* pp. 97–101; Roberta Louis Goodman, "The Neglected Learner: The Adult in Our Reform Community, *Compass* (Fall 1993): 20–21; Seymour Rossel, "Lifelong Learning: The Art of Being Jewish," *Compass* (Fall 1993): 5; Rahel Musleah, "The Identity Superhighway," *Hadassah* (March 1994): 10; Leonard Fein, "Crisis vs. Continuity," *Jewish Journal,* October 28–November 2, 1994, p. 35; Joelle Cohen, "Why Don't Jews Study Torah?" *Jewish Journal,* June 19–25, 1992, p. 25.

14. Deborah E. Lipstadt, "Tradition and Religious Practice," in *Imagining the Jewish Future,* p. 43.

15. Thomas Fields-Meyer, "When Generation X Asks 'Why?'" *Moment* (June 1995): 26–31, 54–55.

16. Yehiel E. Poupko, "Needed: Standards for Jewish Education," *Jewish Education* (Fall 1991): 30; see also Grishaver, *40 Things,* p. 175, in which he tells parents that if they want their kids to be enthusiastic learners, they'd better be learners, too.

17. Tobin covers the same ground in more detail in "The Synagogue's Evolving Mission," a booklet created for the 62nd General Assembly of the VAHC, October 1993 (pp. 6–7).

18. Tobin makes these arguments in a recent policy paper, "Creating New Jewish Organizations and Institutions," as reported in *Brandeis Reporter,* October 20–November 11, 1994. He spoke about the need for synagogues and other Jewish institutions to change at an April 6, 1995, lecture at the University of Judaism in Los Angeles.

19. Shelley Kapnek Rosenberg, "Singles in the Synagogue: Should We Be Paying More Attention?" *Reconstructionism Today* (Summer 1994): 4–5; Sylvia Barack Fishman, "Marginal No More: Jewish and Single in the 1980s," *Journal of Jewish Communal Service* (Summer 1989): 328–31; Stephen Chaim Listfield, "Turning Singles into Spouses," *Moment* (October 1988): 22; Deborah Berger-Reiss, "Single and Jewish: The Twentieth Century Pioneer" (unpublished manuscript); John L. Rosove, "A Synagogue Model for the Single Jew," *Journal of Reform Judaism* (Spring 1986): 29–30; Jack Nusan Porter, "Jewish Singles," *Midstream* (December 1975): 37–40.

20. Laura Geller and Elizabeth Koltun, "Single and Jewish: Toward a New Definition of Completeness," in *The Jewish Woman: New Perspectives,* edited by Elizabeth Koltun (New York: Schocken), pp. 43, 48.

21. Deborah Berger-Reiss, "Dear Deborah" (letter titled "More Weird Men" and signed "Considering a Convent"), *Jewish Journal,* December 4–10, 1992, p. 30.

22. Rachel A. Schwartz, "Going It Alone: Single Parents in a Two-Parent Jewish World," *Jewish Monthly,* December 1994, pp. 14, 16, 35; Michele Alperin, "Keeping the Connection: Single Parents in the Jewish Community," *United Synagogue Review* (Spring 1993): 16–17.

23. Marlene Adler Marks, "An Oddball Life," *Jewish Journal,* January 1–7, 1993, p. 7.

24. Wade Clark Roof, *A Generation of Seekers: The Spiritual Journeys of the Baby Boom Generation* (New York: HarperCollins, 1993), pp. 45, 59, 67, 184–85, 257–59; Jeffrey L. Sheler, "A Rekindling of Faith," *U.S. News and World Report,* October 21, 1991, pp. 78–79; Bradley Shavit

Artson, "Jewish Love, Jewish Law: Why Bother?" *Jewish Spectator* (Fall 1992): 19–20; Edward Hoffman, "Jewish Spirituality," *Sh'ma*, January 25, 1991, p. 44.

25. Jack Wertheimer, *A People Divided: Judaism in Contemporary America* (New York: Basic Books, 1993), pp. 140–49, 152.

26. Sally Friedman, "The Struggle to Prevent Intermarriage" (an interview with New Jersey rabbi Gerald L. Zelizer), *New York Times*, June 28, 1992, sec. XXIII, p. 3.

27. Daniel Schifrin, "The New Reform Movement," *Jewish Week*, April 1–7, 1994, pp. 24–26; Diane Winston, "Searching for Spirituality: Reform Judaism Responds," *Moment* (June 1992): 33–35; Lawrence A. Hoffman, "From Common Cold to Uncommon Healing," *CCAR Journal* (Spring 1994): 19–26; "Myths and Facts," *Reform Judaism* (Spring 1990): 29. There is some concern within the Reform movement that the trend toward greater spiritual expression will weaken Reform's commitment to social activism, as outlined by Leonard Fein in "What Is Required of Us," *Reform Judaism* (Spring 1991): 38–39, 63, and stated to me by several Reform rabbis. Besides the "myths and facts," the Spring 1990 issue of *Reform Judaism* features a short article by Lawrence Hoffman on spiritual renewal ("Beyond the Cat Stand," pp. 26–27) and something of a counterpoint by UAHC trustee Matthew H. Ross ("Reform: A Perspective," p. 27) in which Ross calls the changes being made in Reform worship "pseudo-Orthodoxy."

28. Wertheimer, *A People Divided*, pp. 160–69; "Perhaps You Belong in a Jewish Reconstructionist Community" (promotional brochure); Mordechai Liebling, "Who Are We?" *Reconstructionism Today* (Autumn 1993): 2–3; "What Reconstructionists Believe," flyer distributed at Kehillath Israel, a Reconstructionist synagogue in Pacific Palisades, California; Judy Petsonk and Jim Remsen, *The Intermarriage Handbook: A Guide for Jews and Christians* (New York: William Morrow, 1988), 263–64.

29. Arthur Waskow, "Does the Jewish People Have a Purpose?" *New Menorah* (Summer 1993): 1–2, and "Renewing *New Menorah*: A Letter from the Editor," *New Menorah* (Winter 1994): 1; Rami M. Shapiro, "Toward a New Beginning: The Emerging Judaism of the 21st Century," *New Menorah* (Winter 1993); Wertheimer, *A People Divided*, pp. 77–79; Rodger Kamenetz, *The Jew in the Lotus* (New York: HarperCollins, 1994), pp. 74, 264; Petsonk and Remsen, *The Intermarriage Handbook*, pp. 267–68; promotional brochures from the Network of Jewish Renewal Communities and its parent, ALEPH: Alliance for Jewish Renewal.

30. Wertheimer, *A People Divided*, pp. 76, 79–80; Michael Lerner, "Take Judaism Back from the Right," *Los Angeles Times*, October 5, 1992, p. B7; Charles Familant, "Statement of Purpose of Beit Tephila L'Chol HaAmim" (flyer describing the purpose and objectives of a congregation for interfaith families); Gary A. Tobin, "Will the Synagogue Survive?" *Moment* (August 1990): 45 (reporting on the need for singles congregations).

31. Laura Geller and Sue Levi Elwell, "On the Jewish Feminist Frontier, a Report," *Sh'ma*, November 13, 1992, pp. 1–2; Sylvia Barack Fishman, *A Breath of Life: Feminism in the American Jewish Community* (New York: Free Press, 1993), pp. 124–29; Wertheimer, *A People Divided*, pp. 72–75; Lerner, "Take Judaism Back from the Right," p. B7; Diane Winston, "Women Greet the New Month (Rosh Chodesh) in Dallas," *Moment* (June 1992): 32.

32. Riv-Ellen Prell, "A Judaism of Scale," *Sh'ma*, February 21, 1992, p. 63; Richard Siegel, Michael Strassfeld, and Sharon Strassfeld, *The Jewish Catalog* (Philadelphia: Jewish Publication Society of America, 1973), pp. 278–80; Bernard Reisman, *The Chavurah: A Contemporary Jewish Experience* (New York: Union of American Hebrew Congregations, 1977), pp. 8–12, 32, 39–40, 58–59; Rodger Kamenetz, "Has the Jewish Renewal Movement Made It into the Mainstream?" *Moment* (December 1994): 42–49, 79–81; Mark I. Pinsky, "Havurah: A New Spirit in Judaism," *Los Angeles Times*, October 11, 1986, p. A1; Michele Alperin, "Havurot: A Path to Belonging," *United Synagogue Review* (Spring 1992): 17; Wertheimer, *A People Divided*, pp. 67–68. A more recent full-length book that details the history of the *chavurah* movement and describes how *chavurah* Judaism differs from mainstream American Jewish worship is Riv-Ellen Prell's *Prayer and Community: The Havurah in American Judaism* (Detroit: Wayne State University Press, 1989).

33. Siegel, Strassfeld, and Strassfeld, *The Jewish Catalog*, pp. 281–85; Reisman, *The Chavurah*, pp. 17–20, 80–98, 131–32, 137, 149–51; Prell, "A Judaism of Scale," pp. 62–63; Judy Petsonk, "Renewal, a One-Generation Phenomenon?" *Sh'ma*, January 25, 1991, pp. 41–43; Wertheimer, *A People Divided*, pp. 68–70; Petsonk and Remsen, *The Intermarriage Handbook*, pp. 261–62; Charles Silberman, *A Certain People: American Jews and Their Lives Today* (New York: Summit, 1985), pp. 250–51; Lerner, "Take Judaism Back from the Right," p. B7; Alperin, "Havurot: A Path to Belonging," pp. 17–19; Francine Klagsbrun, column, *Moment* (August 1991): 11, 58; Alan Fisher, "A Place to Grow," *Jewish Journal*, July 22–28, 1994, p. 12; Jonathan Stein, "In Defense of the Congregational *Havurah*," *Journal of Reform Judaism* (Summer 1983): 43–45; Kamenetz, "Has the Jewish Renewal Movement Made It into the Mainstream?" pp. 42–46, 81. Rabbi Mitchell Chefitz sent me *The Havurah Guide: A Handbook of Havurah Dynamics* (Miami: Havurah of South Florida, 1990), the guiding principles and program guide for the Havurah of South Florida, a busy, multifaceted community whose activities revolve around regularly scheduled study sessions and Shabbat and holiday observance, with frequent visits from guest speakers, an annual retreat, and occasional social action projects—an impressive range of Jewish activities.

34. Ephraim Buchwald, "The Beginners' Service Beginnings," *Sh'ma*, February 21, 1992, pp. 57–58; flyer from Fairmount Temple in Ohio, describing its Adult Learners' Service. Rahel Musleah, in "The Identity Superhighway," p. 10, describes how Buchwald's beginners' service has expanded into the National Jewish Outreach Program, which offers crash courses in Hebrew, Judaism, and prayer and which Buchwald estimates has reached 100,000 Jews since it was founded in 1988.

35. When she was staff director for the UAHC Task Force on the Unaffiliated, Rabbi Renni Altman developed a program called "Being Jewish: So What?" modeled after a Denver program that reached out to unaffiliated young adults to let them know that the Reform movement has activities of value to them. She also told me about a large Kansas City, Missouri, congregation that, taking its cue from Chabad, got a grant to remodel an RV as a "shulmobile" and take it to malls and community center parking lots in the suburbs north of Kansas City, where there are no synagogues, and hold classes and services in the RV.

36. Jeffery K. Salkin, "The Jews We Don't See: What to Do about the Unaffiliated," *Reform Judaism* (Winter 1991), p. 39; Gary A. Tobin, "Will the Synagogue Survive?" *Moment* (August 1990): 48.

37. Musleah, "The Identity Superhighway," p. 11 (almost 400 Reform congregations offer Privilege Cards providing a year's free membership, free High Holiday tickets, and other benefits to adults 22–30); Salkin, "The Jews We Don't See," p. 39 (Fairmount Temple in Cleveland has a Young People's Congregation for adults under 36, charging low membership dues; 95 percent of the smaller group join the parent temple); flyer describing the under-30 program of Temple Kol Ami in South Florida, which offers free membership to anyone under 30, with graduated increases in dues after that point.

38. Salkin, "The Jews We Don't See," p. 40; Tobin, "Will the Synagogue Survive?" p. 48. Tobin calls for synagogues to allow Jews to affiliate on a fee-for-service basis.

39. Lavey Derby, "Outreach, Intermarriage, and Jewish Continuity: Toward a New Synagogue-Federation Partnership," *Journal of Jewish Communal Service* (Summer 1992): 332–35; Shrage, "A Communal Response," p. 329; Gary Rosenblatt, "In Search of Our Mission," *Jewish Journal*, February 10–16, 1995, p. 31; David Belin and Paul Menitoff, final report of the UAHC Strategic Planning Task Force for Jewish Continuity and Growth, October 1993, pp. 8–11; Gary Rosenblatt, "Federations Confront Jewish Survival" (p. 40) and "Deja Jew" (p. 10), *Baltimore Jewish Times*, November 20, 1992.

40. Gerald B. Bubis, "Jewish Dollars Drying Up," *Moment* (December 1992): 28–33.

41. Tom Tugend, "A New Era?" *Jewish Journal*, July 1–7, 1994, p. 4.

42. Mark S. Glickman, "Reform Rabbi Offended by Two Articles" (letter), *Moment* (August 1992): 6; see also Yehuda Lev, "Give and Take," *Jewish Journal*, May 6–12, 1994, p. 39.

43. Grishaver, *40 Things*, pp. 10–17. Another book with down-to-earth, real world advice on how to be Jewish when life keeps getting in the way is Steven Carr Reuben's *Raising Jewish Children in a Contemporary World: The Modern Parent's Guide to Creating a Jewish Home* (Rocklin, Calif.: Prima Publishing, 1992).

44. Siegel, Strassfeld, and Strassfeld, *The Jewish Catalog*, pp. 262–73. Countercultural as they were, the catalog authors provided a "reluctant guide" to established Jewish organizations, including names, addresses, and a big chart laying out the structure of the major Jewish religious movements. If the listings have been updated since 1973 (or even if they haven't), it's a good place to start making your way through the maze of organized Judaism.

45. Commission on Reform Jewish Outreach, *Reaching Adolescents: Interdating, Intermarriage, and Jewish Identity* (New York: Union of American Hebrew Congregations, 1990), pp. 31–50, 75–78; United Synagogue of Conservative Judaism, *Intermarriage: What Can We Do?* pp. 13–18; Alan Silverstein, "Causes for Concern" and "It Starts with a Date" (New York: United Synagogue); Barbara Mirel and Jeffrey Mirel, *Relationships: A Jewish View* (Denver: Alternatives in Religious Education, 1981), pp. 8–11, 14–15; materials (discussion questions, role-playing exercises) distributed at a workshop entitled "But Ma, We're Only Dating," at the 1993 UAHC Biennial.

46. See also Jonathan Woocher, "Intermarriage and Jewish Education," *Jewish Spectator* (Winter

1991–92): 12–14; Susan Weidman Schneider, *Intermarriage: The Challenge of Living with Differences between Christians and Jews* (New York: Free Press, 1989), pp. 179–80.

47. *Reaching Adolescents* has a strong and explicit exercise on stereotypes (pp. 75–78), and *Relationships: A Jewish View* addresses the role of media in forming the image of one's ideal partner (p. 10). According to Rabbi Robert Abramson, United Synagogue's education director, the booklet "It Starts with a Date," for use by parents with older teens, touches on the JAP stereotype. An account of how stereotypes are being addressed in the summer camp setting is included in Dubowsky, "Identity Politics at Summer Camp," p. 22. It is difficult to say how widely stereotype-busting programs are being implemented; none of the congregational rabbis or educators I interviewed volunteered stories of attempts to combat stereotypes in their classrooms or youth groups. Abramson said his office has sold more than 100 manuals for a program for 12- and 13-year-olds called "Future Thinking," which focuses on dating and marriage and devotes 2 of its 12 sessions to negative stereotypes.

48. Robert Eshman, "Groovin' at Tatou," *Jewish Journal*, September 2–8, 1994, pp. 17, 50; Naomi Pfefferman, "L.A. Singles: Looking for Love," *Jewish Journal*, March 18–24, 1988, pp. 14–18, 50; Jacqueline Gerstein, "The Singles Dance: 2-Step to the 'Chupah'?" *Jewish Journal*, August 14–20, 1987, pp. 22, 31–32; Debra Hachen, "Playing the Jewish Singles Game," *Sh'ma*, January 6, 1978, pp. 37–39.

49. Avis D. Miller and Sander H. Mendelson, "Twentysomethings Come to Shul," *United Synagogue Review* (Fall 1994): 16–17; Listfield, "Turning Singles into Spouses," pp. 20–22, 25; Rosove, "A Synagogue Model for the Single Jew," pp. 30–33; Robert Rubin, "Successful Singles Programming: Encouraging Jewish Marriage," in United Synagogue of Conservative Judaism, *Intermarriage: What Can We Do? What Should We Do?* (New York: United Synagogue of Conservative Judaism, n.d.) pp. 19–22; Roberta Thisdell, "Camp Romance," *Virginian-Pilot*, September 2, 1992, pp. B1, B7 (an account of an annual Jewish singles weekend in Virginia Beach, Virginia, sponsored by a Conservative synagogue in Norfolk, Virginia). A successful young adults program at The Temple in Atlanta was described at the 1993 UAHC Biennial.

50. Tara Aronson, "BayDates Offers Low-Cost, High-Tech Matchmaking," *Northern California Jewish Bulletin*, October 16, 1992, p. 37.

51. Judith Colp, "The New Shadchens," *Moment* (June 1990): 47–51; Carol Tice, "The Marriage Biz," *Jewish Journal*, August 20–26, 1993, p. 13; Susan Ornstein, "And What's Being Done about It," *Jewish Women's Journal*, February 1993, pp. 8–9; Bob Pool, "The Romance Broker," *Los Angeles Times*, September 17, 1992; pp. B1, B8; William Novak, "Dating Ourselves," *Moment* (January/February 1984): 25–30; Irene Nathan, "Making Jewish Matches: A Calling," *Sh'ma*, January 21, 1983, pp. 46–47; Diana Bletter and Lori Grinker, *The Invisible Thread: A Portrait of Jewish American Women* (Philadelphia: Jewish Publication Society, 1989), pp. 130–32; materials about the Colorado Jewish Social Network, distributed at the 1993 UAHC Biennial.

52. Dorfman, "Jewish Singles and Their Stereotypes," p. 42; Paul Stregevsky, "Oh, Grow Up!" *Jewish Journal*, April 3–9, 1992, p. 44; Andrea Heiman, "Man Trouble," *Jewish Journal*, April 15–21, 1994, p. 34.

53. Yoram Gold, "Aish HaTorah Fires up Judaism," *Ha'am*, October 1992, pp. 3, 14; Andrea Heiman, "A Match Made in Heaven?" *Los Angeles Times*, August 26, 1992, pp. EI, E8; Naomi Pfefferman, "The Twenty-Something Dating Scene," *Jewish Journal*, December 27, 1991–January 2, 1992, pp. 9, 13.

54. Bethamie Horowitz and Jeffrey R. Solomon, "Why Is This City Different from Other Cities? New York and the 1990 National Jewish Population Survey," *Journal of Jewish Communal Service* (Summer 1992): 312, 316–18; Ari L. Goldman, "Religion Notes," *New York Times*, October 23, 1993, p. A8; Jonathan D. Sarna, "Reform Jewish Leaders, Intermarriage, and Conversion," *Journal of Reform Judaism* (Winter 1990): 4.

55. Diane Solomon, "Outreach, Inreach, and Overreach: How Should We Interact with the Intermarried?" *Moment* (February 1995): 52.

56. Phyllis Klasky Karas, "A Mother's Fear," *Jewish Journal*, February 9–15, p. 23, also in many other local Jewish weeklies between January and April 1990. The link between family observance and whom the children from those families marry is hardly absolute. In the Reform movement's study of the delegates to its 1985 biennial, an overwhelming majority of the respondents practiced various home-based rituals, from avoiding bread during Passover to lighting Shabbat candles and observing *yahrzeit* dates. They were *more* observant of these rituals (except for keeping kosher) than their parents had been, and four out of five of those parents, on the average, had practiced those home observances. Moreover, 85 percent of their children had been or were going to be confirmed, completing ten years of formal Jewish education. Still, of the responding delegates' children who had married, 31 percent had married non-Jews (Mark L. Winer, Sanford Seltzer, and Steven J. Schwager, *Leaders of Reform Judaism: A Study of Jewish Identity, Religious Practices and Beliefs, and Marriage Patterns* (New York: Union of American Hebrew Congregations, 1987), pp. 32, 50, 60–61, 65, 69.)

9: A Time to Embrace

1. Commission on Reform Jewish Outreach, *Outreach and the Changing Reform Jewish Community: Creating an Agenda for Our Future* (New York: Union of American Hebrew Congregations, 1989), pp. 131–32; Lawrence J. Epstein, *The Theory and Practice of Welcoming Converts to Judaism* (Lewiston, N.Y.: Edwin Mellen Press, 1992), pp. 90–91.

2. Commission on Reform Jewish Outreach, *Reform Jewish Outreach: The Idea Book* (New York: Union of American Hebrew Congregations, 1988), pp. 212–13; Charles Silberman, *A Certain People: American Jews and Their Lives Today* (New York: Summit, 1985), pp. 321–22; Jack Wertheimer, *A People Divided: Judaism in Contemporary America* (New York: Basic Books, 1993), p. 108.

3. Commission on Reform Jewish Outreach, *The Idea Book*, pp. 211–12; Leslie Goodman-Malamuth and Robin Margolis, *Between Two Worlds: Choices for Grown Children of Jewish-Christian Parents* (New York: Pocket, 1992), p. 58; John D. Rayner, "Jewish Identity: Law and Reality," *Journal of Progressive Judaism* (November 1993): 62; Silberman, *A Certain People*, p. 322. The Reconstructionist movement accepted the principle of patrilineality in 1968 and reaffirmed it in 1979.

4. Joseph A. Edelheit, "Children of Mixed Marriages: A Non-Lineal Approach," *Journal of Reform Judaism* (Winter 1983): 34–37; Robert Gordis, "To Move Forward, Take One Step Back," *Moment* (May 1986): 59–60; Hershel Shanks, "An Unimportant Issue: 'Who Is a Jew?'" *Moment* (February 1994): 4; Kenneth L. Woodward, "A New Definition of Who Is a Jew," *Newsweek*, March 28, 1983, p. 50; Commission on Reform Jewish Outreach, *The Idea Book*, pp. 210–11. The concept of Jewish lineage being conferred by the father but through the mother was presented by Rabbi Mordecai Finley during a study session at the UAHC Kallah, Santa Cruz, California, July 1994.

5. Jakob J. Petuchowski, "Toward Sectarianism," *Moment* (September 1983): 34–36; Gordis, "To Move Forward, Take One Step Back," pp. 60–61; Mark L. Winer, "Our Vision of the Future: Personal Status and K'lal Yisrael," a speech presented to the Central Conference of American Rabbis in 1994; Silberman, *A Certain People*, p. 322.

6. Sheldon Zimmerman, "Raising the Standard," *Moment* (September 1983): 32–34; Edelheit, "Children of Mixed Marriages," pp. 40–42; letters in response to Robert Gordis in *Moment* from Trude Weiss-Rosmarin and Bernard Zlotowitz (October 1986: 4–6), Elias Lieberman (November 1986: 3–4), and George Stern (December 1986: 4, 6). See also Goodman-Malamuth and Margolis, *Between Two Worlds*, p. 67; and Commission on Reform Jewish Outreach, *The Idea Book*, pp. 214–15.

7. Egon Mayer, "The Impact of Intermarriage," *Reform Judaism* (Spring 1991): 32; Egon Mayer, "The Coming Reformation in American Jewish Identity," in *Imagining the Jewish Future: Essays and Responses*, edited by David Teutsch (Albany: State University of New York Press), pp. 179–80; Peter Steinfels, "Beliefs," *New York Times*, August 7, 1993, p. A28. Up to 70 percent of Conservative Jews say they would consider their grandchildren Jewish even if their mother was not.

8. Michael Parks, "Soldier's Death Raises Questions: Who Is a Jew?" *Los Angeles Times*, August 14, 1993, p. 3.

9. Hershel Shanks, "Rabbis Who Perform Intermarriages: Who They Are and Why They Do It," *Moment* (January/February 1988): 14; Roberta Hershenson, "With Interfaith Marriages, Conflict Over Role of Rabbis," *New York Times*, July 9, 1989, sec. XXII, p. 1; Wertheimer, *A People Divided*, pp. 100–102.

10. Irwin H. Fishbein, "Summary of Rabbinic Center for Research and Counseling 1990 Survey on Rabbinic Participation in Intermarriage Ceremonies," December 31, 1990, furnished by author; Shanks, "Rabbis Who Perform Intermarriages," pp. 16–17; Wertheimer, *A People Divided*, p. 37.

11. Maurice Davis, "Why I Won't Perform an Intermarriage," *Moment* (January/February 1988): 20–21; Mark L. Winer, "Should Rabbis Perform Mixed Marriages?" *Reform Judaism* (Summer 1985): 2–3; Hershenson, "With Interfaith Marriages, Conflict over Role of Rabbis," p. 4; Judy Petsonk and Jim Remsen, *The Intermarriage Handbook: A Guide for Jews and Christians* (New York: William Morrow, 1988), pp. 64–65.

12. Hershenson, "With Interfaith Marriages, Conflict over Role of Rabbis," p. 1; Peter Steinfels, "Jews Found Split on Mixed Marriage," *New York Times*, September 18, 1990, p. A25;

Mayer, "The Impact of Intermarriage," pp. 31–32; Marshall Sklare, "Intermarriage and Jewish Survival," *Commentary* (March 1970): 54; Petsonk and Remsen, *The Intermarriage Handbook*, pp. 70–71. The Steinfels and Mayer articles report on a Jewish Outreach Institute study that found 70 percent of Conservative respondents and 90 percent of Reform respondents in favor of rabbinic officiation at an intermarriage if the couple was committed to raising Jewish children. Sklare notes that as early as the 1950s many of his Lakeville subjects were complaining that rabbis wouldn't officiate at their children's weddings to non-Jews.

13. Dannel Schwartz, "The Intermarriage Rip-off," *Moment* (July/August 1978): 62–64; Shanks, "Rabbis Who Perform Intermarriages," p. 17; Winer, "Should Rabbis Perform Mixed Marriages?" p. 3.

14. Irwin H. Fishbein, "Minority Report: Central Conference of American Rabbis Report of Committee on Mixed Marriage," *CCAR Yearbook 1973* (New York: Central Conference of American Rabbis, 1974), pp. 64–67; Albert S. Axelrad, *Meditations of a Maverick Rabbi* (Chappaqua, N.Y.: Rossel Books, 1985), pp. 67–70; Shanks, "Rabbis Who Perform Intermarriages," pp. 17–19; Schwartz, "The Intermarriage Rip-off," p. 64; Allen I. Freehling, "Why I Changed My Mind about Performing Intermarriages," *Jewish Spectator* (Summer 1995): 41–42.

15. Schwartz, "The Intermarriage Rip-off," p. 63; Shanks, "Rabbis Who Perform Intermarriages," pp. 17–19; Fishbein, "Minority Report"; Hershenson, "With Interfaith Marriages, Conflict over Role of Rabbis," pp. 4–5.

16. Egon Mayer and Amy Avgar, *Conversion among the Intermarried* (New York: American Jewish Committee, 1987), p. 33; Shanks, "Rabbis Who Perform Intermarriages," pp. 17–19; letters to *Moment* in response to Shanks's article from Diana Ober and Henry Cohen (April 1988: 6–7) and Marjorie Schonhaut Hirshan (June 1988, p. 8); Michael D'Antonio, "Jewish Husbands, Christian Wives (and Vice Versa)," *Present Tense* (Autumn 1985): 9; Cohen, "Mixed Marriage and Jewish Continuity," p. 51.

17. Winer, "Should Rabbis Perform Mixed Marriages?" p. 2.

18. Rabbi Emily Faust Korzenik of the Fellowship for Jewish Learning in Stamford, Connecticut, wrote a pamphlet called "It's an Intermarriage: We Want to Have a Jewish Wedding but We Can't Find a Rabbi," which describes in detail how to create a traditional Jewish ceremony without a rabbi as officiant. Anita Diamant, in *The New Jewish Wedding* (New York: Summit, 1985), gives advice on how to put Jewish tradition into a civil ceremony (pp. 38–40). Steven Carr Reuben deals sympathetically with interfaith wedding issues in *But How Will You Raise Your Children?: A Guide to Interfaith Marriage* (New York: Pocket, 1987), pp. 96–110.

19. Commission on Reform Jewish Outreach, *Outreach and the Changing Reform Jewish Community*, pp. 132–33; Paul Cowan with Rachel Cowan, *Mixed Blessings: Marriage between Jews and Christians* (New York: Doubleday, 1987), pp. 166–95 (describing the operation of workshops the Cowans conducted at the 92nd St. Y, which Rachel Cowan has continued); Frayda Rembaum, "Communal Programming: A Constructive Response to Intermarriage," *Jewish Intermarriage, Conversion, and Outreach* (New York: Jewish Outreach Institute, 1990),

pp. 42–43; Michael Wasserman, "Outreach to Interfaith Couples," *Conservative Judaism* (Fall 1988): 79–82; Rachel Cowan, column in *Moment* (April 1990): 14; Susan Weidman Schneider, *Intermarriage: The Challenge of Living with Differences between Christians and Jews* (New York: Free Press, 1989), pp. 242–43.

20. United Synagogue of Conservative Judaism, *Intermarriage: What Can We Do? What Should We Do?* (New York: United Synagogue of Conservative Judaism, n.d.), pp. 25–29; Commission on Reform Jewish Outreach, *Outreach and the Changing Reform Jewish Community*, pp. 12–13; Rembaum, "Communal Programming," pp. 43–44, 45–48; Debra Nussbaum Cohen and Leslie Katz, "Intermarriage Alarm," *Jewish Bulletin of Northern California*, September 23, 1994, p. 1; Sally Friedman, "The Struggle to Prevent Intermarriage" (an interview with New Jersey rabbi Gerald L. Zelizer), *New York Times*, June 28, 1992, sec. XXIII, p. 3.

21. Saundra Heller, "Stepping Stones to a Jewish Me," *Jewish Intermarriage, Conversion, and Outreach*, pp. 52–59; "Program Helps Intermarrieds Decide Future for Children," *Jewish Bulletin of Northern California*, October 22, 1993, p. 3A; Rahel Musleah, "The Identity Superhighway," *Hadassah* (March 1994): 12; Schneider, *Intermarriage*, p. 240.

22. Introduction to Judaism and Basic Judaism programs vary widely. Some meet for six or eight weeks and are intended to provide a quick sketch of Jewish history, doctrine, practice, and holidays; others meet weekly for six months or more and go into much more depth. Some programs emphasize academic study, while others are heavy on experiential activities such as learning prayers and carrying out Jewish rituals at home. A really good Intro class will give a student the basic tools to begin to function as a well-rounded Jew in real life: an overview of Jewish history, familiarity with Jewish theology and doctrine, an understanding of Jewish holidays and life cycle, practice in basic Jewish prayers and rituals, and perhaps a little Hebrew.

  Most programs conducted through the Reform movement are based on a curriculum put together by Stephen J. Einstein and Lydia Kukoff, *Introduction to Judaism: A Course Outline* (New York: Union of American Hebrew Congregations, 1983). The Conservative movement has two books that many programs use as texts: Simcha Kling, *Embracing Judaism* (New York: Rabbinical Assembly, 1987), which focuses on Jewish history and doctrine; and Ronald H. Isaacs, *Becoming Jewish: A Handbook for Conversion* (New York: Rabbinical Assembly, 1993), which deals with the nuts and bolts of prayer, holiday observance, and taking on a Jewish identity. See Wasserman, "Outreach to Interfaith Couples," pp. 83–85, for a description of the Derekh Torah program at the 92nd St. Y.

23. Commission on Reform Jewish Outreach, *The Idea Book*, pp. 11–17, 109, 161; Commission on Reform Jewish Outreach, *Outreach and the Changing Reform Jewish Community*, pp. 9–13, 111–13, 115, 124–26; Lena Romanoff with Lisa Hostein, *Your People, My People: Finding Acceptance and Fulfillment as a Jew by Choice* (Philadelphia: Jewish Publication Society, 1990), pp. 139–40.

24. Commission on Reform Jewish Outreach, *Outreach and the Changing Reform Jewish Community*, pp. 111–13, 115–16.

25. Bradley Shavit Artson, "Facing Intermarriage," *Women's League Outlook* (Winter 1993): 19;

Eric Cytryn, "Making All Jews Good Jews," *Sh'ma*, March 8, 1991, p. 68. Some Conservative synagogues do allow non-Jews to join Sisterhood and Brotherhood.

26. David Margolis, "Convention Notes from Palm Springs," *Jewish Journal*, January 17–23, 1992, p. 10.

27. Debra Nussbaum Cohen, "CJF Urges Federations to Serve Intermarrieds," *Jewish Journal*, September 2–8, 1994, pp. 26–27; Cohen and Katz, "Intermarriage Alarm," pp. 1, 40; similarly in other Jewish weeklies nationwide in September 1994.

28. Wasserman, "Outreach to Interfaith Couples," pp. 85–86; Rembaum, "Communal Programming," pp. 42–43; Barbara Mollin Lerner, "JCCs and the Intermarried" (letter), *Moment* (June 1995): 12.

29. Steven Bayme, "Ensuring Jewish Continuity: Policy Challenges and Implications for Jewish Communal Professionals," *Journal of Jewish Communal Service* (Summer 1992): 339.

30. Jonathan Woocher, "Intermarriage and Jewish Education," *Jewish Spectator* (Winter 1991/92): 14.

31. Goodman-Malamuth and Margolis, *Between Two Worlds*, pp. 19, 192ff; Rachel Cowan, column in *Moment* (December 1990): 14–15.

32. Irwin H. Fishbein, "Intermarriage and Outreach: Facing Contemporary Challenges," address to the 24th annual convention of the Federation of Reconstructionist Congregations and Havurot, Buffalo, New York, June 14, 1984.

33. David Belin, "The Intermarriage Crisis: It's Time for Realism," in *Jewish Intermarriage, Conversion, and Outreach*, p. 61; similarly in two guest columns in *Moment* (December 1993: 28–29, and June 1995: 22–23). In the 1993 column, Belin reported the results of a poll conducted by the Jewish Outreach Institute in which almost all the Conservative and Reform Jews and three-fourths of the Orthodox Jews surveyed said they were in favor of programs that would allow the intermarried to "become better acquainted with and attracted to Judaism." When asked whether the Jewish community should devote more resources to such programs, more than 4 out of 10 Orthodox Jews, almost 9 out of 10 Conservative Jews, and almost all the Reform Jews polled said yes.

34. Silberman, *A Certain People*, pp. 315–16; Schneider, *Intermarriage*, pp. 222–23; Barry A. Kosmin and Seymour Lachman, *One Nation under God* (New York: Simon and Schuster, 1993), p. 247; Peter Y. Medding, Gary A. Tobin, Sylvia Barack Fishman, and Mordechai Rimor, *Jewish Identity in Conversionary and Mixed Marriages* (New York: American Jewish Committee/Jewish Publication Society, 1992), pp. 36–37.

35. Epstein, *Theory and Practice*, p. viii (Epstein cites about 3,600 converts per year); Gloria Ulmer, "Congregationalist Came 'Home' to Judaism," *Jewish News* (Cleveland), December 31, 1993, p. 16 (estimates about 4,500 per year); Egon Mayer, in "Why Not Judaism?" *Moment* (October 1991), suggests that by the year 2010 converts may account for 7–10 percent of American Jews (p. 28). Mayer estimated the 3,000–5,000 range during a telephone conversation on May 13, 1995.

36. Conversion rates vary widely from city to city and decade to decade. For example, Cohen Center researchers found that 15 percent of people not born Jewish married to Jews in 1985 had converted to Judaism, whereas 40 percent had done so in Pittsburgh, and 40 percent of

the 30-to-39-year-old age group had in Phoenix. (Hebrew Union College demographer Bruce Phillips said in an interview that cities such as Phoenix and Dallas, which have large populations of conservative Christians, have higher conversion rates than more religiously liberal cities such as Denver and San Francisco because in a religiously conservative area, people will challenge you to declare a religious identity, whereas in more cosmopolitan areas, nobody cares.) Lawrence Epstein estimated a conversion rate of 30–40 percent during the late 1970s and early 1980s. See Epstein, *Theory and Practice*, p. 88; Lawrence Sternberg, "Intermarriage: A First Look," CMJS Research Notes, Cohen Center for Modern Jewish Studies, May 1988; Mordechai Rimor, "Intermarriage and Conversion: The Case from the Boston Data," CMJS Research Notes, Cohen Center for Modern Jewish Studies, December 1988; Kenneth L. Woodward, "Becoming a 'Jew-by-Choice,'" *Newsweek*, January 28, 1985, p. 73.

37. Medding et al., *Jewish Identity in Conversionary and Mixed Marriages*, p. 6 (in about 25 percent of the households in which one partner was not born Jewish, he or she had converted); Gary Tobin, "From Alarms to Open Arms," *Hadassah* (December 1991): 24 (he cites a one-in-four rate); Stephen Fuchs, "Reach Out—but Also Bring In," *Sh'ma*, March 8, 1991, p. 69 (quotes Steven Bayme as citing an 18 percent cumulative rate); Barry A. Kosmin, Sidney Goldstein, Joseph Waksberg, Nava Lerer, Ariella Keysar, and Jeffrey Scheckner, *Highlights of the CJF 1990 National Jewish Population Survey* (New York: Council of Jewish Federations, 1991), p. 13 (a 13 percent cumulative rate). The rate of conversion at or around time of marriage has been low—usually 5–10 percent—for years; converts accounted for about 9 percent of partners not born Jewish married recently to Jews in the 1990 NJPS (5 percent in 57 percent; *Highlights*, p. 14).

38. Tobin, "From Alarms to Open Arms," p. 24; Rahel Musleah, "The New Mosaic," *Hadassah* (March 1994): 19; Epstein, *Theory and Practice*, p. 92.

39. Schneider, *Intermarriage*, pp. 6, 200–201; Kosmin, *One Nation under God*, p. 247; Silberman, *A Certain People*, p. 311; Musleah, "The New Mosaic," p. 20; Steven Huberman, "Jews and Non-Jews: Falling in Love," *Journal of Jewish Communal Service* (Spring 1979): 266.

40. Solomon B. Freehof, "Circumcision of Proselytes," in *Conversion to Judaism in Jewish Law: Essays and Responsa*, edited by Walter Jacob and Moshe Zemer (Pittsburgh: Rodef Shalom Press, 1994), p. 168.

41. Cowan, *Mixed Blessings*, pp. 236–43; Schneider, *Intermarriage*, p. 201; Silberman, *A Certain People*, pp. 312–13; Brenda Forster and Joseph Tabachnik, *Jews by Choice: A Study of Converts to Reform and Conservative Judaism* (Hoboken, N.J.: KTAV, 1991), p. 121; Shoshana Brown-Gutoff, "Dear Ruth: Letter to an Aspiring Convert," in *Lifecycles: Jewish Women on Life Passages and Personal Milestones*, edited by Debra Orenstein (Woodstock, Vt.: Jewish Lights, 1994), pp. 235–39.

42. Mark Washofsky, "Halakhah and Ulterior Motives: Rabbinic Discretion and the Law of Conversion," in *Conversion to Judaism in Jewish Law*, p. 1; Forster and Tabachnik, *Jews by Choice*, pp. 43–44; Brown-Gutoff, "Dear Ruth," pp. 238–39.

43. Marc D. Angel, "Another Halakhic Approach to Conversions," *Tradition* (Winter/Spring

1972): 107–12; Washofsky, "Halakhah and Ulterior Motives," pp. 2, 12–14, 16, 23–24, 26–27; Forster and Tabatchnik, *Jews by Choice*, pp. 45–46.

44. Alan Silverstein, *Are You Considering Conversion to Judaism?* (New York: Rabbinical Assembly, 1992), pp. 12–14; Lydia Kukoff, *Choosing Judaism* (New York: Union of American Hebrew Congregations, 1981), pp. 12–13; Silberman, *A Certain People*, pp. 308–10; Romanoff, *Your People, My People*, pp. 53–54; Forster and Tabatchnik, *Jews by Choice*, pp. 75, 77, 79; Musleah, "The New Mosaic," pp. 19–20; Cytryn, "Making All Jews Good Jews," pp. 67–68; Huberman, "Jews and Non-Jews: Falling in Love," p. 267; Catherine Hall Myrowitz, "Who We Are and What We Need: An Open Letter to the Jewish Community from a Jew by Choice," in *Lifecycles*, p. 250.

45. Andree Brooks, "Motives of Judaism's Converts," *New York Times*, June 22, 1987, p. B9; Forster and Tabatchnik, *Jews by Choice*, pp. 76–79, 140; Romanoff, *Your People, My People*, pp. 56–63; Schneider, *Intermarriage*, pp. 202–5. Although much of the literature on intermarriage warns not to pressure the non-Jewish spouse about conversion, the evidence today is that Jewish partners and in-laws bend over backward not to pressure. In Forster and Tabatchnik's study, 82 percent of the converts surveyed said they had initiated their own conversion process, with fewer than half reporting that their partners played a role in their decision to convert. Mayer and Avgar's 1985 survey of 309 mixed and conversionary couples found that about a third of the respondents not born Jewish had converted; only a third of the rest said they didn't convert because of their own religious convictions, with many reporting that they had received no pressure or even encouragement to convert from their Jewish spouses or in-laws or their rabbis; most of the couples married by rabbis were not even invited to stay in contact with those rabbis' temples. The Reform movement publishes a pamphlet entitled "Inviting Someone You Love to Become Jewish" (as well as another directed toward potential converts, "Becoming a Jew"), and the 1993 UAHC Biennial featured a workshop on the topic.

46. Commission on Reform Jewish Outreach, *The Idea Book*, pp. 235–41; Epstein, *Theory and Practice*, pp. 45–46; Debra Orenstein, "Choosing Judaism," in *Lifecycles*, pp. 232–33. Rabbinic comments supportive of converts from the Talmud and other sources include admonitions not to treat proselytes (denoted by the Hebrew word *ger*, meaning "stranger") as different or less Jewish than born Jews, as born Jews were themselves strangers in the land of Egypt; statements that converts are especially beloved of God and that the Jews were scattered precisely so that strangers would join them; and instructions to receive proselytes immediately and wholeheartedly.

47. Stephen C. Lerner, "Choosing Judaism: Issues Relating to Conversion," in *Celebration and Renewal*, edited by Rela Geffen (Philadelphia: Jewish Publication Society), pp. 78–79; Jack Riemer, "Embracing Converts: A Policy Proposal," *Moment* (October 1982): 62–63; Romanoff, *Your People, My People*, pp. 4–5. Lerner discusses the unwelcoming attitude of Orthodox rabbis toward converts; Riemer notes that his synagogue has three teachers to work with the 45 or so *b'nai* and *b'not mitzvah* each year, but no one to prepare people for conversion, even though at least as many people approach the temple for that purpose.

48. Robert Eshman, "O Come All Ye Faithful," *Jewish Journal*, December 23–29, 1994, p. 9; see also Perry Netter, "Will Your God *Really* Be My God?" *Moment* (January/February 1989): 47; Epstein, *Theory and Practice*, p. 47; Romanoff, *Your People, My People*, pp. 145–46; Forster and Tabatchnik, *Jews by Choice*, p. 133.

49. Bernard Zlotowitz, "Sincere Conversion and Ulterior Motives," in *Conversion to Judaism in Jewish Law*, pp. 68–69; Netter, "Will Your God *Really* Be My God?" pp. 45–46; Eshman, "O Come All Ye Faithful," p. 9; Orenstein, "Choosing Judaism," p. 233. Rabbi Helbo's comment about the troublesome nature of converts compares them in various translations to a sore, an itch, or a skin disease. Other common interpretations of Rabbi Helbo's comment are that converts made trouble for the Jewish community by annoying Roman authorities and that they remind born Jews that they do not have the honor of having chosen Judaism.

50. Romanoff, *Your People, My People*, p. 129.

51. Fink spoke at the November 1994 *Tikkun* conference in New York. Similarly: Steven Huberman, "Preparing for the Jewish Future," *Reconstructionist*, Spring 1993, p. 14; Nan Fink, "Jewish Renewal: Our Current Situation," *Tikkun* (May/June 1994): 25; Romanoff, *Your People, My People*, pp. 79, 86–87; Epstein, *Theory and Practice*, pp. 132–33; Schneider, *Intermarriage*, p. 216; Huberman, "Jews and Non-Jews: Falling in Love," p. 269; Myrowitz, "Who We Are and What We Need," p. 250.

52. Edwin Farber, "Converts Bring Much to the Community," *United Synagogue Review* (Spring 1992): 20–21; Huberman, "Jews and Non-Jews: Falling in Love," p. 267; Medding et al., *Jewish Identity in Conversionary and Mixed Marriage*, p. 18.

53. Epstein, *Theory and Practice*, pp. 138–39; Romanoff, *Your People, My People*, pp. 130–31.

54. Jonathan D. Sarna, "Reform Jewish Leaders, Intermarriage, and Conversion," *Journal of Reform Judaism* (Winter 1990): 5–7; Mark L. Winer, "Will Success Spoil Reform?" *Reform Judaism* (Spring 1991): 26; Forster and Tabatchnik, *Jews by Choice*, pp. 47–48, 88, 97, 100–101, 139–40; Medding et al., *Jewish Identity in Conversionary and Mixed Marriage*, pp. 32, 36–37.

55. Lydia Kukoff, "A Decade of Reform Jewish Outreach: Achievement and Promise," in *Jewish Intermarriage, Conversion and Outreach*, p. 50.

56. Kukoff, *Choosing Judaism*, pp. 48–49, 56; Forster and Tabatchnik, *Jews by Choice*, p. 133; Romanoff, *Your People, My People*, pp. 71–73, 75, 132, 134, 140–41, 237; Cowan, *Mixed Blessings*, p. 198; Schneider, *Intermarriage*, pp. 217–18; Woodward, "Becoming a 'Jew-by-Choice,'" p. 73; Myrowitz, "Who We Are and What We Need," pp. 249–50.

57. Romanoff, *Your People, My People*, pp. 228, 137–43, 162–65, 228; Kukoff, *Choosing Judaism*, pp. 104–12; Joy Levitt, "Will Our Grandchildren Be Jewish?" *Journal of Jewish Communal Service* (Summer 1992): 345; Petsonk and Remsen, *The Intermarriage Handbook*, p. 171; Myrowitz, "Who We Are and What We Need," pp. 250–52.

58. Romanoff, *Your People, My People*, pp. 6–9, 155–62; Brown-Gutoff, "Dear Ruth," pp. 240–43; Petsonk and Remsen, *The Intermarriage Handbook*, pp. 166–67.

59. Lawrence J. Epstein, guest column for *Moment* (October 1994): 28; Petsonk and Remsen, *The Intermarriage Handbook*, p. 167.

60. Commission on Reform Jewish Outreach, *Defining the Role of the Non-Jew in the Synagogue: A Resource for Congregations* (New York: Union of American Hebrew Congregations, 1990), pp. 36–40, 49–55, 56–59, 60, 65–77, 87–90, 92–96, 110–13; Wertheimer, *A People Divided*, pp. 107–8, 110; Nina Mizrahi, "Non-Jews in the Synagogue," *Reform Judaism* (Summer 1992): 5–8, 34; Garth Wolkoff, "Reform Jewry Leader Urges Greater Role for Non-Jewish Spouses," *Jewish Bulletin of Northern California*, October 22, 1993, pp. 1, 50; Na'ama Batya Lewin, "Does Outreach Threaten the Fabric of Jewish Life?" *Washington Jewish Week*, March 17, 1994, pp. 29, 49, 59. A 1991 Reform Outreach census found almost 9 out of 10 Reform congregations allowed non-Jews, usually presumed to be partners of Jewish members, to be listed as members and to serve on all or most committees, but only 62 percent extend voting rights to non-Jewish members. Twenty-seven percent allow non-Jews to hold office. Sisterhood officers must be Jewish. On the ritual side, more than 90 percent allow non-Jews to participate in life-cycle events in some way, although not necessarily in an active or verbal role; 41 percent permit non-Jews to light Shabbat candles in the synagogue (a common role for the mother of a bar or bat mitzvah the Friday night before the ceremony), and 22 percent will allow a non-Jew to say the blessings before and after reading of the Torah. A UAHC publication, *Defining the Role of the Non-Jew in the Synagogue*, reprints a number of responsa, interpretations of Jewish law, and essays by Reform rabbis that come down against permitting non-Jews to become temple members, light Shabbat candles in the sanctuary, or take a speaking role in a child's bar or bat mitzvah. In 1994, former CCAR president Walter Jacob circulated a paper urging that non-Jewish spouses of intermarried couples be denied temple membership.

61. Debra Nussbaum Cohen, "Drawing the Line," *Jewish Journal*, November 5–11, 1993, p. 22.

62. Lawrence Hoffman, "Non-Jews and Jewish Life-Cycle Liturgy," *Journal of Reform Judaism* (Summer 1990): 1–16, reprinted in *Defining the Role of the Non-Jew in the Synagogue*, pp. 65–80; Lawrence Mahrer, "The Role of the Non-Jewish Parent in Synagogue Life-Cycle Ceremonies: A Rabbi's Reflection," *Defining the Role of the Non-Jew in the Synagogue*, pp. 92–97. Objection to Gentiles saying certain prayers as "service leaders" (that is, in front of the congregation) is based on phrases such as "who has chosen *us*," as in the Torah blessing, or "who has commanded *us*," as in the candle blessing, wording that, rabbis claim, excludes the non-Jew. Hoffman argues that many non-Jews feel very much part of the Jewish community and identity with the language in the prayers; moreover, many Jews say Jewish prayers with which they disagree completely. Mahrer points out that the wording of some blessings can be altered slightly to allow non-Jews to participate more actively in life-cycle events.

63. Wertheimer, "Family Values and the Jews," *Commentary* (January 1994): 34.

64. The UAHC Sample Constitution limits membership to "person[s] of the Jewish faith" and states that while the non-Jewish partners of members are considered members and are welcome "to share in the fellowship of the congregation," they cannot vote or hold any kind of office. No provision is made for membership of divorced non-Jewish custodial parents of Jewish children in absence of the Jewish parent or for single non-Jews who may wish to join Reform congregations by themselves, except to say that temple boards may

establish special membership classifications as they see fit. Although an individual Reform synagogue is not required to adopt the Sample Constitution as its own, the Sample Constitution is a model for congregational by-laws and as such stands as a recommendation for how Reform congregations regard the non-Jews among them.

65. In his president's address to the 1993 UAHC biennial convention, Rabbi Alexander Schindler urged member synagogues to permit non-Jews to participate in a wide range of ritual functions. The refusal of many Reform congregations to allow a non-Jewish parent to pass the Torah to a bar or bat mitzvah is based on emotion, not *halacha*; there is nothing in Jewish law that prohibits non-Jews from holding the Torah, he said, and aren't the five books of Moses part of a Christian's religious heritage, too? See also *Defining the Role of the Non-Jew in the Synagogue*, p. 75. The rabbi of a small synagogue in Wisconsin told *Reform Judaism* magazine that by necessity he had several non-Jews teaching in his religious school and pointed out that in small congregations the involvement in leadership roles of committed non-Jews is often essential for the synagogue to function; establishing rigid boundaries might decrease the willingness for such involvement (Mizrahi, "Non-Jews in the Synagogue," p. 8).

66. Commission on Reform Jewish Outreach, *Defining the Role of the Non-Jew in the Synagogue*, pp. 49–52; Epstein, *Theory and Practice*, pp. 68–69; Schneider, *Intermarriage*, pp. 208–9; Ronald M. Brauner, "Ger-Toshav: Reviving an Ancient Status," *Reconstructionist* (April 1982): 28–30.

67. Stephen C. Lerner, "Gerut and the Conservative Movement: An Approach for Our Time," *Conservative Judaism* (Fall 1979): 42–45; Lerner, "Choosing Judaism," pp. 72–77; Epstein, *Theory and Practice*, pp. 34–40, 61–68, 69–80; Robert M. Seltzer, "An Historical Overview of Outreach and Conversion in Judaism," *Jewish Intermarriage, Conversion and Outreach*, pp. 14–17; Bernard J. Bamberger, "Is Judaism a Missionary Faith?" *Reform Judaism* (Fall 1989): 16–17; Mayer, "Why Not Judaism?" pp. 30–31. Estimates of how many Jews lived in the Roman empire range from 4 million to 8 million.

68. The complete text of Schindler's 1978 address to the UAHC board of directors appears in Commission on Reform Jewish Outreach, *Outreach and the Changing Reform Community*, pp. 83–90; most of it was reprinted in *Moment* (Alexander Schindler, "Reaching in, Reaching Out: Dealing with the Jewish Population Problem" [March 1979]: 20–23), and excerpts appear in Aron Hirt-Manheimer, "Why Jews Should Seek Converts," *Reform Judaism* (Spring 1994): 10–12.

69. The March 1979 issue of *Moment* included comments in response to Schindler's proposal by Conservative leaders Wolfe Kelman and Harold Schulweis, law professor Leo Pfeffer, and Reform rabbi Dannel Schwartz. *Reform Judaism* ran a sidebar of rabbinic responses to Schindler's 1993 call for outreach to the general public (and the raising of $5 million as an endowment to provide income to finance it) in its spring 1994 issue ("Jewish Responses," pp. 14–15, 59). Reaction was also reported in Jewish and mass circulation newspapers.

70. "Jewish Responses," pp. 15, 59; similarly from Wolfe Kelman's "Comment," *Moment* (March 1979): 24–25; and Eshman, "O Come All Ye Faithful," p. 9.

71. Peter L. Berger, "Converting the Gentiles?" *Commentary* (May 1979): 35–39; Lerner,

"Gerut and the Conservative Movement," pp. 46–47; Epstein, *Theory and Practice*, pp. 129–32. The spring 1994 issue of *Reform Judaism* also contained a compilation of comments on Schindler's 1978 and 1993 remarks from Christian leaders, some of whom recommended caution, but most of whom were warmly supportive. "The mainline Christian churches are in a state of theological exhaustion and are most unlikely to be roused from it by a little Jewish proselytizing," Berger wrote in his *Commentary* piece. The Conservative movement insists that a recently established toll-free number through which people interested in conversion can obtain information does not constitute proselytizing (Gustav Niebuhr, "Conservative Judaism Reaches Out," *New York Times*, May 6, 1995, p. 9).

72. W. C. Wasserkrug, letter to *Reform Judaism* (Summer 1994): 4; similarly from Seymour Prystowsky, "Jewish Responses," p. 59; Leo Pfeffer, "Comment," *Moment* (March 1979): 26.

73. In 1958, Conservative rabbi Robert Gordis proposed, in the pages of *Time* magazine, that the leaders of the major Jewish movements unite "to consider the founding of a missionary program among the unaffiliated gentile population in the Western Hemisphere and Japan" (Dannel Schwartz, "Comment," *Moment* [March 1979]: 28). During the 1960s, engineer Ben Maccabee ran the Jewish Information Society, which invited the general public to learn more about Judaism but languished for lack of support from the Jewish community (Evelyn Lauter, "Trend toward Conversion TO Judaism, Not from It," *National Jewish Monthly* [July/August 1969]: 9). In 1975, Conservative rabbi Gilbert Kollin urged that Jews make conversion "accessible, convenient and honorable," advocating schools and reading rooms for prospective converts ("The Advisability of Seeking Converts," *Judaism* [Winter 1975]: 57).

74. Mayer, "Why Not Judaism?" pp. 39–42.

75. Harold Schulweis, "Comment," *Moment* (March 1979): 27; see also Lawrence J. Epstein, letter to *Commentary* (April 1994): 8; Epstein, *Theory and Practice*, pp. 116–19; Lerner, "Gerut and the Conservative Movement," pp. 47–48; Michael Lerner, *Jewish Renewal: A Path to Healing and Transformation* (New York: Grosset/Putnam, 1994), pp. 273–76; Egon Mayer, "Strategies for Taking Judaism Public," *Moment* (August 1992): 38–41.

Index